DIMENSIONS OF THE HOSPITALITY INDUSTRY

Third Edition

DIMENSIONS OF THE HOSPITALITY INDUSTRY

Paul R. Dittmer

John Wiley & Sons, Inc.

Library of Congress Cataloging-in-Publication Data:
Dittmer, Paul.
  Dimensions of the hospitality industry : an introduction/
Paul R. Dittmer.—3rd ed.
    p. cm.
  Includes index.
  ISBN 0-471-38479-8 (cloth : alk. paper)
  1. Hospitality industry—Management. I. Title.
TX911.3.M27 D583 2001
647.94'068—dc21   2001017913

Printed in the United States of America.

10 9 8 7 6 5 4 3 2

This text is dedicated to Gerald Griffin, coauthor of the two previous editions, who passed away shortly before the start of this revision. His lifelong dedication to excellence in education and his willingness to devote his time and energy to the betterment of the hospitality industry will not soon be forgotten.

CONTENTS

Preface   *ix*

Acknowledgments   *xi*

PART I
INTRODUCTION   1

Chapter 1   Dimensions of the Hospitality Industry:
A Career Overview   3

PART II
FOUNDATIONS   27

Chapter 2   Hospitality Foundations: Early Development of the
Hospitality Industry   29

Chapter 3   The Hospitality Industry in the United States:
The Twentieth Century   67

PART III
FOOD AND BEVERAGE PERSPECTIVES   109

Chapter 4   Dimensions of Food and Beverage   111

Chapter 5   Food and Beverage Facilities   143

Chapter 6   Food and Beverage Operations   173

PART IV
LODGING PERSPECTIVES   201

Chapter 7   Dimensions of Lodging   203

Chapter 8   Lodging Facilities   231

Chapter 9   Lodging Operations   259

PART V
HOSPITALITY MANAGEMENT PERSPECTIVES   289

Chapter 10   Hospitality Operations Management   291

PART VI
TRAVEL AND TOURISM PERSPECTIVES   333

Chapter 11   Dimensions of Travel and Tourism   335

Chapter 12   Travel Services   365

Chapter 13   Recreation, Entertainment, and Other Tourism
               Attractions   391

PART VII
FUTURE PERSPECTIVES   417

Chapter 14   Hospitality and Tourism Tomorrow:
               An Issues Overview   419

Glossary   441
Index   463

This text is intended for courses that introduce students to the broad world of hospitality and tourism and to the curricula that will prepare them for managerial careers in these fields. This revised edition consists of 14 chapters, divided into 7 parts. Each part covers a primary area commonly treated in introductory courses, as indicated below:

Part	Area Covered	Number of Chapters
I	Introduction/Overview	1
II	Historical Foundations	2
III	Food and Beverage	3
IV	Lodging	3
V	Hospitality Management	1
VI	Travel and Tourism	3
VII	Future Perspectives	1

The number of chapters is meant to facilitate the use of the complete work in a one-semester course. The strong positive features of the first two editions have been retained, and the material has been updated and altered where necessary. These features include Newsflashes, Technology Gateways, and Biographical Summaries throughout the work. Newsflashes, excerpts from current periodicals, provide industry-based illustrations of material in the chapters. Technology Gateways demonstrate technological applications of significant points in the chapters. Biographical Summaries, which appear in the historical chapters only, offer interesting sketches of some of the giants who have made dramatic and lasting contributions to our field.

In addition, this revised edition features case studies at the end of each chapter. Identified as Moments of Truth, these provide opportunities for students to engage in chapter-related critical thinking under the guidance of their instructor and to discuss their varying views in the classroom. Finally, the end of each chapter contains Internet exercises, intended to introduce students to many of the Web sites in Hospitality and Travel and Tourism.

Flexibility is a key feature of this edition. For example, elimination of any one of the seven major parts will not make it difficult to use others. Thus, instructors in programs who do not include foodservice courses can choose to ignore part III, "Food and Beverage Perspectives." In programs without lodging courses, instructors may prefer to skip Part IV. Likewise, in programs without travel and tourism components, instructors can disregard Part VI.

Although instructors in many programs will choose to include the parts of the text that introduce the principal areas covered in their curricula, some may prefer to take a contrary approach: to assign the parts *not* linked to the specifics of their programs. Instructors in programs that do not offer courses in food and beverage management, for example, may choose to assign the relevant chapters in this text to provide their students with some introduction to this important area. In addition, because the number of end-of-chapter questions is more than most instructors will be inclined to assign, they can be used selectively for written response or in-class discussion.

Answers for all end-of-chapter questions can be found in the *Instructor's Manual* (0-471-20635-0), which also includes other materials designed to assist instructors with their classroom preparation. The *Instructor's Manual* is available to qualified adopters on request from the publisher: John Wiley & Sons, 605 Third Avenue, New York, NY 10158–0012, or contact your local Wiley sales representative.

The following is an overview of the text:

Part I gives a profile of the hospitality industry and is intended to provide a sense of its scope. At the same time, it introduces the three principal areas addressed in college majors—foodservice, lodging, and travel and tourism—and two key concepts: moments of truth and cycles of service. Finally, it addresses issues of particular concern to students—career opportunities, education, and experience required to pursue those opportunities—and both the advantages and disadvantages of working in these fields.

Part II traces the history and development of travel and hospitality in the western world. The first section of Chapter 2 sketches the growth of travel and hospitality from earliest times through the Greek and Roman empires, the Middle Ages, and the period up to the Industrial Revolution in England. The second section of this chapter traces the hospitality industry in the United States from colonial times to the twentieth century. Chapter 3 deals exclusively with hospitality in the United States during the twentieth century.

Part III offers a broad introduction to food and beverage. Chapter 4 identifies the size and scope of the industry, describes characteristic types of food and beverage operations, and explains a system for classifying establishments in the foodservice industry. Chapter 5 deals with food and beverage facilities and defines the terms *product line* and *service product*. Chapter 6 describes food and beverage operations from purchasing through service.

Part IV provides a general introduction to lodging. Chapter 7 identifies the size and scope of the industry, describes many characteristic types of lodging and establishments, and discusses various ways of classifying and rating establishments. Chapter 8 deals with lodging facilities and shows how the terms *product line* and *service product* relate to the lodging industry. Chapter 9 describes the basic operations that all lodging establishments require and identifies services found in a number of lodging operations.

Part V introduces operations management in the hospitality industry. Using examples from the world of foodservice and lodging, Chapter 10 introduces operations management in the following key areas: management, marketing, human resources, accounting, and computers.

Part VI introduces travel and tourism. Chapter 11 discusses travel motivators, describes the role of governments in travel and tourism, and identifies the size and scope of the industry as well as its several components. Chapter 12 focuses on the people and businesses that sell travel, defines the term *package*, and describes types of travel packages. Chapter 13 defines the terms *recreation* and *entertainment* and describes many tourism attractions on which the travel industry depends.

Part VII consists of a single chapter devoted to significant issues likely to be of increasing concern to managers in the hospitality and tourism industries in the years ahead.

ACKNOWLEDGMENTS

In developing this text, we were fortunate to have the cooperation and assistance of many people. Some of these individuals may feel their contributions were minor. We strongly disagree; even brief comments and the most casual of conversations can suggest ideas and change views and, thus, have a profound impact on a work in progress. With that in mind, we sincerely and publicly acknowledge and thank the many people, including users of earlier editions, who were kind enough to send us their comments and suggestions.

PART I
Introduction

Dimensions of the Hospitality Industry:

A Career Overview

CHAPTER 1

▶ Learning Objectives

After reading and studying this chapter, you should be able to:

1. Distinguish between the products, service, and government sectors in an economy.

2. Define hospitality and describe the scope of the hospitality industry.

3. Identify the two principal segments of the hospitality industry and list the major types of businesses in each.

4. Describe the relationship between the hospitality industry and the travel and tourism industry.

5. Discuss the historic role of entertainment in the hospitality industry.

6. Distinguish between travel agents and tour operators.

7. List and explain the elements that make the hospitality industry unique.

8. Discuss the special characteristics that distinguish hospitality and other service businesses from those that manufacture products.

9. Define the terms *moment of truth*, *cycle of service*, and *employee empowerment*, then discuss the significance of each for the hospitality industry.

10. Identify the principal thrust of total quality management and its significance for hospitality management.

11. Discuss career opportunities in the hospitality industry and the qualifications commonly sought by hospitality employers.

12. Describe the advantages and disadvantages associated with careers in the hospitality industry.

INTRODUCTION

Imagine yourself in an occupation that allows you to work in almost any part of the world, giving you the chance to meet famous people—movie stars, recording artists, political leaders, and others—offers an elegant work environment in luxurious surroundings, and lets you climb that well-known ladder of success, advancing in rank and position as fast as your abilities will allow. Don't think of it as only a dream: it's reality for many people just like you—people who decided on careers in hospitality, a globe-spanning industry that continues to grow faster than most people can imagine and cries out for young men and women to help manage the hotels, restaurants, and related businesses springing up in every corner of the world. A vast number of opportunities is available to anyone interested in people and willing to work hard. Hospitality is one of the most interesting industries in the modern world economy.

Hospitality is just one part of a larger group of enterprises that make up the service sector of the economy. We can divide the economy into three major sectors. The first consists of organizations and businesses that produce and manufacture products. The second comprises those individuals and businesses that provide services. The third is government.

The first sector includes companies and individuals that make or grow real physical items that people can touch; these are known as *products*. This sector includes manufacturers of automobiles, furniture, computers, toys, and so on, as well as farmers who grow corn, wheat, and other farm products. The second—the service sector—is made up of individuals and organizations that perform services for people and businesses. The service sector includes a broad range of fields, including law, interior decorating, dentistry, accounting, nursing, automobile repair, foodservice, haircutting—and the list goes on and on, almost without end. Hospitality is a major part of the service sector. The third sector is government—national, state, and local. Governments at all levels also perform services. They run national and state parks, they provide passports and visas, they inform the public about health hazards, they gather and publish statistical data on population and the economy, and they perform a great number of other services, including protection, trash collection, and so on. However, governments are noncommercial; that is, they do not operate for a profit, whereas most other services do. Because of this, government is typically treated as a separate part of our economy.

In years past, the products sector was the major force in the economy, accounting for the largest part of the economic growth that so changed the United States in the nineteenth century and the first half of the twentieth century. However, in the years since 1950, the service sector of our economy has been growing much faster than the manufacturing sector—and the hospitality industry has been growing faster than most other service industries. All kinds of career opportunities are opening up every day in every part of the hospitality industry, and the number of jobs keeps growing.

Since the 1950s, hospitality has been a key industry in the economic life of many nations. It has become a world leader in providing jobs and new opportunities for people from every age group and from all ethnic, racial, and socioeconomic groups. Most economists predict that hospitality will continue to grow worldwide in the years ahead. That would mean ever greater numbers of career possibilities for the men and women who train to become hospitality professionals and prepare to seize these new opportunities.

The first chapter of our investigation of the hospitality industry is devoted to basic elements: identifying the scope of the industry, contrasting it to other industries, and pointing out its distinctive characteristics. Finally, we point out opportunities the hospitality industry offers the men and women who prepare to take advantage of it.

A DEFINITION OF HOSPITALITY

The word **hospitality** has ancient roots, dating from the earliest days of Roman civilization. It is derived from the Latin verb *hospitare*, meaning "to receive as a guest." Several related words come from the same Latin root, including *hospital*, *hospice*, and *hostel*. In each of these, the principal meaning focuses on a host who receives, welcomes, and caters to the needs of people temporarily away from their homes. The phrase "*to receive as a guest*" implies a host prepared to meet a guest's basic requirements. The requirements of a guest are, traditionally, food, beverages, and lodging or shelter. Additionally, many hosts provide some form of entertainment. However, entertainment has become a large separate industry that includes major undertakings such as theme parks, major musical and sports performances, fairs and festivals, and parades. Because entertainment is primarily associated with travel and tourism and is not a necessary ingredient to satisfy a traveler's basic needs, we treat it as part of travel and tourism rather than food, beverage, and lodging—the basic elements of hospitality.

THE BASICS OF THE INDUSTRY

The traditional view takes us to the heart of the hospitality industry. If the word *hospitality* refers to the act of providing food, beverages, and lodging to travelers, then the **hospitality industry** consists of businesses that do this. This brings up two important distinctions between the hospitality industry and other service enterprises:

1. The hospitality industry provides food, beverages, lodging, or some combination of the three that other businesses provide only on the most incidental basis.

2. The hospitality industry provides services primarily to travelers, in a broad sense of the term. By contrast, other service businesses deal primarily with customers who are local residents and who are at home rather than in the

process of traveling. Thus, the typical barber or beauty shop normally caters to the local community. Travelers are normally a small part of their business.

Our definition also distinguishes the hospitality industry from the products and government sectors of our economy. Manufacturers and producers of products do not normally sell services. Instead, they make or produce products that are sold to consumers through regional systems of local wholesalers and retailers, or directly to the consumer via mail or private delivery service. Governments are essentially nonprofit organizations and, with some exceptions, are not designed to provide for the essential needs of the traveler.

The astute student will be quick to point out a potential problem with the above view of the hospitality industry. Clearly, services provided for travelers are frequently also provided to local residents. Restaurants and hotels are excellent examples of facilities that provide food and lodging to local residents in addition to travelers. Additionally, many businesses provide food to employees who live locally. Those concerned with the question of the residential or nonresidential nature of customers in a hotel dining room, local restaurant, or employee cafeteria will soon recognize the futility of attempting to make useful distinctions. Regardless of where the customers live, the staff of a hotel or restaurant must offer the same menus and provide a level of service to all. Even if a business provides food to employees in a cafeteria and does not cater to travelers, the food and service may not differ greatly from a cafeteria organized to cater to travelers. In other words, the essential nature of the foodservice is the same regardless of the clientele. Although the hospitality industry evolved as a means of providing food, beverages, and shelter for travelers, these services appealed to local residents as well, and increasing numbers have come to take advantage of them. Today, some hospitality enterprises service local residents only and never attend to the needs of travelers, as is the case in an employee cafeteria. For practical and definitional purposes, then, those providing food, beverages, and shelter, or some combination of these, are considered part of the hospitality industry whether or not their customers are actually travelers.

SCOPE OF THE HOSPITALITY INDUSTRY

From the above material, it is apparent that there may be any number of businesses in the hospitality industry. The definition is really quite broad; therefore, at this point we discuss some of the varied enterprises that make up each of the two principal segments of the industry—food and beverage, on the one hand, and lodging, on the other.

Food and Beverage Segment

Everyone is aware of the seemingly limitless array of organizations that provide food and beverage service to the public. Today, these include every conceivable type of establishment, from a brightly colored fast food restaurant (many of these establishments prefer to be labeled fast service restaurants rather than fast food restaurants) to a quiet dining room offering elegant, ultraexpensive continental or French cuisine. No matter what type of food travelers and nontravelers alike desire, food service must be available to them at the appropriate hour for breakfast, lunch, dinner, supper, snacks, and so on. The public looks for foodservice everywhere: hotels, motels, factories, dormitories, highways, cruise ships, city streets, trains, offices, airlines, national parks, airports, bus terminals, shopping malls—any place outside the home where people can be found shopping, driving, working, playing. Commercial restaurants of every description are around us every day: fast-service restaurants selling hamburgers, chicken, pizza, pasta, or hero sandwiches; ethnic restaurants selling Chinese, Mexican, Italian, Latin American, German, Indonesian, Indian, and dozens of other types of meals; specialty restaurants serving seafood, steaks, pasta, chicken, or vegetarian items; restaurants organized around

No matter what style or type of food is desired—fast food, specialty foods, or fine dining—the restaurant industry provides these facilities for patrons.
(Photos courtesy of Radisson Hotels and Resorts; MGM Grand; Doctor's Associates, Inc.; and White Castle Systems, Inc.)

themes, such as railroad cars, English pubs, railroad stations, medieval pageants, opera, or the circus; and a range of others—expensive, inexpensive, noisy, quiet, elegant, dingy, brightly lit, or dark, and serving great food, decent food, terrible food, and every other kind you can imagine.

All sorts of foodservice establishments exist outside the usual restaurant settings. Examples are found at Disney World and other theme parks, in schools and colleges, in hospitals and homes for senior citizens, in prisons and halfway houses, in shelters for the homeless. There are carts in the streets and vending machines everywhere; even supermarkets and other food stores offer in-store foodservice.

Those familiar with the history of our industry recognize that taverns traditionally sold both food and beverages and provided some form of entertainment, however limited. Some taverns even made overnight accommodations available for travelers. In fact, in the seventeenth century, laws were passed in New England requiring that each community provide a tavern for the "entertainment of travelers." .

The tavern, pub, inn, alehouse, or public house served as a social center—a place to which travelers and local residents could go to find "entertainment." It served society in this manner throughout the eighteenth and nineteenth centuries, long before the invention of such pervasive modern devices as phonographs, movies, radios, televisions, videos, tape decks, and compact disk players. People gathered in the taverns, where local residents could mingle with travelers to share news of wars, plagues, famines, or natural disasters, to discuss politics, or gossip about their neighbors. Sometimes people wanted only to find a quiet, warm place by the fire; normally, being at a tavern created an occasion for a mug of beer, a tankard of ale, or even a glass of wine.

During the twentieth century, the role of the establishments selling beer, ale, wine, and other beverages changed, to some extent, as the role of taverns expanded and evolved. In the twenty-first century, taverns are meeting new needs in society—needs that did not exist before the introduction of some of the modern world's technological innovations. Most taverns are now known as bars, clubs, and cocktail lounges.

Hotels and restaurants also have long been in the business of selling drinks—as accompaniments to food, or because their customers began to expect it, or because they discovered it was profitable. The terms *food* and *beverage* became ever more closely linked, and both hotels and restaurants began to use terminology that illustrated the linkage; *food and beverage manager* and *food and beverage department* became common terms, and remain so. Because our industry treats food and beverages together as one segment of the industry, we do the same in this text.

Lodging Segment

The lodging segment of the hospitality industry includes the more familiar kinds of establishments that have long offered shelter to travelers—the hotels and motels we see on city streets, along highways, near beaches, and close to airports, ski slopes, theme parks, lakes, and national parks. Those less familiar with the industry may not realize that some lodging facilities called inns, motor hotels, lodges,

The hotel industry caters to most travelers, with facilities that meet their needs. Shown are the Woodbury Inn; Mexico City's Four Seasons Hotel; Chateau Lake Louise, a resort hotel; and a Radisson Suite hotel.

(Photos courtesy of Carlson Hospitality Worldwide; photograph of the Four Seasons Hotels, © 2000 Four Seasons Limited. Used by permission; Fairmont Hotels and Resorts; and Radisson Hotels and Resorts)

or motor inns are simply hotels or motels using different names. However, some lodging establishments do use distinctive terms and sell lodging concepts unlike those of the traditional hotels and motels. Examples are bed-and-breakfast, resort hotel, resort condominium, conference center, extended stay, time-share, and all-suite—all terms that must be addressed in a discussion of the lodging segment. Additionally, some lodging establishments are known for the special facilities they offer: ski lodges in Colorado and casino hotels in Las Vegas and Atlantic City are good examples. Definitions and discussion of the various types of lodging establishments are found in Chapter 7.

In many ways, campgrounds and transient trailer parks are lodging establishments, and so are school and college dormitories, summer camps, and health spas. All attend to the lodging needs of those away from home.

Outside the United States, the signs for lodging establishments may display unfamiliar words. Examples include *parador*, an old Spanish monastery or castle converted to use as a hotel; *pension* or *pensione*, a French or Italian home at which guests are provided with room and board; *chateau*, a French castle or elegant country home used as a hotel; *ryokan*, a Japanese inn at which traditional customs are observed; and *hostel*, a lodging facility at which inexpensive accommodations are provided for students and others, typically on a nonprofit basis.

Lodging signs also bring us some of the world's best-known names in hospitality: Hilton, Sheraton, Holiday Inn, Marriott, Ramada, Days Inn, Quality Inn, and Hyatt, to name just a few. All these, and many others, help make up the dynamic and growing lodging segment of the industry.

TRAVEL AND TOURISM

Two key terms that arise in any discussion of the hospitality industry are **travel** and **tourism.** They are typically used together as an umbrella term to refer to those businesses providing primary services to travelers. These include the traditional hospitality businesses (hotels and restaurants) and related enterprises in the fields of entertainment, recreation, and transportation, travel agencies and tour operators, as well as segments of national, state, and local governments.

Entertainment and Recreation

Entertainment has its roots in the traditional duty of a host to entertain his guests, whether neighborhood residents or travelers from afar. Beginning centuries ago, innkeepers, tavern keepers, and their descendants have attended (in varying degrees) to guests' needs for entertainment. Some simply talked to their guests; others told stories (some truthful, others interesting or humorous lies); some provided games (darts, draughts, backgammon, or chess, for example); others hired jugglers and traveling minstrels.

Today, guest entertainment includes the modern equivalents of these ancient traditions, but it is not limited to these. The concept of entertaining guests is far broader. Guests are offered all manner of inducements in the form of entertainment and recreational activities to attract them to particular properties. Golf, tennis, casino gambling, backpacking, concerts, swimming, boating, and handball are all examples of this.

Disney World has taken a logical next step, developing a resort environment that includes a vast array of food and beverage, lodging, and entertainment facilities. The entertainment facilities include shows, rides, and exhibits so spectacular that guests have no interest in looking for any entertainment outside the Disney environment during their visit. This is one example of a complete recreational center that, in itself, has become a travel destination. To guests, the food, beverage, and lodging is relatively incidental; they travel to Disney World for the spectacle of it all.

Transportation

All travelers require some means of getting from one place to another. That is a major purpose of the transportation business—making it possible for people to go from one place to another. There are many ways to do this, from the primitive and simple to the modern and complex. One can ride on the back of an animal, or in a supersonic jet, or select from any number of other possibilities. The more common options are automobiles, recreational vehicles (RVs), buses, ships, trains, and airplanes.

People preparing for professional careers in the traditional hospitality industry should be aware of the long-standing importance of transportation to the survival of hotels, motels, restaurants, and closely related enterprises. Links between the transportation and hospitality businesses are as old as history, and developments in either have normally brought about changes in the other. Nations and states with the best transportation networks usually develop the healthiest economic systems and the most advanced hospitality industries.

Travel Agencies and Tour Operators

Travel agencies and tour operators are comparatively modern additions to the world of travel and tourism. Neither existed before the middle of the nineteenth century, but both have become central to the survival of many businesses in the hospitality industry.

A **travel agent** is one who sells travel services in a travel agency. Transportation—air, train, bus, cruise ship—and lodging are the most common services they sell. Although a travel agent makes a large number of individual reservations for airline tickets and hotel rooms for some clients, much of the business volume in travel agencies normally consists of selling travel services assembled by others into packages. In the travel business, a **package** is a bundle of related travel services offered to a customer at a single price.

Many types of packages are available through travel agencies. Some include only a limited number of services—an airline ticket and a rental car, for example, or a hotel room and tickets for a ski lift. Other packages are more inclusive, providing the buyer with a round-trip airline ticket, rental car, hotel room, all meals, access to golf courses and tennis courts, and tickets to various events.

Most travel agencies selling packages do not put the packages together. This is done by **tour operators**—wholesalers who make the necessary contacts with hotels, airlines, and other providers of travel services. Tour operators devise packages that they believe will appeal to retail buyers. Like all wholesalers in all businesses, they are volume purchasers who are able to negotiate lower prices because of their high-volume purchases. They are typically able to offer any collection of travel services at a price lower than the individual consumer or his travel agent would be able to arrange.

Many resorts owe their survival to travel agents and tour operators. So, too, do other hospitality enterprises that depend on the sales volume provided by guests at these resorts. Resorts on some of the Caribbean islands, for example, find that up to 80 percent of their guests are booked by travel agents. The vast majority of other international travel arrangements are made by travel agents.

National, State, and Local Governments

Governments at all levels are involved in travel and tourism. For example, in the United States, at the federal level, the National Park Service operates all of the parks that come under its jurisdiction. States operate state parks and, in addition, have departments charged with the mission of attracting tourists and travelers to the state. At the local level, many chambers of commerce and convention bureaus work to bring tourists to their towns and cities.

In some cases, governments and businesses work together to turn communities into desirable destinations for travelers. For example, casino gambling and celebrity entertainment are two of the principal reasons that people go to Las Vegas. The success of Las Vegas would not be possible without the cooperation, participation, and encouragement of state and local government.

THE IMPORTANCE OF SERVICE IN HOSPITALITY MANAGEMENT

People who manufacture durable goods almost never meet the final purchasers of their products. Toy manufacturers do not see the children who use their toys and seldom know the real extent to which children are pleased or disappointed with them. Some customers may write the toy manufacturer to express pleasure or disappointment, and some may return toys to the manufacturer for repair or replacement, but that is usually the extent of their customer contact.

By contrast, people in the service industries typically deal directly with their customers, meeting them face to face on an ongoing basis. Hotel employees, for example, provide services directly to customers. They are in daily contact with guests and often receive immediate feedback about the hotel's quality of service. Many customers express their feelings about the service by complimenting or complaining to the staff. For many customers, the level of service is defined by a

Las Vegas, Nevada, is an excellent example of state and local governments working together with business to bring tourism to its location. Shown in the picture is the famous Las Vegas Strip.
(Photo courtesy of Las Vegas Convention and Visitors Authority)

specific event or by contact with a particular member of the staff. A clean room may lead a guest to believe that he is staying in a hotel that offers excellent service. Poor service in the dining room may lead another guest to think that all service in the hotel is poor. A friendly and helpful desk clerk or a housekeeper unwilling to provide extra towels may make a world of difference in the minds of guests distinguishing between excellent and poor service.

One of the primary features of a restaurant is its service. When discussing restaurants, people everywhere judge them by the quality of their service—professionalism, courtesy, and speed.

A customer expects a particular level and quality of service. If the service meets or exceeds those expectations, the customer is likely to be satisfied. If not, he or she is likely to be unhappy. In fact, an opportunity to transform a first-time customer into a loyal customer may be lost because of poor service. The quality of service is critical to the success and survival of a hospitality business.

Hospitality managers have traditionally tried to ensure a high quality of service by training their staff, the goal being uniformity. Most believed that, by training each staff member to use specific service techniques and procedures, they were establishing standards for excellent service.

Some hospitality managers—the more enlightened ones—have come to realize that service need not necessarily be exactly the same for every customer. Service should be of high quality, of course. But some managers find it advantageous to tailor service to the specific needs and perceptions of individual customers.

Moments of Truth

Jan Carlzon, former president of Scandinavian Airlines, wrote a book in which he employs the term "**moments of truth**." (1) It describes contacts between customers and businesses that give customers impressions of the businesses and from which customers make judgment about the businesses.

A customer makes a judgment about a business each time he or she has contact with any element of that business. For example, in a hotel, a guest may first make contact with the hotel business when her taxicab stops in front of the entrance. The initial impression made by the outward physical appearance of the building may be the first moment of truth. If the guest expects the taxi door to be opened by a doorkeeper, his presence or absence may be the next moment of truth.

The next may be found in the doorkeeper's attitude or demeanor, or the manner in which the job is performed. Other moments of truth come from guests' contacts with desk clerks and bellstaff, a ride in the self-service elevator, and their first reaction to their assigned rooms. Many other moments of truth occur during the course of these guests' stay in the hotel. Finally, their overall impressions reflect every contact made during the period and includes a number of judgments about the business: how efficiently it is run, whether or not it is customer oriented, how competent the employees are, how well the establishment meets the needs of its customers, and the level of its service quality. In a fully occupied hotel of 500 rooms, thousands of moments of truth occur every day.

In restaurants, moments of truth are equally applicable. Customers experience moments of truth when they arrive at the establishment. If the appearance of the building is pleasing or if there is sufficient parking, positive moments of truth are recorded. Upon entering the restaurant, customers note its atmosphere—the lighting and decor as well as the noise level. The promptness with which they are seated, the location of the table, and its proximity to other tables offer other moments of truth. Next, the menu—its appearance, prices, number and desirability of items—is judged. The server's appearance, demeanor, and professionalism constitute other moments of truth. The speed with which the customers receive their food and, of course, the quality of the food itself constitute important moments of truth.

The sum of the customers' moments of truth become the perception and impression of a hospitality business and its service quality. If the majority of customers judge the moments of truth to be positive, the business will have a positive reputation. If not, the business's reputation will be negative, and decreasing levels of sales will be likely.

Cycles of Service

Karl Albrecht, in his book *At America's Service*, carries this concept further (2). He states that a customer views an organization in terms of the chain of events from the beginning of his experience with an organization to the end of the experience. He refers to this chain of events as a "**cycle of service**." Albrecht states that

HOTELS CHECK IN GUESTS
BEFORE THEY SET FOOT INSIDE

The hotel front desk is no longer the only place where travelers check in and get their room keys. Many hotels are shortening front desk lines and creating more positive moments of truth by preregistering guests by phone or the Internet and then having them pick up their keys at a special counter in the lobby. Other hotels provide curbside check-in where bags are taken and keys to rooms issued. A few hotels allow guests to register and receive room keys at satellite lobbies in the airports. Some even allow guests to register on the shuttle bus ride from the airport to the hotel. In such cases, hotel employees are alerted and meet guests with room keys outside the hotel when they take their bags.

Source: Adapted from an article in *USA Today,* 2 November 1999.

a cycle of service "is a natural, unconscious pattern that exists in the customer's mind, and it may have nothing in common with your 'technical' approach to setting up the business."

Albrecht points out that service businesses are often set up and run in a fashion designed to achieve specific goals established by owners or managers, and that working to achieve these goals may impede one's ability to provide positive moments of truth and satisfy customers' needs. For example, a hotel may be run to achieve maximum profit. Managers may therefore establish policies that would minimize staff and maximize efficiency. This may mean that customers desiring to check into the hotel have to wait in line because an insufficient number of clerks is on duty. This approach may mean establishing policies in the kitchen and bar that do not allow servers to take orders for items other than those listed on the menu. It may lead to minimizing supervisory staff to a point where customer problems cannot be appropriately handled. Guests, however, are not aware of these policies and are concerned with their own comfort and enjoyment of the hotel facility. They experience moments of truth from the beginning of their stay to their departure and, taken together, these represent a cycle of service that leaves an overall impression of satisfaction or dissatisfaction with the hotel.

It is important to note that the policies identified above may work well in an enterprise producing durable goods. There, a good manager may be considered one who is best able to establish and carry out specific policies and routines that minimize costs and maximize output. In the production of durable goods, important goals include producing appropriate numbers of units, each of which meets the quality standards established for the item, at minimal cost. In that setting, disaffected workers and difficult working conditions may not be of real consequence, as long as the products sold to customers meet the quality standards established by management and production volume can be maintained at suitable levels.

The results of such policies in a service enterprise, however, are necessarily different. In hospitality, where our product is service, policies must be customer oriented and service oriented. If both managers and staff members do their best to generate positive moments of truth for customers, the resulting cycles of service are more likely to produce satisfaction. Policies and procedures must be sufficiently flexible for staff members to have the ability to provide individualized service for guests.

Total Quality Management

In recent years, growing numbers of hospitality managers have begun to take the moments of truth concept seriously and are now working to ensure that more of the moments of truth in their establishments are positive. To accomplish this, many have changed the way they go about managing. A number of managers and organizations have adopted a management style that some refer to as **total quality management** (TQM). Some use the term **service quality management** (SQM) to refer to the same set of basic ideas. Regardless of the term one uses, the underlying principles are the same.

One of these principles is considered key: offering customized rather than standardized service—in other words, tailoring service to the needs of guests and customers. To accomplish this, management must delegate the authority to satisfy guests' needs to the employees who come into direct contact with guests: servers, housekeepers, desk attendants, and so on. Managers give employees in these and similar jobs wide latitude to do what is necessary to meet guests' needs and solve their problems without obtaining specific permission from management. The term used to describe this is **employee empowerment**. Employees are said to be empowered when they have the power to make decisions about how best to meet the particular needs of a guest or customer in a particular instance. One effect is to provide employees with the ability to transform guests' moments of truth from negative to positive.

Empowerment does not mean that employees have unlimited power to make any changes they choose in any phase of operations. Reasonable limits apply. Employees are usually limited to making decisions about their own jobs. Additionally, there are commonsense boundaries: housekeepers can satisfy the needs of guests who request extra towels, but they cannot respond positively to a transient guest's request for the walls of his room to be painted a different color.

While the details of TQM programs vary from one establishment to another, an example drawn from a luxury hotel in an eastern city serves as a useful illustration. At this hotel, high standards of service are the norm. New employees are required to complete a weeklong training program during which they are instructed that all guests' needs should always be anticipated and satisfied. They also learn that any employee who receives a request or complaint from a guest "owns" that request or complaint; he or she is expected to fulfill that request or satisfy that complaint, even if the employee must interrupt other work to do so. If the request can be met only by an employee of another department and therefore must be turned over to another employee, the first employee is responsible for verifying that appropriate action is taken.

Another feature of TQM programs is their approach to problem solving. Committees are formed to deal with operational problems. In hotels, the mem-

SWEET DREAMS ARE MADE OF THIS

Many hotels are providing more positive moments of truth by supplying more comfortable beds, allowing guests to get a better night's sleep. Weston Hotels has installed a multilayer bed called the "Heavenly Bed" in its rooms. Ritz-Carlton has installed feather beds and offers its guests a menu of different pillows in some of its properties. Hilton has created "Sleep-Tight Rooms" in some of its properties; these rooms have fancier beds as well as noise- and light-dampening features.

Source: Adapted from an article in *USA Today*, 31 August 1999.

bers of these committees are drawn from several departments. The committees meet regularly to discuss changes in policies and procedures that might improve employees' abilities to serve the guests' needs. They have the authority to reach decisions and to implement new policies and procedures, as long as it can be demonstrated that guest service will improve.

It is important for hospitality operations to operate in a manner that maintains service quality at suitable levels. This is one of the great challenges in hospitality management, a field that demands great dedication and a commitment to solving problems positively. For those prepared for the challenges, the rewards can be great.

At this point, it is useful to look at some of the many opportunities available to those who plan careers in the hospitality industry.

CAREER OPPORTUNITIES IN THE HOSPITALITY INDUSTRY

Until several years ago, management personnel in the hospitality industry were rarely college educated. Those interested in hospitality management typically began their careers by taking lower-level jobs to learn about the industry and eventually worked their way up through the organization. This process often took many years. In hotels, men typically started as elevator operators, information clerks, or bellmen; by contrast, women began as reservations clerks or typists. Career development followed much the same approach in restaurants; people started as servers, order clerks, or bookkeepers, then progressed slowly to jobs with higher levels of responsibility and higher salaries.

Educational Requirements

Although it is still possible to begin a career in hospitality without formal education in the industry, such opportunities are diminishing each year. Today, people starting careers in hospitality management are more and more likely to have some formal education obtained in one of the postsecondary programs developed over the last 75 years to prepare men and women for hospitality careers. Whether they have earned certificates, diplomas, or degrees at the associate, baccalaureate, or graduate level, growing numbers of hospitality managers and management trainees have studied formally to prepare for their chosen careers.

Experience Requirements

It is important to note that starting positions are not typically filled solely on the basis of educational background. Experience in the field is still an important consideration to many employers, and many students find that good work experience gained while attending classes is instrumental in their finding good jobs after graduation. In many instances, those in the industry insist that graduates gain real work experience in conjunction with education, and most hospitality management students today should seek part-time employment during the academic year or full-time employment in the summer. Potential employers are typically more inclined to offer good starting jobs to students with valid work experience. For example, a student who worked on the front desk at a local hotel while earning a degree is much more likely to obtain a favorable position in the front office of a hotel upon graduation than one without prior front office experience.

Entry-Level Management Positions

The multifaceted nature of the hospitality industry suggests that opportunities are available in a number of different areas. In hotels, individuals might be given such job titles as management trainee, assistant front office manager, night auditor, banquet sales representative, assistant restaurant manager, assistant food and beverage controller, assistant housekeeper, and assistant steward. In some motels and smaller hotels, the available job titles could include assistant manager, banquet manager, and assistant food and beverage manager. In restaurants and similar foodservice operations, analogous positions might carry such titles as management trainee, assistant manager, dining room manager, unit manager, steward, bar manager, banquet manager, or food and beverage cost controller, depending on an individual's level of experience.

The size of an operation often determines the job title, and the authority and responsibility associated with a job title vary greatly with the size of a property. For example, an assistant manager in a 50-room motel might be the only person on duty in the front office and, therefore, would be responsible for taking reservations, operating the switchboard, checking guests in and out, and solving guests' problems. An assistant manager in a 500-room hotel would have very different, higher-level responsibilities, such as supervising a sizable staff of specialists, each of whom is responsible for one of the many tasks required in lodging operations.

The specific job that an individual is offered may be heavily dependent on her overall qualifications. After all, employers are likely to consider many aspects of an applicant, trying to match her to the requirements of a particular job. In order to do this successfully, they must attempt to assess all of an applicant's attributes, not simply her technical knowledge.

THE NUMBER OF LODGING JOBS PROJECTED TO INCREASE AT A RAPID RATE THROUGH THE YEAR 2008

The U.S. Labor Department projects that the number of jobs in the hotel and motel industry will increase by 312,500, or 17.6 percent between the years 1998 and 2008. Some specific jobs and their percentage of increase for that period are listed below:

Job Title	Number of Additional Jobs	% Increase Between 1998 and 2008
General managers and top executives	8,110	26.2%
Desk clerks	21,419	13.5%
Accountants and auditors	2,530	24.0%
Human resource managers	1,292	32.0%

Source: U.S. Department of Labor Web site.

Qualifications and Employer Assessment

Factors commonly considered when assessing potential candidates include grades, outside interests, participation in organizations, employment record, ability to communicate effectively, attitudes, and interpersonal skills. Each employer weighs them differently. Some emphasize good grades, others employment record, and still others look for good communications skills as a primary ingredient.

Good grades demonstrate dedication to achievement and willingness to work hard as well as ability. A broad range of interests in sports, music, drama, and other areas normally indicates that the applicant is well rounded. Participation in organizations such as fraternities and sororities, student government, and professional groups gives the employer some idea of a person's social skills and leadership abilities. Past employment is examined to see if the applicant has a stable work record, which can be indicative of future reliability.

Employers also assess the attitudes of applicants, looking for people willing to devote the necessary time and effort to a task, even if it means temporarily sacrificing other activities. They look for applicants who are willing, cooperative workers, able to do the work required of them.

Finally, employers search for people with good interpersonal skills. During the course of a typical workday, hospitality employees are likely to come in contact with a diverse population. This includes guests from many regions of the country and from many parts of the world as well as coworkers whose native language is different from their own. Because hospitality is a service business that requires ongoing contact with a variety of people, it is critical that employees are able to communicate effectively with guests as well as with coworkers.

THE NUMBER OF FOODSERVICE JOBS PROJECTED TO INCREASE AT A RAPID RATE THROUGH THE YEAR 2008

The U.S. Labor Department projects that the number of jobs in the foodservice industry will increase by 1,321,400, or 17 percent, between the years 1998 and 2008. Some specific jobs and their percentage of increase for that period are listed below:

Job Title	Number of Additional Jobs	% Increase Between 1998 and 2008
Foodservice managers	54,252	20.2%
Cashiers	149,422	32.8%
Accountants and auditors	1,623	15.7%
Human resource managers	425	23.1%
Waiters and waitresses	325,287	19.4%

Source: U.S. Department of Labor Web site.

ADVANTAGES AND DISADVANTAGES OF WORKING IN THE HOSPITALITY INDUSTRY

All jobs have positive and negative elements, and those in the hospitality industry are not exceptions. But people view the characteristics of jobs differently. Although one aspect of a given job may be considered positive by one individual, another may view that same aspect in a negative light. For example, evening work suits some people well, but others dislike it intensely. Similarly, clerical work suits many, while others find it tedious. The following is an outline of the conditions generally found in the industry. Each person must judge for himself if these conditions are appealing.

Wages and Salaries

Generally, wages and salaries are determined by such factors as the adequacy of the labor supply, the level of skills required for particular jobs, the extent to which unions influence wages, and regional considerations. The hospitality industry is labor intensive, and many of the jobs require relatively low levels of skill and education. Generally, entry-level jobs requiring neither specific education nor previous experience tend to command the lowest wages. Jobs that do require specific training or previous experience, such as cook or night auditor, pay somewhat higher wages. Starting salaries for recent college graduates with majors in hospitality management tend to be average when compared with similar jobs in other industries. Salaries for jobs in middle and upper management are often considered quite good, and many regard them as excellent. In general, larger organizations often pay more than smaller organizations for similar work and, within a given region, wages and salaries in affluent urban areas tend to be higher than those offered in rural and poorer urban areas.

Work Environment

The work environment in the hospitality industry can be quite good compared with other industries. For example, first-class and luxury hotels are often considered fine places to work, with their opulent surroundings and clean environment. The idea of spending one's working hours in contact with wealthy and famous guests is appealing to many. In better properties, employees are typically provided with excellent meals, and some management employees may be permitted to eat in the dining rooms of the hotels. Further, some hospitality organizations provide exceptional work sites: Caribbean beaches; resort areas with pools, tennis courts, golf courses; and a host of other superior facilities.

On the other hand, conditions can be viewed as less than satisfactory in some older, poorly maintained hotels, and in a sizable number of individually owned restaurants. The front offices of some hotels lack air conditioning, which can be unpleasant in sultry summer months. Aging equipment that continually breaks down can present unsatisfactory working conditions. Kitchens with poorly maintained equipment and improper ventilation can be uncomfortably hot and difficult to work in.

Hours and Days of Work

Because the industry caters to travelers, who may seek hospitality services at any hour of the day or night, a vast number of hospitality operations are open when other businesses are closed. Except for a relatively few resort properties that are closed during the off-season, hotels are open and staffed 24 hours a day, seven days a week, including holidays. New employees, including managers, are often required to work evenings and weekends. Employees typically have one or two days off each week, depending on the establishment. The days off are not likely to be Saturdays or Sundays for new employees; weekend days off are usually reserved for employees with seniority. On the other hand, some consider working on weekends an advantage. It gives them time off during the week, when shopping malls and recreation facilities are often least crowded. By the same token, those who work evening shifts look forward to having daylight hours for activities that would be difficult or impossible at night—boating, golf, and tennis, for example. In some cases, employees work according to a system known as *alternating watches*, where an individual may work a normal day shift for one or two weeks, then an evening shift for a similar period. This provides variety and satisfies the lifestyles of many. Employees in the resort industry often work hard during times when their friends are playing but are able to take vacations when others cannot—between vacation seasons, when workers in some other industries cannot possibly get away from their desks. This also gives them opportunities to vacation when resort areas are least crowded and rates are lowest.

Much of the work in the restaurant industry involves evening and weekend hours. This is because evenings and weekends are the most popular times for eating out. There are, however, notable exceptions. Most employee restaurants are open only during working hours and frequently are closed on the weekend. Restaurants in locations that cater primarily to the breakfast and luncheon crowd tend to be open during those mealtimes and closed during the evening. One excellent example of this is New York's financial district. Many restaurants there are open only during the days when the stock markets are open.

New managers in the hospitality industry are often asked to work longer hours than they would in other industries. A workweek of 50 to 60 hours is not uncommon. Neither are workdays of 10 to 12 hours. However, because much of a hospitality manager's workday involves talking to interesting guests, most who do this have no complaints about the length of the day.

It should be noted that the spouses and family members of some hospitality managers object to the specific hours, or the long workdays, or the somewhat unusual days off that can be common in this industry. However, the family members of anyone aspiring to a successful career in management in any field must recognize that long hours are likely to be among the requirements. Hospitality is not unique in that respect.

Travel Opportunities

One of the attractions of a career in the hospitality industry is the potential it offers for travel. A number of chain organizations in the hotel/motel segment of the industry customarily transfer management employees from one property to another every few years. Some restaurant chains do so as well. Both lodging and foodservice chains are more likely to transfer management employees during periods of expansion, when their expertise is needed in new units. Some transfer management-level employees at the time of promotion; others transfer managers periodically to reduce the risk of long-term managers becoming stale.

Another advantage of a career in hospitality is that job opportunities are not restricted to particular cities or regions, as they are in many manufacturing industries. Hospitality businesses can be found in literally every region, city, and town, and individuals can find positions available wherever they choose to live, regardless of climate or geography. Hospitality is very much an international profession.

Some hospitality professionals choose their careers specifically because of the travel opportunities the industry provides. There are even some who take advantage of the travel opportunities by working winter jobs in warm resort areas, such as Florida, and summer jobs in the cooler resorts of New England and the North Central or Rocky Mountain states. For those who enjoy travel, a career in hospitality can satisfy a need that might be difficult to meet in some other field. Frequently, employees who work for chain operations find that they can obtain substantial discounts when traveling to other properties within the chain. This obviously reduces the cost of travel considerably.

Other travel industry workers truly dislike travel and may take all possible steps to avoid it. Many in the hospitality industry have families and find it difficult to move, particularly when school-age children or elderly parents are involved. Many are settled members of their communities and have close ties they are unwilling to break. A substantial number own homes that they are unwilling or unable to sell. Others merely prefer to stay in communities where they have lived for many years.

People who prefer not to move from one region to another must be more particular about the types of positions they seek or the organizations from which they seek employment. It is possible, after all, to work for an independent city or resort hotel or motel or for an individual foodservice establishment for many years without facing the prospect of moving to a new geographical area.

Opportunities for Advancement

In a number of businesses, youth is traditionally a barrier to rapid advancement. Promotions in these businesses are slow, and managers on the higher levels are normally close to retirement age. It may be necessary to wait, sometimes for years, until openings occur within the company and advancement becomes possible. Generally, this is not the case in the hospitality industry.

The hospitality field enjoys a long tradition of mobility. Employees at all levels have almost always found it possible to change jobs readily, and many have done so with great regularity. The transient nature of the industry has generally meant that opportunities for higher-paying jobs are continually available to qualified individuals. Thus, if an individual working in a given hotel or restaurant decides she has little possibility of promotion, she can readily find another position—often a better one—in another hotel or restaurant.

The hospitality industry offers ample opportunities for people of all ages. It is not uncommon for restaurant managers, resident managers, marketing directors, food and beverage managers, executive housekeepers, and others in equally responsible positions to be in their mid- to late twenties. At the same time, many hospitality employees are in their second or third careers—people who discovered the appeal of a career in hospitality after a number of years in some other, possibly less interesting field. Except for the extremes, neither youth nor age is a disadvantage in this industry.

A PEOPLE-ORIENTED PROFESSION

Because the hospitality industry serves the needs of the traveling public, the majority of its workers—and virtually all of its managers—are in constant contact with guests and customers. Ours is a people-oriented profession. Individuals preparing for careers in hospitality must understand that their responsibilities are likely to include daily interaction with customers to meet their needs and to solve their problems. Social skills and the ability to communicate effectively are important assets for anyone planning such a career. Understanding the needs and views of people from the many and varied cultural, ethnic, racial, and religious backgrounds that make up our international mosaic is a clear asset. So, too, is an ability to communicate well in writing and in speech—to select and use words and phrases that do not offend those with backgrounds different from one's own. In addition, one should understand that facial and other physical expressions have meaning, and that the meaning one intends may not be the meaning conveyed to people of different backgrounds. It has been said that diversity is a major factor in American society today. Nowhere is this truer than in the hospitality industry.

If a number of your interests and preferences match those detailed in this chapter, you may find the hospitality industry a suitable career choice. If so, you are likely to find many exciting and rewarding career opportunities available to you. Reliability, dedication, willingness to work hard, and an interest in meeting customers' needs and solving their problems are the primary requisites for success in this field.

SUMMARY

In this chapter, distinctions among the product, service, and government sectors of an economy are drawn, and the scope of the hospitality industry within the service sector is defined and described. The relationships between the hospitality industry and travel and tourism—travel agents, tour operators, transportation, entertainment, and elements of government are explored. The characteristics of the hospitality industry that make it unique are identified, as are the characteristics that distinguish hospitality and other service enterprises from manufacturing. The terms *moment of truth*, *cycles of service*, and *empowerment* are defined and discussed, and their significance for the hospitality industry is described.

Total quality management is cited as an important means for reducing negative moments of truth. Career opportunities available in the hospitality industry and both the advantages and disadvantages of hospitality industry employment are explored. Finally, a variety of skills and values are identified as important assets for those planning careers in hospitality management.

KEY TERMS

Cycle of service
Employee empowerment
Hospitality
Hospitality industry
Moment of truth
Package

Service quality management
Total quality management
Tour operator
Tourism
Travel
Travel agent

DISCUSSION QUESTIONS

1. Distinguish among the manufacturing, service, and government sectors in an economy.

2. Define the terms *hospitality* and *hospitality industry.*

3. Identify the two principal segments of the hospitality industry and list the major types of businesses in each.

4. What is the scope of the travel and tourism industry? What is the relationship of the hospitality industry to the travel and tourism industry?

5. Historically, what kinds of entertainment have hospitality enterprises provided for travelers?

6. Discuss the relationship and the importance of transportation to the hospitality industry.

7. Define the terms *travel agent* and *tour operator.*

8. List and discuss two distinctions between hospitality and other services.

9. What special characteristics of the hospitality and other service industries distinguish them from the product sector?

10. Define the terms *moment of truth* and *cycle of service* and discuss the significance of each for the hospitality industry.

11. Does the study of hospitality management appear to be more important or less important today than in the past? Why do you suppose this is the case?

12. What is total quality management? Of what significance is it to hospitality operations?

13. What advantages would you expect graduates of hospitality programs to have in applying for their first management training positions? Why?

14. List several jobs that a new graduate of a hospitality management program could reasonably expect to be offered as a first job in a 1000-room hotel? In a 50-unit motel? In a fast service restaurant?

15. List and explain the significance of six qualifications hospitality employers commonly look for in applicants for management trainee positions.

16. For you, personally, what are the positive, appealing aspects of a career in the hospitality industry? What are the negative, unappealing aspects?

17. Why are social and communications skills important for people working in the hospitality industry?

MOMENTS OF TRUTH

1. You are working as a server in the Collins Hotel. One entrée on the dining room menu is sea scallops, which are breaded, then deep-fried. A guest in the dining room asks the server if she can have the scallops broiled instead. You

ask the chef, who informs you that he will not permit any changes to menu items. Discuss this in terms of moments of truth, cycle of service, and empowerment.

2. You are the morning desk clerk in a large motel just off an interstate highway. A guest has just come to the desk to check out. He is complaining that he could not sleep because of noises in the next room that continued until after 3:00 A.M. He claims that repeated calls to the desk produced no result. What would you do to change these negative moments of truth into a positive outcome?

3. You are the desk clerk at a seaside hotel. Half the rooms and suites face the sea; the other half face inland. One guest who was checked in by a clerk on an earlier shift assigned the guest to a room with an inland view. The rate is $85. This guest is now at the desk stating that he had reserved a room with a view of the sea. The reservation record confirms his statement, but you have no sea view rooms available. However, three suites with sea views are available, but all have rates over $150. What would you do?

INTERNET EXERCISES

1. Go to www.edfound.org. Search the Web site for career opportunities in food-service. List three jobs shown on that site that you would be qualified to perform in a hotel or restaurant upon graduation.

2. Go to www.careers.msn.com/ on the Internet. Select three hospitality jobs you would like to have upon graduation. Write a short description of each and explain why these jobs appeal to you.

End Notes

1. Jan Carlzon, *Moments of Truth* (Cambridge, Mass.: Ballinger, 1987).
2. Karl Albrecht, *At America's Service* (Homewood, Ill.: Dow Jones–Irwin, 1988) 33.

PART II
Foundations

Hospitality Foundations I

Early Development of the Hospitality Industry

► Learning Objectives

After reading and studying this chapter, you should be able to:

1. Explain the historical relationships between travel and the hospitality industry.

2. Identify the types of hospitality enterprises common in the Egyptian, Greek, and Roman empires and describe their principal characteristics.

3. Describe the hospitality services generally available to travelers in the period between the fall of Rome and the Renaissance.

4. Discuss conditions faced by travelers in Western Europe during the Renaissance.

5. List and explain the principal political, economic, and social developments that led to improvements in travel and in the hospitality services available to travelers between A.D. 1600 and 1800.

6. Identify the principal changes in the hospitality industry that resulted from the development of rail travel.

7. Identify and describe the earliest types of hospitality establishments in the United States.

8. Identify the historic significance of each of the following hotels and restaurants: Coles Ordinary, Fraunces Tavern, City Hotel, Tremont Hotel, San Francisco's Palace Hotel, Denver's Brown Palace, The Greenbrier, Ye Olde Union Oyster House, Delmonico's.

9. Discuss the impact of railroads on the development of both city hotels and resort hotels in the nineteenth century.

10. List and discuss the characteristics of nineteenth-century American city hotels that made them unique in their time.

11. Describe the dimensions of the fire problem in city hotels in the nineteenth century.

12. List and discuss the economic and social conditions that fostered the growth of the foodservice industry in the nineteenth century.

13. Name six types of foodservice establishments common in major American cities in the nineteenth century.

14. Identify the following individuals and describe the principal contributions of each to the development of the hospitality industry: Samuel Coles, Samuel Fraunces, Isaiah Rogers, Harvey Parker, Henry Flagler, and Fred Harvey.

INTRODUCTION

Everyone planning a career in the hospitality industry should be interested in both the present state of the industry and its history—a rich history that explains a lot about the field today. Hospitality managers, as educated persons, should have some understanding of the historical development of the industry so they can appreciate its continuing development and the progress made over the years. In our view, managers should be able to discuss any aspect of our industry, current or historical, with coworkers, superiors, and subordinates.

This chapter and Chapter 3 discuss the industry's classic and historic roots. They do not constitute a complete and comprehensive history of the hospitality industry worldwide, nor its many manifestations. Such a history would require volumes. However, the material presented here provides a suitable foundation for understanding the development of our industry and may impel students who find themselves intrigued to study the history of our industry further at the undergraduate or the graduate level.

OVERVIEW

Those beginning to study the history of the hospitality industry soon recognize that its development is inexorably tied to the development of transportation and the economic growth of cities, regions, and even nations.

Transportation and economic progress are clearly interdependent; they tend to develop together. Historically, nations that achieved high economic status in a given era had transportation networks more advanced than those of other nations. Examples of economic prosperity and superior transportation abound; the Roman Empire of 21 centuries ago and the British Empire of the nineteenth century are excellent examples. By contrast, and in our own time, nations that are part of the so-called Third World offer typical examples of inadequate transportation networks and relative economic distress. To the student of hospitality history, it soon becomes clear that growth and development in our industry has tended to occur most commonly in those nations that (1) were the most economically successful at the time and (2) had the most highly developed transportation networks.

From the earliest days of human history, much travel has been dependent on roads of one sort or another. Whether people traveled on foot, on the backs of animals, or in vehicles pulled by animals, or by train or automobile, roads were a key element in the development of travel and transportation systems. As we shall see, each segment of the hospitality industry changed and grew as roads improved.

Nations with the most advanced economies and the best infrastructure have had the most tourists. Shown are an inn and a road as they might have looked during the Roman Empire.
(Photo courtesy of E.N.I.T. Chicago)

BEGINNINGS

Human population has existed for hundreds of thousands of years in all parts of the world. For example, Cro-Magnon man was active in Europe and the Middle East at about 40,000 B.C. At about 20,000 B.C., early humans crossed the Bering Land Bridge from Asia to America. At about 10,000 B.C., Jericho, the oldest known city, was built in the Middle East. However, there was relatively little travel as we know it today and no known hospitality industry until relatively recently in human history.

The Sumerians

The recorded history of the hospitality industry begins with the Sumerians, a group of people who inhabited an area known as Mesopotamia, near the Persian Gulf, by about 4000 B.C. Much of this area, covering part of the modern state of Iraq, was particularly fertile, allowing many of the Sumerians to become skilled farmers and cattle breeders. Some also became relatively prosperous.

The Sumerians' skill at farming enabled them to raise and harvest sufficient grain to support artisans and craftsmen who could devote their time and talent to other activities—tool making, building, and pottery making among them. The Sumerian farmers were eventually able to produce so much grain that they had a surplus available to trade. Sumerians are often credited with inventing money and writing, both critical elements in the evolution of business.

In addition to growing and trading grain, the Sumerians became skilled at converting it to alcoholic beverages, primarily beers. These became the most widely and commonly consumed beverages at all levels of Sumerian society. The Sumerian grain beverages were probably safer to drink than their water.

Local Sumerian taverns were probably among the first hospitality businesses. These were drinking establishments that catered to people who lived in the immediate neighborhood. The taverns served various beers and provided a gathering place for local residents to discuss the issues of the day.

Early Traders Needed Hospitality Services

By 2000 B.C., a considerable amount of trade had developed among the peoples of the Middle East. Many earned their living from trade and followed established routes to trade for exotic goods. They needed places to stay and eat on these long journeys, and enterprising individuals set up hospitality businesses to meet the needs of travelers. Known as **caravanserai**, these businesses were early inns, providing food and shelter. Their reputation was similar to those of taverns of the period: dirty, bug-infested places that travelers preferred to avoid whenever possible.

EMPIRES: 3200 B.C. TO A.D. 476

While several civilizations were thriving in the region around the Persian Gulf, others were developing around the Mediterranean Sea between 3200 B.C. and A.D. 476—a period known to historians as the **Empire era**. During this time, three significant empires flourished around the Mediterranean: the Egyptian, the Greek, and the Roman.

We do not mean to suggest that these parts of the world were the only areas where civilization was developing, nor are we implying that these were the only areas where trade, travel, and the conditions for the evolution of a hospitality industry could be found. History clearly indicates otherwise. There is evidence, for example, that a road system was built in China around the year 2300 B.C. and that small road systems existed in northern Europe as early as 4000 B.C. There are also clear indications of developing civilizations in India by 2400 B.C. These examples show that civilizations were developing around the world during this period.

However, because of the advanced levels of their civilizations, the wealth of information available about them, and the direct influence they had on the development of the hospitality industry in Europe, we restrict our discussion to the Mediterranean empires of Egypt, Greece, and Rome. Each of these built and improved transportation systems and developed hospitality services for increasing numbers of travelers. These developments reached their zenith during the Roman period with the creation of a transportation network that surrounded the Mediterranean and extended to such distant points as England, France, and Germany.

Egypt

The Egyptian empire developed over a period of several thousand years. By about 3200 B.C., various groups had been united under one government. The Egyptians are considered the first people to have created a political entity we could recognize as a single nation rather than a group of city-states. They developed a government to rule a large number of people in an organized manner, with a hierarchy of civil servants dividing responsibilities for various aspects of governing. The government was headed by a pharaoh, their term for a king.

The famed pyramids were built as tombs for the pharaohs. These were constructed as early as 2700 B.C. and became tourist attractions that people traveled great distances to view. They may well have been the first man-made tourist attractions!

Travel was not uncommon in ancient Egypt. In addition to traveling to see the pyramids, people traveled to see other sights, to trade goods, to transact government business, and to attend religious festivals. Evidence suggests that the ancient Egyptians may have been the first to organize festivals, religious and otherwise, and to see that foodservice and lodging were provided for the crowds attending. Thus, the ancient Egyptians may have been responsible for beginning the activity we now call tourism.

Pyramids in Egypt might have been the first man-made tourist attractions. They remain the primary reason tourists visit Egypt today.
(Photo courtesy of PhotoDisc, Inc.)

Greece

Ancient Greek civilization began to develop about 1100 B.C. It evolved in the form of independent city-states that tended to be fiercely competitive. In the early years, major battles took place between the peoples of two of these, Sparta and Athens. No unified Greek nation developed until the middle of the third century B.C., when Philip of Macedon united the city-states. His son, Alexander the Great, built an empire that surrounded the Mediterranean and extended as far east as India.

The Greeks were great travelers. By 356 B.C., their travels over land and sea made them dominant in the Mediterranean region. They established colonies that stretched their empire as far west as Spain and even to the north coast of the Black Sea. Travel to these distant colonies was risky at best; common dangers at sea included shipwreck and piracy.

On land, robbery was a constant threat. In spite of the danger, many Greeks traveled to great religious centers, particularly Delphi and Olympia, to take part in games and competitions and to consult their oracles.

While good restaurants served the needs of travelers in major cities, Greek inns and taverns were reputed to be dreadful places. The proprietors were considered among the lowest forms of human life. Innkeepers commonly adulterated drinks with water and engaged in criminal activities. Some were particularly good at extortion and espionage. They were almost universally despised by citizens with wealth, status, and power, who would not enter inns and taverns under any circumstances. If a government employee visited one, he risked his colleagues having nothing further to do with him.

The two most important contributions the Greeks made to the development of the hospitality industry were:

1. Their language, which became universally accepted as the language of international trade

2. Their currencies, which were widely circulated, accepted, and trusted as the medium of exchange for monetary transactions

The general acceptance of the Greek language and currencies throughout the empire made travel and trade comparatively easy and thus played an important role in increasing the volume of both. As travel and trade increased, so did the demand for the hospitality services of food and lodging.

Rome

The Roman Empire dates from the time peasant farmers from central Europe settled at approximately the site of present-day Rome. By about 500 B.C., the Romans had established a government that provided for the election of some officials by citizens. The Romans were ambitious and pursued international power by both military and nonmilitary means. They aggressively increased their territory and, as they did so, their influence grew. In 146 B.C., after many years of conflict, the Romans were finally victorious over the Greeks. Roman efforts at territorial expansion continued and, by the time Rome conquered most of Western Europe and the Middle East, inns and taverns were well established throughout the empire.

Travel within the empire was relatively safe and easy, compared with earlier times, because:

1. The traveler needed only one currency—Roman coins—to travel anywhere in the empire.

2. The excellent system of roads the Romans built throughout Europe made travel faster and easier.

3. The traveler needed to know only Latin or Greek, the languages of business and government, to communicate fairly easily in any part of the empire.

These factors contributed to the development of an economic prosperity that surpassed any previously known. Goods of all kinds were sent to Rome from every part of the known world—some because of conquest, most because of trade. As a result, many citizens of Rome became wealthy.

A few good inns were reserved for military and government personnel and a very few fine resorts, available only to the wealthiest of citizens, existed, but the general quality of the taverns and inns accessible by the public was poor. Although there were many inns along the great Roman roads, the upper classes did not patronize them if they could find any conceivable alternative.

Roman food, by contrast, was often excellent. Good food was not consumed in their inns, however. The Romans, particularly the wealthy, had lavish meals at home and at banquet facilities adjacent to the public baths.

The Roman public restaurants of the day served more ordinary food to the population. In the ruins at Pompeii are a number of small restaurants reminiscent of present-day fast food establishments. They share a single basic design and appear to have been set up to prepare and sell essentially the same, very limited menu. They may have been operated by one person, or by one small group, much like a modern small chain. It is thus conceivable that these Romans should be credited with the establishment of the first restaurant chain!

By the late fifth century A.D., the Roman Empire was in serious decline. In A.D. 476, the last of the Roman emperors was deposed by the Byzantines, who ruled much of the area to the east and south of present-day Italy—lands that had once been part of the Greek, then the Roman empires. The Byzantine empire dominated the eastern Mediterranean for the next thousand years.

DECLINE AND REVIVAL: 476 TO 1300

After the fall of the Roman Empire and the decline in international trade, fine foods disappeared from the Western European diet. These were replaced by basic foods grown at home. About 90 percent of the population returned to farming and other forms of agriculture. Cities began to crumble and some virtually disappeared. Trade nearly ceased and the middle class disappeared. This period was marked by invasions into areas of Europe that had once been the Roman Empire. The invaders were so-called barbaric tribes of north central Europe. Travel and tourism, whether for business or pleasure, virtually ceased. Travel was undertaken primarily for religious reasons; some brave souls made pilgrimages to Rome and to the Holy Land. Innkeeping nearly disappeared, except for local taverns and a few inns scattered throughout Europe. This was the age of **feudalism**, a system whereby land was given by a ruler in return for loyalty and service.

Throughout this period, the Roman Catholic Church was thriving, gaining both spiritual and political power over the life of Europe. The Church, through its monasteries, filled the vacuum created by the demise of the commercial hospitality industry. In effect, the Church took over the job of feeding and housing travelers. The monasteries of the Church were self-sufficient enterprises. Members of the religious orders were skilled farmers, growing vegetables and herbs within the monastic walls, and members of the orders raised animals for meat and grew grapes for wine.

RENAISSANCE: 1350 TO 1600

The term **Renaissance** refers to the period of European history from the early fourteenth century to the late sixteenth century. It is derived from the French word for rebirth and originally referred to the revival of artistic values, especially in Italy. Later, the term came to mean a distinct historical period characterized by the rise of the individual, scientific inquiry, and growth of worldly values.

Renewed Travel and Trade

By about 1350, some degree of safety had returned to the roads, and travel and trade increased, creating conditions that led to the rise of the middle class in the economic life of Europe. In this period, the monasteries continued to be the principal providers of hospitality services to travelers in all economic strata.

Commercial Accommodations for Travelers

Gradually, taverns, inns, and wine shops began to make accommodations available to middle-class travelers, and the Church began to take the position that because the middle classes could afford to pay for the hospitality services available outside the monastery walls, it was proper to direct these travelers to such establishments. Thus, the Church played a role in the development of the hospitality industry during this period. The number of inns began to grow. They were very small by today's standards; an inn of 25 to 30 rooms was considered large. Standards of comfort and cleanliness varied greatly from country to country and region to region.

Tavern Signs

During this period—until the nineteenth century, in fact—most people could neither read nor write. Taverns and inns developed signs with distinctive pictures so that people could identify and direct other people to them. The signs varied, but usually depicted animals or birds. A weary traveler would be directed to the sign of the bull, the black swan, the lion, or the duck. These signs survive today and are found on many taverns and inns, particularly in the United Kingdom.

The Discomforts of Travel

Traveling was uncomfortable at best. Many roads of the period were more like trails, and travelers intending to go any distance rode horses. Women normally did not travel because of the discomforts of the road and the dangers associated with travel. Therefore, inns did not have provisions for women. It was not unusual to find the bedroom of an inn furnished with one or more large beds, each of which meant to sleep five or six people. In such places, the traveler would go to bed fully dressed in street clothes and share the bed with several strangers. The realities of travel were so unpleasant that women avoided it until the late nineteenth century.

Foodservice During the Renaissance

During this period, there were no restaurants as we know them. No dining rooms offered meals to the public at large. In England, there were taverns, public houses (pubs), alehouses, and inns. None of these were primarily dining establishments; to the extent that they served food, the food was intended only for travelers who had no other place to eat. As in other times and places, inns were ordinarily avoided by the wealthy upper classes, who dined and entertained in their homes.

Innkeeping

The monasteries that had housed travelers since the fall of Rome continued to do so. When they could find it, travelers preferred this free housing to local inns. Innkeepers resented this unfair competition and, as students of the Reformation know, at this time, a number of Church practices were considered offensive. In England in 1539, Parliament passed an act that suppressed the 608 religious houses. Under Henry VIII, the monasteries were closed and the lands given to many of the king's supporters, which helped ensure the unification of England under one strong government. One unintended consequence of this upheaval was that travelers could no longer find accommodations in monasteries. This greatly stimulated the innkeeping business and dramatically increased the number of inns in England.

Tourism in the Sixteenth Century

The sixteenth century also saw the beginnings of an activity known as the **grand tour**. Wealthy English would send their sons to tour Europe to "finish their education" on a tour that might last as long as three years. Paris was a favorite destination, as was the Italian peninsula. Young men might spend an entire year learning about the arts and humanities.

EARLY MODERN: 1600 TO 1800

The period from 1600 to 1800 was particularly important in the evolution of the hospitality industry. One critical element was the beginning development of roads, which facilitated the use of the stagecoach between cities. Roads built by the Romans before A.D. 500 had not been maintained and thus had decayed. Moreover, after the fall of Rome, there had been no comparable central government in Europe to build or maintain road systems. At the start of this period, roads were likely to be little better than trails. With continued use, a trail would come to resemble the primitive dirt roads found in rural communities. However, because no government was responsible for roads, maintenance was left to the discretion of the owners of the land through which a road passed. Therefore, although it was possible to go from one place to another by stagecoach, it was usually difficult and dangerous because of the condition of the roads. By the end of the period, roads became more passable, and stagecoach travel increased.

Another important development was English common law, which forms the basis of U.S. law and which has special significance for the hospitality industry today. Early common law required that innkeepers receive all travelers, providing they had space and the travelers were in a fit condition to be received. This meant that innkeepers could not refuse accommodations to travelers without a good reason and that the time of arrival of a traveler was not a consideration, even if he arrived at the inn at 3:00 A.M. Further, because some innkeepers were unscrupulous—they were in league with highwaymen or with guests who would steal from other unsuspecting guests—the law required that innkeepers be insurers of guests' property while at the inn. This meant that if property were stolen, the innkeeper was liable for its value. These principles are still reflected (with modifications) in our laws today.

Introduction of the Stagecoach

With the introduction of the stagecoach, regular stagecoach routes were established and so-called **coaching inns** soon followed. At the coaching inns, tired horses were exchanged for fresh horses and stagecoach passengers were fed and given opportunities to rest, frequently overnight. Travel was difficult, as the roads were often mud-soaked and full of potholes. One can imagine how uncomfortable it was to ride in a stagecoach all day. By the 1700s, the inns in England were much safer and more comfortable, although the standards varied from one inn to another.

Posthouses

The mails were an important factor in the development of the hospitality industry during this period. Until the late 1700s, the mail in England was carried on horseback by messengers known as postboys, who were able to ride about 6 miles per hour. Letters usually took several days to go even 100 miles. With the development of stagecoaches, mail carrying was gradually transferred to stagecoach lines. These had established routes and contracts that provided that mail be delivered within specific amounts of time. Because of these provisions, stagecoaches began to travel faster. Teams of horses were run at full speed for approximately 10 miles, at which point the stage stopped at a **posthouse** to change horses. A new team was hitched to the stage and the process repeated.

Posthouses were much like the coaching inns described earlier. They were equipped to feed drivers and passengers or to accommodate them overnight. Locating the inns along coach routes ensured that the inns served a steady supply of customers arriving by stagecoach. Even in the eighteenth century, location was an important element in the success of a hospitality enterprise.

Foodservice in Coffeehouses and Taverns

After the fall of Rome and until the late eighteenth century, no public restaurants existed as we know them today. England, however, had establishments known as **coffeehouses**, where one could get light snacks, and taverns that served a daily **ordinary**, which was a main meal at a fixed price. Most people consumed their meals at home. The wealthy had their own cooks and, when they entertained, they usually did so in their own homes. Inns were primarily for travelers and did not normally serve meals to local residents.

Restaurants

The foodservice element of the hospitality industry changed dramatically and forever in Paris in 1765. A man named Boulanger operated a small business selling soups and broths. These were known as *restaurants*, a French word meaning restoratives. Soups and broths have long been noted for their ability to fortify the weary or to restore energy, and Boulanger was one of many such sellers of soups and broths at the time.

For reasons that are unclear, Boulanger decided to add an item to his product line—a dish made of sheep's feet with a sauce. Perhaps some had requested it; perhaps he was merely trying to make his small business different from others. In any event, the **traiteurs**—members of a caterers' guild who prepared roasts and meats for consumption in private homes—objected on the grounds that he was preparing and selling a ragout, and that only traiteurs were permitted to sell ragouts and similar foods under existing French law. They took him to court.

After careful study of the traiteurs' position, the court decided that Boulanger had not violated any law. The case created much publicity and interest and led to a decree authorizing both traiteurs and restaurateurs to serve guests within their establishments. After a while, this resulted in the development of public dining rooms in which guests could be seated and served the food and drink of their choice.

Boulanger is usually credited with creating the first **restaurant**, which has come to mean an establishment with a dining room open to the public where varied foods may be purchased and consumed. Technically, however, he merely reinvented a form of foodservice enterprise that had existed many centuries earlier but had disappeared during the Dark Ages. After all, the forerunners of Boulanger's restaurant had existed in ancient Greece and Rome.

In the late eighteenth century, the restaurant business took another leap forward. During the French Revolution, the common people of France revolted against the monarchy, taking control of the government and the properties of wealthy aristocrats, many of whom were executed. Cooks and chefs who had been employed by the aristocrats were suddenly out of work. They had to find ways to earn a living, and many opened foodservice establishments. After the French Revolution, the number of restaurants in Paris and other parts of France began to grow dramatically.

Another type of foodservice establishment that emerged in France at this time was the **café**. *Café* is the French word for coffee, and it is probable that cafés were the French equivalents of the English coffeehouses. At first, they may have served snacks only, just as the English did. It is likely that the proprietors of these establishments soon began to use their highly developed culinary skills to prepare more elaborate items—certainly to the delight of their customers.

These developments in France in the late eighteenth century mark the beginnings of the modern restaurant industry, which embarked on a period of growth and development in the early nineteenth century that continues to this day.

THE INDUSTRIAL ERA: FROM 1800

The Industrial Revolution, which dates from the mid-1700s, started in England with the development of machines to do work that formerly was done by hand. This period was an age of invention. Machines and the developing concept of the factory were key elements that changed forever the way work is accomplished. It was no longer necessary to depend on water and water wheels for power. With steam engines, power could be made available in locations that had no access to water transportation. This led to the development of mill towns—later, cities—in many new locations across England and Scotland. The greatest period of growth for these new communities and work sites followed the invention of the railroad in 1825. This new form of transportation started a network designed to move raw materials and finished goods from place to place.

Rail Travel and the Hospitality Industry

The significance of the railroad to the development of the hospitality industry cannot be overemphasized. It quickly became apparent that railroads could transport people as well as goods and thus reduce traveling time. Passengers could reach their destinations quickly and in relative comfort. For example, the trip from London to Bath, a distance of 110 miles that required 11 hours to travel by stage-coach, took only 2.5 hours by rail.

As the rail network grew, stagecoach operators began to lose much of their business. Government contracts to carry the mail were not renewed. New contracts were negotiated with the railroads, which before long controlled the principal postal routes. People soon abandoned stagecoach travel as well. This led to the demise of most stagecoach lines in a very few years. As the coach lines disappeared, the coaching inns lost their traditional sources of business and were forced to find new markets or close.

The development of railroad networks—first in England, then in other nations—had a greater effect on the hospitality industry than had any other single development since the fall of the Roman Empire. Passenger rail traffic led to the establishment of railroad stations, which became obvious locations for new hospitality businesses. Inns, taverns, restaurants, and, later, hotels opened in or near railroad stations. In England, examples include the Charing Cross Hotel and the St. Pancras Hotel in London and the Queens Hotel in Birmingham. Scotland had St. Enoch's Hotel in Glasgow and the Station Hotel in Perth. Later U.S. examples include the Biltmore Hotel and the Commodore Hotel, built in New York City near Grand Central Station.

Public Dining

In the last years of the nineteenth century, important changes began to appear in the European hospitality industry. Until then, eating meals away from home was done of necessity rather than by choice. Business travelers and people working in factories, shops, and offices ate meals away from home because they could not return home during the working day. Whenever possible, people preferred to dine in domestic privacy. Because public dining was not popular, many hotels were constructed without dining facilities. The custom was for hotel guests to have meals in their rooms—room service, in today's terms. In the hotel dining rooms that did exist, the patrons were all men. It was not customary for women to dine in public.

By 1880, dining out had begun to gain acceptability and some small measure of popularity. One of the first steps taken in that direction occurred in 1875 in the Albemarle Hotel, London, when a dining facility was opened for the "accommodation of both ladies and gentlemen." By this time, the term *restaurant* had come into common English use but referred to the dining room of a hotel.

In London, new, luxurious hotels were built. Some of them were known both for the excellence of their guest accommodations and the superiority of their food. One of the best known of these was the Savoy, opened by an entrepreneur named Richard D'Oyly Carte in 1889. In the Savoy, D'Oyly Carte employed two men who would become famous throughout the world: César Ritz and Auguste Escoffier.

CÉSAR RITZ (1850–1918)

César Ritz was born in 1850 in Switzerland, the thirteenth child in a large family. His early days in the hospitality industry did not suggest that his was to be a brilliant future. He was dismissed from his first two jobs, one as an apprentice wine waiter and the other as an assistant waiter. After this inauspicious beginning, Ritz drifted to Paris, where he obtained and lost other jobs before taking a waiter's job in the most fashionable establishment in Paris at that time, the Voisin. He quickly learned that the wealthy in Paris wanted, demanded, and appreciated excellent service. Soon, the wealthiest and most famous of the Voisin's clientele were asking for him by name. His reputation grew, and he became a maître d'hôtel, then restaurant manager at the Grand Hotel at Nice. Because of his superior abilities to please the wealthy, he was always able to work in the finest properties, some of which were used by Thomas Cook's organization to accommodate travelers on luxury tours of Europe.

Before long, he progressed to hotel manager and, in 1870, at the age of 27, Ritz was offered a job managing the Grand National Hotel in Lucerne, Switzerland. The hotel was not a profitable venture when he assumed the manager's job, but Ritz was able to turn it into one with his deft management skills. He inspired the staff and the chef with his enthusiasm and principles of good service, and he organized luxurious and fabulous entertainments for his guests. Soon the hotel became one of the most popular in Europe, and César Ritz became one of the most respected hoteliers on the continent.

The Ritz name today is a symbol of superior products and luxury hotels. The Ritz chain has hotels throughout the world and includes the Ritz-Carlton in Boston, the Chicago Ritz, and the Ritz-Carlton in Laguna Niguel, California. Other Ritz hotels are located in Atlanta, Barcelona, Cleveland, Hong Kong, Houston, Hawaii, San Francisco, Sydney, and elsewhere.

HOSPITALITY IN AMERICA

The development of the hospitality industry in the United States has been unique, having no precise parallel in any other country. There appears to be a number of contributing reasons, including the vast size of the country, the multinational character of the people, the formation of the transportation system, and the unique political and economic systems operating in America. The factors listed below set the American hospitality experience apart from that of the rest of the world.

1. Since the time of the earliest settlements in the late sixteenth century, a larger proportion of the American people have traveled greater distances than have the people of other nations; consequently, Americans have patronized hotels and restaurants in greater numbers.

2. The American political and economic systems have made it possible for financially successful people to build grand hotels as monuments to their success, even if the properties they built were unprofitable. These systems have also enabled ambitious, hard-working people of limited means and little education to become successful in hospitality businesses.

AUGUSTE ESCOFFIER (1846–1935) ◄

Auguste Escoffier was four years older than César Ritz. His career as a chef began in Paris, and he was soon employed at some of the finest properties of the time in France. Escoffier and Ritz worked together at the Grand Hotel, Monte Carlo, before Ritz became manager of the Savoy in London. Recognizing the need for a superior chef to enliven a dull menu in this new luxury hotel, Ritz sent for Escoffier.

Escoffier is noted for his many contributions to the improvement of cuisine and service. He is the only chef ever to be given membership in the French Legion of Honor, a distinction bestowed on him by the president of France in 1920. His principal contributions include:

1. Simplifying classic cuisine.

2. Simplifying menus.

3. Reorganizing the kitchen staff into the classic brigade. He divided the staff into specialized departments on the basis of types of foods prepared; the earlier method, which he discarded, had each chef prepare an entire meal from appetizer onwards.

4. Revolutionizing banquet service by serving only one or two dishes at a time, rather than the older, established practice of serving a whole table full of dishes at once.

5. Naming dishes after famous people (Melba toast, Peaches Melba, and Melba Sauce were named for the opera star Nellie Melba).

6. Writing *Le Guide Culinaire*, a culinary text and collection of recipes used by several generations of chefs.

Following the success of the Savoy, a number of other luxury properties opened in London, including the Waldorf, the Strand Palace, and Claridge's, to name but a few. All of these survive to this day.

Auguste Escoffier is perhaps the most famous and most respected chef of all time. He had a greater impact on the culinary arts than any one else.

3. Innkeeping has always been considered an honorable and respected profession. This is in stark contrast to the tradition of innkeeping in other nations, where innkeepers were commonly relegated to the lowest classes of society.

4. American hotels have always been public places—establishments used by local residents as social centers and places for entertaining. In other nations, inns and hotels were used only by travelers, at least until the late nineteenth century. In these countries, the local populace frequented taverns, but not hotels.

5. The multicultural nature of the American population has led to a greater diversity in the kinds of restaurants established here, in contrast to those established in other countries.

6. Although other nations have long relied on railroads as their major means of intercity travel and transportation, at the end of World War II, the United States began to rely heavily on automobiles and airplanes instead. Today, automobiles account for over 80 percent of all U.S. intercity travel. Airplanes

account for approximately 17 percent and railroads less than 2 percent. The major difference between these modes of transportation and those used in other nations has caused American hospitality operations to develop very differently.

7.   Several unique hospitality concepts originated in the United States and were later imitated in other nations. These include:
   • Large grand hotels
   • Restaurant chains
   • Franchises
   • Motels

Ordinaries, Taverns, and Inns in Early America

The earliest known example of an American hospitality enterprise existed in Jamestown, Virginia, in 1610. Because the Jamestown settlement did not survive, there is no reliable information about it. Therefore, the beginning of the American hospitality industry is usually said to be 1634, when Samuel Coles opened an establishment in Boston that was named Coles Ordinary. It was a tavern—the first tavern of record in the American colonies, and probably the first inn as well. It was quite successful, lasting well over 125 years. When John Hancock became governor of Massachusetts in the eighteenth century, Coles Ordinary, still in business, was renamed Hancock's Tavern.

The terminology used in the colonial period to identify these establishments can be confusing. Throughout the period, the terms *ordinary*, *tavern*, and *inn* were all used to refer to the same basic institution—an enterprise established to provide food, drink, overnight accommodation, or some combination of these to travelers, local inhabitants, or both. Over time, *tavern* became the more common term from New England to New York; *inn* became favored in the Pennsylvania region; *ordinary* was more common in the South.

The word *ordinary* is an old term, used originally in Great Britain to describe a midday meal served at a fixed price in a tavern to the local inhabitants. The term also came to mean the tavern itself. The ordinary offered no menu and no choice: the tavernkeeper served whatever he decided to prepare for that day. Ordinaries in New England were under strict Puritan guardianship and were not allowed, at one point, to charge more than 6 pence for a meal and 1 penny for a quart of ale or beer.

Opening and closing hours were enforced by the Puritans, and men who drank too much were punished. The punishment could be severe; miscreants could be put in bilbos—long iron bars with shackles that slid back and forth—set in the stocks, and whipped. Records show that one Robert Wright was fined 20 shillings and put in the stocks for an hour for being "twice distempered in drink." Robert Coles—no relation to Samuel Coles—was fined 10 shillings and ordered to wear a sign on his back that read DRUNKARD in large letters. Unfortunately, this penalty did not cure him. A year later he was at it again, and that time the badge of disgrace was made permanent. He was ordered to wear a large *D* around his neck. Lists of names of drunkards such as Coles were given to taverns in other towns and the proprietors warned not to serve liquor to them under penalty of losing their license.

The number of ordinaries in the New England colonies grew. They were considered important establishments, and sometimes the courts directed that ordinaries or public houses be opened in communities where they did not exist. For example, in 1656, the General Court of Massachusetts made towns responsible for sustaining an ordinary. Concord, Massachusetts, was fined by the court for not having an ordinary and was directed to open one. In 1644, the colonial records of Connecticut ordered "one sufficient inhabitant in each town to keep an ordinary, since strangers were straitened for want of entertainment." It was recognized early in the colonial period that travelers needed a place to eat, drink, and find accommodation. Inducements were offered to a person willing to keep an ordinary. These included exemption from church rates and school taxes as well as grants of land or pasturage for cattle.

Early ordinaries existed not only to accommodate travelers but also to serve as gathering places for the local townsfolk. They were important centers for the exchange of news and served as places where public questions could be debated or public opinion sampled. In addition, they were places for local residents to seek refreshments—ale, beer, and cider among them. In wintertime, taverns were particularly popular. For example, people became very cold during services in the unheated churches and meetinghouses while they sat listening to long sermons. After the services, the men flocked to a welcoming nearby tavern to warm up.

Innkeeping in the Colonies

Unlike the innkeepers in England, American innkeepers have always been respected members of the community, and inns located in cities and towns were generally clean and well run. When one traveled into rural areas, however, the quality of the taverns and inns was less reliable, ranging from very uncomfortable to quite nice. In these areas, anyone who could both build a log hut and supply liquor could put up a tavern sign. Those who did would then go to the woods nearby, kill some game, and put it into a pot to cook. The result was used to feed the guests and was known as **potluck**. The practice of sharing a bed with strangers had disappeared in Europe by the 1700s, but it persisted in America, particularly in rural establishments.

The Oldest Continually Operating Tavern in America

New York City, one of America's oldest cities, has had its share of firsts. One of special interest to the student of hospitality history is Fraunces Tavern, located in the lower part of Manhattan in the area known as Wall Street, now New York's financial center. Located at the corner of Broad and Pearl streets, Fraunces Tavern has the honor of being the oldest continually operating tavern in the nation and has some interesting history associated with it.

The building was constructed in 1719 as a private residence, which it remained until about 1757, when the owner moved uptown to a better neighborhood, a practice that persisted in New York City for generations. In 1762, the house was sold to a West Indian named Samuel Fraunces, who converted it to a tavern that he named the Queen's Head. After operating it for a short time, he leased it out for several years but returned to operate it in 1775 because he was unable to sell it. He continued to run it throughout the Revolutionary War, but it was not actually known as Fraunces Tavern until 1783, after the war.

One of his customers was George Washington, whom Fraunces served when the general met with his staff at the tavern to plan war campaigns. When the British occupied New York City, Fraunces continued to operate the tavern. Although his customers were then British generals, Fraunces remained loyal to the revolutionary cause, serving as a spy for the American Army. Fraunces frequently sent word about British plans to General Washington. In fact, Fraunces has sometimes been characterized as the first American intelligence agent!

The First Hotel Building in the United States

In 1794, the first structure designed specifically as a hotel was constructed in New York City near Wall Street. Aptly named the City Hotel, it occupied a large site on the island of Manhattan, on the west side of lower Broadway near Trinity Church. The hotel had 73 guest rooms and was the largest hotel in New York until 1813. It was simply furnished, was spacious and comfortable, and offered room service to its guests. For $2, it offered a room and meals—breakfast at 8, dinner at 3, tea at 6, and supper at 9. Its two proprietors were men named Jennings and Willard. Willard served as host, room clerk, bookkeeper, and cashier, while Jennings supervised food preparation and the operation of the dining room. Both were said to be good at remembering names and faces and were generally considered excellent proprietors. For several years, the City Hotel was the social center of New York, the setting for many important banquets, dances, and political events. Although it survived until 1849, it had long since lost its early splendor.

There has always been an important difference between American hotels and those of Europe. From their earliest days, American hotels—the City Hotel and its successors—were considered gathering places for the local community, whereas European hotels were not considered such until the twentieth century.

THE HOSPITALITY INDUSTRY IN THE NINETEENTH CENTURY

The nineteenth century was a notable period for the hospitality industry in the United States. The expanding railroad network caused considerable travel and spawned the building of excellent city hotels and resort hotels. Many important restaurants were established. It can be said that the nineteenth century saw the travel and hospitality industry develop at a greater rate than at any prior time.

City Hotels in the 1800s

From 1800 to approximately 1880, a large number of city residents lived in hotels or in rooming houses and boardinghouses that closely resembled small hotels. Those who could not afford private homes had no other choice. There were no apartments as we know them today; the first apartments in America were constructed in New York City in 1880. Consequently, over 50 percent of the rooms in the typical city hotel were occupied by permanent residents. Hotels were available for people of various income levels, and virtually everyone in need of rooms could find something affordable. Some hotels appealed to people employed in the immediate area; others catered to those in particular professions or income strata. All were usually busy. We know most about those that earned grand reputations as the finest available in their times and comparatively little about the others.

"Palaces of the Public"

Those famous American hotels of the past about which much information survives have been dubbed "**palaces of the public**," a title that refers not only to the public nature of American hotels but also to their elegance. In many small cities, the local hotel was the finest, most splendid structure in the city. In larger cities, several hotels commonly competed to be the best, installing the latest in modern conveniences and, often, becoming self-sufficient cities within cities. Many featured such amenities as barber shops, libraries, billiard rooms, hair salons, ticket offices, florists, and cigar stands. Some eventually provided dining service for over 20 hours a day.

It is particularly interesting that the palatial hotels of this nature—the so-called grand hotels—were found only in the United States, until the later years of the nineteenth century. Grand hotels were clearly an American invention.

The Tremont Hotel, Boston

The first of the truly grand hotels in America was the Tremont Hotel, a purpose-built property that opened in Boston at the corner of Tremont and Beacon Streets in October 1829. By every standard of the time, it was a luxurious enterprise. The designer of this remarkable property was a young man of 27 named Isaiah Rogers. The Tremont was three stories high and boasted 170 guest rooms and a dozen public rooms. It was the first hotel to have:

- Bellboys
- Clerks whose responsibilities were limited to the front desk
- A carpeted lobby and a large carpeted (200-seat) dining room, both with gaslit chandeliers
- Bathing rooms (eight)—probably steam baths—located in the building
- Private rooms—both singles and doubles—all equipped with doors having locks and keys for guests

- French cuisine
- A washbowl and pitcher in each room, plus a free bar of soap
- The first inside toilets, called water closets, located in the basement of the building
- A mechanical device known as an annunciator in each room, which made it possible for a guest to signal the hotel front office merely by pushing a button

The ceilings of the Tremont were exceptionally high, and any floors not carpeted were made of black and white marble. The furniture was native carved walnut. Although the list of firsts above may not connote a very luxurious operation by today's standards, one must remember that we are describing a property that was constructed 30 years before the Civil War—long before the advent of electricity, modern plumbing, and telephones. The Tremont was an extraordinary, luxurious hotel in its time.

The Astor House, New York

John Jacob Astor, a well-known American business tycoon, watched the success of the Tremont with great interest and decided that if a luxury hotel could succeed in Boston, one could do so in New York. Moreover, Astor decided to build a hotel in New York that would exceed the luxury of the Tremont. He proceeded to plan the Astor House, which was completed in 1836.

To design his hotel, Astor employed Isaiah Rogers, who was rapidly becoming known as the premier hotel architect in America. Rogers designed a hotel that was more grand than his Tremont. In addition to all the features that first appeared in the Tremont, the Astor House contained not eight but 17 bathing rooms, larger public rooms, and two new devices known as showers, which were located in the basement. The guest rooms were furnished with black walnut, and the floors were covered with Brussels carpets. In addition, all rooms were provided with gaslight; in fact, the Astor House was the first hotel to be fully illuminated with gas.

The Astor House was a hotel of 309 rooms on five floors. One of the more interesting problems in operating the hotel involved the gaslights. Guests were not used to gaslight, which was a new invention at the time. They were accustomed to candles, which were normally extinguished when people went to bed. Guests accustomed to extinguishing their candles by blowing them out sometimes took the same approach with gas fixtures, often with disastrous results. Failing to realize that raw gas was escaping from the unlighted fixtures, substantial numbers died—some from asphyxiation, others from explosions that occurred when they lit matches to reignite the gaslights.

Other Grand Hotels of the Era

The Tremont in Boston and the Astor in New York established models for more ostentatious American hotels. In Boston, grand hotels constructed included the

Adams House in the latter 1840s, the Revere House in 1847, and the original Parker House in 1855. New Yorkers were awed by such properties as the Howard Hotel in 1839, the New York Hotel in 1844, the Metropolitan in 1852, and the St. Nicholas in 1853. The St. Nicholas was the first hotel costing more than a million dollars to build—nearly $2 million, actually—and became the largest in the city after an 1856 addition increased its size to 500 rooms.

Similar growth and development was occurring in other cities as well. In New Orleans, both the St. Louis Hotel and the St. Charles Hotel opened in the late 1830s, soon after New York's Astor House. Philadelphians witnessed the opening of the American House in 1844 and the Washington House in 1845. In Buffalo, the American Hotel opened in 1836, the same year as the Astor House. Farther west, the citizens of St. Louis were justly proud of their Planters' Hotel, which opened in 1841.

In Boston, after its 1855 opening, the original Parker House became very popular and was considered far more modern than the Tremont Hotel. This perception was one of the factors that led to the decline and eventual closing of the famed Tremont. Charles Dickens, the famous British novelist and lecturer, spent several days in the Parker House when he was on a lecture tour of the United States in 1867. Local newspapers reported that he caused a sensation when people lined up at the hotel to obtain his autograph.

None of the grand hotels of the period, including those discussed above, was more than five stories high. There were two reasons for this. First, the hotels were built of wood, and wood construction is not suitable for tall buildings. Of equal importance was that the elevator had not yet been invented, so guests had to climb stairs to get to their rooms. This made the rooms located on the upper floors less popular and less expensive than those on the lower floors. The absence of elevators helps to explain the popularity of bellboys in the luxury hotels; guests no longer had to carry their own baggage up flights of stairs to their rooms. Years later, after the first elevator installations in hotels, about 1859, the industry witnessed reversal in the rates for rooms. Those on higher floors became more popular, and more expensive, than the less popular rooms on lower floors.

Fire was a constant danger in these wood buildings. The situation was serious enough when rooms and corridors were lighted with candles, which could accidentally start fires if knocked over or if placed too close to flammable materials. The problems were considerably worse when the newly invented gaslight became the principal means of illumination. With candles, fire was an obvious threat, and both guests and employees were vigilant; the introduction of gas brought the added threat of explosions, which might precede and precipitate devastating fires. During this period, before water was available above the first-floor level of buildings, raging fires in which many lives were lost regularly destroyed hotels. Seeing a hotel destroyed by fire, then watching it be rebuilt to open the following year was a normal experience for the citizens of large American cities.

It is important to understand that this period, between the opening of the Tremont (1829) and the start of the Civil War (1860), was one in which more new hotels were opened than at any time in our history until the 1920s. This could not and would not have occurred without a dramatic increase in the number of people traveling. This increase was directly related to the development of a network of railroads that became the primary means of transportation for people seeking to go from one to another of the growing cities in the United States. As in England, locations near railroad stations were quickly seen to be ideal for hotels, and the race was on in every city and town with a railroad station to build hotels close by. Tired travelers, emerging from the stations after long journeys on trains, typically sought the nearest hotel to find food, shelter, and rest.

Chicago's Hotels

Perhaps the most important railroad center of the age developed in Chicago. As the city and the railroad industry grew, so did the hotel industry. In 1837, the entire population of Chicago was only 4170. By 1860, the city had grown to over 200,000 and had a sufficient number of first-class hotels to be able to host the second Republican national convention, the one at which Abraham Lincoln was nominated. The list of grand hotels in Chicago at that time included a new Tremont, opened in 1850 to replace a prior Tremont that had burned, and which, in turn, replaced yet another Tremont that had also burned! The new Tremont cost $750,000 to construct and was, at first, considered too palatial for Chicago. Nevertheless, it quickly became a grand success and was enlarged twice. By 1868, it had reached nearly 300 rooms.

The Palmer House, Chicago

Another of Chicago's first luxury hotels was the original Palmer House, a 227-room property that opened in 1870. In 1871, a great fire swept through Chicago, destroying most of its hotels, including the Palmer House. After the great Chicago fire, the city began to rebuild, and many new hotels appeared. Twenty-three new first-class hotels opened within two years, including the Palmer House, the Grand Pacific, the Tremont, and the Sherman, which collectively became known as the Big Four. By then, Chicago had a population of over 300,000.

San Francisco's Hotels

The success of the hotel industry in Chicago was paralleled in San Francisco. In 1848, San Francisco was a small western town, still part of the Mexican Territory. The hospitality industry consisted of one small tavern that was just one-and-one-half stories high. In 1849, when gold was discovered in that part of California, the gold rush brought millions of people to the area to make their fortunes. In the next 25 years, the population of San Francisco grew to 160,000. As the population grew, so did the hospitality industry. New hotels, restaurants, taverns (saloons, actually), and other enterprises, which can best be described in a book of this nature as "entertainment centers," opened almost daily.

One of the earliest hotels in San Francisco was another Parker House, built in 1849 by Robert Parker—who, coincidentally, had come from Boston. San Francisco's Parker House was noted for its high prices, its gambling hall, and its large ballroom. It set the standard for prices and, when similar properties were built, they, too, charged very high prices. With gold fever in the air, people were not concerned about high prices. A cigar stand at the Union Hotel reportedly rented for $4000 a month, and the operator of the cigar stand, even at that high rent, was still able to make a handsome profit.

By 1859, a number of other grand—even opulent—hotels had been built, including the Occidental (400 rooms) and the Cosmopolitan, both of which opened in 1859. Perhaps the most expensive hotel constructed in San Francisco during this period was the Grand Hotel, built in 1869 at a cost of more than $1 million for a property of just 200 rooms!

Transcontinental railroad service began in 1869 with the joining of the Central Pacific and Union Pacific railroads. As one might expect, a number of fine hotels were constructed along this route to the West. By the end of the century, cities west of the Mississippi boasted the finest hotels. In fact, a reporter for one of Chicago's newspapers, the *Century*, wrote that two of the three best hotels in the country were located in the west. One was the Palace Hotel in San Francisco; the other was the Brown Palace in Denver. Perhaps not surprisingly, as the third in this trio of best hotels in America, the reporter chose one in his native Chicago—the Auditorium.

The Palace Hotel, San Francisco

The Palace Hotel was completed in 1875 at a cost of almost $5 million. It contained 755 rooms and boasted of having the same elegant features offered by the best of the New York and Boston hotels—and a few that they lacked. It was said that the Palace was so large that some guests had difficulty finding their rooms. One writer offered advice for those who experienced this problem: The best plan was to "pretend you are full, let yourself loose, and cuss. Someone will come and guide you to your room."

The rooms in the Palace Hotel were 20 feet square—very large rooms, even by today's standards. The dining room was 155 feet by 55 feet, the largest in the world at the time. The hotel had a large number of private dining rooms, reading rooms, and parlors, and even card rooms. The Palace was furnished with upholstered furniture made with native hardwood.

Operations were not profitable for the first ten years because of the huge cost of constructing the hotel. However, over the years, it became extremely successful. The Palace was the pride of San Francisco and was said to be earthquake proof, earthquakes having been a matter of concern as early as the late nineteenth century. Although it did survive the historic earthquake that rocked San Francisco on 18 April 1906, it burned to the ground in the ensuing fire that leveled the city.

Grand City Hotels Constructed During the 1890s

The Brown Palace, Denver

The Brown Palace had only 440 rooms, compared with 755 in the San Francisco Palace, but was as elegant as any hotel in the world when it opened in 1892. The immense lobby was eight stories high, with a stained-glass interior roof, onyx walls, and tile floors with elaborate Greek designs. The public rooms in the Brown Palace were dispersed throughout the building rather than concentrated on one floor—the usual practice in hotels built both before and after the Brown Palace. These public rooms were grandly decorated in the Louis XVI style. The hotel featured five honeymoon suites, known as bridal chambers and described by hotel management as "too beautiful and delicate for use." The daily rates for these suites were outrageously high—as much as $100, the equivalent of more than one year's salary for many American workers at that time! The other bedrooms in the hotel, half of which had private baths and many of which had fireplaces, were decorated in 50 shades of yellow, from cream to gold.

The Waldorf-Astoria, New York

As a fitting climax to the nineteenth-century growth of the hotel industry in the American city, two hotels were built in New York City on Fifth Avenue between 33rd and 34th streets on the sites of mansions owned by feuding members of the Astor family. The first, opened in 1893, was the Waldorf, built on the site of William Waldorf Astor's mansion at the corner of 33rd Street; the second, opened in 1897, was the Astoria, built on the site of the mansion owned by Colonel John Jacob Astor at the corner of 34th Street. Colonel Astor was the grandson of the John Jacob Astor who had been responsible for the original Astor House over 60 years earlier.

The two properties were joined by a passage from the day the Astoria opened. In addition, their names were soon joined by a hyphen, and the Waldorf-Astoria quickly became one of America's finest and best-known hotels. The Waldorf-Astoria occupied the 34th Street site for over 30 years, but it closed in 1928 when real estate taxes rendered its operation unprofitable. The site was sold to a new corporation that planned to build the world's largest office building. That building—the Empire State Building—occupies the site to this day. The Waldorf-Astoria was rebuilt in 1932 on Park Avenue between 49th and 50th streets.

Resort Hotels in the 1800s

In the nineteenth century, while the great and growing network of American railroads was providing the means for the economic development of regions, cities, and towns, it was also putting in place a mechanism that would make possible a new period of growth and development for a group of hospitality operations that came to be known as resort hotels.

Railroads and Resort Hotels

The resort hotel industry in the United States could not have developed without railroads. The reason for this is apparent when one considers the distance of many nineteenth-century resort hotels from population centers, as well as their relative inaccessibility by any other means of transportation.

In this period, it was not uncommon for families of means to spend entire summers or winters at resort hotels. A mother and her children—sometimes with servants—would remain at the resort hotel from week to week. The father would spend only weekends with his family, traveling by train from a city to the resort at the end of the workweek and returning to the city on Sunday evening or Monday morning to earn the money to pay for it all.

Early Resort Hotels

By the beginning of the nineteenth century, the resort hotel industry had begun its earliest period of development in the East. By 1789, for example, weary city dwellers in New York were being advised in advertisements to seek relaxation at Deagle's Hotel, far from the noise and crowds of the city, in a then-rural part of Manhattan Island near what is now 155th Street and Amsterdam Avenue. Deagle's, the earliest known resort hotel on Manhattan, offered harassed New Yorkers opportunities for quiet fishing and other ways to relax, and ushered in a period of growth for this new form of American hotel enterprise.

The Homestead was one of America's earliest resorts. Shown in the picture is the Homestead as it appeared in 1857.
(Photo from The Album of Virginia *by Edward Byer, courtesy of The Homestead, LC)*

The 1800s saw the opening of many of America's important resort hotels and resort areas. In Cape May, New Jersey, the Congress Hotel was in operation in 1812 and was known for its sweeping verandas, which made it possible for resort guests to enjoy the cooling ocean breezes in summer. The Catskill Mountain region, located in an area between 70 and 130 miles northwest of New York City, traces its resort beginnings to the opening of the Catskill Mountain House in 1823. By the 1820s, White Sulphur Springs, in what later became West Virginia, had begun to develop its reputation as a spa.

The Homestead, Hot Springs, Virginia

An early and very famous resort hotel was The Homestead. The property was acquired in 1832 by Dr. Thomas Goode, who planned and developed it and continually made improvements to the property. By 1850, The Homestead was said to have approximately 15,000 visitors annually. Even today, it continues to be one of America's premier resorts.

The Greenbrier, White Sulphur Springs, West Virginia

In White Sulphur Springs, located in Virginia until West Virginia became a state in 1863, the mineral waters were said to have wonderful curative powers. This attracted people to the area, including presidents of the United States, as well as wealthy individuals with various illnesses. The growing popularity of the waters resulted in the eventual building of the original Greenbrier Hotel, then called the Grand Central Hotel, in 1857. Several of the buildings had been constructed many years earlier, including the Greenbrier Museum, built as a private home in 1816. Many wealthy and famous people who had heard of the mineral waters and their alleged healing powers rented rooms there. The Grand Central Hotel was seldom called by its given name. Guests usually referred to it as "The White," or "The Old White," either in reference to its white-colored exterior or to its location in White Sulphur Springs.

Guests of The Old White included such notables as President Martin Van Buren, Senator Henry Clay, the future King Edward VII, and General Robert E. Lee. It was renamed The Greenbrier in 1861 but was closed during much of the Civil War. Over the years, The Greenbrier has gone through several periods of financial difficulty and has been owned by a number of individuals and corporations. The original property has been entirely reconstructed. A new 250–room building was added in 1913 and expanded to 580 rooms in 1930. The Greenbrier was one of the first resorts to be classified as a five-star property—a rating it has earned every year since. It now contains 531 rooms and suites, 121 guest houses, and 4 estate houses, along with three championship golf courses.

The Balsams, Dixville Notch, New Hampshire

In New England, another interesting resort property was developed in northern New Hampshire near the Canadian border. Named the Balsams, it was built in 1866 and was under continuing development up to the beginning of World War I. For over 100 years, The Balsams has been considered one of the finest resorts

HENRY FLAGLER, RESORT DEVELOPER ◀

For most of the resort hotels of the nineteenth century, the railroad was the principal means of access. The close relationship between railroads and resort hotels can perhaps best be illustrated by examining the business career of Henry Flagler.

Flagler, who was a partner in John D. Rockefeller's Standard Oil Company, became wealthy and was able to retire at the age of 53. He went to Florida to relax in 1883, but like so many successful entrepreneurs before and since, he could not leave business behind. He was enchanted by the Florida climate and by its unspoiled beauty and decided to investigate the possibilities for profitable real estate development. In 1885, he began construction of the Ponce de Leon Hotel in St. Augustine, on the Atlantic coast. He planned that the hotel would cater to the wealthy but soon realized that it would be difficult to attract the clientele he wanted because of the poor transportation in the area. He started to buy the small railroads in the region and eventually controlled most railroad service in the state.

With his control of an excellent transportation network, Flagler was able to build a number of fine resort hotels throughout Florida, including such well-known properties as the Palm Beach Hotel, the Royal Poinciana, and the original Breakers in Palm Beach.

in the region. Although the majority of the grand summer resorts of New England have long since closed because of their inability to operate profitably as summer-only ventures, The Balsams was able to convert to year-round operation successfully and is still considered a premier resort. In addition to its summer activities, The Balsams has excellent winter sports and has gained a reputation for its outstanding cuisine.

The Grand Hotel, Mackinac Island, Michigan

Farther west, in Michigan, a beautiful resort called the Grand Hotel is located on Mackinac Island in Lake Huron. No automobiles are permitted on the island, which makes this a unique resort. Transportation is by horse and carriage or bicycle only. The hotel, billed as the largest summer hotel in the world, first opened for business in 1887. It was a retreat for wealthy and famous people from Chicago and other nearby areas.

Mackinac Island is only 3 miles long by 2 miles wide, and the hotel is situated to provide guests with spectacular views of the lake. The Grand Hotel is still in operation and still quite popular.

RAILROAD NETWORKS

By the end of the nineteenth century, entrepreneurs in the United States had developed a network of rail lines for both passengers and freight that was second to none in the world. Today, it may be difficult to comprehend the importance and complexity of the rail system, most of which has vanished. For example, the

Mount Washington Hotel in New Hampshire's White Mountains was easily accessible by rail from all major cities in the Northeast. Guests typically checked in for all or part of the summer, arriving by train with trunks full of their summer wardrobes. Today, although the hotel is still in operation, the passenger trains no longer come, and guests arrive by automobile and bus. The passenger rail networks serving our resort areas—the Catskill Mountains, the New Jersey shore, and many others—are gone now, and the names of the railroad companies, once household words, are nearly forgotten. The Hudson River Railroad; the Ulster and Delaware River Railroad; the New York, Ontario, and Western Railroad; the Delaware and Hudson Canal Company Railroad; the Delaware, Lackawanna, and Western—these, and hundreds of others, with thousands of miles of track, are now just names for historians. But they were once lifelines for the guests and employees who made America's resort hotels the great successes they were in the nineteenth century.

RESTAURANTS IN THE 1800s

Restaurants in the United States are generally considered to have their origins in the ordinaries, inns, and taverns of colonial America. These older terms persisted through the seventeenth and eighteenth centuries. By the beginning of the nineteenth century, *ordinary* had all but disappeared as a synonym for inn or tavern, and a comparatively new foodservice term of French origin—*restaurant*—was becoming dominant. By the beginning of the nineteenth century, inns, taverns, and restaurants had become common in the major American cities and were thoroughly integrated into the fabric of American society.

Factors Affecting Restaurant Development

The development of the restaurant business in urban America is closely linked to the Industrial Revolution. By the early nineteenth century, two factors were beginning to have significant impact on the development of restaurants:

1. Manufacturing industries were expanding, creating a growing need for labor in cities and towns.

2. Agricultural methods and technology were improving, resulting in increased farm production on the one hand and less need for farm labor on the other. Those who left rural America to seek jobs in cities faced the problem of locating living quarters; this became increasingly difficult as the urban population grew. The first apartment buildings did not appear until about 1880. Until that time, people lived either in private homes, which were expensive, or in less expensive alternatives—rooms they rented in early hotels, in boardinghouses, or in lodging houses. Boardinghouses included meals in their rates. Some gave guests excellent meals, whereas others served food of very poor

quality. Many hotels and lodging (or rooming) houses did not provide meals, and residents typically had no access to cooking facilities. This led them to seek food in the various kinds of restaurants that developed in this period.

The Variety in City Restaurants

The vast majority of these establishments tended to be simple and plain, serving basic, inexpensive meals to those who needed them: factory and office workers, most of whom lived too far from their jobs to go home for their midday meal. Other regular customers were people who did not have facilities for meal preparation at home. After all, cooking stoves were first patented in America about 1815 and did not become common in home kitchens until about 1850.

In the last half of the nineteenth century, a wide variety of foodservice enterprises were found in America's growing cities: street vendors; lunch carts and lunch wagons; lunch rooms in office buildings; taverns, both common and elegant, offering "free lunch"; hotel dining rooms; ethnic restaurants in ethnic areas; sandwich shops; cheap restaurants, known as 5-cent houses, and 15-cent houses which served a portion of hot meat with potatoes, pickles, bread, and butter for that price. These and many others were common.

Oyster Houses

One of the most popular and inexpensive American foods of the period was the oyster, found in the Atlantic Ocean in large beds near the East Coast. Oysters appealed to people of all backgrounds and were as popular in their time as hamburgers are in ours. They were very cheap, and the types of establishments that specialized in serving them were known by many names; **oyster house**, *oyster cellar*, *oyster saloon*, and *oyster wagon* were all common terms. People consumed oysters in vast numbers, to the extent that many of the oyster beds were depleted. As this occurred, the price of oysters rose and they began to lose their popularity, except in a few superior establishments.

One of these was Boston's Ye Olde Original Oyster House, now known as Ye Olde Union Oyster House, which opened in 1826. It is one of the oldest continuously operating restaurants in America, with an extensive menu that includes a large number of seafood entrées in addition to the oysters for which it is named. The semiprivate stalls, or booths, and the oyster bar itself are reported to be original furnishings.

Changing Service Techniques

One particularly important development in the nineteenth century was a change in the techniques of service. Until about 1830, hotels and boardinghouses served **table d'hôte** meals, meaning a complete meal for one price, just as inns and taverns had done for generations. Meals were included in the room rate, and each meal was served at an appointed hour. Guests were seated at long tables preset

The Union Oyster House is said to be the oldest continually operating restaurant. It is shown here as it appeared in the early 1800s.
(Photo courtesy of Union Oyster House)

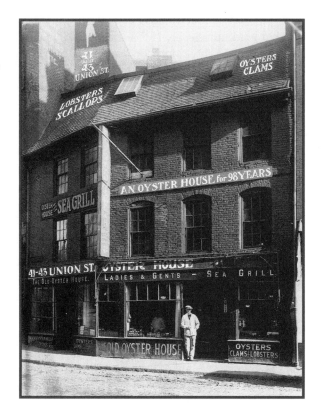

with all foods constituting the meal. They helped themselves from platters, bowls, tureens, and other serving dishes. Competition among diners for the choicest foods could be fierce, and entire meals were frequently consumed in ten minutes or less.

In hotels, a later and more civilized approach was to divide the meals into courses that were served by waiters. Meals were still served at appointed hours and guests were still seated at long tables, but the earlier every-man-for-himself approach was eliminated. Waiters moving with military precision served each course to one guest at a time. The foods typically were placed on sideboards to which waiters went to select the items requested by each guest.

Later, the **European plan** was introduced. Meals were not included in the room rate. Printed menus were offered, giving diners opportunities to select their foods. With this development, both fixed hours for meals and long tables for guests began to disappear. Eventually, dining rooms were open for meals for periods of several hours, and guests dined at hours they chose.

Cities Known for Numerous Fine Restaurants

By the last years of the nineteenth century, all of America's great cities were able to boast about the quality of the meals available in some of their restaurants. The cities with truly outstanding reputations for fine dining were San Francisco, New Orleans, and New York.

San Francisco

After the gold rush, the population of San Francisco grew dramatically, setting the conditions for equally dramatic growth in the restaurant industry. Within a few years, San Francisco was noted for its variety of fine restaurants, including Lazzuro's (Italian), Manning's (oyster house), the Mint (Southern), Zinkand's (German), and Jacques' (French).

New Orleans

In New Orleans, one of the fine old establishments is Antoine's, which opened in 1840. Known for its superior seafood specialties, Antoine's is owned and operated by the family of the original owner, Antoine Alciatore, an immigrant from Marseilles, France. Other popular establishments included Moreau's, Begue's, Les Quatre Saisons, and Le Pelerin.

New York

Perhaps the most important American city for fine dining throughout the nineteenth century was New York, which took pride in its many restaurants. The list was long and varied, and included such famous names as Taylor's, Sherry's, and Rector's. Von Mehlbach's opened in 1842 but changed its name to Luchow's in 1882. It operated under von Mehlbach's name until it was purchased by a young, industrious waiter named August Luchow, who had emigrated from Hanover, Germany, a few years earlier.

Delmonico's. Perhaps the most famous, and certainly the most interesting, of New York's restaurants was Delmonico's, originally located on William Street in lower Manhattan, near Wall Street. Delmonico's opened as a simple coffee and pastry shop in 1827 and grew to be a vast restaurant and private catering establishment. Reportedly the best and most expensive restaurant in the country, it was operated for several generations by members of the Delmonico family. As the commercial center of the growing city continued to move, the owners of Delmonico's kept pace by changing the location of the restaurant. In 1897, Delmonico's made its last move, to Fifth Avenue and 44th Street, where it prospered for many years. Eventually, surviving members of the family grew tired of the restaurant business, and Delmonico's closed forever in 1923.

Delmonico's was the first restaurant to print its menu in both French and English. It boasted an unusually long menu—327 items, each of which was available every day, assuming that the necessary supplies could be purchased. Delmonico's also played a role in the emancipation of women; it provided both room and food for luncheon meetings of an organization of prominent women in an acceptable social setting, thus enabling the members for the first time to appear unescorted in a public restaurant.

The Earliest American Restaurant Chains

A particularly interesting chain of restaurants was started along the southwestern route of the Atchison, Topeka, and Santa Fe Railroad in 1876 by an immigrant from England named Fred Harvey. He had extensive experience in foodservice and as a railroad mail clerk. He had observed the poor food and terrible service provided for railroad passengers traveling to the West, and he devised a system to improve it.

Under contract with the railroad, he established restaurants at stations for passenger dining. Railroad personnel were trained to distribute menus to passengers, record their selections, and inform the restaurant staff of these selections before the train reached the station. This was accomplished by means of a complex system of whistle signals. Meals were cooked to order and were nearly ready for passengers when trains reached the stations. Waitresses who became known as Harvey Girls served them quickly and efficiently. The delays resulting from passenger dining were kept to an absolute minimum. Harvey's standards were high, and the meals were considered excellent. They were also inexpensive, because the Atchison, Topeka, and Santa Fe did not charge Harvey for shipping his food supplies by rail.

The first restaurant in the Harvey chain opened in Topeka, Kansas, in 1876. By 1883, Harvey owned a total of 17 restaurants and hotels. Among his contributions to the growth of chain restaurants were centrally developed menus, identical uniforms for all waitresses in the organization, a central commissary, and strict quality control.

Another interesting chain grew from a single restaurant in New York City operated by William and Samuel Childs, called Childs' Restaurant. By 1898, the Childs brothers were successfully operating nine restaurants in the city. That year, they introduced a new concept in restaurant dining: the cafeteria. Customers selected foods from long counters, placed their selections on trays, and paid for the foods at the end of the counter. This was a great success and widely imitated by foodservice operators across the nation, including Horn & Hardart, Bickford's, and others.

Restaurants in Hotels

Perhaps the most important restaurants in the United States during the 1800s were not the independent, individually owned establishments but those located in the principal hotels of major American cities.

Because these hotels could afford to hire the finest chefs from Europe and because they were the social centers of their cities, where the elite entertained, their foodservice eclipsed that available in most private restaurants. For example, the Parker House in Boston had an unsurpassed reputation for fine food. The owner, Harvey Parker, paid the chef $5000 per year in a time when a good chef could be hired for less than $500.

The Waldorf-Astoria was another hotel known internationally for its excellent cuisine. In fact, at one point in its history, the original Waldorf-Astoria was better known for its exceptional food than for its fine accommodations. Food service has been supervised by some of the best people in the field. The Waldorf-Astoria was the setting in which Oscar Tschirky, known worldwide simply as Oscar of the Waldorf, catered brilliantly for many years to the wealthy and famous personalities who frequented the hotel.

Another hotel noted as much for its haute cuisine as for its grandeur was the Palace Hotel in San Francisco. The Palace maintained a staff of 150 waiters, and management claimed that the Palace chefs could prepare the national dishes of any country in the world, without exception, in the manner of chefs of that country. On many occasions, they proved that they could.

SUMMARY

In the first section of this chapter, the historical development of the hospitality industry is explored, from the earliest civilizations in the Middle East through Egypt, Greece, Rome, and Western Europe, with special attention to developments in England from the fifteenth to the late nineteenth centuries. Economic links between hospitality and several other industries are described, and improvements in methods of transportation and the economic development of population centers are illustrated.

Various types of early hospitality enterprises are described, along with the principal characteristics of the establishments and their owners. The growth of the industry through the fall of Rome, the role of the Church in providing hospitality services during the Dark Ages, and the importance of several social and economic phenomena in the rebirth of the hospitality industry during the Renaissance are traced. Finally, various elements that fostered dynamic change in the industry during the early modern period are illustrated, including the development of road networks, stagecoaches, and postal networks, the reinvention of the restaurant in eighteenth-century France, and the extension of English common law to the business of innkeeping. The growth of the hospitality business in the Industrial Era is described, and the invention of the steam engine, the development of railroad networks, and the acceptance of dining out by the public at large are cited as principal determinants of the industry's development.

In the second section of this chapter, the earliest types of hospitality establishments in America are identified and described. The impact of railroads and railroad travel in the nineteenth century on the hospitality industry in general, and on city hotels and resort hotels in particular, is examined in detail. Significant hotels of the nineteenth century are identified and the characteristics that made them unique described. These include hotels erected in major cities, such as New York, Chicago, Boston, and San Francisco, as well as major resort hotels in various locations in the East and the Midwest. The problem of hotel fires is also discussed. Economic and social conditions that fostered the growth of the foodservice industry are listed and described, and types of foodservice establishments common in the period are named. In addition, the following individuals are identified and their principal contributions to the hospitality industry enumerated: Samuel Coles, Samuel Fraunces, Isaiah Rogers, Harvey Parker, Henry Flagler, and Fred Harvey.

KEY TERMS

Café	Feudalism	Potluck
Caravanserai	Grand tour	Renaissance
Coaching inn	Ordinary	Restaurant
Coffeehouse	Oyster house	Table d'hôte
Empire era	Palaces of the public	Traiteur
European plan	Posthouse	

DISCUSSION QUESTIONS

1.   The history of the hospitality industry is tied closely to the development of transportation. Explain.

2.   What contributions did the Sumerians make to the development of the hospitality and travel industries?

3.   What kinds of establishments were probably the first hospitality businesses?

4.   What were the characteristics of a typical inn of the year 2000 B.C.?

5.   Identify one important contribution of ancient Egypt to the development of the hospitality industry.

6.   What were the two most important contributions of ancient Greece to the development of travel?

7.   Were Greek inns generally clean and well run? How good were their restaurants?

8.   Of what significance was the Roman road system to the development of travel?

9.   Some Roman inns were clean and offered excellent accommodations to one special group of travelers. Explain.

10.   Why did the business of innkeeping virtually disappear during the period A.D. 476 to 1300? Where did travelers stay?

11. What was the grand tour?

12. What impact did an A.D. 1539 act of the English parliament have on the innkeeping business of that era?

13. During which period in European history did the stagecoach become a common method of transportation? What effect did this have on innkeeping development?

14. When and where did public restaurants first become common? What caused them to increase in numbers?

15. How did the invention of the railroad and the development of railroad networks affect the development of the hospitality industry?

16. Why did the Industrial Revolution increase the number of inns in Europe?

17. Define the term *ordinary*. What was the role of an ordinary in the life of a seventeenth-century community?

18. What difference was there between the status of the early American innkeeper and that of his counterpart in Europe?

19. Discuss the role of Samuel Fraunces and his tavern during the Revolutionary War.

20. Hotels in the United States have always been considered "palaces of the public." Explain.

21. What was the first purpose-built hotel structure in the United States? Where was it located and when was it built?

22. Name the property considered America's first luxury hotel. Where was it located? When was it built? List five features that made it an outstanding hotel for its time.

23. Name the New York hotel designed and built to rival the luxury of the Tremont. Who designed it? How was it illuminated?

24. Why were none of the hotels built in the early nineteenth century above five floors in height?

25. The period between 1830 and 1860 was one in which more new hotels were opened in America than at any other time until the 1920s. Why?

26. What characteristics of the hotels built before the Civil War made fire a constant danger?

27. What was the impact of railroad development on Chicago in the 25-year period between 1835 and 1860?

28. What characteristics of the Palace Hotel, San Francisco, and the Brown Palace, Denver, led to their being known as grand hotels?

29. Why were railroads important to the development of the resort hotel industry?

30. How does the career of Henry Flagler illustrate the close relationship that developed between railroads and the resort hotels in the nineteenth century?

31. Describe early nineteenth-century changes in agriculture and manufacturing that set the stage for significant growth in the restaurant industry.

32. Discuss the role of boardinghouses and lodging houses in the development of the foodservice industry from 1800 to the start of the Civil War.

33. List six types of foodservice establishments found in major American cities in the period after the Civil War.

34. Which three American cities were reputed to have the best restaurants in the late nineteenth century? List the names of three restaurants in each city during this period.

35. Which restaurant had the reputation of being the finest restaurant in the United States in the late nineteenth century? Why?

36. What were the contributions of Fred Harvey to the development of the restaurant industry in America?

37. Why were the grand hotels in nineteenth-century America able to develop reputations for providing food and service of a quality exceeding that available elsewhere in major American cities at the time?

38. What distinguished the foodservice operation of San Francisco's Palace Hotel from that of other American hotels of the late nineteenth century?

MOMENTS OF TRUTH

1. You are assistant to the president of an international hotel chain. The president is interested in expanding its operations into more countries and is considering several of the less developed countries in Africa. You have been assigned the task of researching these countries and reporting on their potential for travel and tourism. Based on the knowledge you gained from reading this chapter, what are the most important topics to research about any country you might consider?

2. You have been discussing career opportunities with a friend and have told him you are currently taking a course in hospitality that includes a sizable amount of history of the industry. He tells you that you are wasting your time studying history because it will be of no use to you in your career. How do you respond to this argument?

INTERNET EXERCISES

1. Search for the Web site for The Greenbrier. What do you see as the attractions of this resort hotel?

2. Search for the Web site of The Balsams. What features of the hotel allow it to remain open year-round?

3. Search for the Web site of Antoine's Restaurant and study the dinner menu. How is the menu priced? How many soups, salads, and entrées are listed? About how much would you expect to pay for a full meal consisting of appetizer, soup, salad, entrée, and one vegetable?

The Hospitality Industry in the United States:
The Twentieth Century

C H A P T E R 3

▶ Learning Objectives

After reading and studying this chapter, you should be able to:

1. List the important inventions of the late nineteenth century and describe the impact of each on the hospitality industry.

2. Identify three major reasons for the growth in mass travel after World War II.

3. List the principal appealing features of a vacation cruise.

4. Discuss the importance of railroads to travel in the United States during the first half of the twentieth century.

5. Identify Amtrak and trace its development.

6. Discuss the early history of aviation and explain the importance of mail contracts to airline development.

7. List and discuss three results of the Airline Deregulation Act.

8. Describe, in general terms, the principal developments in the three major segments of the industry—restaurants, hotels, and resort hotels—from 1900 onward.

9. Identify each of the following and describe their principal contributions to the development of the hospitality industry: Ellsworth M. Statler, Conrad Hilton, Howard Johnson, J. Willard Marriott, Kemmons Wilson, Ray Kroc.

INTRODUCTION: AN OVERVIEW

The golden age of invention in the late nineteenth century was followed by dramatic changes in American life. Electricity, for example, began to replace gas in illuminating homes and offices. Henry Ford and others were further developing the recently invented automobile, which promised new and improved methods of motor transport. Streets and roads were paved and otherwise improved in cities, towns, and rural areas so that people could take full advantage of the new vehicles. The telephone was becoming common, making voice communication possible over long distances, just as the railroads had made rapid transit between cities and regions a reality. These and other important developments moved America toward becoming the world's foremost economic power. The dramatic increase in economic development gave rise to more travel for Americans than they had ever known before, setting the stage for the major developments in America's hospitality industry.

The first third of the twentieth century was a time of rapid growth for American business. This growth produced an increase in travel, particularly business travel. Long-distance trips were still made primarily by train, but use of the automobile was increasingly common. New paved roads were constructed in the early part of the century, and more and more of the older unpaved roads were paved. By 1920, it was possible, in many parts of the country, to drive an automobile from one city to another without using the dirt roads of earlier decades.

The first recorded journey across the United States by automobile was undertaken in 1903 by a physician from Vermont named Nelson Jackson. It took Dr. Jackson 69 days—from 23 May to 1 August—to drive from New York City to San Francisco. Many of those days were spent in hotels, waiting for the automobile to be fixed and for parts to be shipped. America's roads were not yet well suited to long-distance driving.

World War II marked a turning point in travel and hospitality. After 1945, the hospitality industry embarked on a period of dramatic change that was unequaled and unparalleled in any time in history. Travel, transportation, foodservice, and lodging—literally every aspect of travel and hospitality—were affected.

In the nineteenth century and the first half of the twentieth, the average American did not engage in long-distance travel for pleasure. The only people to travel long distances frequently were businessmen and theatrical people, who could not earn their living without traveling, and the wealthy, who had the time and money to travel for pleasure. The workweek for the average American was five and one-half or six days, and few Americans were able to take vacations. Those who could were not necessarily given vacations with pay. The cost of long-distance travel for vacations was quite beyond the financial ability of most Americans. For the majority, travel might mean an occasional trip to the seashore or a not-too-distant lake, or a short journey to visit relatives in a nearby community.

Mass Travel

After World War II, great numbers of Americans began to travel. Three of the many reasons for this were of special significance for the hospitality industry:

1. Economic life was changing for many Americans. More industries were becoming unionized, and the contracts that resulted from collective bargaining provided for shorter workweeks, higher wages, and more fringe benefits. Vacations with pay became nearly universal for both unionized workers and for nonunionized white-collar workers who had held their jobs for the stipulated prerequisite periods; one year was a typical minimum. In general, Americans in all walks of life began to have more leisure time than ever before. This set the stage for increased travel.

2. Modes of transportation were changing. America's railroads were in decline, and the automobile became the primary means of private transportation for local and long-distance travel. The airplane was increasingly regarded as the major means of public transportation for long-distance travel. With increased volume and improved technology, travel also became more affordable. This led to the development of new travel destinations.

3. Major improvements were made in America's highways. With the decline of the railroads and growing reliance on motor vehicles—both trucks and cars—the development of a national network of superior, limited-access highways became an important public concern. There had been major highways for a number of years in all regions of the country. There had never been, however, any coast-to-coast, border-to-border network of limited-access interstate highways. Planning for this national system began during President Eisenhower's administration, and construction proceeded in the following years.

In the balance of this chapter, we take a closer look at the various elements of the travel and hospitality mosaic to illustrate the more important changes that took place in the twentieth century—changes affecting the hospitality industry in ways that are evident today.

TRAVEL AND TRANSPORTATION IN THE TWENTIETH CENTURY

The decline of passenger ship and railroad travel, and the development of the automobile and airplane, were major factors in the changing American life of the twentieth century. We begin with a look at the role of passenger ship transportation.

Passenger Ships

Until the twentieth century, all travel and transportation between the United States and nations overseas was by ship. There was no other means for transporting people and goods between Europe and America, or between Asia and America. Ships dominated intercontinental travel and transportation in much the same way that railroads dominated domestic travel and transportation.

World War II brought a halt to most scheduled passenger shipping. Many passenger ships were used for troop transports, and some were sunk by enemy submarines. After the war, passenger service resumed. The luxurious SS *France* was built in 1961, and the *Queen Elizabeth II* went into service in 1968. Although the United States has never invested heavily in passenger ships, it did build the *United States*, a superliner, in 1952. At the time, this was the fastest liner afloat, capable of a speed of 35 knots. However, the days of transatlantic passenger ships were numbered, and the *United States* never carried the numbers of passengers that might have been possible some 30 years earlier. By the late 1960s, the *United States* had to be taken out of service for lack of passengers.

The beginning of the end of transatlantic passenger crossings came in 1957, the first year more people crossed the Atlantic by plane than by ship. Travelers no longer wanted to spend five to seven days traveling to Europe by ship when a plane would take them across the ocean in a matter of hours. The last ship to provide scheduled transatlantic service was the *Queen Elizabeth II*, and this was only during the summer months.

Today, most of the grand transoceanic liners are gone. The *Queen Mary* is permanently docked in Long Beach, California, as a tourist attraction. The original *Queen Elizabeth* sank in Hong Kong harbor. The *France* was sold to the Norwegian Caribbean Line, was refurbished, and is now sailing as the cruise ship *Norway*. The *Queen Elizabeth II* is used almost exclusively for long-distance vacation cruising.

Vacation Cruising

Vacation cruising goes back 110 years to 1891, when the P&O line began to offer vacation cruises to distant parts of the world. For generations, taking a cruise meant boarding a ship in Boston, New York, Los Angeles, or some other city, then sailing to ports around the world.

The scheduled lines—those that provided scheduled transoceanic service—had specific year-round routes. However, sales always decreased in winter, which was never a good time to travel by ship. The seas were rough, the winds were fierce, and the temperatures could be frigid. In the mid-1930s, owners of lines that crossed the Atlantic Ocean started scheduling ships for winter vacation cruises to keep them going during the cold months when there was limited demand for transatlantic service. These ships carried passengers from cold-weather ports to warmer climates. New York City was the major port of embarkation. Ships that normally traveled from New York to Europe went on vacation cruises to the Caribbean, South America, and the Mediterranean.

Today, the large seagoing passenger vessels are used almost exclusively for vacation cruising. They are concentrated in the Mediterranean, Caribbean, and on the U.S. West Coast, although it is possible to take a vacation cruise in almost any part of the world—the South American coast, the African coast, etc. The typical cruise is three, four, seven, or eight days long, although cruises of 10 to 15 days are not uncommon. Extended vacation cruises to distant ports of call are still available on ships such as the *Queen Elizabeth II*, but the greater demand is for short-term cruises that are within the budgets of the average working person.

Although the ages of vacation cruise passengers are younger and the length

**CRUISE ABOARD
RADISSON'S *NAVIGATOR***

The *Seven Seas Navigator* has taken her honored place in a small class of remarkable ships dedicated to the quest for excellence. The smallest suite (there are no staterooms) is a generous 301 square feet, and the largest measures 1173 square feet, including balcony. She offers her 490 guests an unusual level of luxury—all ocean-view accommodations, superb cuisine, complimentary wines with dinner, and peerless service. Another plus is the delightfully roomy bathroom, which features a full-sized soaking tub and a separate glass enclosed stall shower.

The *Navigator* has accommodations, cuisine, service, and entertainment equivalent to a five-star hotel.

Source: Adapted from an article in the *Arizona Republic* by Michael Christopher, 30 March 2000.

of the cruises is shorter, the appealing features of cruises have not changed over the years. They continue to be:

- Food
- Activities and entertainment
- Weather
- Elegance and comfort

The level of service on many ships is as high as that in luxury hotels. Cabin stewards are available 24 hours a day and provide turn-down service in the evening. Food and beverage service is commonly available day and night, and all sorts of recreational activities are available at any given time. Pursers are on board to store valuables, cash checks, and convert currencies. Because of the high level of service, a cruise on one of these luxury liners can be an elegant and refreshing experience.

Railroads

In the United States today, the railroad plays only a minor role in intercity passenger traffic, accounting for about 1 percent of long-distance trips. Nevertheless, the historical role of railroads in the expansion and development of many parts of the United States cannot be ignored. In the previous chapter, the importance of the railroads was discussed. Railroad stops were natural locations for hotels, and resort hotels were natural destinations for railroads. In some cases—Henry Flagler's hotels, for example—reaching existing hotels was the chief reason a railroad was built.

The number of miles of railroad track in the United States reached a peak in 1916. However, the railroads were still the primary means of long-distance public transportation for many years thereafter. All through the 1920s, the 1930s, and most of the 1940s, American railroads provided excellent passenger service. In fact, the railroad cars were generally considered more comfortable than other means of transportation, and the staff was efficient and polite. Trains generally ran on time, and food served in the dining cars of some trains was as good as that served in fine restaurants. During the period of their greatest popularity, railroads accounted for as much as 70 percent of all intercity traffic.

The best intercity trains were named, just as cruise ships are named. In fact, the practice of naming trains continues with Amtrak. Famous trains of the past include:

The Twentieth Century Limited: The deluxe train of the New York Central Railroad, providing service between New York City and Chicago. It was introduced in 1902 and made its last run in 1967.

The Broadway Limited: Inaugurated in 1902 by the Pennsylvania Railroad between New York City and Chicago as competition for the Twentieth Century Limited. Amtrak retained a train with this name until 1995.

The Panama Limited: Started by the Illinois Central Railroad in 1912. It ran between Chicago and New Orleans.

The Super Chief: Inaugurated in 1936 by the Santa Fe Railroad to provide service between Chicago and Los Angeles.

After World War II, competition from airlines and private automobiles led to a decrease in the number of railroad passengers. Passenger service has never been highly profitable, and decreased ridership caused the railroads to operate at a loss. As a result, passenger service began to deteriorate; service was perceived as less friendly, cars were not kept in the best condition, and food in dining cars was not up to previous standards. Roadbeds for the railroad track were not well maintained, and train travel was less comfortable than it had been. Railroads were required by law to maintain passenger service, but because it was not profitable, they spent less money on the service—with predictable results.

Creation of Amtrak

In an attempt to preserve long-distance train service, the federal government formed **Amtrak** in 1971. Amtrak is a national passenger train service, but it differs in organization from railroad service in other countries. Amtrak is a quasipublic corporation that is neither nationalized nor completely private. It is independent of the federal government, having its own board of directors and nongovernment employees. At the same time, it receives capital support from the federal government, which regulates it.

Amtrak has never made a profit and, like every form of transportation in America, including highways, aviation, mass transit, and the marine industry, is subsidized each year by Congress. Since 1971, Congress has given Amtrak between $500 million and $800 million each year. This represents 16 percent of its total revenues. In 1997, Congress provided Amtrak with a $2.2 billion in capital and

The most modern of Amtrak's trains is the *Acela Express*, shown in this picture.
(Photo used with permission of Amtrak)

passed legislation that required Amtrak to become the first passenger railroad in the world to be operationally self-sufficient by the end of fiscal year 2002.

In the attempt to become self-sufficient, Amtrak has added new service that will allow it to develop express and parcel services along with its passenger service, modernized its fleet of trains, and upgraded its service. In the fall of 2000, Amtrak put its new 150-mile-per-hour Acela Express train into service. The Acela travels between Boston, New York, and Washington, D.C., cutting the time of travel considerably. In addition, these new trains offer business-class seating with audio and power jacks, special check-in areas, concierge service, and pub-style café cars with meeting tables and upgraded menus.

Early Air Service

The invention of the airplane and the development of commercial passenger airlines have had the greatest influence on long-distance travel since the invention of the railroad. Air travel may be the most important transportation development in the history of mankind.

Lighter-than-Air Craft

The first airline, Deutsche Luftschiffahrts AG, was founded on 16 November 1909. It was more commonly known as Delag. Headquartered in Frankfurt, Germany, its purpose was to operate **zeppelin** airships. These were a particular type of lighter-than-air craft known as *dirigibles* or *blimps*. They were similar in appearance to those seen today in the skies over major sports and entertainment events advertising Goodyear, Met Life, and other companies.

Lighter-than-air craft were around for many years prior to Delag. The first successful one was constructed and flown as early as 1852, by Henri Giffard, from Paris to Trappe. The term *zeppelin* comes from Count Ferdinand von Zeppelin, who designed many successful lighter-than-air craft, constructed of a lightweight frame covered by a thin exterior skin of aluminum and powered by internal combustion engines. These were an important part of early aviation and transported many passengers throughout Europe and across the Atlantic. The popularity of the zeppelin reached a high point in commercial aviation in 1929 when the Graf Zeppelin, a large version of the original zeppelin, made an historic round-the-world flight—taking 21 days, 7 hours, and 31 minutes. The Graf Zeppelin flew until 1940, when it was finally retired. Between 1928 and 1940, it completed 590 flights, including 140 Atlantic crossings, and carried 13,100 passengers.

Commercial Airplane Service

The first scheduled air service on a commercial airplane was 1 January 1914, from St. Petersburg to Tampa, Florida. It was accomplished by the newly formed St. Petersburg–Tampa Airboat Line in a single-engine biplane (a plane with two sets of wings) that was open to the sky. The venture appeared to be successful but, for unknown reasons, the airline continued operations only until the end of March of that year. During its existence it carried a total of 1024 passengers.

The first international commercial flight was on 10 January 1919 from London to Paris. It was established by the British Royal Air Force primarily to provide transportation for government officials attending the Paris Peace Conference. Flights continued until September 1919. A total of 749 flights were made.

Another attempt at scheduled passenger service in the United States was made by Ryan Airlines in 1925. This West Coast airline flew from Los Angeles to San Diego; service lasted about a year. Continual scheduled passenger service did not begin until 1927, when it was started by Colonial Air Transport, an airline that had a contract to carry the mail from Boston to New York. Colonial was one of the many airlines that had been carrying mail for the U.S. Postal Service since 1918. In 1926, Congress passed the **Kelly Act**, which authorized long-term mail contracts for airlines. The passage of the Kelly Act led to the founding of many airline companies. All were competing for the contracts to carry U.S. mail and many, like Colonial Air Transport, carried passengers as well. Many of these new airlines failed, some succeeded, and many of them merged. By 1931, these mergers had resulted in the establishment of such well-known airline carriers as American, Eastern, TWA, and United.

One important airline in American aviation history is Pan American, which began regular mail service between Key West, Florida, and Havana, Cuba, on 28 October 1927. Passenger service on that route began in January 1928. Travelers were charged $50 for a one-way ticket. Over the next few years, Pan American expanded its routes to other Caribbean islands and into South America. By 1934, it was operating 85 aircraft and carrying over 100,000 passengers a year.

Martin M-130 China Clipper

In November 1935, Pan American inaugurated transpacific mail service with its new four-motor seaplane, the Martin M-130 China Clipper. It departed from Alameda, California, for Manila, the Philippines, and arrived there almost 60 hours later. Paying passengers were allowed on this flight beginning 21 October 1936. Pan American's new long-distance seaplanes were named the China Clipper, the Philippine Clipper, and the Hawaii Clipper. They could carry 41 passengers and had a cruising speed of 157 mph. Pan American subsequently extended this service to Hong Kong.

Boeing 314: Yankee Clipper

Airline service over a portion of the Atlantic began on 16 June 1937, when Imperial Airways inaugurated service between Bermuda and New York. Pan American began its passenger service between New York and Southampton, England, on 8 July 1939, with the Yankee Clipper, another new long-distance plane. It was a Boeing 314, which carried 17 passengers, each paying a fare of $375.

In October 1936, international airline passengers began flying in four-motored seaplanes, called "clippers." Pan American Airlines was the foremost international airline at that time.
(Photo courtesy of Pan American Airways Collection Archives and Special Collections Department, Otto G. Richter Library, University of Miami, Coral Gables, Florida)

PAN AMERICAN CLIPPER
PASSING THROUGH GOLDEN GATE
ON INITIAL FLIGHT
TO HONOLULU
APRIL 16, 1935

DC-3

Most of the planes used on domestic airline routes during the later 1920s and the 1930s were small, accommodating 8 to 15 passengers. They cruised between 100 and 135 mph. In 1934, Douglas Aircraft introduced its DC-2, a twin-engine plane that could travel at a cruising speed of 196 mph. Douglas soon produced a larger version, the DC-3, with a cruising speed of 186 mph. The DC-3 was the workhorse of civil and military passenger service for many years. It is said that the DC-3 was the first plane that could operate profitably without the benefit of a mail contract. A total of 10,655 DC-3s were built, and many of them are still flying today.

Commercial Jet Aircraft

An important development that had profound effect on the hospitality industry was the introduction of commercial jet aircraft in 1958. Because of their faster speed, jet flights between cities took less time and were less arduous a form of travel than ever before. This improved people's perceptions of travel. More people began to travel by air and, as new—and, later, larger—models of aircraft were introduced, the relative cost of long-distance travel began to decrease. Round-trip fares between cities became less than one-way fares had been when piston aircraft were used, and the time to travel between cities was cut by nearly half.

Perhaps one of the most important developments in air travel was the introduction of wide-bodied aircraft. The first of these was the giant Boeing 747, which went into service with Pan American World Airways on 22 January 1970. The aircraft had 58 seats in first class and 304 in economy class, and a maximum cruising altitude of 45,000 feet. More recent versions of the 747 accommodate as many as 500 passengers.

The 747 is too big and costly to operate on short flights, however; it is designed for long-distance routes. Smaller and less costly wide-bodied aircraft were manufactured about the same time. These include the DC-10, which has a seating capacity of 270 passengers, and the Lockheed L1011, which can carry 330 coach passengers or 272 passengers in a mixed configuration. The DC-10 went into service on 5 August 1971 and the L1011 on 26 April 1972.

In June 1995, the Boeing 777 was introduced. It is a large two-motored aircraft that can carry 292 passengers. It was designed in cooperation with airline representatives and contains many new features for the comfort and safety of passengers. Each of its two motors is larger and generates more thrust than each of the motors on the 747. Other smaller aircraft have been introduced to serve short- to medium-range flights relatively inexpensively. These include the Boeing 737, 757, and 767, the McDonnell Douglas MD-80, and the European Airbus. These smaller planes are also now used for long-distance flights when there is a limited number of passengers. They feature fuel-efficient engines and many modern advances in airline technology.

Supersonic Concorde

Perhaps the most interesting aircraft is the Supersonic Concorde, a joint development of Britain and France. It underwent many years of design and testing before it was put into service. It first flew on 2 March 1969, but was not put into service until January 1976. This remarkable plane cruises at an amazing 1332 mph. It is a slim delta-winged aircraft that accommodates relatively few passengers. It can fly from western Europe to New York in about three hours, enabling it to arrive in New York at a local time earlier than its local time of departure in Europe. It is also costly to operate; therefore, compared with fares on traditional jet aircraft, the Concord is very expensive.

Airline Regulation

The airline industry in the United States was highly regulated until 1978. The Civil Aeronautics Board (CAB) allocated routes, approved fares, and ruled on mergers. Relatively little competition existed among airlines. Comparatively few were allowed to serve major routes. For example, direct service from New York to Los Angeles might be awarded to only two airlines, which would submit proposed fares to the CAB for approval. Knowing the number of potential passengers between New York and Los Angeles, they would submit fares that would guarantee a profit. In return for limited competition, airlines were required to serve cities with few potential passengers, where service was unprofitable.

The Airline Deregulation Act of 1978

The Airline Deregulation Act of 1978 led to major changes in the airline industry. It eliminated the CAB and transferred its responsibilities to the Federal Aviation Administration (FAA) and the Department of Transportation (DOT). The Act was designed to increase competition and to provide the airlines with more freedom to choose routes and set rates.

The Airline Deregulation Act of 1978 had significant consequences. Major airlines eliminated unprofitable routes, and hundreds of small commuter airlines were born to fill the need for commuter service from smaller cities. Consolidation of airlines soon followed, and financially weak airlines went out of business.

Competition has driven the price of airline travel down, and more people are flying than ever before. The industry is still evolving; it appears that a few very large long-distance carriers will dominate the industry. Smaller commuter airlines will be tied closely with the larger airlines, which may control or own them.

Frequent-Flyer Programs

With increased competition and in an effort to develop a loyal customer base, the airlines have instituted **frequent-flyer programs**. These are incentive programs that award mileage for travel on their airlines and provide various rewards for the accumulation of miles. The awards may include upgrades to first-class seats, free flights, free car rentals, and free hotel rooms.

Airport Clubs

In addition to frequent-flyer programs, airlines have also established airport clubs, which are, essentially, comfortable separate passenger lounges. Club members typically obtain free beverages and frequently receive other benefits such as upgrades, access to a range of gifts, and reductions on hotel room and rental car rates.

Yield Management

It costs airlines about the same amount to fly a plane half full or with a full complement of passengers. Thus, airlines make a concerted attempt to fill all of their flights. They know that if they lower the price of an airline ticket sufficiently, many more customers will book passage than if the standard price is charged to everyone. The process they use to keep flights as full as possible is called **yield management**.

Airlines assess the potential demand for each flight. When flights will not be full at the standard rate, they set aside a number of seats at much lower prices for people who are unwilling to pay the higher price and who can make their reservations far in advance. The tickets issued at these lower fares are typically nonrefundable and require the ticket holder to stay over a Saturday night. These restrictions are called fences because they prevent the person who must travel and who cannot stay over a weekend or who makes a reservation at the last minute from getting a lower rate. The bulk of discounted tickets are purchased by customers for personal travel and by persons who have greater flexibility in their travel schedules. The customers who normally pay the higher airfare are businesspeople. They frequently cannot make their travel plans far in advance, and they typically travel during the week so that they can be home on the weekend. Furthermore, business travel expenses are generally not as price sensitive as personal travel. Thus, businesses are more willing to pay higher fares than persons traveling for pleasure.

Hub-and-Spoke Routing

Another effort to fill the maximum number of seats on each flight and to simplify scheduling is a system of routing aircraft commonly referred to as **hub-and-spoke routing**. Each airline utilizes several major airports as hubs providing meeting points for planes coming from outlying cities (spokes). Flight schedules are established so that many planes arrive at the hub at about the same time. Passengers then change planes and proceed to their final destinations as shown in Figure 3.1. Delta, for example, has a major hub in Dallas. Many flights originating in Boston, New York, Philadelphia, Pittsburgh, Washington, Atlanta, and elsewhere fly directly to Dallas. They are scheduled to arrive in Dallas within approximately one-half hour of each other. On arrival, passengers change planes and proceed to their final destination. Not all flights on an airline are scheduled this way, of course. A number of them still operate as direct flights.

The hub-and-spoke method has advantages over direct routing. The major advantage to the airlines is that flights can be more fully booked. For example, suppose that in a certain period of a day, Delta has sold 300 tickets on flights from Boston: 100 for Los Angeles, 100 for San Francisco, and 100 for Seattle. If it scheduled three direct nonstop flights, one to each of the three cities, each plane would

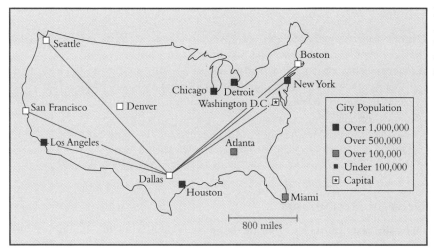

FIGURE 3.1
Airlines commonly use the hub-and-spoke method to route aircraft, as illustrated here.

be only about half full. However, using the hub-and-spoke method, only one wide-bodied plane need be used. It could be scheduled to go, for example, to Los Angeles. The plane would stop first in Dallas, where it would meet planes coming from New York, Washington, and other cities. Those passengers continuing to Los Angeles would stay on board, whereas those for Seattle and San Francisco would transfer to other planes that had come from New York and Washington. The Los Angeles plane would be filled from passengers transferring from the New York and Washington flights.

From the viewpoint of the passenger, the advantage of the hub-and-spoke method is that one can fly to virtually any city in the Delta system with only one stop and a change of planes. The disadvantage is that the stop at the hub makes the time to fly from one city to another somewhat longer than a direct flight would be. For some flights, one must fly extra distance because it is necessary to go to a hub airport that may be inconveniently located for the passenger. In addition, for those passengers changing planes, there is an increased chance that baggage will be lost. In the event that one incoming flight is delayed or canceled, passengers due to transfer from that flight will miss their connection and be delayed in Dallas until the next scheduled departure for their intended destination.

RESTAURANTS IN THE TWENTIETH CENTURY

The early twentieth century saw the development of new foodservice establishments, such as diners, drive-ins, hamburger restaurants, roadhouses, and ice cream stands. These years also gave rise to trends that became increasingly important. The growing popularity of the automobile, for example, led to the development of different kinds of restaurants along the highways of America. Roadside diners and drive-ins were typical.

Diners

Diners became common after 1897, when the cities of Boston, New York, and Philadelphia began to replace their old horse-drawn trolleys, called *horse cars*, with the new electric variety. Many of the horse cars were sold to dealers who refitted them with stoves and dishes, then resold them as lunch wagons. Later, after World War I, larger, well-lighted, furnished, and fully equipped versions were manufactured especially for use as diners—restaurants that were seen by many as imitating the glamour that had once graced the dining cars on the railroads. By 1930, dozens of manufacturers were building diners, which became typical features of the highways, cities, towns, and villages of America. They were everywhere.

Drive-in Restaurants

Drive-in restaurants were an important development of the automobile age. J. G. Kirby of Dallas is credited with the idea for the drive-in restaurant. In 1921, he opened the first of a chain of these, calling it Pig Stand. These were small restaurants within large parking lots that featured food served to customers in their parked automobiles. The idea was widely copied. Orders were taken by young men and women, conveyed to the kitchen, and served when ready. The food was served on special trays that hooked onto the frame of the open automobile window, and customers could eat without leaving their cars. In some drive-ins, servers were equipped with roller skates to speed service. Drive-ins were popular from the 1920s until nearly 1960.

Other Types of Restaurants

Other establishments that developed during the period following World War I included those that were acceptable to unescorted women, typically shoppers: tearooms, women's exchanges, and the restaurants found in department stores.

Prohibition

By the end of World War I, a long-standing political disagreement between two groups of American voters was about to be resolved—at least temporarily. The groups were the drys and the wets—those in favor of prohibiting the sale of all alcoholic beverages, and those opposed. By 1919, a sufficient number of states had ratified an amendment to the U.S. Constitution that made the manufacture, transportation, and sale of alcoholic beverages illegal. This amendment, the eighteenth, ushered in Prohibition, a period later known as the Noble Experiment. Prohibition went into effect in 1920 and lasted until 1933. Its impact on the restaurant industry was profound.

Speakeasies

Prohibition led to the demise of a number of established restaurants. Unable to sell wine, spirits, and beer, some could not attract sufficient customers by serving

WHITE CASTLE: THE FIRST FAST-FOOD HAMBURGER CHAIN

The origins of the hamburger restaurant chain can be traced to Wichita, Kansas, and the opening of the first White Castle in 1921. This featured a portion of ground beef cooked on a grill and served between halves of a sliced roll with fresh onion. No one knows who originally invented the hamburger, or where, or in what year, but it is certain that Walter Anderson and E. W. (Billy) Ingram, the founders of the White Castle system, were responsible for the first fast-food hamburger restaurant chain.

White Castle had many imitators, the best known of which was the White Tower. White Castle considered the White Tower imitation flagrant and sought the assistance of the courts to stop it. White Castle sued White Tower in the Minnesota courts, and White Tower sued White Castle in the Michigan courts. At the request of White Castle, the case was transferred to federal court. Hearings, decisions, and appeals consumed several years. Finally, in 1937, the U.S. Court of Appeals affirmed a lower court decision in favor of White Castle, ordering White Tower to stop operating its business in such a manner as to confuse the public by making it difficult to distinguish between the identity of restaurants in the White Castle system and those of the White Tower.

food alone; others were not able to earn sufficient profit without selling drinks. Customers looking for drinks by the glass or alcoholic beverages by the bottle soon found them available in a new, illegal, and highly profitable type of establishment known as the **speakeasy**. The number of these grew quickly. Soon millions drank in the speakeasies; millions more drank at cocktail parties in private homes. By 1929, the police commissioner of New York estimated that there were approximately 32,000 speakeasies in the city, about twice the number of licensed and unlicensed saloons before Prohibition. Some speakeasies survived both Prohibition and repeal and have become particularly well known. These include two of New York's finest—the famed 21 Club and El Morocco.

Roadhouses

Prohibition led to the development of an establishment known as the **roadhouse**—a roadside restaurant that sold alcoholic beverages, alone or to accompany meals, and that provided live or recorded music for dancing. These were formidable competitors for restaurateurs who chose not to break the law. After the repeal of Prohibition, many roadhouses continued in operation as legitimate restaurants.

Other Restaurants of the Prohibition Era

Some of America's best-known restaurants opened in this period. In New York, these included Pavilion, the Stork Club, and the Rainbow Room; in New Orleans, Galatoire's, Arnaud's, and Brennan's; and, in San Francisco, Taidsch Grill, Schroeder's, and Marchand's.

The first fast-food hamburger res-
taurant chain in the world was
White Castle, founded in 1921 by
Walter Anderson and E. W. (Billy)
Ingram. Shown in this picture is
one of the chain's earliest stores.
*(Photo courtesy of White Castle System,
Inc.)*

Marriott and the Beginning of Restaurant Franchising

Another chain to develop in the 1920s had some units that were drive-ins and
others in which the customers walked up to outdoor stands to order a specific
product: root beer. Roy Allen and Frank Wright established the organization in
California, and the root beer was called A&W, for Allen and Wright. They were
successful and soon developed the idea of selling franchises—contracts that permit others to use the name of the parent company and to sell its products or services under conditions defined in a contract. In 1926, two young men became
partners in the purchase of the A&W franchise for Washington, D.C. One was a
young college graduate named J. Willard Marriott; his partner was Hugh Colton.
They opened their first store in the summer of 1927. By fall, with the arrival of
cooler weather, sales began to drop, and Marriott quickly decided to enlarge the
product line. He removed the A&W logo and adopted the name Hot Shoppe,
principally because of the spiced Mexican foods he was selling. From this simple
beginning came the Marriott Corporation, one of the world's leaders in the hospitality industry.

Howard Johnson

The first entrepreneur to promote franchises aggressively was Howard Johnson,
founder of the company that bore his name. The first franchised Howard Johnson

restaurant opened in Massachusetts in 1935. Under the contract, it was owned and operated by the builder, Reginald Sprague, who purchased ice cream and other products from Johnson's firm. By 1940, there were over 130 Howard Johnson restaurants along the eastern seaboard.

World War II brought problems for the foodservice segment of our industry, and Howard Johnson's restaurants were hard hit. The federal government imposed gasoline and food rationing during the war. Food rationing limited the menu choices available to foodservice operators. Gas rationing restricted the distance that people could drive, which kept potential customers from many of the Howard Johnson's restaurants located along highways. Many were closed for the duration of the war because of lack of business. After the war, Americans resumed the practice of driving for pleasure, which they had been forced to curtail. Many people stopped at restaurants on these trips away from home. A substantial number were uncomfortable with the idea of eating in strange establishments and elected to stop at the familiar and trusted Howard Johnson's, with its orange roof.

Howard Johnson's restaurants reopened, heralding a period of great prosperity for the chain. The Howard Johnson name and reputation were already well established, and the organization was able to compete favorably for new locations on the developing interstate highway network and elsewhere. Because of their standard physical features—including the orange roof—excellent ice cream, and reputation for products of consistent quality, the Howard Johnson restaurants became a model organization for others.

FOODSERVICE INDUSTRY AFTER WORLD WAR II

After the end of World War II in 1945, the foodservice industry entered a period of development that was linked to changes taking place both in American culture and in other segments of the hospitality industry. The most significant of these were women in the work force and economic expansion.

Women in the workforce: This important change had its origins during World War II. When men were drafted into the armed forces, labor shortages occurred in business and industry. The only reasonable solution was to hire women to fill the jobs, so that, by war's end, millions of women were employed full time. Many of these women had never before been employed. A great many discovered that they enjoyed working, they liked earning money and the sense of independence it gave them, and they did not want to be full-time homemakers or housewives.

Economic expansion: After the war, men discharged from the armed forces returned home to resume their lives. Considerable economic disruption was expected but comparatively little took place. The economy expanded to meet the demand for consumer goods resulting from the end of the war. Gasoline, for example, had been rationed during the war, and automobiles had not been produced for the consumer market in 1943, 1944, and 1945. Demand in this area was very strong in the years immediately following the war, and the number of jobs for workers in automobile plants expanded considerably.

The Restaurant Industry Grows

Gradually, the interaction of an expanding economy, higher levels of disposable income, increased leisure time, and greater numbers of automobiles on the road led to significant growth in the restaurant segment of the hospitality industry. As automobile travel increased, the traveling public wanted more restaurants at which to stop. Local restaurants often were not convenient to travelers, who also found it difficult to determine food quality and prices of restaurants they had not previously visited. This set the stage for nationally recognized images and price structures that the traveling public could rely on.

New Chains Develop

In the 1940s and 1950s, a number of foodservice chains were developed that employed some of the same techniques as Howard Johnson. Creating brand names—which came to represent in consumers' minds a particular product, price, level of quality, and type of service—was one technique. Another was to build into each restaurant physical characteristics that made it instantly recognizable as one of the units in a particular chain. To be successful with these techniques, millions of dollars were spent on advertising—especially using the new national medium that had become commercially available in 1947: television. Some of the organizations to do this were Kentucky Fried Chicken, Dairy Queen, Denny's, Dunkin' Donuts, Burger King, Jack-in-the-Box, and Googie's. With the establishment of this general operating pattern, the era of so-called fast food had begun.

McDonald's

Of all the fast-food companies to develop in the United States, the most clearly and consistently successful has been McDonald's. Interestingly, Ray Kroc, who was responsible for its ultimate success, was not its founder. The original idea and the early development of the chain was the work of two brothers, born in Manchester, New Hampshire, after whom the company is named—Richard and Maurice McDonald.

The McDonald brothers had been in the restaurant business for some years by 1948, which turned out to be an important year for our industry. They had become tired of the personnel problems common in the restaurant business and were looking for a new method of operation to free them of the burden. After considerable discussion and planning, they attempted an operating method that reduced their former dependence on highly skilled staff members. Their method was similar to the assembly line used in manufacturing industries. They devised an operation offering a limited menu of products prepared by unskilled workers who were carefully trained to perform simple tasks in a repetitive manner. Each product was thus the result of a number of simple tasks performed by several workers. It became possible to hire people with limited educational background and no foodservice experience and to train them quickly. Because of the assembly-line format, it was easy to respond to demand by producing large numbers of products quickly, and to do so at low labor cost. Because the jobs were unskilled, wages and labor costs were very low compared with competitors'. The McDonald brothers were successful, and they were beginning to sell franchises when their success came to the attention of Ray Kroc.

Ray Kroc and McDonalds

Ray Kroc was one of the most influential restaurant operators in the history of our industry. He was 52 years old in 1956 when he noticed, during a trip to San Bernardino, California, people lining up to purchase hamburgers from a stand owned and operated by the McDonald brothers. He learned that they were sell-ing franchises, and he bought a franchise that allowed him to open McDonald's restaurants anywhere in the state of Indiana. Over the next few years, Kroc opened a number of units but had numerous disagreements with the McDonald brothers over various policies and procedures. Eventually, Kroc offered to buy the business from the McDonalds, and they accepted his offer and retired from the business.

Under Kroc's management, McDonald's became extraordinarily successful, in-ternationally as well as within the United States. His strengths were in organiza-tion, standardization, and marketing. He made franchising common in the restau-rant business. Today, the company he founded accounts for a greater dollar volume of sales than any other restaurant company in the world.

The Growth of Additional Specialized Chains

By the third quarter of the twentieth century, the seeds had been sown for still more national foodservice chains, many of which grew by selling franchises. The chains typically offered limited menus of specialized, standardized items for con-sumption, either on the premises or for takeout, as the customer preferred. These organizations included Arthur Treacher's Fish and Chips, Kentucky Fried Chicken, and Pizza Hut. Some chains developed around themes—Victoria Station, the Magic Pan, Trader Vic's, and the Red Barn, for example—whereas others were defined by the specialty foods they offered—Taco Bell, Red Lobster, Steak and Ale, Spaghetti Factory, and more. Another group catered to families—Friendly's and Denny's were two. Some of these chains have not survived—Arthur Treacher's and Victoria Station, for example—but others continue to succeed.

Changing Tastes in Dining Out

The variety of restaurants in the preceding discussion suggests that Americans showed a broad taste in their restaurant selections in the years since World War II and that the industry responded with many types of restaurants. Prior to 1940, dining out was reserved for special occasions for most Americans. As our standard of living has risen, dining out has become more common. For many people, din-ing out is now considered an everyday experience, part of a normal lifestyle. The term *dining out*, however, conveys varying images to people. A dining-out experience that some might consider pleasant can induce horrified groans in others. The beauty of a dining-out experience, like beauty itself, is in the eye of the beholder.

The trend toward dining out has caused the restaurant industry to expand in size and scope and to become one of the fastest-growing industries in the United States. In the following chapter, we discuss the lines along which the restaurant industry has developed as a result of the growth in demand for foodservice.

CITY HOTELS IN THE TWENTIETH CENTURY

The twentieth century brought major changes to city hotels. The first half of the century was perhaps the most important in the history of the hotel industry in the United States. The last half also saw significant changes take place.

From 1900 Through World War II

The first half of the twentieth century saw both unprecedented growth and, later, an economic depression that led to many hotel company failures. One hotel organization, founded by E. M. Statler, began and grew dramatically in the early years of the century, survived the economic downturn, and managed to prosper in the years that followed.

The Buffalo Statler, Buffalo, New York

This 300-room hotel opened on 18 January 1908, and is considered to be a milestone in the history of the hotel industry. The Buffalo Statler was one of the first modern commercial hotels to cater to the ever-growing number of traveling businessmen, offering them the following:

- Private bath in every room
- Circulating ice water in every bathroom
- Telephone in every room
- Full-sized, lighted closet in every room
- Light switch on the wall just inside the door of each room
- Free newspaper delivered to every guest's room each morning. Doors were especially constructed so that a newspaper could be slipped underneath.
- Mail chute that ran from the top floor to the lobby, so that guests could post letters without leaving their floors

The above list of features may not seem to reflect a modern hotel by today's standards. However, in 1908, these features were unusual. For example, other hotels had a pull chain hanging from the light fixture that guests had difficulty locating in the dark. Telephones were still a relatively new invention. Only luxury hotels had large closets in guest rooms. The Statler was therefore modern by standards of the time. The advertising motto of the hotel was "A room with a bath for a dollar and a half"—an incredible value for travelers. The Buffalo Statler was successful, and E. M. Statler began to open additional hotels bearing his name, thus creating a group of properties assigned the modern term *chain*. Eventually, he owned and operated properties in Cleveland, Detroit, New York, Boston, and most other major American cities. When he died in 1928, Statler controlled more hotels than anyone in the history of the industry.

The Plaza Hotel, New York

During the years when Statler was developing his Buffalo property and expanding his holdings, many individuals, partnerships, and corporations were designing and building new hotels in cities all across America. In New York City, nearly a mile from the nearest railroad, a new hotel opened in 1907. Named the Plaza, it was actually the second hotel of that name to occupy the site. The first, erected only 17 years earlier, was torn down so that the new 800-room Plaza could be built.

The world-famous Plaza is a particularly notable establishment, an excellent example of the great American "palaces of the public." Interestingly, it is one of the few successful hotels anywhere to operate without a sign. In addition, the Plaza has been continuously operated as a luxury hotel since 1907—an unusually long period. Managers of the hotel have been known to boast that those who would

New York City's luxury Plaza Hotel is one of the few hotels that does not have an identifying outside sign. Management has boasted that those who would not recognize the hotel without such a sign do not belong there.
(Photo courtesy of Fairmont Hotels and Resorts)

not recognize the Plaza without a sign clearly do not belong there. In the early years, up to 90 percent of the rooms and suites in the Plaza were occupied by permanent residents. This provided financial stability and helped assure the hotel of a prosperous future.

Other Well-Known Hotels

Other important hotels constructed in the period before World War I included the Copley Plaza (1912) in Boston; the McAlpin (1912) and the Biltmore (1916) in New York City; the Willard (1901) in Washington, D.C.; and Statler properties in Cleveland (1912), Detroit (1915), and St. Louis (1918).

The Golden Age of Hotels

The decade of the 1920s—popularly known as the Roaring Twenties—was a particularly important period of hotel development. It has been characterized as the golden age of hotels because of the large number of hotels constructed, their size, and the high occupancy rates they were able to maintain.

Occupancies during the 1920s were the highest the hotel industry had ever known. Annual guest occupancy rates for many American hotels averaged above 80 percent during this period. New hotels were almost instant successes, and it seemed as though hotels could not be built quickly enough to satisfy the increasing demand for rooms. This high demand was one consequence of a booming economy that led to great increases in travel for business purposes. Given the improvements in railroads, automobiles, and roads, long-distance travel was far easier than ever before.

The curtain had gone up on the era nearly a year earlier than the 1920s in New York City with the opening of the Pennsylvania, a 2200-room hotel located just across the street from a major railroad terminal—the famed Pennsylvania Station. The Pennsylvania opened for business in January 1919 and was the world's largest hotel at the time. Although the building was owned by the Pennsylvania Railroad, it was operated by E. M. Statler. It was his first venture in New York City.

The Pennsylvania was a vast enterprise. When it opened, the chef's staff was reported to consist of "9 bakers, 10 pastry bakers, 4 ice-cream chefs, 9 butchers, 12 cold meat cooks, 9 roast cooks, 12 sauce cooks, 9 fry cooks, 6 vegetable girls, 4 soup cooks, 4 banquet chefs, 8 pot washers, 4 cleaners," and others too numerous to list. Many years later, it became a Hilton hotel—the Statler-Hilton—when Statler's chain was purchased by Conrad Hilton in 1954. It has changed ownership several times since then, a pattern not unusual in the hotel industry.

Many important hotels were built during the 1920s, including the Ritz-Carlton (1927) and the Statler (1927) in Boston; the Roosevelt (1924) and the New Yorker (1927) in New York City; the Biltmore (1927) in Santa Barbara; the Mayflower (1925) in Washington, D.C.; and the Palmer House (1924) and the Stevens (1928) in Chicago. The Stevens, a 3000-room property, was later purchased by Hilton and renamed the Conrad Hilton, after the founder of a company that

CONRAD HILTON (1887–1979) ◄

Hilton is one of the most recognized names in the history of the hospitality industry. The chain that bears this name was founded by Conrad Hilton, who had embarked on a successful career prior to going into the hotel business. He was a banker in New Mexico and purchased his first hotel—the Mobley, in Cisco, Texas—in 1919 with an investment of $5000. This was a time when much oil was being discovered in Texas, and the owner of the Mobley decided to try drilling for oil rather than stay in the hotel business. Hilton happened to be in Cisco on bank business at the time and discovered the hotel was for sale.

Hilton was successful at operating the Mobley. He used some of the techniques employed by innkeepers over many centuries. He increased occupancy by renting each room to two, three, or even four persons every night. They were prospectors and oil field workers who did not know one another, but they were all desperate for sleeping accommodations, which were in short supply in the area. Hilton, who lived in the hotel, was even known to rent his own bed and sleep in a lobby chair on occasion. He was obviously able to achieve maximum revenue from the hotel under these circumstances.

Hilton acquired seven hotels in the area in a short time, expanding as fast as his credit rating would permit. He knew the banking business well, and he maintained contacts who loaned him the funds to make the necessary down payments on hotel properties. His business philosophy was to borrow as much as possible on each of his hotels in order to expand as rapidly as possible. This worked well as long as hotel occupancy rates were high. However, when occupancy rates dropped during the depression of the 1930s, Hilton was unable to meet the payments required by this heavy debt and lost several of his properties in bankruptcy proceedings.

symbolized the hotel industry for many Americans from the 1930s through the 1960s. The Conrad Hilton long served as the headquarters of the Hilton organization and was the world's largest hotel for many years.

The Great Depression

The Great Depression began in October 1929 and continued for the next decade. During this period, banks failed and firms large and small went out of business. Because the government did not insure against bank failures, many people lost their life savings. Unemployment rose to alarming rates and people were sometimes out of work for years. Nature compounded the economic problems in some parts of the country. Prolonged drought was followed by dust storms, and land that had once been fertile could no longer be used for agriculture or to support livestock.

During the Depression, the hotel industry experienced the same problem as other industries—sharply reduced sales volume. The hotel business closely follows business cycles and, therefore, is profitable when the economy is healthy and unprofitable during economic downturns. The explanation is fairly simple. Profitability in the hotel business is closely linked to travel. During periods of prosperity, more people travel, for business and pleasure. During a recession or depression, individuals and businesses reduce the amounts they spend on travel and related expenses, including food, beverages, and lodging. As a consequence, hotel occupancy rates plunge. Occupancies for those hotels that were able to survive the Depression were often below 50 percent, a level typically below the break-even point for most hotel operations.

One of the few hotels to open during the Great Depression was the world-famous Waldorf-Astoria, which opened in New York in 1932. The new location was 301 Park Avenue, between 49th and 50th streets. Actually, it was the second hotel to use that name, the first one being located farther downtown (see Chapter 2).

The End of the Depression

Some limited economic recovery began in 1933 and slow progress continued. However, historians tend to agree that the Great Depression continued until the production demands of World War II (which the United States entered in 1941) reduced unemployment and brought the nation a measure of prosperity. Virtually all economic activity was directed toward the war effort and many products, including building materials, were unavailable for civilian use. Thus, no commercial hotel construction took place. At the same time, there was a dramatic increase in travel by civilians and by government personnel, including the military. Gasoline was rationed, so people relied increasingly on public transportation for long-distance travel.

World War II brought renewed prosperity to the hotel industry. Many hotels had failed during the Depression, and a number of these hotel buildings had been converted to other uses. Consequently, the supply of hotel rooms was inadequate to meet the wartime demand. Many hotels in major cities had higher rates of occupancy than ever before or since. The existing hotels were busier than anyone had thought possible. Day after day, hotel desk clerks spent eight hours facing unending lines of weary travelers wanting rooms. Travelers to many of the major cities—New York and Washington, most notably—found it nearly impossible to get rooms. Many hotels failed to honor reservations; others would not even take reservations. It was a desperate time for travelers. National hotel occupancy percentages reached a record annual average well above 90 percent.

AFTER WORLD WAR II

The Development of Motels

After World War II, travel continued to increase. Greater amounts of leisure time, ease of travel, and increased disposable income created a growing number of actual and potential customers for hospitality services. By the early 1950s, the increasing numbers of Americans traveling by automobile and airplane no longer found the grand old hotels located near major railroad stations appealing or convenient. People traveling by automobile sought accommodations in new, more convenient locations.

The new American traveler—both working class and middle class—was not accustomed to the formality of the traditional hotel, nor was he willing to pay the prices and tip the great numbers of uniformed hotel employees found in traditional establishments. Moreover, the traditional city hotel did not provide on-premises parking. This new traveler wanted a clean, comfortable room at an affordable price, and he wanted ready access to his automobile. The business traveler, who had formerly used the train, was also becoming a confirmed automobile traveler. He could carry more in the trunk of his car than he could by train. He found it easier and cheaper to travel by car.

The demand for convenient accommodations for automobile travelers led, inevitably, to the development of the motel. Establishments had provided roadside accommodations for motorists since the earliest use of the automobile for long-distance travel in the 1920s. These were of two types: groups of small individual cabins, known as **tourist courts**, which offered parking space near the cabins; and private homes, known as **guest houses**, in which spare bedrooms were rented to transient guests. Neither of these forerunners of the motel constituted a significant element in the lodging industry.

Early Motels

Early **motels** were usually built, owned, and operated by individuals or couples, not by chains. They were typically purpose-built, single structures, all on one floor. Parking was free and convenient. Cars were normally parked just outside the door of the rented unit. The motel was informal; the motorist without a coat and tie did not feel out of place. He stopped at an office to check in, pay for his accommodations, and pick up the key, then he drove to the room, parked his car, and carried his own luggage. There was no one to tip. There were seldom foodservice facilities as part of the motel, so the traveler had to walk or drive to a restaurant to eat. These motels were simple, and they were inexpensive compared to the price of hotels, but they were few. The best and most sought-after location for a motel at the beginning of the motel age was on a main highway close to a city or town. It was generally agreed that a motel should be located on the right-hand side of a road because travelers driving toward a city would be more inclined to turn right into a motel parking area than to turn left across oncoming traffic. As the interstate highway network was developed, the exits from these highways became the preferred locations for motels.

Kemmons Wilson and the Holiday Inns

In the early 1950s, a building contractor named Wilson from Memphis, Tennessee, while driving with his wife and children on a family vacation, took special notice of the difficulty they had finding acceptable, reasonably priced places to spend the night. He conceived of an improved motel that offered many of the services of the traditional hotel but was situated more conveniently for the increasing numbers of people who traveled by automobile. When he returned home, Wilson began

Holiday Inn was the first national chain of motels that offered full service to business travelers. Shown here is an inn as it appeared in the 1950s.
(Photo courtesy of Bass Hotels and Resorts, Inc., successor of Holiday Inns, Inc.)

to plan the construction of a motel that was to become the first Holiday Inn. It opened in 1952 in Memphis.

Kemmons Wilson's Holiday Inn was so successful that he constructed another nearby. Thus began the development of an organization that eventually controlled more guest rooms than any other in the world. Wilson's special talent was in identifying sites for the location of successful motels. The growth of his chain kept pace with the development of the interstate highway system. Wherever an exit was planned, Wilson was one of the first to determine if that exit were an appropriate location for one of his Holiday Inns. To keep pace with the development of the highway system, it was necessary for Holiday Inns to franchise its operations.

Franchising

Although franchising had existed in the restaurant industry for many years, as previously described, it was not an important phenomenon in the lodging industry until it was adopted by Holiday Inns. A **franchise** is a contract between two parties, a franchisor and franchisee, that allows the franchisee the right to use the franchisor's name, sell its products, and participate in its programs and services under set, specific conditions. In the lodging field, the franchisor may own and operate many of the establishments bearing its name. The franchisor seeks independent affiliates—franchisees—for two main reasons: (1) so the franchisor can expand its network of establishments at a more rapid rate than would otherwise be possible, and (2) so the franchisor can increase revenues through the fees it collects from its franchisees without actually owning additional properties. The fees generally include a percentage of sales, an advertising fee, a fee for access to the reservations network, and, sometimes, other fees.

The advantage to the franchisee is as follows: The franchisee's property is part of a chain that is known, has the ability to profit from regional or national advertising campaigns conducted by the franchisor, and obtains access to professional management and management training (in most franchises) as well as to a national reservation network.

Older Hotels Begin to Change

While Wilson and others were building motels in the 1950s and 1960s, the established center-city hotels, many of them near the railroad terminals, were aging and becoming more costly to maintain. Some were indifferently maintained, and most were losing much of their business to the new booming motel industry.

A number of the older, decaying properties were finally forced to close; they simply could not compete. In other properties, management added staff to the sales departments and began to look for new ways to survive. Some hotels sought to lure long-term residents by advertising appealing weekly and monthly rates. Some attempted to compete directly with the new motels by merely changing their signs. Many—typically those that lacked meeting and banquet space but had access to parking—began to call themselves motor hotels and motor inns, to suggest that automobile travelers would be as satisfied in these accommodations as they were in a motel.

Many of the hotels that had served the individual commercial traveler attempted, often successfully, to develop tour business—groups of vacationers traveling together, typically by bus or airplane. At about this time, tour wholesalers started to reserve large numbers of rooms at these older hotels because they were able to negotiate comparatively low rates.

Hotels with adequate meeting and banquet space made efforts to attract special varieties of group business—conventions and business meetings. These ranged from sales meetings to trade shows, from fraternal to political meetings, and from alumni reunions to educational seminars. Center-city hotels became increasingly popular sites for all of these.

Finally, older center-city hotels attempting to survive adopted any combination of techniques to fill the vacant rooms. It was not unusual to find a hotel sales staff aggressively competing for both convention and group business while the banquet manager sold wedding parties and the front-office manager sold rooms on weekly and monthly rates. Many of these hotels were very large, and great amounts of skill and imagination were required to produce adequate sales volume from the vast number of banquet, meeting, and sleeping rooms they contained.

Hotel Construction Begins Anew

Unfortunately for the older center-city hotels, their competition was not limited to the new motels being constructed at the perimeters of cities. A new and lively threat was developing much closer than the outskirts of the city. Builders and developers had started a new era of hotel construction. For most cities, this was the first hotel construction since the earliest days of the Great Depression, 30 years before. New hotels were being built and opened at a record pace. In New York, for example, new properties constructed between 1960 and 1965 included the New York Hilton, the Americana, the Summit, the Regency, and the City Squire, all of which continue to thrive, although some have new names and new owners.

A number of the new center-city hotels constructed during this period were purpose-built, designed specifically to cater to large groups of people. They were truly convention hotels in every sense, with meeting rooms for hundreds of people and banquet rooms for thousands. For many of these, convention and other group business accounted for at least 80 percent of the sales.

International Operations

The introduction of commercial jet aircraft in 1957 also made international travel for masses of people a practical possibility for the first time in history. Americans began to travel abroad in great numbers, and visitors from other countries began to come to America. This led to more business for the lodging properties in many cities—particularly, at first, those on the East and West coasts with international airports. Later, when international arrivals and departures became common at other airports, hotels in those cities were also able to benefit.

One of the outcomes of increased international air travel was the development of international hotel operations; American hotel chains that had formerly restricted themselves to domestic operations began to expand abroad. Until the 1950s, only two major American hotel companies operated abroad. Intercontinental Hotels, a subsidiary of Pan American Airlines, had been international since 1947, when the United States government suggested that the company construct hotels in Central and South America as an aid to the economic development of those regions. Hilton Hotels also became international in 1949 with the opening of the Caribe Hilton in San Juan, Puerto Rico. Most hotel companies focused on the burgeoning American market during the early 1950s and were slow to go into the international area. Eventually, others did so, and today, most American hotel chains are international in scope. Principal examples include Marriott, Hyatt, Hilton, Sheraton, Holiday Inns, Ramada, and Best Western. Today, these names are clearly visible on lodging signs around the world, and there is no evidence that the American hotel and motel industry will retreat from its international leadership role in the years ahead.

Computers in the Lodging Industry

In the early 1980s, an additional important development began to take hold in the lodging industry. Hotels and motels started to become fully computerized.

Computers had been around for many years and many hotels had tried them out. However, until the early 1980s, computers were not successful in lodging properties because they were not reliable enough for lodging operations that were open 24 hours a day, seven days a week. Further, they were expensive and bulky. As early as the late 1960s, the New York Hilton hotel opened with a complete IBM computer operation. However, after only a short period, the system was scrapped and a traditional system put in place. Other hotels ran traditional systems side by side with computers because they were afraid that the computer system would crash and they could not check in or check out guests. A source problem was that hotel people had little computer expertise and computer people had little understanding of the hotel industry. It took some years to get past that.

By the early 1980s, computers were more reliable, less expensive, and more powerful. Furthermore, growing numbers of hotel operators learned a great deal about how computers could improve operations, and many computer experts acquired sufficient understanding of lodging operations to develop useful systems. Hotel and motel companies began to adopt computer property management systems. Today, virtually all properties with more than 50 rooms are computerized.

Market Segmentation

Most businesses, including the hotel business, must decide on specific types of individuals they wish to attract. For example, two **market segments** for hotels might be categorized as travelers seeking luxury accommodations and many services and who are willing to pay high prices for them, and travelers seeking only basic accommodations and who are willing to pay only moderate prices. Until the 1980s, most lodging companies operated properties that appealed to one or two specific types of travelers. Some operated only luxury hotels. Other companies specialized in economy motels or budget motels. Still others restricted their operations to first-class hotels catering primarily to business travelers, vacationers, or tours.

In the early 1980s, lodging organizations began to change their approach. They made serious efforts to attract more than one segment of the travel market. Over time, operators established a number of types of properties to appeal to a large number of segments. Market segments became more clearly defined and new types of properties were built. Examples include all-suite hotels for guests who want separate living and sleeping accommodations with limited cooking facilities, and residence motels for guests who intend to stay more than one or two nights.

Some lodging companies became multisegmented, with various brand names for their products. One good example is Marriott. In addition to first-class and luxury Marriott hotels and resorts, Marriott developed the following brands for other segments of the lodging market:

Courtyard: A midpriced chain of first-class hotels and motels

Residence Inns: A chain of first-class accommodations catering to travelers staying more than one or two nights

Fairfield Inns: A chain of limited-service budget motels

Spring Hill Suites: Moderately priced all-suite hotels

Town House Suites: Moderately priced suite hotels for those staying a week or more

Marriott Executive Apartments: Apartments for traveling executives

Marriott Conference Centers: Establishments catering only to groups holding meetings and conferences

Recent Hotel Construction

In recent years, many new large hotels were built throughout the United States. A number of these were constructed in the larger American cities, many of which have new or renovated convention centers or exhibition halls. In Philadelphia, for example, Marriott opened the largest hotel in Pennsylvania adjacent to the new Pennsylvania Convention Center. Hyatt built the 2000-room Hyatt Regency in Chicago, the home of McCormick Place, America's largest exhibition center. Large new properties were built in one of America's key resort and convention cities, Las Vegas, including the Luxor, New York, New York, and Bellagio. At present, the world's largest hotel is in Las Vegas: the MGM Grand Hotel, with 5005 rooms and suites. It is more than a hotel; it can perhaps best be described as a complete entertainment center that includes shops, stores, restaurants, lounges, pools, a health club, a casino, a 33-acre theme park, and a showroom.

RESORT HOTELS IN THE TWENTIETH CENTURY

By the early years of the twentieth century, several important factors affected the quality of life for the American workforce—changes that became significant for the operators of resort properties as the years wore on.

Leisure Time in America

Early in the twentieth century, some Americans began to have measurable amounts of leisure time. Most had very little, but it was more than their parents had known. At the same time, some had enough disposable income to be able to make plans for their newly found leisure hours. For most, there was little time and little money, but they went about enjoying the little there was. They took day trips by train or by boat, and, later, by car as well. The seashore, a park, a zoo, a historic site—Americans visited them all. These activities introduced new possibilities, including hotels, rooming houses, and boardinghouses catering not to business travelers but to people with a day, a weekend, or a week of leisure time. Increasingly, those who could afford it began to stay weeks or months.

Vacations

By 1915, growing numbers of white-collar and government workers received paid vacation time of one or two weeks a year and many, with their families, began to take vacations—a nearly revolutionary concept in the industrialized world. As unionized industrial workers obtained increased benefits through collective bargaining, many began to pressure their union leaders for vacations with pay. Although it was not easy for the unions to win paid vacations at the bargaining table, they were making gradual progress in this area by 1929.

As time went by, people who could afford to, began to travel somewhat farther away. The New York area, for example, offered a number of possibilities: for those of limited means, a day at the beaches of Coney Island; for others with greater incomes, the extensive rail network offered opportunities for weekends or weeks at destinations in the nearby Catskill Mountains of southern New York and the Pocono Mountains of eastern Pennsylvania. By the mid 1920s, over 200 resort properties in the Catskills alone catered to holiday seekers, principally from New York City.

There were other possibilities, as well. The beaches along the New Jersey coast were always popular with New Yorkers and Philadelphians. President Grant had said of Long Branch, one of the New Jersey resorts, "In all my travels I have never seen a place better suited for a summer residence." In the early twentieth century, packed trains from New York City arrived at the New Jersey resort towns on summer weekends at the rate of 12 or more each hour.

The Grand Resorts

The resort hotels developed during this period were many and varied. Many of those enjoyed by white-collar and blue-collar workers have not survived. However, it is likely that they attempted to imitate elements of the grand resorts, described in the following sections, all of which continue to operate.

The Broadmoor Hotel, Colorado Springs, Colorado

One of the premier resort properties in the United States is located in Colorado near Pikes Peak. Near the bottom of this 14,000-foot mountain, in Colorado Springs, stands this classic example of the elegant resort hotels of the West. The Broadmoor Hotel was founded by Spencer Penrose, an entrepreneur who had attempted to purchase the Antlers, a hotel in downtown Colorado Springs. He had not been able to do so and had decided instead to purchase another property outside of town. This had once been an established hotel operation but had burned down, been rebuilt, failed, and been converted to a girls' school. Existing facilities were inadequate for the resort, so construction began in 1917, and the new resort hotel opened in 1918. It was one of Colorado's first nationally known resorts. The architects were the firm of Warren and Wetmore of New York City, designers of New York's Grand Central Station, Biltmore Hotel, and Ritz-Carlton Hotel, among other important buildings. The Broadmoor quickly became a success. All through the 1920s, the Penroses entertained many wealthy and famous people, and their Broadmoor became a fashionable place for New York society. It is said that one reason for this success was Penrose's preparation for Prohibition. The Broadmoor allegedly had on hand one of the largest liquor supplies in the United States when Prohibition began in 1920.

This period of success for the Broadmoor ended with the onset of the Depression. Occupancy rates and guest counts dropped sharply, and Penrose was forced to reduce operating costs. He cut the size of the staff drastically, and it is reported that bellmen and waiters earned only their tips.

After World War II, improving economic conditions brought prosperity back to the hotel. New facilities and new rooms were added, and today the Broadmoor has 700 rooms. It has been a five-star and five-diamond resort ever since the awards were started.

The Arizona Biltmore, Phoenix

Another of America's grand resorts, the Arizona Biltmore, is located just 800 miles south of Colorado Springs in Phoenix, Arizona. It was built in the style of America's best-known architect, Frank Lloyd Wright, who participated in its design. At the time the hotel was built, Phoenix was a small community in a large valley—Paradise Valley, which was, essentially, desert. The Biltmore was situated on a large tract of barren land in the northeastern part of the city, near the foothills of the mountains.

The Biltmore was designed and constructed by Albert Chase McArthur, an architect and disciple of Wright. It opened in 1929 and was sold later that year

The Arizona Biltmore Hotel is one of the twentieth century's classic resort hotels that still is in operation. It is shown here as it appeared during the 1930s. *(Photo courtesy of Arizona Biltmore Resort and Spa)*

to William Wrigley Jr., the chewing gum manufacturer. Wrigley built a mansion for his personal use on a knoll overlooking the hotel. His home was visible for miles around; the resort hotel was not.

After World War II, the population of Phoenix began to increase dramatically. As the city grew, the Biltmore was eventually surrounded by newly constructed homes and businesses. In 1973, the Wrigley family sold it to Talley Industries. That summer, while the hotel was closed for the installation of a sprinkler system, a major fire damaged the property. Repairs were made promptly, and it reopened for the start of the guest season later that year. Talley Industries no longer owns the property, and it has changed hands several times over the years.

Interestingly, the Arizona Biltmore was originally open only during the winter months. Phoenix is normally extremely hot during the summer months, and only the development of suitable air conditioning systems made it possible for resort hotels in the region to stay open year round.

The Arizona Biltmore is typical of resorts that found it increasingly difficult— in some cases, impossible—to survive solely on individual guest business. The seasons are too short to generate the necessary sales volume. In order to remain open year round, the Biltmore began booking conventions and other group business. The hotel, however, enjoys a reputation for restricting its group business to periods of the year when comparatively few individual reservations are booked.

The Boca Raton Hotel and Club, Boca Raton, Florida

Another five-star hotel built during this period is the fabulous Boca Raton Hotel and Club, which originally opened in 1926. It was envisioned as a palatial establishment by Addison Mizner, a successful architect who became famous in Florida for designing many of the homes and other properties there. He wanted to turn the 17,500-acre site into "a happy combination of Venice and Heaven, Florence and Toledo, with a little Greco-Roman glory and grandeur thrown in." His grand plan included a castle with a drawbridge, set in the middle of a man-made lagoon—for himself! He was not able to construct all he originally had in mind, but all that he did build used the best and most expensive materials available. One of his creations was a luxurious 100-room hotel that cost $1.5 million dollars to build—a fortune in those days for such a small establishment. He named it the Cloister Inn. He used this name again later for a property he designed in Sea Island, Georgia.

The Cloister Inn was not financially successful; it was open for only three months before it was forced to close. It was sold to Charles Dawes, a former vice president of the United States. It was sold again, in 1928, to Clarence H. Geist of Philadelphia. Geist closed the hotel and spent millions of dollars converting it to a private club by adding rooms, swimming pools, and other features to the original building. He brought the total number of rooms to 400 and reopened the facility in 1930 under a new name: the Boca Raton Hotel and Club.

During World War II, the hotel was taken over by the United States Army and used as a training facility. In 1956, the Boca Raton Hotel and Club was purchased by Arthur Vining Davis, who set up a corporation, called Arvida, to own and operate it. Arvida built a 27-story tower, which added new guest rooms and a convention center. The property has been under continuous development since and now is one of the larger resorts in the area, with 1000 guest rooms, 29 meeting rooms, 4 outdoor swimming pools, 7 dining rooms, an 18-hole golf course, 22 tennis courts, and a half-mile of private beach.

The Impact of Changing Transportation Modes on Resort Hotels

We have observed how the decline of the railroads and the increased use of automobiles began to affect traditional hotels in the cities and towns of America after World War II. These developments also had a significant and lasting impact on the nation's resort hotel industry.

In New England, for example, the summer resort hotels historically catered to guests who arrived by rail and stayed for weeks and months. With changes in transportation, it become more difficult—eventually impossible—to reach these properties by rail, and more guests began to arrive by car, particularly as the quality of the roads improved. Because people in cars have greater mobility, guests tended to stay for shorter periods. Instead, they used their newfound mobility to visit other areas, see new sights. Some of the New England ski areas, formerly accessible principally by train, were much easier to reach by car, particularly as train service deteriorated. Guests with private cars also found that the car simplified the daily transit problem of getting from hotel to ski slope. As time went on, developers began to plan and construct hotels closer to the slopes and accessible only by car, which helped sound the death knell for rail travel in the ski areas. Later, the automobile gave impetus to the development of new ski areas that would clearly not have been built if rail travel had remained the primary means of access.

As people began to accept air transportation as a common means of travel, various changes took place in the resort hotel industry. Just as the acceptance of air travel occurred gradually, so did these changes:

1. Resort hotels accessible with reasonable ease by rail or by automobile—including many fashionable properties in the East—gradually lost their traditional business. Many of their former guests found new destinations easily reached by air. These included Caribbean islands, South Pacific beaches, and historic cities and sights of Europe.

2. Resort hotels in remote locations—including many in the West—that were difficult to reach by ground transport were readily accessible by air. It became convenient for residents of the East Coast, for example, to fly to Colorado in the winter to ski, or to Arizona to bask in the warm sunshine. Previously, such trips took more time and were less comfortable. People who made such trips tended to stay longer to justify the time and trouble the journey represented.

3. Some resort areas that had remained small because of the time and cost incurred by travelers in reaching them began to grow as air travel made them more accessible and the cost of flights decreased. Some destinations—the

Hawaiian Islands and Las Vegas, for example—grew quickly. After the intro-duction of commercial jet aircraft in 1958, the number of visitors to Hawaii increased, reportedly by 500 percent between 1959 and 1967.

4. Later, as remote areas became accessible, imaginative developers began to plan and construct resort hotels—and even new resort areas—in places where none had previously existed. Vail, Colorado, is an excellent example. So are Maui, Hawaii, and Cancun, Mexico.

5. Operators of chain hotels, recognizing the outstanding potential for growth in resort areas, gradually developed various types of properties in domestic and international locations. Privately developed resort hotels began to include the names Sheraton, Hilton, Marriott, and Hyatt. Many independent resorts were sold to the chains or were managed by them. Camelback Inn, a five-star resort, for example, was sold to Marriott Corporation.

6. In order to remain competitive, to retain their capable staffs, and to generate sufficient dollar volume to meet growing overhead costs, seasonal resort hotels—both the older traditional properties and their newer competitors—increasingly began to remain open year round.

7. In order to generate volume in their off seasons, resort hotels began to move into markets that had formerly been the provinces of the large center-city hotels: conventions and other business meetings. To survive, many resort prop-erties competed with commercial hotels for as much convention and meet-ing business as they could attract. Eventually, many resort operators found that they grossed more money on this kind of business than they did from their traditional customers—families and individual guests.

8. An era of instant resort development began. Developers acquired large areas of land and created complete resorts, with the typical amenities, all within a short period. Complete resort operations—the Dorado Beach Hotel built by Rock Resorts, for example, and such theme parks as Sea World and Disney World—became both popular and successful. Many of the earlier, more tra-ditional resort hotels, started as small operations, expanded as their fame and success increased. By contrast, many of these new resorts are large operations when they open—grandly and imaginatively designed and constructed for in-stant and continuing success.

Two examples of new properties in the resort world illustrate dramatically some of the differences between traditional resorts, such as the Broadmoor and the Arizona Biltmore, and the exciting new players in today's resort industry.

Marriott's Desert Springs, Palm Desert, California

In the deserts of southern California, over 100 miles from the Pacific coast, lies a resort area known as Palm Springs. The region has been popular with celebrities for years, and developers have built important golf resorts in the area. One of the more interesting of these is Marriott's Desert Springs, a beautiful four-diamond

Palm Desert resort and spa created on desert land. There, with the aid of modern irrigation, Marriott developed a lush, green resort property that includes a main hotel building of more than 900 rooms and a series of villas. Special features include 36 holes of golf, a 20-court tennis complex, a 27,000-square-foot European-style spa, and a number of elegant restaurants. One of the most interesting features is the unexpected series of lakes and waterways that offer incredible views and improbable possibilities for boating in the middle of the desert. In fact, the waterways extend into the main lobby of the hotel, which has a dock for launches that transport guests from the main building to two of the restaurants located across the lake.

Prince Resorts Hapuna Beach Prince Hotel, Hapuna Beach, Hawaii

In 1994, on the island of Hawaii, Prince Resorts created a new 350-unit property in which all rooms and suites face the white sands of Hapuna Beach, considered America's best beach by many discriminating travelers. Special features include five restaurants, a golf course designed by Arnold Palmer, tennis courts, a swimming pool, and a health and fitness center.

Typical of many new resort properties, the designers included features and facilities to attract meeting and convention business. These include over 14,000 square feet of function space, an 8400-square-foot grand ballroom, four smaller meeting rooms, and two executive boardrooms. With the addition of facilities of this type, today's resort hotel operators need not depend exclusively on reservations from individual vacationers, as did the operators of resort properties in the past. Today, the operator of a modern resort hotel is prepared to compete for business with operators of any kind of hotel properties.

Time-Shares

A relatively new concept in resort development is sharing the cost and use of a property with others—the **time-share**. The idea came from the computer industry during the 1960s, when computers were big and expensive. Many companies that wanted computers, but could use them for a limited time only each day, decided to share the cost of purchasing and maintaining them by inviting other companies to participate in their use for a period of time each day. Gradually, the idea caught on with other expensive products—condominiums, recreational vehicles (RVs), boats, apartments, and so on. Many older hotels doing poor business or looking to modernize decided to time-share part or all of their property in order to raise funds. The new industry has grown over the past 30 years. More than two million households now own a vacation time-share. In the lodging industry, time-shares generally take one of the following forms:

- **Fee ownership time-share:** This is a form of ownership where each owner purchases a unit of time in a property and shares the cost of its maintenance. Time can be purchased in a condominium, individual house, apartment, or hotel. Owners purchase as many weeks as they wish at a specific cost for each week. The cost per week varies according to the time of year. For example, a person purchasing a time-share in Florida for the first week in March will pay more than a week time-share at the same property during August. Like any other property owned, a time-share can be sold, given away, or willed to an heir. One of the oldest companies dealing in this category of time-shares is Fairfield Communities, which has over 20 locations and over 260,000 members and property owners.

- **Right-to-use time-share:** This form of time-share does not involve ownership but, rather, is a long-term lease on a piece of property. The lease may be for 15, 20, 25, or 30 years, or any other period. The lease may be for a specific property or for use of an unspecified unit in a larger property. A maintenance fee is charged each year and, at the end of the lease, the time-share expires. Right-to-use time-shares typically cost less than fee ownership and are very popular. Many companies deal in this form of time-share, including Silverleaf Resorts, which owns 23 resorts.

- **Vacation club time-shares:** This is the newest form of time-share. It requires purchasers to buy "points," which can be spent in a variety of ways and for any of the specified locations. For example, if someone purchases 150 Disney vacation club points (for about $9750), that person can split his time between Disney World and Disney's Old Key West Resort. Major hotel companies are now into vacation time-shares, including Marriott, Hilton, Ritz-Carlton, and Hyatt.

Under fee ownership and right-to-use time-share arrangements, an attractive feature provided by all larger companies is the ability to exchange one's time for time in another unit in a different location. For example, someone who owns a time-share in a Caribbean island can exchange his week for a week in Mexico.

SUMMARY

In this chapter, late nineteenth-century inventions that helped change the hospitality industry are identified and the impact of each is described. Ships and trains are identified as the principal means of travel in the early years of the century, prior to the development of automobiles and planes. The development of the airline industry is discussed in detail. Its growth and importance to travel are examined and the effects of deregulation detailed. The significance of current methods of routing aircraft and frequent flyer programs are explained.

Significant developments are discussed that occurred in three segments of the industry—restaurants, hotels, and resort hotels—from the turn of the century onward. Economic and social factors that led to increased travel by Americans after 1945 are identified and discussed, as are the principal changes that took place in restaurants, hotels, and resort hotels in the same period. Factors include the impact of chain operations, the role of franchising and market segmentation, the importance of computers, the impact of changing transportation modes, and time-sharing. The contributions of several important figures—including Ellsworth M. Statler, Conrad Hilton, Howard Johnson, J. Willard Marriott, Kemmons Wilson, and Ray Kroc—are also examined.

KEY TERMS

Airline Deregulation Act of 1978   Market segment
Amtrak   Motel
Diner   Right-to-use time-share
Drive-in   Roadhouse
Fee ownership time-share   Speakeasy
Franchise   Time-share
Frequent-flyer program   Tourist court
Great Depression   Vacation club time-share
Guest house   Vacation cruising
Hub-and-spoke routing   Yield management
Kelly Act   Zeppelin

DISCUSSION QUESTIONS

1. List three important inventions of the late nineteenth century and briefly describe the impact of each on the hospitality industry of the early twentieth century.

2. Identify the three major reasons cited in the text to explain the growth in mass travel after World War II.

3. Why are vacation cruises becoming increasingly popular?

4. List the four main attractions of vacationing on board cruise ships.

5. Why did the number of railroad passengers decline after World War II?

6. What is Amtrak? When and why was it created? Has it been profitable? What is Amtrak doing to become self-sufficient?

7. What is a zeppelin? In which decades of the twentieth century were zeppelins used for commercial passenger service?

8. Of what significance was the Kelly Act of 1926 to the development of passenger airlines?

9. When was Pan American's first international passenger flight? its first Pacific passenger flight? its first Atlantic passenger flight?

10. In what year was the Boeing 747 introduced into commercial service? What was the impact of this plane on air travel? Which airline was first to use it?

11. In what year was the Concorde supersonic jet introduced into commercial service? Why was the introduction of this new plane significant? How fast does it fly?

12. List and explain three effects of airline deregulation.

13. What is the hub-and-spoke method of routing aircraft? What are the advantages and disadvantages of this method over direct routing of aircraft?

14. List and describe four types of restaurants that developed in the early twentieth century.

15. What was Prohibition? What was the impact of Prohibition on each of the following: taverns, fine restaurants, roadhouses?

16. Name the first fast-food hamburger chain. When was it started?

17. Who founded the Hot Shoppe restaurants? What circumstances led this individual to start the first of these establishments?

18. What were Howard Johnson's principal contributions to the restaurant industry?

19. After World War II, the interaction of several forces led to significant growth in the restaurant industry. List two.

20. Who founded McDonald's? Who first sold McDonald's franchises?

21. What were Ray Kroc's two principal contributions to the development and eventual success of McDonald's?

22. Identify four specialty food restaurant chains that developed after World War II.

23. What were E. M. Statler's principal contributions to the development of the hotel industry?

24. Name the property that is generally considered the first modern commercial hotel and describe five features that distinguished it from competitors. What was the advertising motto of the hotel?

25. Name the world-famous New York City hotel that has operated without an identifying exterior sign throughout its history.

26. List three reasons that the 1920s were considered the golden age of hotels.

27. What effect did the Great Depression have on the hotel industry? What happened to levels of occupancy during this period?

28. Are hotels affected by recession, depression, prosperity, and other changes in the economy? Why?

29. What caused the high levels of hotel room occupancy during World War II?

30. Why did the motel segment of the lodging industry experience rapid growth in the period following World War II?

31. What contribution did Kemmons Wilson make to the development of the motel segment of the industry?

32. What is a franchise? What are the advantages of franchise arrangements for the franchisor? The franchisee?

33. Faced with declining business volume after 1950, older center-city hotels devised ways to attract new business. List three.

34. Why did American hotel chains begin to move into international markets in the 1960s? Identify five chains that are engaged in international hotel operations today.

35. What factors made it possible for lodging companies to take advantage of computer systems in the 1980s?

36. What is market segmentation? Why did lodging companies begin to move toward multisegmentation?

37. In the early twentieth century, some American workers began to have measurable amounts of leisure time. What kinds of activities does the text indicate were available to the American worker on his day off?

38. Name three five-star resort properties built and opened between 1900 and 1930.

39. The text identifies eight significant changes in the resort hotel industry that have occurred since 1945. List and discuss five of these.

40. What features of Marriott's Desert Springs property set it apart from older, more traditional resorts?

41. What is time-sharing? List and explain the differences among the three most popular forms of time-sharing.

MOMENTS OF TRUTH

1. You have just been appointed assistant to the general manager of a 150-room motel with foodservice, bar, convention facilities for 200 persons, swimming pool, and exercise room. The motel is an independent operation located on the outskirts of a midsize city. Occupancy and profit at the motel has not been good. One of the options to improve occupancy and profit is to become a franchisee for a well-known chain. The general manager has asked you to investigate this option. How could this option help? Do you see any advantages to remaining independent rather than becoming a franchisee?

2. You intend to travel by air from Boston, Massachusetts, to Seattle, Washington. Your airline tells you that there is no direct flight between these two points. You will have to fly to Dallas, Texas, change planes, and then fly to Seattle. What benefits do you suppose that airlines gain from this arrangement? Do you see any benefits to travelers?

3. The president of a chain of high-priced first-class hotels knows that many travelers are looking for first-class accommodations but unwilling to pay first-class prices. They are willing to give up some services and amenities in order to pay less for their rooms. What steps would you recommend he take to gain a share of this business?

INTERNET EXERCISES

1. Find the McDonald's Web site. What is Hamburger University? How many people have graduated from it? Go to the job search page and find an opening you might consider on graduation. Write a paragraph outlining the requirements for the job.

2. Find the Web site for Camelback Inn. How many rooms does the facility contain? List the various types of accommodations it offers and write a brief description of each.

3. Go to www.silverleafresorts.com, a time-share company. Write a brief description of its locations, facilities, and programs.

PART III

Food and Beverage Perspectives

Dimensions of Food and Beverage

► Learning Objectives

After reading and studying this chapter, you should be able to:

1. Cite the percentage of gross domestic product (GDP) attributable to food and beverage service.

2. Identify the importance of the food and beverage industry as an employer of women, minorities, and teenagers.

3. List and discuss the three principal reasons cited in the text for increased demand for foodservice.

4. Define *foodservice* and a foodservice enterprise.

5. List and discuss the five most important characteristics of a foodservice operation.

6. Describe each of the characteristic types of foodservice establishments presented in the chapter.

7. Define *beverage service* and a beverage service operation.

8. List nine reasons for patronizing beverage service establishments.

9. List and discuss the three terms used to describe the focus of beverage service establishments.

10. Identify the major categories in the National Restaurant Association's classification system for reporting industry sales.

INTRODUCTION

Immigrants from Europe recreated in America the eating and drinking establishments of their homelands in the seventeenth century. These establishments have always enjoyed a high degree of popularity in America. As we discussed in previous chapters, seventeenth- and eighteenth-century taverns sold alcoholic beverages of various types—beer, ale, wine, and rum among them—and most served food as well. Many served a midday meal, known in some parts of the country as an ordinary. Many were popular social centers in their communities.

In the nineteenth century, the number and variety of food and beverage operations grew at an amazing pace. This was when the foundations of the modern food and beverage industry were developed. Restaurants and taverns of all sorts served meals relatively inexpensively. People who lived in lodging houses, where there were no cooking facilities, ate many of their meals in inexpensive restaurants. At the same time, hotels and restaurants provided the finest of food and wines in luxurious surroundings to the growing number of wealthy Americans.

By the beginning of the twentieth century, Americans had access to many types of restaurants—diners, cafeterias, roadhouses, and hamburger stands, to name a few. The concept of dining out—making an important occasion out of the dining experience, with the finest of food and beverages served in a pleasant environment—began to play a growing role in American life.

THE SIZE OF THE INDUSTRY

The foodservice industry ranks as one of the largest in the United States (1). Recent publications of the **National Restaurant Association** (NRA), the industry's principal trade association, state that "eating and drinking places are first among all retailers in the number of establishments and the number of employees." Nearly 30 percent of all retail establishments are eating and drinking places. Over 840,000 eating and drinking establishments employ 11.3 million people in the United States. NRA projects that the number of employees will rise to 12 million by 2006. That is about 8 percent of all U.S. employees.

On a typical day, almost half (46 percent) of all adults in the United States are restaurant patrons. The typical restaurant serves 11 percent of its customers with breakfast, 37 percent with lunch, and 52 percent with dinner. One must remember, however, that few restaurants are typical. Some are open only for dinner, some only for breakfast and lunch, and others for all three meals. Saturday is the most popular day to eat out, and Monday is the least popular.

Information published by the NRA reveals that the foodservice industry employs more women, more teenagers, and more members of minority groups than any other industry in America. Approximately 58 percent of foodservice workers are female and 70 percent of all supervisors are women. Twelve percent of employees are African American, and 17 percent are of Hispanic origin.

The growth of food and beverage sales has been continuous. In 1970, NRA figures placed foodservice sales at $42.8 billion. By 1975, sales volume had grown to $70.3 billion. By 1980, it had grown to approximately $120 billion, and the 1980 figure nearly doubled by 1990. By 2001, sales were in excess of $395 billion. This was 4 percent of the gross domestic product (GDP)—generally defined as the value of all goods and services sold. By any measure, this is a major industry.

Some foodservice establishments boast sales of $30 million or more each year. However, most foodservice establishments are small operations. Two out of three eating and drinking places have annual sales of less than $500,000. Approximately three out of four are single-unit operations. More than four out of every ten are sole proprietorships, establishments owned by one individual.

Although a great number of establishments in our industry offer both food and beverages to their customers, the practice is not universal. The majority of foodservice operators do not sell alcoholic beverages. Because of this, and because there are significant differences between food operations and beverage operations, we discuss the foodservice and beverage service segments of the industry separately in this chapter.

FOODSERVICE

As suggested by the statistics of the NRA, the demand for foodservice has grown at a rapid pace in recent years. In today's world, even children patronize foodservice establishments at very early ages—having their "Happy Meals" at McDonald's—then continuing to patronize McDonald's and other fast-food restaurants as adults. Today, many adults eat out several times each week, more than ever before in our history. The NRA reports that 45.8 percent of the money Americans spend on food is spent in foodservice establishments.

In addition, the frequency of eating out is increasing. Americans consume more meals away from home each year and, nationwide, foodservice sales continue to increase dramatically. Experts predict that Americans will soon be eating half of all meals away from home.

Several reasons are commonly cited for America's increased demand for foodservice. These include (1) increased discretionary income, (2) smaller families, and (3) changing lifestyles.

Increased Discretionary Income

The first reason for America's rising demand for foodservice is significant. The average American has more discretionary income than ever before. Individuals have more money to spend as they choose, and growing numbers are spending a substantial amount of it in foodservice establishments. For most Americans today, having a meal or a snack in one of the restaurants or other foodservice operations that we see everywhere is an unremarkable, everyday occurrence.

Smaller Families

Another reason that Americans patronize foodservice operations more frequently is a decrease in the size of the family. One explanation for this is that more women are in the workforce and choose to postpone having children. In fact, many choose to have fewer children altogether. In two-earner households, with both adults tired at the end of the day, going out to eat or having a meal delivered has become an acceptable alternative to preparing the evening meal at home. Also, it is probably easier and certainly more affordable to go out to dinner with a small family than with a large one.

Changing Lifestyles

The daily routines of families are considerably different from those of 30 or more years ago. The term *two-earner household* implies that one individual no longer stays at home all day to take primary responsibility for food shopping, meal preparation, and cleaning up after meals. As a result, Americans are less inclined to prepare evening meals at home.

Another change in lifestyle that affects the foodservice industry is that neither young people attending school nor working adults carry their lunches from home to the extent that they did in years past. Students and workers have foodservice readily available at low cost at school, at work, or at any number of fast-food establishments nearby. Similarly, each individual in today's family has a greater degree of independence than in the past. Each makes more personal decisions about his or her life than before. More family members have automobiles and can easily decide to go out for a quick meal with friends rather than eat at home. In some households, it is difficult to identify an evening meal period at all. Family members may come home at different times and either prepare their own meal or elect to go to a restaurant to eat. This would have been unusual a generation ago.

At the same time, the increase in the number of wage earners in America has led to a decrease in the number of family members trained in the art and science of food preparation. In many households, no one is able to prepare an excellent meal. Thus, for holiday meals and other occasions for celebration, many depend on restaurants.

FOODSERVICE DEFINED

Foodservice may be defined as providing fully prepared foods for immediate consumption on or off premises. Foodservice establishments are those engaged in providing foodservice. These establishments include not only the obvious examples of restaurants and college dining halls but also the salad bars and sandwich counters in food markets and such distant relations as food vending machines.

Foodservice enterprises range from full-service restaurants to self-service buffets, from fine restaurants to take-out operations, and from company cafeterias to hamburger stands. Foodservice operations may be either **commercial**—those operated with the aim of earning a profit—or **noncommercial**—those operated primarily for the convenience or welfare of those served rather than primarily for profit. In the sections that follow, we examine in more detail the kinds of foodservice establishments and the kinds of service they offer.

VARIATIONS AMONG FOODSERVICE ESTABLISHMENTS

Anyone who has observed the variety of foodservice establishments will agree that there are significant differences from one to another. These differences are the result of decisions made by owners and managers about the five most important characteristics of a foodservice operation:

1. Menu items

2. Food quality

3. Menu prices

4. Service

5. Ambience

Menu Items

Perhaps the most important difference among foodservice enterprises can be found in the menu items they offer. Some establishments present the customer with a menu consisting of several pages and listing many kinds of dishes. This is common in establishments open for long hours daily and serving a varied group of customers. By contrast, other foodservice operations offer a limited menu, one that may include only a very few luncheon or dinner items—two appetizers, three entrées, and two desserts, for example.

Some establishments specialize in particular menu items, such as ethnic or regional dishes. Ethnic dishes are those associated with a particular culture; regional dishes are those characteristic of a particular geographic area—New England or the South, for example.

Regional establishments sometimes cater to the tastes of those living in the region in which they are located. A menu for a restaurant in the South might feature catfish, black-eyed peas, and hush puppies. These items would not normally be found in the North, except in establishments specializing in regional southern dishes. Similarly, a substantial number of restaurants on the coast of New England sell Maine lobster, New England clam chowder, and New England boiled dinner—items one would not commonly find on menus in the South.

Some establishments restrict their menus to specialty foods. Specialty foods belong to a particular food family, such as vegetarian, seafood, or pasta. Others do not specialize but instead offer menus that appeal to a broad range of customers.

EL POLLO LOCO KNOWS WHAT IT DOES BEST AND KEEPS DOING IT

Irvine, California–based El Pollo Loco has been in business for 20 years and is now a chain of 270 units. Although it is a Mexican restaurant chain serving the usual tacos and burritos, the item that has set it apart from other Mexican fast-food establishments is Crazy Chicken. In fact, *el pollo loco* means crazy chicken in English.

Crazy Chicken is marinated chicken that's flame broiled. Food critics rave about it and management has no intention of changing it. It is the cornerstone of their business.

El Pollo Loco is an excellent example of the importance of menu items and food quality in restaurant success.

Source: Adapted from an article in *Nation's Restaurant News*, 25 May 2000.

School and college foodservice operations typically take this approach. They try to serve foods that appeal to many groups of students.

Food Quality

Food quality is defined as the degree of excellence in food products. Food quality may vary greatly from one foodservice establishment to another. In the final analysis, variations in quality result from decisions made by management to establish a given level of quality. In general, the level of quality is determined by the interplay of three elements:

1. The quality of the food ingredients used

2. The professional skill of those preparing the food

3. The time and effort expended on food preparation

The quality of the food products prepared is determined largely by the quality of the ingredients used. For example, no one can prepare an appealing tossed green salad using wilted lettuce and unripened tomatoes, or an excellent fisherman's platter using fish caught several days before and refrigerated improperly. In addition, a foodservice operator must know that many fresh foods are graded for quality and that items of a given quality may be inappropriate for use in certain dishes. For example, oranges used for freshly squeezed juice may be entirely unsuited to display on a buffet or use in fruit baskets delivered to guests' rooms in a hotel.

Another important element in determining food quality is the professional skill of those preparing the food. Some food preparers are trained in one of the excellent colleges and institutes offering culinary degrees and diplomas or in one of the splendid apprenticeship programs in Europe. Others learn on the job from mentors willing to train them. Some claiming to be professionals have never really learned much about food preparation but only pretend to know. Still others lack the ability or the will to excel at food preparation.

Each foodservice operator must determine the amount of time and effort that should be devoted to preparing food for customers. As a general rule, food prepared on premises from fresh ingredients should be better than food purchased in a frozen, canned, or other pre-prepared state. The latter is known as **convenience food**, a term used to refer to food products processed before purchase, thus reducing in-house preparation time. The reasons for not preparing all food products from fresh ingredients vary. In some establishments, the kitchen staff lacks the professional skill to prepare products equal to the convenience items. In others, hiring skilled personnel would make the cost of labor too high and would cause menu prices to be higher than customers would pay. For many, convenience items are of acceptable quality. In fact, sometimes convenience foods are of better quality than those foods available fresh. For many chain operations, in which management wants products of uniform quality used throughout its chain, convenience foods provide the most reasonable means of achieving uniformity.

Menu Prices

Menu prices can vary greatly from one foodservice operation to another. On one hand, some establishments charge low prices and attempt to be successful by making a small profit on each of a large number of sales. Others charge low prices for different reasons; they may provide a service for a specific group of people—club members or hospital patients, for example—and no attempt is made to earn a profit. On the other hand, some establishments charge high prices knowing that they will attract fewer customers. Each sale, however, normally results in a comparatively high profit, enabling the operator to prosper with fewer customers than the lower-priced establishment. Other reasons for variations in menu prices relate to differences in operating costs, numbers of customers required for profitability, and the image the operator intends to project for the establishment.

Service

Foodservice operators may provide a number of service arrangements for their customers. Establishments are often differentiated on the basis of these service arrangements, which include table service, counter service, room service, self-service, and take-out or delivery service.

Table Service

For **table service**, servers normally take customers' orders selected from menus or their equivalent, then deliver the foods to the customers seated at their tables. There are many variations on this basic procedure, as well as several specific forms of service, including those known as American, Russian, French, and English. These are described in greater detail in Chapter 6.

Counter Service

For **counter service**, customers are served food across a level surface called a *counter*. They may be either seated at the counter or standing, and they may consume the food at the counter or at some other location within the establishment.

AMBIENCE IS KING AT THE BELMONT

The Belmont is the most elegant restaurant in Cheltenham in the United Kingdom. It is a Regency-style restaurant combining contemporary and traditional cuisine.

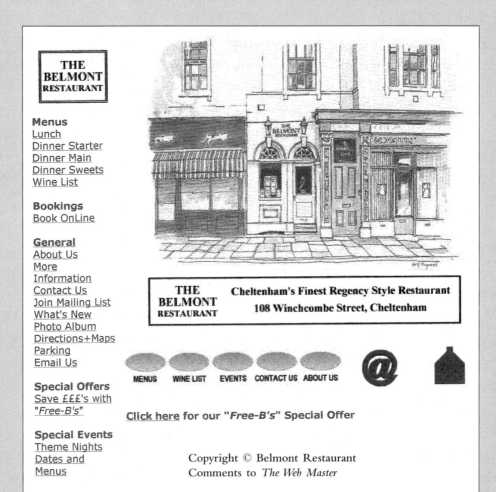

The entrance is identified by two distinctive brass carriage lamps set on either side of the door, which conceals a charming bar leading to the dining area. The interior is decorated in ocher, terra cotta, and cream, with crystal chandeliers giving sparkle to the silver table.

The Belmont is an excellent example of the importance of ambience in distinguishing one restaurant from others.

Source: Taken from the Web site of The Belmont Restaurant, 30 May 2000.

Room Service

For **room service**, customers are situated away from a normal dining area, typically in a hotel room or a hospital room. Food is transported to the individual's room and served.

Self-service

For **self-service**, customers select foods from an array of displayed items; they carry the items, with or without a tray, to some location in the establishment to consume them. Cafeterias, buffets, and salad bars are three common examples of self-service arrangements.

Takeout or Delivery Service

Takeout or delivery service differs markedly from the others. The menu items are expected to be consumed off premises and are packaged accordingly. With takeout, the customer collects the food on premises and carries it out before consuming it. With delivery service, the customer places an order by telephone or fax, then waits for the food to be delivered. Some establishments offer take-out service only, others offer only delivery, and others offer both.

There are no general rules about the types of service offered by foodservice establishments. Some offer only one type—table service, for example. Others provide more than one type—possibly table service and counter service. Still others may employ all of these in their efforts to please the greatest number of customers.

Ambience

In the foodservice industry, *ambience* is a term used to refer to the aesthetic or emotional impact of an establishment on its customers. It has any number of elements—furnishings, lighting, sound, decorations, themes, table settings, employees' appearances and attitudes, and so on—all aspects of the establishment's environment. In a professionally designed restaurant, the ambience is never left to chance. It is carefully crafted to achieve a particular impact. One of the reasons that the units in a chain operation are the same is that this helps ensure that all have a similar ambience.

The elements of ambience vary greatly from one establishment to another. Some, often family restaurants, are typically bright, cheerful, and informal. Others are far more formal featuring subdued lighting, crisp white linen, fine china and glassware, highly polished silver, and a professionally trained staff. Still other establishments—those that cater to college students, for example—are more likely to be lively, noisily informal, and feature popular music. Restaurants attempting to create romantic settings may be dimly lighted and provide soft background music.

Ambience is one of the key features that differentiate one restaurant from another. Shown here is the interior of a restaurant at the Regent Beverly Wilshire Hotel.
(Photo courtesy of Regent International Hotels)

CHARACTERISTIC TYPES OF FOODSERVICE ESTABLISHMENTS

Because of the large number of variables in foodservice establishments, most attempts at classifying them are not successful. The classifications are either too simple to be of any value—"with or without parking," for example—or too complex to be useful, with categories based on the many possible variations in menu, food quality, service, atmosphere, and so on. One useful exception is classification based on price. Many restaurant guides classify restaurants according to how expensive they are, typically using dollar signs ($, $$, $$$, or $$$$) to indicate the relative prices of the menus. This type of classification is simple yet informative to customers. Guides also rate establishments according to an overall evaluation of quality. Restaurants are typically awarded one or more stars, up to four or five stars. Neither of these two rating systems, however, indicates the type of restaurant or food served without further explanation.

Nevertheless, because people discuss foodservice establishments, describing and comparing them, some terms have become commonly accepted. Those that follow are characteristically regarded as describing types of foodservice establishments. One must remember, however, that they do not constitute any real system of foodservice classification because they are not mutually exclusive. To describe a single foodservice operation, it is usually necessary to use more than one of these terms.

Fast Food

Fast-food establishments are those that serve foods for which there is little or no waiting. Many such establishments are beginning to identify themselves as *fast-service* or *quick-service* restaurants in recognition of the fact that the service is fast, not the food. The food may take some time to prepare.

In fast-food restaurants, customers wait on line for access to a counter at which they order food from a limited menu. Often, the food is prepared and packaged ahead of time, and the customer's choices need only be picked up by a server and delivered to the customer—on a tray or in a bag, depending on whether the customer intends to consume the food on or off premises. Fast-service operations are relatively low priced. Examples include McDonald's, Burger King, Dunkin' Donuts, Kentucky Fried Chicken, Wendy's, Roy Rogers, and Nathan's. So that the concept works, a high degree of standardization is required. Management typically sets rigid standards for procedures, portion sizes, and packaging. *Procedures* are methods for doing work; *portion sizes* are the quantities of specific menu items served each time a given item is ordered; *packaging* is the particular container or wrapping in which a single portion of a given menu item is served. Other prerequisites to successful operation of a fast-food restaurant typically include an almost inflexible menu, specialized equipment for preparing the foods on the menu quickly, and a staff properly trained to use the equipment efficiently and to serve a large number of customers in a short time. A fast-service restaurant is a well-organized enterprise designed to operate with staff who can be trained quickly and easily.

Table Service

A **table service restaurant** is one in which customers are seated and served at tables. Individuals may be escorted to their tables by an employee known by a title, such as host or hostess, or may select their own tables. They may be given printed menus from which to select foods or may select them from an equivalent device, such as a sign or a chalkboard, or from the server's description. At the customer's table, an employee may suggest particular menu items and, normally, makes note of the item or items selected.

The selections are conveyed to the kitchen, where the food is prepared. Selections are served to customers when prepared, with the delivery suitably timed if several items are ordered by one individual. The individual doing the serving (waiter or waitress or server) is typically the one who took the customer's order.

In most table service restaurants, the customer is presented with a bill at the conclusion of service. The bill is commonly called a **guest check**, and the customer is expected to pay, charge, sign, or otherwise attend to the bill at that moment. In some establishments, the bill is settled directly with the server; in others, it is settled with a cashier, typically stationed near the exit. Exceptions occur in operations that include meals with room prices.

Ethnic

An **ethnic restaurant** specializes in foods associated with a particular culture. Among the most common of these are Chinese, Mexican, Greek, French, Japanese, German, Italian, Spanish, Thai, and Indian. Ethnic restaurants vary considerably in menu, food quality, menu prices, service, and ambience, even within a specific ethnic grouping. Chinese restaurants, for example, may serve foods from one or more of four regional cuisines—Peking, Szechwan, Canton, and Shanghai—each of which is distinct. Some Chinese restaurants offer table service; others offer counter service or takeout. In recent years, buffet service has become more common. Some ethnic restaurants use high-quality ingredients and prepare the finest of foods; others use food of lower quality in order to keep menu prices low.

Specialty

A **specialty restaurant** features foods of a particular type, such as seafood, pancakes, chicken, vegetables, steaks, doughnuts, omelettes, or sandwiches. The possibilities for specialties are many and varied, as are the establishments that feature them. Some limit their menus almost exclusively to the specialty, while others use the specialty item as the focal point of the menu but add other items to broaden the establishment's appeal and attract additional customers.

Specialty restaurants can vary considerably in their menu items, food quality, menu prices, service, and ambience. Long John Silver Restaurant is an excellent example of a restaurant that specializes in seafood items.
(Photo courtesy of Long John Silver's Inc.)

Specialty restaurants vary considerably in menu items, food quality, menu prices, service, and ambience; this is true even within one specialty. For example, some seafood operations specialize in shellfish; others feature a more varied assortment of fish and shellfish on one menu. Some have extensive menus limited only by the availability of particular items in the markets; others restrict their menus to a few items that are always available. Some operators insist on purchasing fresh seafood daily for their establishments; others use frozen products. In some parts of the country, one or another item may be readily available and popular with diners, while that item may be rare or virtually unsalable in another geographic area. Other differences among specialty establishments can be easily observed with respect to menu prices, service, and ambience.

Fine Dining

Fine-dining establishments emphasize high-quality foods, expertly prepared and professionally served. Few convenience foods are used, and most foods are prepared from fresh ingredients. Such restaurants are typically among the most formal and often among the most expensive.

Service is a particularly important element in the fine dining experience, but the type varies from one restaurant to another. Some offer elegant French service, others Russian or American.

The term *fine dining* gives no indication of the nature of the foods served. The menus may be ethnic, such as Swiss or northern Italian; they may feature specialties, such as seafood; or they may rely on the skill of a chef to prepare dishes unique to the restaurant. Other possible variations among fine-dining establish-

Service is a particularly important element in the fine-dining experience, as shown in this picture of Four Seasons Hotel's restaurant service.
(Photo courtesy of the Four Seasons Hotels, © 2000 Four Seasons Limited. Used by permission.)

ments include the number of items on the menu; many restaurants offer extensive menus with a few special creations that change frequently, whereas others—often among the finest restaurants in an area—offer only one or two entrées that change daily. In some, which typically require reservations, customers are given no choice at all; they are served the several courses that constitute the dining experience planned by the chef.

Limited Menu

At an establishment that offers a **limited menu**, management has made a conscious decision to restrict the number of items on the menu. This may be a small but varying number, or it may be a specific, unchanging number, as in a steak house that offers only three entrées, all of which are sirloin steaks of varying weights. Some restaurants offer only one basic menu item, such as pizza or hamburger, for which a large number of variations are available—often in the form of toppings. Other kinds of restaurants with limited menus feature chicken, hot dogs, lobster, omelettes, or roast beef, among other possibilities.

The quality of the food in limited-menu establishments varies considerably. The steak house may offer the finest aged beef in the state, or the steaks may be of a quality such that miniature hacksaws are required to cut them. Menu prices in limited-menu establishments vary as well, from the minimum common in hot-dog stands to extraordinarily high prices in some of the finest steak houses. It also should be apparent that ambience varies as dramatically from the hot-dog stand to the steak house.

Chain Restaurants

Chain restaurants are linked in some way. For some, ownership provides the link; two or more establishments that may or may not resemble each other in any way have common ownership. For others, common name, appearance, and products, or some combination of these, provides the link. For restaurants in the well-known national chains—Wendy's, Pizza Hut, and Kentucky Fried Chicken, for example—all three apply. In some instances, all units in a given chain are under common ownership; more frequently, groups of units in one geographical area may be commonly owned by some entity other than the national organization. For example, Burger King owns some, but not all, of the restaurants bearing that name; groups of Burger King restaurants are owned by other companies, and some are owned by individuals.

Chain restaurants vary considerably in their other characteristics as well. Their menu items range from pizza to steaks and from hamburgers to seafood. Some, such as McDonald's, are relatively inexpensive; others—Olive Garden or Houlihan's, for example—are moderately priced. Food quality and service vary too. Some restaurants offer table service; others, only counter service. Some feature takeout; others do not. Nevertheless, the ambience in chain restaurants affiliated by product is typically the same from one unit to another.

Boston Market Restaurant is an example of a restaurant chain. Some of their restaurants are franchised, and others are owned by the chain.
(Photo courtesy of Boston Market Corporation)

Theme Restaurants

A **theme restaurant** is designed around a particular theme, which is used or reflected in every element of the establishment's ambience. For example, if the circus were selected as the theme, the interior of the restaurant might be decorated to resemble some idealized version of the interior of a circus tent, complete with trapeze; the servers might be costumed as circus performers; the menu might be printed to look like a circus program; and the menu items might be named for circus acts—a hamburger special described as the "Lion, King of the Burger Jungle." Other possibilities for themes are railroad cars or stations, antique automobiles, colonial America, the Old West, medieval dining, World War II, kitchenware—the number is endless, limited only by human imagination.

Theme restaurants, naturally, differ from one another in the ambience. The developer of a theme restaurant or chain must make every effort to avoid resemblance to any other foodservice establishment. Menu items and service must be closely linked to the theme and the atmosphere. Food quality and menu prices vary considerably from one theme establishment or chain to another.

Tops

A **tops restaurant** is a food and beverage operation situated on the top floor of a hotel or other tall building, usually located in some part of a major city where the view is interesting or spectacular. One of the finest examples can be found at the top of one of the twin towers of the World Trade Center in New York: Windows on the World, a luxurious restaurant on the 107th floor that offers a stunning view of the city and its harbor. Some tops restaurants are specially constructed so that either the floor or the entire room turns, giving customers panoramic and ever-changing views of the city as they dine.

Tops vary as greatly as do other foodservice operations. Some offer foods and service of excellent quality, while others do not. Similarly, some present a formal atmosphere and select menu items accordingly, while others strive for a high degree of informality in atmosphere and menu to attract younger customers.

Menu prices vary among tops restaurants but, as a group, their prices tend to be higher than those in similar restaurants not located at the top of a building. Menu prices in tops reflect the higher costs of construction and operation as well as the premium one would expect to be charged for the privilege of dining at an establishment that may represent not only the pinnacle of a building but also the essence of business or social success.

Family Restaurants

A **family restaurant** caters to family groups—parents with children and other contemporary family groupings. In order to appeal to families, operators must make important decisions with respect to menu, food quality, menu prices, service, and ambience.

Family restaurants usually include a sufficiently broad range of items on the menu so that something will appeal to everyone, from parent to child to grandparent. Some have special menus for children under a given age. These menus may be separate from the regular menu or may be in one section of it. Family restaurant menu items are typically low to moderate in price, tacitly recognizing that the American family faces difficult collective financial burdens and is either unwilling or unable to spend large amounts of the family's limited disposable income on restaurant meals. Menu prices reflect food quality, and owners usually attempt to match food quality to their customers' perceptions of quality. Atmosphere in family restaurants tends to be informal. At their best, they are cheerfully decorated, bright, and well lighted, and they radiate a sense of welcome to their customers.

Cafeteria

A **cafeteria** is a foodservice establishment that permits the customer to see the foods available and to make selections from among those displayed. In many cases, this makes it possible for the customer to select the actual portion he or she will consume. Cafeterias impose a greater degree of self-service on their customers than most other restaurants. Food portions are individually plated and priced; and the customer is typically expected to take a tray through an area where foods are displayed, make selections, place them on the tray, and carry the tray to a station where the prices are totaled. In some establishments, the customer pays for the food at that point; in others, the customer is given a bill that must be paid at the exit. In either case, the customer carries the tray to another part of the establishment, where the food is either consumed or packed for takeout.

Buffet

A **buffet** is a type of service characterized by one or more tables on which a selection of varied foods are attractively displayed on platters, in bowls, and in other suitable vessels. Frequently, entrée and salad items are placed on one table and desserts on another. Each diner typically carries a plate, determines selections, places desired quantities of selected foods on the plate, and then takes the plate to a table. A set price is usually charged for each person regardless of particular foods or quantities selected, and diners are commonly permitted unlimited access to the buffet. This is to encourage diners to take smaller portions and revisit the buffet as desired.

Catering

Catering is preparing and serving food to groups of people gathered for a specific purpose, such as attending a meeting or celebrating a wedding. Some caterers prepare and serve food only in their own halls; others prepare food in their own kitchens but serve only on premises provided by their clients. Some both prepare and serve in facilities provided by the client. Some agree to any of these arrangements. People in the catering business are normally flexible and willing to meet reasonable requests for particular foods. Most are prepared to offer the client preplanned menus at various price levels for various types of functions and to adjust any of these to meet the client's needs or desires.

Catering has several advantages over normal restaurant operations. Functions are always booked in advance, so management knows the number of people to expect and can easily determine the proper quantity of food to serve. Staffing and food purchasing, therefore, can be planned precisely, making it possible to estimate costs accurately in advance and thus plan a predetermined profit on each function.

A large number of restaurants are simultaneously in the catering business. Some restaurants have separate rooms used primarily for catering, and others are able to close off part of the public dining area to accommodate groups. The food for these groups is typically prepared in the restaurant's single kitchen; no special kitchen is set aside for catering. Many city hotels are in the catering business. These hotels often have both special kitchens and dining facilities for catering. In the hotel business, catering is done by what is commonly known as the **banquet department**. This represents one part of hotel food and beverage operations that is typically quite profitable. Some hotels staff their banquet operations with part-time or full-time employees who work only in this area.

Institutional Foodservice

Institution is a term used to refer to a wide variety of service organizations, public and private, that attend to one or another of many possible public needs. Schools, colleges, hospitals, nursing homes, and prisons are common examples of institutions. An **institutional foodservice** operation is one whose principal purpose is preparing food for people associated with a particular institution. Students in grade schools, patients in hospitals, and inmates in prisons are all examples of those served by institutional foodservice operations.

Institutional foodservice operations are established primarily to meet the needs of the institutions in which they operate by providing food to those working in or using the services of the institution, willingly or otherwise. In some instances, people being served are confined to the institutions and must be provided with foodservice, as in hospitals, nursing homes, and prisons. In others, because of institutional decisions or public policy, foodservice is made available for those who want it, as in schools, colleges, and similar settings.

Institutional foodservice operations are run on either a for-profit or not-for-profit basis and managed either by the institution or by an outside foodservice contractor. Institutional foodservice operations are similar to several other types of foodservice operations—business and industry foodservice and airline catering are two examples. None of these is operated primarily for public dining; each is intended to provide foodservice for a particular group—children in a school, passengers on an airplane, or employees of a corporation.

Business and Industry Foodservice

Business and industry foodservice operations provide food during working hours for employees of particular firms in their offices or factories. As in the case of institutional foodservice, these facilities are operated on either a for-profit or not-for-profit basis and managed by the firm whose employees they serve or by an outside foodservice contractor.

In large firms, it is not uncommon to find several foodservice operations at one site preparing foods at several levels of quality for various types of service and price levels and for different groups of employees. For example, within a specific building, one might find a cafeteria serving adequate foods at moderate prices for workers earning modest salaries, a table service restaurant with more elaborate meals at higher prices for midlevel managers, and a fine-dining facility for the executive staff.

Airline Catering

Airline catering is the business of providing food prepared and packaged for service by an airplane crew during a flight. The food is prepared by an airline catering organization at a central facility, called a **commissary**, where it is suitably packaged in serving containers. It is transported to planes in storage units that keep food warm or cold, as required, until it is served. The storage units are stowed in specially designed cupboards on the plane and served by flight attendants at appropriate times. An airline catering operation may be owned by the airline it serves, by another airline, or by one of the hospitality firms, large and small, in this specialized business. Marriott, Sky Chefs, Dobbs, and Trust House Forte are some of the leading names in this field.

Club Foodservice

Club foodservice operations provide foodservice in membership establishments known as clubs. Many types of clubs—golf, tennis, athletic, luncheon, college alumni, fraternal, and social, to name a few—are organized to appeal to people with some common interest.

Foodservice operations in clubs range from simple and inexpensive to those that provide the finest food and service available—from hot-dog stands near a swimming pool to spectacular dining rooms with fine linen, china, and glassware, and elegant professional service. Private clubs restrict service to members and their guests; some clubs, however, are open to the general public.

Stand

A **stand** is a stationary, open-air foodservice establishment without a dining room facility. Customers walk to a counter to order and obtain foods, then consume them at the counter or elsewhere, as they prefer. Examples include hot-dog stands at beaches and roadside stands selling ice cream, hamburgers, or cider, among other possibilities.

Coffee Shops

Traditionally, a **coffee shop** was a limited-menu establishment to which customers typically went to order coffee and some other item such as a doughnut, a sandwich, or a slice of pie. Coffee shops did not provide full meals. They tended to be small, usually offering seating on stools at a counter. Some provided a limited number of tables or booths. Today, many have more extensive menus resembling those of diners, as described below.

Diner

A **diner** is normally a moderately priced full-service restaurant, typically open long hours—sometimes 24 hours a day—and serving breakfast, lunch, and dinner from a single multipage menu. In most diners, the customer can order any meal at any hour—breakfast at 11 P.M., for example.

The modern diner is a direct descendant of the establishments discussed in Chapter 3. The exterior design evolved from trolleys and railroad dining cars of an earlier period, but only older diners display the characteristics of the diners of earlier times. There is little physical similarity between today's diner and one built 60 years ago.

Neighborhood Restaurant

A **neighborhood restaurant** caters to the needs, tastes, and preferences of people who live or work nearby. In general, each reflects the character of the neighborhood in which it is found. Some are inexpensive, and others less so. Some are actually quite expensive, depending on the neighborhood. More than any other type of establishment, the neighborhood restaurant depends for survival on repeat

The modern diner is a moderately priced, full-service restaurant that stays open long hours and serves breakfast, lunch, and dinner from a multipage menu. The Tick Tock Diner in Clifton, New Jersey, is one example.
(Photo courtesy of Tick Tock Diner, Clifton, New Jersey)

business from people in the area. Thus, owners of neighborhood restaurants must pay particularly close attention to their customers' likes and dislikes. Failure to do so has a greater negative impact with more immediate consequences than is the case in other types of establishments.

Drive-Through

A **drive-through** is an operation at which a customer can drive a vehicle to a window to obtain and pay for food without leaving the vehicle. Having received the food, the customer drives away to consume the food elsewhere. In effect, drive-throughs can be considered the descendents of the drive-in restaurants of the 1950s and 1960s. The process limits the kinds of foods that can be sold. They tend to be preportioned items, prepared in advance and easily packaged for takeout—in other words, the typical products of the fast-service restaurants. In fact, a number of the chain restaurants specializing in fast-service products have been successful in providing drive-through service for their customers.

Takeout

A **takeout** is an operation that prepares foods for consumption off premises. Foods for takeout may be fully prepared in advance, then merely packaged when ordered by a customer, or not prepared until ordered. Takeout merely means that food leaves the premises where it is sold. The food may be picked up and transported by the purchaser or delivered, depending on the nature of the operation. Some do both. Many pizza establishments deliver; those offering hamburgers or chicken typically do not. Some take-out establishments have no facilities for on-premises consumption; they operate exclusively as takeouts. Some are parts of a broader foodservice operation that provides seating for customers.

These are some of the terms used in general conversation to identify or describe various kinds of foodservice establishments. However, one can readily see that no single term fully describes a given establishment. For example, the term *fast service* conveys that a customer should be able to obtain food quickly in such an establishment, but it does not provide information about the kind of food served or the extent of the menu. To describe the establishment more completely and usefully, we would have to say, for example, that it is a fast-service restaurant with a limited menu, specializing in chicken. Similarly, to describe a particular restaurant as dedicated to fine dining is to imply that it features foods of high quality, that it is probably expensive, and that it offers table service. But the term *fine dining* tells us nothing about the kind of food served, the type of service, or the ambience. Because the quality of ethnic, specialty, and all other restaurants can vary so greatly, simply stating that a particular establishment is Italian tells us next to nothing about it. We need to know a great deal more to describe it fully.

BEVERAGE SERVICE

Society has not always viewed the consumption of alcoholic beverages favorably. On the whole, however, American society has generally tolerated "drinking" and has even encouraged it under some circumstances, provided it was not done to excess. Many today believe alcohol has therapeutic value when consumed in moderation. Everyone recognizes its dangerous and debilitating effects when consumed to excess.

As discussed in the previous chapter, the sale of alcoholic beverages was illegal in the 1920s under the provisions of the Volstead Act. Nonetheless, this did not stop Americans from drinking. Drinking establishments called *speakeasies* were popular. Making alcoholic beverages at home—the so-called bathtub gin, for example—was a hobby for many Americans, and illegally transporting and selling alcoholic beverages—bootlegging, in the vernacular of the period—made rich men of many underworld characters.

After the repeal of the Volstead Act in 1933, the authority to regulate the sale and consumption of alcoholic beverages was returned to state and local governments. Laws passed in the years since have resulted in great variations from one state to another, and even from one community to another within a state. The extent of these variations is so great that it is quite beyond the scope of any introductory text. A few examples illustrate.

All states and almost all local communities allow properly licensed establishments to serve alcoholic beverages in one form or another—by the glass or by the bottle, or both of these. In a few communities, the sale of alcoholic beverages in any form remains illegal. In some of these, however, a customer can bring his own alcoholic beverages to a restaurant, and the establishment will provide the glassware, ice, mixer, or whatever combination of these the customer requires. In some states, customers cannot be served alcoholic beverages unless they are seated. In others, customers are not permitted to order drinks at a bar, then carry them from the bar to a table; an employee must serve them. In some states, it is illegal to have more than one drink in front of a customer at any given time. In others, a customer can carry a drink to his table, but only one. If the customer wants a drink for a companion, he cannot have it; the companion must get his own. All states now prohibit the purchase of alcoholic beverages by anyone under the age of 21 years. This was the result of a decision by the federal government to withhold federal highway funds from any state that did not raise the drinking age to 21.

Beverage Service Defined

There are several possible ways to define beverage service. In this text, we define **beverage service** as providing alcoholic and related beverages for consumption on premises. The term *beverage* includes all alcoholic beverages and any nonalcoholic beverages typically prepared by bartenders. The **beverage service establishment** provides beverage service for its customers. In many cases, the beverage service establishment provides food as well. Food sales may even constitute the major source of sales revenue.

Reasons for Patronizing Beverage Service Establishments

Commonly cited reasons for patronizing beverage service establishments include:

- Dining
- Seeking entertainment
- Socializing
- Discussing business
- Meeting new people
- Getting away from home
- Killing time
- Relaxing
- Drinking

These are some of the many possible reasons for going to beverage service establishments. For most people who patronize these establishments, drinking appears to be a secondary consideration. In fact, data reveal that sales of alcoholic beverages in beverage service establishments have actually decreased in recent years, whereas sales of nonalcoholic drinks have increased a great deal. This may indicate that patrons of beverage service establishments are switching from alcoholic to nonalcoholic beverages because they never had been drawn to these establishments, in the first place, primarily to consume alcoholic drinks. There are, doubtless, reasonable numbers who patronize these establishments primarily to purchase and consume alcoholic beverages. They appear to be a minority, however. To the extent that such customers abuse alcohol, the social pressures to modify their behavior continue to grow, particularly for those who drive.

THE FOCUS OF BEVERAGE SERVICE ESTABLISHMENTS

Because customers patronize beverage service establishments for different reasons, operators feature or emphasize those elements that they hope will attract customers. These elements can be grouped into three categories, each of which we characterize as a focal point for operations.

Beverage service establishments can be distinguished from one another on the basis of this focus. Each beverage service operator establishes one of the following as primary:

- Food
- Entertainment
- Beverages

Food

Many establishments that provide beverage service place primary emphasis on their food. These tend to be foodservice establishments that provide beverages as accompaniments to food. Many of the characteristic types of foodservice establishments described earlier in the chapter—ethnic, theme, family, fine dining, tops, neighborhood, and others—have this focus. They make beverages available before, during, and after meals. Customers may order cocktails before dinner, wines with the meal, and after-dinner drinks, such as liqueurs and dessert wines. To many cus-

Customers patronize beverage service establishments for various reasons. Shown here is the cocktail lounge at a Fairmont Hotel. *(Photo courtesy of Fairmont Hotels and Resorts)*

tomers of these establishments, beverages are integral parts of the dining experience. Many would probably not return if the establishment no longer offered beverages with the food. Therefore, these businesses may be regarded as both foodservice and beverage service establishments. They serve beverages to satisfy the expectations of their customers and because drink sales are profitable, but their emphasis, their principal business focus, tends to be the food, which normally provides greater revenue than the beverages. Some of these establishments may also offer entertainment—live piano music during dinner, for example—but only as a secondary element. The principal focus is food.

Entertainment

In other establishments, primary emphasis is placed on entertainment. Entertainment is a broad term, encompassing any number of possibilities. It can range from sports events on television to professional musicians—bands, pianists, or singers—from coin-operated games to horse races at a track, or from professional team sports to theatrical companies. Establishments such as nightclubs, gambling casinos, theaters, piano bars, racetracks, and sports arenas provide beverage service to customers who have come for the entertainment. For many customers, the beverages are an indispensable element of the entertainment. Some of these establishments do not charge for the entertainment; the cost to management is so low that there is no need to recover any of it from customers. This is the case when, for example, the entertainment consists of sports events on television.

However, professional entertainers can be costly, and the owner of an establishment featuring professional groups might attempt to recover the cost of the entertainment by selling tickets or by imposing either a cover charge or a minimum. A cover charge is an amount per person added to the total bill incurred for food and drink. A minimum is the least amount each customer is permitted to spend; those spending less are charged the minimum. Many of these establishments also offer food—excellent food, in some cases. For example, some dinner theaters feature professional performances of musical productions. They offer food and beverages as well, but their principal focus is clearly the entertainment.

Beverages

In a vast number of beverage service establishments, the primary emphasis is clearly and conspicuously on the beverages themselves. Some places give away simple salty foods to stimulate beverage sales. Others provide entertainment in the form of background music from a radio. The focus of these establishments is clear and simple: they sell beverages and have little or no interest in any other possibilities. Many neighborhood bars are of this type. Closely related are the typical bars at airports or railroad stations that cater to travelers waiting to board planes or trains. Some beverage service establishments, although focusing primarily on beverages, make some attempt to broaden their appeal. They may, for example, provide a wider range of foods than salty snacks—sandwiches, hamburgers, or a few hot foods in a steam table located near the bar—but the food is typically of secondary importance. Some establishments attempt to provide a limited kind of entertainment for their customers—coin-operated games, for example. In all of these, however, the principal focus is on neither the food nor the entertainment; it is on the beverages.

Several terms are used to identify establishments in which beverages are the primary focus, including tavern, inn, saloon, cocktail lounge, and bar. Historically, the distinctions among these were well known and generally accepted. That is no longer the case. It is perfectly possible, today, to see an establishment identified by its owner as a tavern, then to find another nearby, virtually a duplicate of the first, called a cocktail lounge. The terms are not readily distinguished from one another any longer.

Strange as it may seem, few people ever speak of a beverage service industry. In the hospitality industry, beverage service is treated as part of foodservice; and the data related to establishments selling beverages and to beverage sales are commonly reported with foodservice data. Thus, when an individual mentions the foodservice industry, it is unlikely that he means foodservice alone; he is probably referring to the combined industries known by the single term *foodservice industry*.

NATIONAL RESTAURANT ASSOCIATION CLASSIFICATION

Years ago, the **National Restaurant Association** (NRA) developed a classification system for the foodservice industry, primarily to report information about the industry's total sales. Table 4.1 illustrates the NRA's classification system and provides interesting data about total food and drink sales for the years shown.

Note that all food and beverage enterprises are divided into three groups. Group I is the largest, representing the majority of both food and beverage establishments and sales. It encompasses those establishments whose primary business is foodservice, beverage service, or some combination of both. All are commercial foodservice operations—that is, they are profit oriented. This does not mean that every one of them actually earns a profit but that they are being operated with the intention of profitability.

Within Group I, the largest category is eating places. This includes establishments operated primarily as foodservice businesses, not those that are part of other businesses. No attempt is made to differentiate among them on the basis of size, type of food served, or food quality. Eating places are divided into several types, including full-menu restaurants, limited-menu restaurants, cafeterias, caterers, and ice cream stands. Bars and taverns are separately listed in this category.

The second category in Group I is food contractors. These are commercial firms that provide foodservice in other establishments (commercial and noncommercial), such as banks and other financial service operations, office buildings, factories, hospitals, colleges, primary and secondary schools, transportation services, and recreation and sports centers.

The third category in Group I is foodservice operations in lodging places.

TABLE 4.1

Restaurant Industry Food-and-Drink Sales Projected Through 2001

	1998 Estimated F&D Sales ($000)	2000 Projected F&D Sales ($000)	2001 Projected F&D Sales ($000)	2000–2001 Percent Change	2000–2001 Percent Real Growth Change	1998–2001 Compound Annual Growth Rate
Group I—Commercial Restaurant Services[1]						
Eating Places						
Fullservice restaurants[2]	$117,774,378	$134,461,359	$143,335,809	6.6%	4.0%	6.8%
Limited-service (fast-food) restaurants[3]	98,120,395	107,252,460	111,971,568	4.4	1.8	4.5
Commercial cafeterias	2,432,636	2,241,857	2,132,006	−4.9	−7.5	−4.3
Social caterers	3,233,426	3,653,667	3,880,194	6.2	3.6	6.3
Snack and nonalcoholic-beverage bars	10,569,734	12,204,545	13,168,704	7.9	5.3	7.6
Total Eating Places	**$232,130,569**	**$259,813,888**	**$274,488,281**	**5.6%**	**3.0%**	**5.7%**
Bars and taverns	11,497,815	12,257,084	12,453,197	1.6	−1.3	2.7
Total Eating and Drinking Places	**$243,628,384**	**$272,070,972**	**$286,941,478[4]**	**5.5%**	**2.8%**	**5.6%**
Foodservice Contractor-Managed Services[5]						
Manufacturing and industrial plants	$5,769,060	$6,220,545	$6,538,976	5.1%	2.5%	4.3%
Commercial and office buildings	1,694,899	1,856,094	1,922,913	3.6	1.0	4.3
Hospitals and nursing homes	2,264,182	2,478,430	2,589,959	4.5	4.7	4.6
Colleges and universities	5,068,280	5,933,374	6,384,310	7.6	4.4	8.0
Primary and secondary schools	2,006,215	2,407,837	2,648,621	10.0	7.1	9.7
In-transit restaurant services (airlines)	2,150,510	2,501,544	2,649,045	5.9	3.3	7.2
Recreation and sports centers	3,037,927	3,445,689	3,642,093	5.7	3.1	6.2
Total Managed Services	**$21,991,073**	**$24,843,513**	**$26,375,917**	**6.2%**	**3.7%**	**6.2%**
Lodging Places						
Hotel restaurants	$16,344,294	$18,312,310	$19,319,487	5.5%	2.9%	5.7%
Motor-hotel restaurants	151,154	140,611	134,986	−4.0	−6.6	−3.7
Motel restaurants	362,471	348,819	342,889	−1.7	−4.3	−1.8
Other accommodation restaurants	295,420	317,991	329,439	3.6	1.0	3.7
Total Lodging Places	**$17,153,339**	**$19,119,731**	**$20,126,801**	**5.3%**	**2.7%**	**5.5%**
Retail-host restaurants[6]	$13,134,666	$14,947,202	$15,862,998	6.1%	3.5%	6.5%
Recreation and sports[7]	4,456,362	4,868,366	5,065,854	4.0	2.1	4.4
Mobile caterers	867,536	963,758	1,012,910	5.1	2.5	5.3
Vending and nonstore retailers[8]	7,584,910	8,354,247	8,797,022	5.3	2.7	5.1
Total—Group I	**$308,816,270**	**$345,167,789**	**$364,182,980**	**5.5%**	**2.9%**	**5.6%**

	1998 Estimated F&D Sales ($000)	2000 Projected F&D Sales ($000)	2001 Projected F&D Sales ($000)	2000–2001 Percent Change	2000–2001 Percent Real Growth Change	1998–2001 Compound Annual Growth Rate
Group II—Noncommercial Restaurant Services[9]						
Employee restaurant services[10]	$1,119,828	$989,649	$934,171	−5.6%	−8.1%	−5.9%
Public and parochial elementary, secondary schools	4,947,567	5,063,346	5,098,996	0.7	−2.2	1.0
Colleges and universities	4,789,582	4,996,758	5,070,468	1.5	−1.7	1.9
Transportation	1,034,538	1,191,681	1,290,086	8.2	4.7	7.6
Hospitals[11]	9,801,367	10,067,591	10,208,537	1.4	1.6	1.4
Nursing homes, homes for the aged, blind, orphans and the mentally and physically disabled[12]	5,047,315	5,401,485	5,595,938	3.6	2.2	3.5
Clubs, sporting and recreational camps	3,046,543	3,571,611	3,783,913	5.9	3.3	7.5
Community centers	1,238,558	1,361,586	1,425,580	4.7	1.8	4.8
Total—Group II	**$31,025,298**	**$32,643,707**	**$33,407,689**	**2.3%**	**0.6%**	**2.5%**
Total—Groups I and II	**$339,841,568**	**$377,811,496**	**$397,590,669**	**5.2%**	**2.7%**	**5.4%**
Group III—Military Restaurant Services[13]						
Officers' and NCO clubs (Open mess)	$818,053	$905,343	$948,799	4.8%	2.2%	5.1%
Military exchanges	399,244	436,815	457,345	4.7	2.1	4.6
Total—Group III	**$1,217,297**	**$1,342,158**	**$1,406,144**	**4.8%**	**2.2%**	**4.9%**
Grand Total	**$341,058,865**	**$379,153,654**	**$398,996,813**	**5.2%**	**2.7%**	**5.4%**

NOTES:

1. Data are given only for establishments with payroll.

2. Waiter/waitress service is provided, and the order is taken while the patron is seated. Patrons pay after they eat.

3. Patrons generally order at a cash register or select items from a food bar and pay before they eat.

4. Food-and-drink sales for nonpayroll establishments should total $6,744,110,000 in 2001.

5. Also referred to as onsite foodservice

6. Includes health- and personal-care-store restaurants, general-merchandise-store restaurants, variety-store restaurants, food-store restaurants and grocery-store restaurants (including a portion of delis and all salad bars), gasoline-service-station restaurants and miscellaneous retailers

7. Includes movies, bowling lanes, and recreation and sport centers

8. Includes sales of hot food, sandwiches, pastries, coffee and other hot beverages

9. Business, educational, governmental or institutional organizations that operate their own restaurant services

10. Includes industrial and commercial organizations, seagoing and inland-waterway vessels

11. Includes voluntary and proprietary hospitals; long-term general, TB, nervous and mental hospitals; and sales or commercial equivalent to employees in state and local short-term hospitals and federal hospitals

12. Sales (commercial equivalent) calculated for nursing homes and homes for aged only. All others in this grouping make no charge for food served either in cash or in kind.

13. Continental United States only

The final category in Group I is a collection of commercial foodservice operations that do not belong in other categories, including restaurants in drugstores, food stores, and recreation centers, as well as mobile caterers and vending machines.

Group II is for foodservice establishments operated by organizations whose primary focus is in some other field. Foodservice is not their primary business, but they choose to operate their own foodservices for the convenience of employees, students, patients, or customers rather than have firms from Group I run them. Some are operated for profit; others are not. Those not operated for a profit are considered noncommercial foodservice operations. This group includes school, college, and university foodservice, and foodservice provided by hospitals and nursing homes, providing they operate their own foodservice.

Group III is military foodservice, a relatively small part of the industry. It includes only those military foodservice enterprises where people pay for food—officers' clubs, NCO clubs, and the like. Because people in military service do not purchase their meals, the vast number of meals prepared daily for those in the military are not reflected.

Note that some operations listed in Group I appear, at first glance, to be duplicated in Group II. For example, colleges and universities are listed in both Group I and Group II. The colleges and universities listing in Group I include foodservices operated by an outside profit-oriented food contractor, such as Saga or Canteen. Listings in Group II, however, are for colleges and universities that operate their own foodservice establishments.

The principal reason for developing the NRA system was to provide a means for reporting quantitative data about industry size and dollar sales. Establishments are divided into specific categories, and information about each establishment is classified accordingly.

Because this system is not and cannot be concerned with the real and significant qualitative differences among establishments evident in our industry, we must use other terms to take these into account—family restaurant offering table service, moderate prices, and ethnic Italian food, for example, or cocktail lounge focusing on entertainment and featuring live piano music. We must use the kinds of terms discussed earlier in the chapter to make meaningful distinctions among the various types of foodservice and beverage service operations. Both approaches are useful. The first enables professionals and the public at large to distinguish one operation from another, and the second facilitates the collection and reporting of statistical information about a vast and important industry.

SUMMARY

In this chapter, the size of the food and beverage industry is illustrated. Three explanations for the increase in public demand for foodservice are offered and discussed. A definition is provided for the term *foodservice*, and five important elements of foodservice operations that differentiate one from another are discussed in detail. An extensive list of characteristic types of foodservice establishments is provided, and each is described in detail. Beverage service is defined, and the principal reasons for patronizing beverage service establishments are listed. A rationale is presented for distinguishing one beverage service establishment from another on the basis of focus. Finally, the classification system used by the National Restaurant Association to collect and report statistical information is presented and explained.

KEY TERMS

Airline catering
Banquet department
Beverage service
Beverage service establishment
Buffet
Business and industry foodservice
Cafeteria
Catering
Chain restaurant
Club foodservice
Coffee shop
Commercial foodservice operation
Commissary
Convenience food
Counter service
Diner
Drive-through
Ethnic restaurant
Family restaurant

Fast-food establishment
Fine-dining establishment
Food quality
Foodservice
Guest check
Institutional foodservice
Limited menu
National Restaurant Association
Neighborhood restaurant
Noncommercial foodservice operation
Room service
Self-service
Specialty restaurant
Stand
Table service
Table service restaurant
Takeout
Theme restaurant
Tops restaurant

DISCUSSION QUESTIONS

1. About how many eating and drinking places are there in the United States? How many people do they employ?

2. What percentage of adults in the United States patronizes foodservice establishments on a typical day?

3. What are the projected sales of the restaurant industry for 2001?

4. What are the three reasons commonly cited for America's increased demand for foodservice in recent years?

5. Define foodservice. What is a foodservice enterprise?

6. What are the five most important characteristics of a foodservice enterprise? Illustrate by example how changes in each can affect the character of a foodservice enterprise.

7. Define each of the following characteristic types of foodservice establishments and cite one example of each: fast service, table service, ethnic, specialty, fine dining, limited menu, chain restaurant, theme restaurant, top, family restaurant, cafeteria, buffet, catering, institutional foodservice, business and industry foodservice, airline catering, club foodservice, stand, coffee shop, diner, neighborhood restaurant, drive-through, takeout.

8. Cite a particular foodservice establishment in your area, an adequate description of which requires the use of four of the terms in question #7.

9. Define beverage service. What is a beverage service enterprise?

10. List nine common reasons for patronizing beverage service establishments.

11. Identify three beverage service establishments that attract customers by featuring or emphasizing entertainment.

12. Identify three beverage service establishments that attract customers without featuring either food or entertainment. Do these provide any food? What kind?

13. Distinguish between a commercial and a noncommercial foodservice operation.

14. Which of the three major groups in the National Restaurant Association's foodservice classification system accounts for the greatest dollar sales annually? The least? What is the principal difference between the establishments in Group I and Group II?

MOMENTS OF TRUTH

1. Imagine you are a regular customer of a restaurant near your home. The restaurant caters primarily to your community, has an extensive and varied menu of items appealing to both adult and children, is moderately priced, is informal, offers both table service and take-out service, is well lighted, and uses some convenience foods to make food preparation easier. Using the terms for restaurants described in this chapter, characterize the restaurant.

2. Identify three beverage service establishments in your area that attract customers by featuring or emphasizing food. Indicate how each differs from the other two with respect to menu items, food quality, menu prices, service, and ambience—the five most important elements of a foodservice operation.

3. Your friend wants to open a restaurant and has enough money to do so. She is unsure of the type of restaurant she should open, but has found an available location at a busy intersection on the outskirts of a midsize city with a population made up primarily of middle-class families. There is plenty of space

for a large parking area. Assuming that there would not be extensive competition from other restaurants, what characteristic types of restaurants would you suggest?

INTERNET EXERCISES

1. Find the National Restaurant Association Web site. Note the statistical data shown. How have they changed from those quoted in this text?
2. Find the Pizza Inn (Pizzainn.com) Web site. Where are their restaurants primarily located? What types of pizza facilities do they operate? What employment positions are currently open?

End Note

1. Statistical information in this chapter comes from several NRA publications. Most of the information is documented in NRA's 2001 Restaurant Industry Forecast and is used with their permission.

Food and Beverage Facilities

► Learning Objectives

After reading and studying this chapter, you should be able to:

1. Define the term *concept* and describe its significance in food and beverage layout and design.

2. Discuss the need for owners and managers of food and beverage facilities to have some understanding of the laws and regulations affecting their operations.

3. Define the term *product line* and identify the elements in the service product line offered by food and beverage operations.

4. List and discuss six principal considerations in the layout and design of food and beverage facilities.

5. List and discuss the major activities that commonly take place in the food area of a food and beverage facility.

6. List and discuss the major activities that commonly take place in the beverage area of a food and beverage facility.

7. Identify the three types of bars.

8. List and describe the three principal parts of a front bar.

The previous chapter was devoted to examining the size and scope of the food and beverage industry and to imparting some sense of its great importance in American life. With that objective accomplished, we now turn to a discussion of food and beverage facilities, a subject that introduces the remaining chapter in this section. The purpose of this chapter is to identify and describe the work areas that tend to be common to all food and beverage facilities and to explain the interrelationships among them. The following chapter discusses operational aspects of food and beverage facilities.

It is first necessary to address three key topics fundamental to the layout and design of food and beverage facilities:

1. Concept

2. Legal requirements (local, state, and national)

3. Product line

Concept

Every food and beverage operation is—or should be—established around a **concept**—an imaginative and unifying idea that serves to focus the type of operation, its potential customers, and its location. This concept originates with the owner or with some other individual or firm commissioned to create it.

Type of Operation

A number of possible types of operations were discussed in Chapter 4, including fast-service operations, fine-dining establishments, family restaurants, cafeterias, ethnic restaurants, specialty restaurants, bars, taverns, and cocktail lounges, among many others. The type of operation is a key element in developing the concept of an establishment.

Potential Customers

Each type of operation can attract specific customers. Ethnic restaurants, for example, attract those who seek the particular foods characteristic of a given ethnic group—Chinese, Italian, Greek, or Indian, among many other possibilities. Fine-dining establishments typically attract customers who have the financial means and the desire for the higher-quality foods and more elegant service they offer. Specialty restaurants attract diners looking for the specialties offered—steak, seafood, pasta, pancakes, or some other type of food. Some foodservice operations, such as those in schools, colleges, nursing homes, and hospitals, typically serve people who have little or no choice of places to eat. Similarly, neighborhood taverns and bars tend to attract customers who live nearby, and airport bars typically attract transient customers who are waiting for planes to arrive or depart. Each establishment attracts customers because of the food, or the beverages, or the service, or the atmosphere, or the location, or some combination of these, and because they are willing to pay the prices charged by the operator.

Location

For a food and beverage operation to be successful, an adequate number of potential customers within a reasonable distance must be willing to patronize it. Some locations do not provide sufficient numbers of potential customers to support particular types of establishments. For example, fine-dining establishments are normally unsuccessful in working-class communities, principally because community residents cannot afford to pay the prices such establishments must charge to be profitable. In addition, local residents sometimes dislike the food such restaurants offer and the service they provide. Similarly, some ethnic restaurants fail to succeed in certain locations because the type of food they offer does not appeal to a large enough segment of the population. By the same token, bars and taverns are typically unsuccessful in communities where the consumption of alcoholic beverages is discouraged by social or religious custom.

To assess the potential for successfully operating a particular type of food or beverage establishment in a specific location, it is advisable to obtain such relevant information as the number of potential customers for the type of food, beverages, and service planned; the extent to which there are competitive establishments; the cost of constructing the necessary facility; the availability of a suitable labor pool; the dollar amounts potential customers are likely to spend; and the potential for profitable operation at the projected level of revenue and expense. All the relevant considerations are included in a **feasibility study**—the name given to an investigation of a given project's likelihood for success.

Location, then, is a key element in determining whether or not a given type of establishment will succeed and is an important part of the initial concept.

Legal Requirements

A potential operator must become familiar with laws and regulations affecting food and beverage operations. All applicable laws and regulations—federal, state, and local—must be taken into account. Health codes, fire codes, building codes, zoning regulations, and licensing requirements are among the most common. Each of these provides specific direction about what an owner can and cannot do in creating and operating a food or beverage enterprise. Legal requirements vary considerably from one state to another and even from city to city within a given state. For example, health codes in some states require that operators provide the staff with lavatories other than those intended for customers. A facility built without staff lavatories would probably require costly reconstruction before it would be permitted to open. This is just one example among many possibilities.

Before proceeding to open a facility, individuals lacking full knowledge of the laws and regulations that apply in given locales must seek professional advice from lawyers, architects, food and beverage consultants, and others with the necessary expertise. Failure to take this information into account can lead to costly errors.

For purposes of the present chapter, we assume that the individual establishing a food or beverage operation has developed a concept that has the potential to be successful, has constructed or purchased a facility that works as a restaurant, and has become familiar with the various local, county, state, and national laws that affect the enterprise. Having attended to all these necessary prerequisites, as discussed above, the next step is to direct attention to the products to be offered to customers of the establishment.

Product Line

Product line is a term used in marketing and retailing to refer to a group of products having similar characteristics. Common examples of product lines are shoes, luggage, and jewelry. Foodservice has borrowed the term from retailing and uses it to mean the group of service products that a hospitality enterprise offers, based on the concept developed for the establishment.

The product line of a food or beverage operation is more than just the foods or beverages it offers for sale. It also includes the services and the ambience of the facility. This is because most customers are attracted to a specific food or beverage establishment for more than one reason. For purposes of the following discussion, the product line of a food or beverage operation has three components:

1. Food and beverages

2. Services

3. Ambience

Food and Beverages

Every foodservice operation has a group of potential menu items that includes all the food products the operator intends to offer, at present and into the future. Some operations, such as Kentucky Fried Chicken and Red Lobster, specialize in one type of food—chicken, fish, or some other—and offer additional items to serve as accompaniments. Any number of specialized food products can be found as key elements in food operations today. Sandwiches, pasta, pizza, hamburgers, crepes, ice cream, and hot dogs are all good examples. Other foodservice operations have a more generalized list of potential menu items—family restaurants, for example.

Bars and taverns specialize in beverage products. This is an entirely different product list, consisting of beverages rather than food. In some establishments, both food products and beverage products are available to customers. In a restaurant devoted to fine dining, for example, the operator typically offers both beverage products and food products. Similarly, some taverns also offer meals to their customers.

Whatever constitutes the food and beverage component of the product line to be offered by a particular operation, it is desirable that all elements be identified and defined in advance because the equipment to be purchased and the layout of the facility is based on them. The specific food products are the basis for the menu that will be offered to customers, and detailed information about these items determines the proper kitchen equipment and layout. The question of whether or not a given piece of equipment should be purchased can best be answered by referring to the list of foods and beverages that will be served. If it is needed to prepare items on the list, the equipment should be purchased. If no menu selections require its use, it should not be purchased unless a specific future need can be predicted.

For example, an establishment that serves only pizza obviously needs kitchen equipment that is very different than that required in a luncheonette serving only soups and sandwiches. An ethnic restaurant serving Chinese food prepared in woks needs different kitchen equipment than does a neighborhood restaurant offering an Italian menu. Similarly, a restaurant specializing in deep-fried and broiled menu items needs different equipment than one offering convenience foods heated in microwave ovens. Kitchen equipment, once purchased and installed, limits the possibilities for adding new items to the list of food products. Great care must be exercised in determining the selections to be offered—on both the original menu and future variations. Therefore, establishing the list of food products is clearly the first key component of a food and beverage facility. This list will be much larger than the menu offered to customers on any given day. Menus change, and the list of items that constitute the menu for a particular day should be drawn from the predetermined list.

It is important to recognize that the list of items that constitute the food and beverage components of the product line never reaches a state in which it can be considered final or complete. Change is constant and continuous in hospitality operations. Dishes are added to and removed from the list of food products. New drinks and brands are added to the list of beverage products, while others are eliminated. Any number of changes can affect the service and the ambience. It is critical, however, to develop preliminary lists of the particular items that will constitute the product line at opening because of their central role in the facility.

In establishing the list of food products for a particular operation and the subsequent menu that will be offered, the operator should have knowledge of:

- Food and service preferences of customers
- Prices acceptable to customers
- Skills required to prepare selected items
- Availability of labor with the necessary skills at suitable wage rates

The success of a foodservice operation is determined by the willingness of potential customers to patronize the establishment. If the foods on the product line are not those that the potential customers want, or if the prices of the menu items are too high, the establishment will not attract sufficient numbers of customers to be successful. Additionally, the product line must be prepared by employees with sufficient skill to meet the standards of the establishment; therefore, the operator must know what skills are required to prepare each item. If the operator is unwilling or unable to pay sufficient wages to attract employees with the necessary skills, or if employees with necessary skills are not available, the quality of the products produced will not be acceptable to customers.

➤ **FRENCH RESTAURANTS ARE SERVING
FOOD FRENCH PEOPLE EAT EVERY DAY**

Once dominated by formal restaurants employing servers who were dressed in formal wear and were reluctant to explain any part of the menu, French cuisine in the United States has climbed down from its lofty heights and has started to serve food that French people actually eat every day.

Casual French restaurants are opening across the country. They are called *brasseries* and *bistros*. These restaurants serve such items as roast chicken, steak au poivre, steak béarnaise, and french fries with a relaxed American attitude.

Casual food is much easier to put together, according to chefs. High-end French food requires a certain chef, and it is prepared for individual customers to their own taste. In bistros, people can come in and talk loudly and be themselves instead of conforming to the very formal atmosphere in the traditional French restaurant.

Service is also much easier and much less costly than traditional French service. This allows for a less expensive menu and makes the food affordable for the average customer.

Source: Adapted from an article in *Nation's Restaurant News*, 7 March 2000.

Over the long term, many food and beverage operations elect to change the original product line, adding and deleting a few items or even making more radical changes. This may be much harder to do than one might imagine. A change in the product line may make it necessary to teach the staff new skills so that they can prepare new menu items; major changes may make it necessary to purchase new equipment or even to redesign some parts of the facility.

Once the product line is established, it is possible to determine which of the items in the product will be listed on a menu for a given day or meal. There is no more important selling device in any foodservice operation than its menu. A good menu requires considerable time and effort to produce, but is well worth the expenditure. Menu development is an interesting combination of art and science and clearly one of the keys to successful foodservice operation. Discussion of menu development is deferred to the next chapter.

Services

Another important component of any food or beverage service product line is the range of services associated with the specific food and beverage products. This second component includes all the services the operator intends to offer to customers, now and into the future. The more obvious services are the styles of service adopted for dining rooms—American, French, or some other—as well as variations on the basic styles, such as weekly buffets, possible use of dessert carts, or occasional use of tableside cooking. (Styles of service, a vast and complex topic, is addressed in detail in the next chapter.) Other services include food preparation in the kitchen, friendliness on the part of the staff, dishwashing, valet parking, attended coatrooms,

BREW MOON TAKES OFF, ←
ROCKETS INTO ORBIT

Brew Moon Restaurant and Microbrewery, one of several restaurants in this chain, captures the romance and mystery of the faraway workplace of the astronauts and ties it to the earthly practice of making beer. Elliot J Feiner, president and chief executive of Brew Moon, says, "There are two kinds of restaurants: those people talk about and those people eat in. We want to be the kind people eat in."

The concept for the restaurant is best described on the front of its menu, which states, "A vision for food. A passion for beer." The restaurant makes its own beer and creates menu items that go with it. They offer everything from classic Buffalo wings to molasses and cumin-charred pork tenderloins.

The menu changes every six months, and Brew Moon's new restaurants reflect their different markets. It is estimated that menu offerings vary by 35 percent from restaurant to restaurant.

Source: Adapted from an article in *Nation's Restaurant News*, 14 March 2000.

background music, special attention to birthday celebrants, complimentary photographs of customers, even entertainment—musicians, clowns, or magicians, for example.

Ambience

The third component of the hospitality service product line in food and beverage operations is perhaps best identified as the ambience of the establishment. This includes those essential details—some tangible, some intangible—that give a specific food and beverage operation its distinctive character. These essential details include theme, lighting, uniforms, furnishings, cleanliness, fixtures, decorations, table settings, and related features that customers see or sense and that contribute to the total atmosphere of the establishment.

These components—food, beverages, services, and ambience—are offered by all food and beverage operations. Some choose to add such other product lines as retail foods, gifts, or souvenirs. In this text, we limit our discussion to the primary service product line cited above and treat all others as outside the normal scope of food and beverage operations.

To comprehend the discussion of food and beverage facilities that occupies the balance of this chapter, the student may find it useful to refer to particular food and beverage operations. To meet that need, Case Studies 5.1, 5.2, and 5.3 are provided below. These describe three food and beverage operations that, at first glance, differ markedly from one another. The case studies help make the point that these three seemingly different operations—and any others the student may know from firsthand work experience—have much in common. The first of these, the Steak Shack, is an independently owned specialty restaurant with a limited menu. The second is an employee foodservice facility operated for a bank by Marecki Foods, an independent-business foodservice company. The third, Frog's Pub, is an English-style pub specializing in imported beers and ales, and offering very limited food service.

CASE STUDY 5.1

The Steak Shack

The Steak Shack is a family-owned and -operated restaurant located in a middle-class suburb, 23 miles from a city of 250,000. It is open six days for dinner only and closed all day Sunday. The goals of the Steak Shack include meeting the dining needs of local residents seeking steaks and a limited number of related items, moderately priced menus, and efficient, friendly service. The restaurant is the sole tenant in a purpose-built, stand-alone building surrounded by parking for up to 50 cars. The interior consists of a dining room; a cocktail lounge and bar; a production area consisting of food preparation, dishwashing, and storage areas; offices; dressing rooms and lavatories for staff; and men's and women's rest rooms for customers. The dining room seats 100 at tables for two, four, or six people, and the tables can be combined when necessary for larger groups. The cocktail lounge, adjacent to the dining room offer seating for 30 at tables for two or four; it is used principally by customers having before-dinner drinks. In this cocktail lounge is a bar that seats 12. During busy periods, two bartenders at this bar prepare all drinks for the bar, the cocktail lounge, and dining room.

The production area includes facilities for receiving, storing, and issuing foods and beverages. In addition, this area has facilities used to prepare food for cooking, ranges and other equipment for cooking, and counters for dispensing finished food products to servers. The production area also includes facilities and equipment for dishwashing, pot washing, and waste disposal. Office space is limited. The manager and bookkeeper share one office, where the computer is located. The other office is used by the chef, who manages kitchen operations and does all purchasing, except for beverages, which are purchased by the manager. The menu consists of six appetizers, three soups, two salads, and ten entrées—five steak, two poultry, one roast beef, and two seafood. In addition, the chef prepares three special entrées each night. Customers are given a choice of french-fried or baked potatoes and either of the two vegetables of the day. Desserts include three pies, one layer cake, cheesecake, and eight flavors of ice cream. Coffee, tea, and milk are available. The customary selection of beers, wines, and spirits and mixers is available at the bar. Figure 5.1 is a floor plan of the Steak Shack, showing the food area, the dining area, and the beverage area.

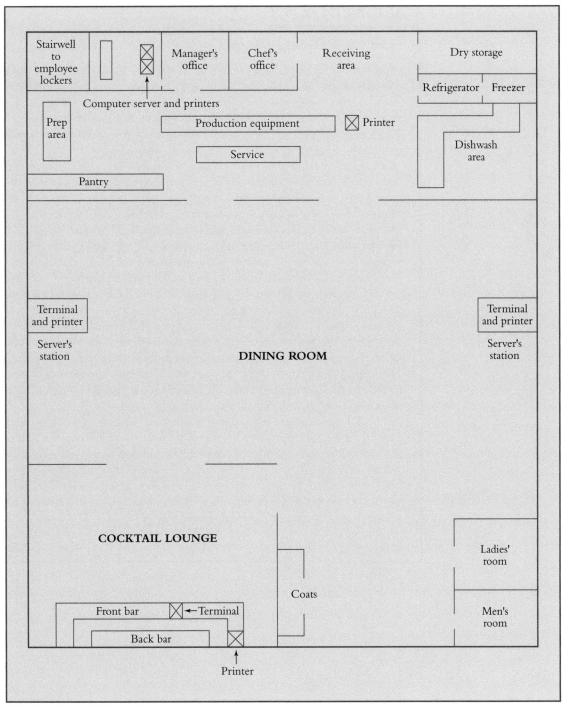

FIGURE 5.1
Floor plan of the Steak Shack

CASE STUDY 5.2

The Staff Dining Room

The staff dining room is a foodservice facility located in the corporate head-quarters of the Mountain Bank and Trust Company in a large city in the West. In compliance with various laws, smoking is not permitted in the staff dining room. The facility is not open to the public; it is provided by the bank as a service for the staff. One of the bank's goals is to provide staff members with good food at reasonable prices during working hours so that they do not have to leave the premises for meals. Another is to provide efficient service so that staff members can eat within the allotted time. The service is operated by Marecki Foods, a regional company specializing in business and industry foodservice. Marecki has a contract to provide the service for a set fee per month. The facility is located on the second floor of the bank's new head-quarters building, constructed just four years ago. The dining, kitchen, and storage facilities are all attractive and modern, and the bank insists that they be properly cleaned and maintained by the foodservice contractor.

The facility is open from 7 A.M. to 3 P.M., and limits service to breakfast and luncheon. Menu selections are limited. Breakfast items include juices, cold cereals, muffins, pastries, eggs, bacon, sausage, and the usual breakfast beverages. Daily luncheon items include a choice of three sandwiches, extensive salad bar, two hot entrées, several desserts, and choice of beverages. Employees pay as they enter. At breakfast, they pay $1.25 for cold selections with beverage and $2.50 for full breakfast. At luncheon, they pay $4.00 regardless of their selections. At the end of each month, the foodservice contractor bills the bank for the difference between revenues and expenses, plus the monthly fee. Employees take trays, flatware, and napkins at the entrance to the facility. Foods are attractively displayed on several buffet islands. Employees make their selections and carry them to tables in the dining room, which seats 120 persons at tables for two and four. Employees bus their own trays, but two food-service employees in the dining room clean tables. Figure 5.2 is a floor plan of the facility operated by Marecki Foods for the Mountain Bank and Trust Company, showing the food area and the dining area. This operation has no beverage area.

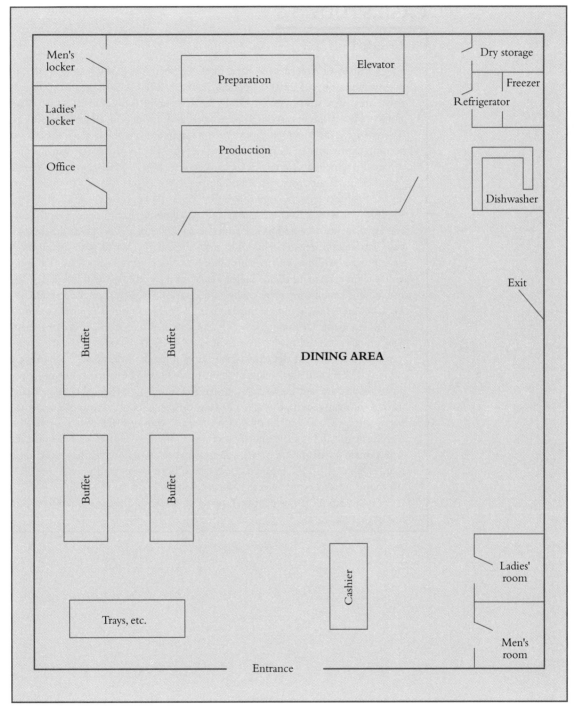

FIGURE 5.2
Floor plan of the staff dining room at the Mountain Bank and Trust Company

CASE STUDY 5.3

Frog's Pub

Frog's Pub is an American version of an English pub, located in a prosperous and growing city of 250,000 people in the Middle West. It is in the downtown area on a street known locally as Restaurant Row, and it attracts large numbers of customers at lunch, after work, and throughout the evening hours. The owner's goals include providing an eating and drinking place for people seeking something out of the ordinary. Another is to provide a casual atmosphere in which customers relax and feel at home. Frog's occupies rented premises in a four-story brick building.

Customers enter a large room that gives the appearance of an authentic English pub, with a long bar along one side. The bar has stools to seat 30 customers. Seventy-five additional customers can be seated at tables. At the bar, two bartenders prepare drinks for customers at the bar as well as for those seated at tables. Table service is provided by three servers, aided by one individual who clears and cleans tables. Food is prepared in a small kitchen at the rear of the establishment by a chef who has one assistant. A small dishwashing machine is operated by a third individual. All food and beverages are stored in the basement. Dressing rooms for the staff and a small office for the manager are also located in the basement.

Frog's is different than any other establishment in the region. It offers 36 imported beers and ales, many of them English. While spirits and some wines are available, the vast majority of customers order the specialty beers and ales in spite of relatively high prices per glass or bottle. Food accounts for a comparatively small percentage of dollar sales, and the food menu is restricted. It includes eight items that serve as accompaniments to drinks or as appetizers. The remainder of the menu includes several sandwiches and three hot items that are changed daily. Limited desserts and both coffee and tea are available. All menu items have names that sound British.

Figure 5.3 is a floor plan of Frog's Pub, showing the combined food and beverage area.

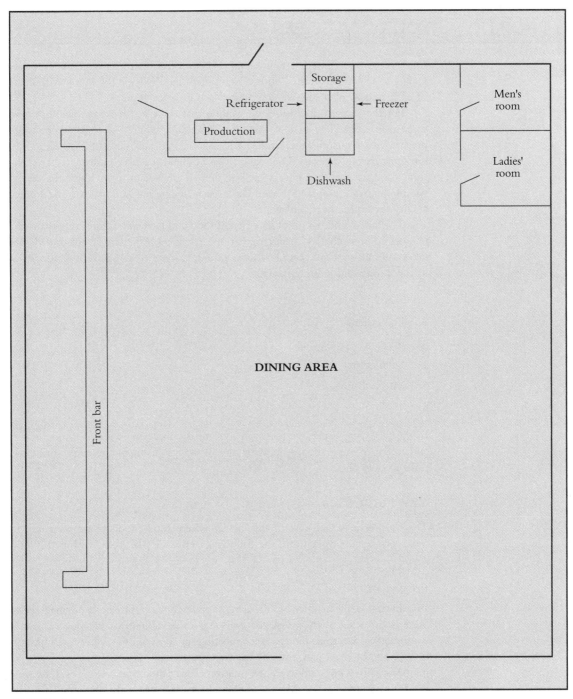

FIGURE 5.3
Floor plan of Frog's Pub

FACILITY LAYOUT AND DESIGN

Once the product line is established, it becomes feasible to design an appropriate facility, to select the specific kinds of equipment required and the number of pieces of each, and to plan suitable equipment layout for each area.

For the present discussion, we assume that food and beverage facilities have three main areas. The first of these is a food area, where the food products are prepared. This includes the kitchen and such related facilities as food storerooms, refrigerators, and freezers. The second is a dining area where customers may consume food, or food and beverages. The third is a beverage area, where the beverage products are prepared. This includes at least one bar and at least one storage facility for liquor, beer, and wine.

The layout and design of an efficient food and beverage facility, one that contributes to smooth day-to-day operation, is critical. Efficient layout and design takes into account six considerations, although some of these are less significant in the dining and beverage areas.

1. Space

2. Equipment

3. Lighting

4. Ventilation

5. Materials flow

6. Traffic flow

In the following pages, we focus on each of the three main areas—food, dining, and beverage—and discuss applying the most significant of these six considerations to each area.

The Food Area

The food area is that part of the facility where food products are prepared. In most foodservice operations, the following activities take place within the food area.

Purchasing

Purchasing is the activity of procuring supplies and equipment. It normally takes place in an office with a desk for working, a file cabinet for keeping records, a computer workstation, and space for meeting quietly with the sales representatives of vendors. In years past, most foods were purchased via telephone or by meeting personally with vendors' representatives. Today, much purchasing is done over the Internet and by fax. Major suppliers have Web pages that list items for sale and their prices. Purchasing personnel are able to e-mail or fax orders directly to purveyors. Thus, the telephone and meetings with sales representatives are used less and less as means of purchasing foods.

Foods are frequently stored on rolling carts and moved directly into walk-in refrigerators, as shown in this picture.
(Photo courtesy of Intermetro Industries Corporation)

Receiving

Receiving activity is conducted in an area that contains equipment used to verify that the goods received conform to the orders placed. Quantity, quality, and price must all be checked. To do this properly, it is necessary to plan an area that is easily accessible to delivery drivers and large enough to hold an entire normal delivery.

Storing and Issuing

Storing and **issuing** require three types of facilities: dry, refrigerated, and frozen. A dry storage facility, typically called a *storeroom*, is maintained at normal room temperature. It is used to keep a reasonable supply of bags, bottles, boxes, and jars of food that need not be refrigerated or frozen. This storeroom must be large enough so that shelves can be constructed and foods stored in an orderly manner. Refrigerated facilities—reach-in and walk-in refrigerators—are used to store meats, fish, vegetables, dairy products, and any other foods that spoil if not kept cold. Freezers—reach-in and walk-in types—are required to store items purchased in a frozen state.

Producing

In a foodservice operation, the term **producing** refers to food production that takes place in the kitchen. Most kitchens require two production areas: one for advance preparation and another for the final preparation of foods immediately

A restaurant's product line determines the type of kitchen equipment that it requires for food production. Shown here is a variety of kitchen equipment, manufactured by the Vulcan Hart Company.
(Photo courtesy of Vulcan Hart Company)

before they are served. The advance preparation area is for basic preparation of foods that are later transferred to another area for final preparation. The final preparation or finishing area is for making foods ready for service.

Serving

Serving is defined as the transfer of finished products from preparation staff to servers. This occurs even in self-service operations—cafeterias and buffets among them—where the customers are also the servers.

Layout and Design Considerations in a Food Area

Space

If the facility is to run efficiently, adequate space must be provided for the activities associated with the food area. The amount of space allocated for the food area varies from one establishment to another, depending on such considerations as products, type of service, type and amount of equipment, and number of personnel required to work in the area. For example, the Steak Shack is a full-service restaurant with relatively more space devoted to food preparation than is the case in Frog's Pub, which offers a very limited menu. While it may be possible to plan sufficient space for every kitchen need in a new facility, older facilities being converted to foodservice use may lack the ideal amount of space for a specific use. In such circumstances, compromise is necessary.

Equipment

Many considerations determine the equipment required in a food area. The two most important are product line and preparation methods.

Product Line. Product line is a key determinant in equipment selection. If the product line includes Chinese food, the equipment needs are different than those in operations featuring French or Italian food. Similarly, specialty restaurants serving pizza require different equipment than those serving hamburgers. In contrast, family restaurants with varied menus require more varieties of equipment than do specialty restaurants.

Preparation Methods. The equipment in food areas varies considerably from one establishment to another. In some, such as the Steak Shack, one sees stockpots, kettles, mixers, steamers, and the other heavy equipment characteristic of kitchens preparing food from raw primary ingredients. This equipment may include broilers, ranges, conventional ovens, microwave ovens, deep-fat fryers, and other possibilities. In other establishments, the equipment may be limited to a few counters used to arrange food on small platters just before they are microwaved. In Frog's Pub, the kitchen equipment is simple and basic because the menu is limited. Needs vary from one operation to another, and choice of equipment should be based on the food products prepared.

Many food items can be prepared in a number of ways, and it is important to establish the preparation method for each food item before purchasing equipment. Chicken, for example, can be fried, sautéed, deep fried, baked, roasted, boiled, or broiled. If an operation establishes deep frying as the proper preparation method for a particular chicken entrée, then a deep fryer—or more than one—should be on the list of equipment to purchase. Similarly, if soups are to be prepared from stocks made in the establishment, as is the case in the Steak Shack and the Mountain Bank Staff Dining Room, then suitable equipment to produce the stocks—stockpots or steam kettles, depending largely on volume—should be on the list. If the product list includes a large number of frozen convenience foods, it is necessary to purchase a larger freezer than would be required if the restaurant were to use mostly raw, fresh ingredients. The number of examples illustrating this point is infinite.

The arrangement of equipment in each part of the food area is influenced by the extent of the work to be done there and the number of staff members available to do it. A large establishment may set up a specific station for broiling, another for frying, and yet another for sautéing, and provide each of these with appropriate equipment. Smaller establishments, not having the volume of work to justify a specific station and staff, may combine these three in a single station. That station would clearly have less equipment of any one type than each of the three stations in the larger establishment.

It is important to recognize that once equipment decisions are made and the equipment purchased and installed, it may be extremely difficult to change the product line in any significant way. For example, some specialty restaurants have found it impossible to enlarge or change their menus because they have neither the appropriate equipment nor space in the kitchen to install it.

Lighting

For employees to work efficiently, they must have sufficient light. Light is required so that employees can attend to the detailed work required for the elegant presentation of foods. It is also required so that employees can read portion scales and be certain that they are providing the correct number of ounces or grams in a portion.

Many considerations must be taken into account when making decisions about the lighting for a work area. The amount of light reaching a particular workstation is considerably less than the amount available at the lighting source itself. Also, the color of the walls and ceiling influence the amount of light available at a workstation. More light is available if wall and ceiling surfaces are in light colors; light colors reflect light, while dark colors absorb it. The amount of light on a surface, such as a worktable, is measured in **lumens** per square foot, or foot-candles. A **foot-candle** of light is the amount of light that can be measured at a distance of one foot from an ordinary candle. One lumen per square foot is equal to one foot-candle, a term whose origin precedes the invention of electric lights. Lighting experts suggest that employees need at least 60 foot-candles of light for ordinary work and about 110 foot-candles of light for detailed work, such as cake decorating.

Ventilation

Adequate ventilation is another basic requirement for work areas. The air that foodservice employees breathe should be clean—free of smoke and other pollutants. The climate should be at a temperature at which staff can work in reasonable comfort.

Because kitchens produce smoke and odors, the air must be replaced continually. If not, air quality deteriorates as levels of smoke and odors rise. In addition, temperatures in the kitchen rise quickly from stoves, ovens, and other heat-producing equipment in use, and the air may become unhealthy. The proper rate of air exchange in a kitchen is determined by the type of cooking, the type and amount of equipment used, and the height of the ceiling. In heavily used kitchens, the rate of air exchange may be as high as 50 times per hour. Fresh air may come from any of three sources: other rooms in the facility, outside, or a ventilation system in the establishment.

Materials Flow

Work areas and equipment should be arranged so that foods can proceed smoothly and logically from the receiving area to the storing and issuing area. From there, foods should move smoothly to the producing area for advance preparation and final preparation, and from there to the serving area.

To facilitate this smooth and even flow, the receiving area and all equipment required for receiving are typically located near a rear entrance to a foodservice facility. The storing and issuing area and the attendant equipment and facilities—storeroom, refrigerators, and freezers—should be located close to the receiving area. The producing area and its equipment should be located close enough to the storing and issuing area that advance preparation and final preparation can be expedited. The serving area should be close to the finishing area so that foods can be served as quickly as possible once they are ready. Note the arrangement of the equipment on the floor plan of the Steak Shack, found in Figure 5.1. Food deliveries come to the receiving area at the rear of the building, then move to one of the storage facilities nearby, from which they are transferred to the food preparation area as needed. The preparation and finishing areas are close to one another to facilitate quick service of the finished product to guests in the dining room.

Dishwashing equipment traditionally has been placed in a part of the kitchen that is near the entrance from the dining room so that servers returning to the kitchen with soiled china, glassware, and flatware can place these things in a convenient spot before proceeding to pick up food. However, because the noise associated with the handling of dishes can often be heard in the dining room, some establishments install conveyor systems. This is the approach taken in the Steak Shack. With these systems, dishwashing areas can be located some distance from the kitchen entrance; soiled items move to the dishwashing area via the conveyor belt.

Traffic Flow

People working in food areas must be able to move around without interfering with the work of others. They are all working in aisles, real or potential. In general, there are two kinds of aisles: traffic aisles and working aisles. The two should not coincide. Employees moving about the food area in traffic aisles should not interfere with people storing, issuing, or preparing food in working aisles. Traffic aisles should be wide enough to permit the passage of personnel and equipment. Working aisles should be wide enough to allow employees to move with reasonable freedom as they work. Note the wide aisles in the kitchen facility at the Mountain Bank Staff Dining Room, illustrated in Figure 5.2. Serving areas must accommodate both personnel returning soiled china and linens from a dining room and those picking up foods to be served in the dining room, and space must be adequate for the anticipated number of personnel to work without being crowded.

In planning a food area, then, adequate space and suitable equipment must be provided for purchasing, receiving, storing, issuing, producing, and serving food. Similarly, adequate lighting and ventilation must be provided. Finally, the food area should be arranged to facilitate efficient movement of personnel and materials.

The Dining Area

The dining area is that part of the facility where food and beverage products are consumed by customers. It normally includes tables, counters, or similar surfaces on which the products are placed, and chairs, stools, benches, or other seating arrangements for customers to use as they consume the products. It may also include such items as salad bars, buffet tables, and other items designed for customer self-service.

The amount of space devoted to seating in the dining area is determined by the type of service, the variety and mix of table sizes, and decisions that must be made regarding space between tables.
(Photo courtesy of The Red Lion Inn)

Layout and Design Considerations in a Dining Area

Space

The amount of space devoted to seating in the dining area is determined by the type of service, the variety and mix of table sizes, and decisions about space between tables.

Type of Service.   Some types of service require more space than others. French service (discussed the next chapter), for example, requires considerable space between tables so that the gueridons characteristic of French service can be moved tableside. American service (discussed in the next chapter), on the other hand, requires comparatively little space between tables—just enough for servers to walk quickly carrying plates or trays. In the Mountain Bank Staff Dining Room, where self-service is the rule, aisles in the dining area can be much narrower than at the Steak Shack. There, servers require considerable space to move large trays of hot foods quickly from kitchen to customers.

Variety and Mix of Table Sizes.   Table sizes and the mix of table sizes in the dining area also influence the amount of space required to accommodate a given number of diners. Tables for two, four, six, or eight customers require varying amounts of floor space. Round tables require a bit more of space than square or rectangular tables. Knowledge of the number of tables of each shape and size helps determine the total number that can be accommodated in a dining area of a given size. It takes only about half the space to seat eight persons at one table as it does to seat the same eight persons at four separate tables accommodating two persons each. Tables intended to seat two persons can be purchased in standard sizes ranging from 24 × 24 inches to 30 × 36 inches. Establishments catering to families require a greater number of tables accommodating larger parties than do those catering to couples. Establishments offering luxurious evening dining require larger tables than do those offering only breakfast or lunch. Frog's Pub has no real need for large tables because customers do not ordinarily order full meals. Consequently, the tables are small, selected because they provide enough table area for beverage products, rather than food products, which tend to be secondary in Frog's Pub. The tables in the Steak Shack are larger because customers normally order full meals. In a sense, beverage sales are secondary in the dining room of the Steak Shack.

Decisions About Space Between Tables.   The distance between tables influences the number of customers who can be accommodated in a given area. Many managers see no difficulty in having customers seated close to one another. Others prefer to seat customers at greater distances from one another and to preserve the privacy of their conversations. Under the former policy, a greater number of customers are seated; under the latter, fewer are seated.

Equipment

The equipment required in the dining area is determined by the type of service and management decisions concerning the need for buffet stands, serving stands, coatracks, and the like. In the Mountain Bank Staff Dining Room, considerable space is devoted to three buffet islands, pieces of equipment not found in Frog's Pub.

Lighting

The two primary considerations in dining area lighting are the amount and the type. The decision to have a well-lit dining area, as opposed to a dim one, is based on the atmosphere management is attempting to create. Some establishments—Frog's Pub, for example—keep lighting levels low to create an intimate atmosphere. In some, the lighting level is so low that older customers have difficulty reading a menu. By contrast, other establishments, the Mountain Bank Staff Dining Room and the Steak Shack among them, are brightly lit. Sometimes this is because they are family establishments; other times, it may be because they feature an interesting or unique theme.

The two basic types of lighting are direct and indirect. The bulbs providing direct lighting can be seen, and their light shines directly into a room. For indirect lighting, bulbs are not visible. Indirect light shines toward the ceiling and walls and is reflected back into the room. Direct lighting produces shadows, but less light is required to achieve a given degree of brightness. Indirect lighting is softer and produces no shadows, but more is required to reach a particular level of illumination than would be required with direct lighting.

Ventilation

Adequate ventilation is another basic requirement for a dining area. The air in a dining area should be at a temperature at which people can dine in reasonable comfort. Today, with the growing tendency to provide smoke-free areas for diners—especially when required to do so by local laws—ventilation has assumed greater importance than in previous years. If smoking is permitted, air quality deteriorates as levels of smoke and odors rise. Therefore, the owners of the Steak Shack provide a separate smoking area along with equipment to ensure that smoke is vented outside. This is not a consideration in the Mountain Bank Staff Dining Room, where smoking is not permitted. However, temperatures in a dining area rise quickly without adequate ventilation, and the air becomes unhealthy. Fresh air may come from any of three sources: other rooms in the facility, outside, or a ventilation system. It is important to note that the air pressure in the dining room and other rooms should be higher than that in the kitchen. This causes air to flow from the dining room to the kitchen, not the other way around. If air pressure were higher in the kitchen, the smoke and odors from the kitchen would soon flow into the dining room, making it uncomfortable for diners.

Traffic Flow

Traffic in a dining area must move smoothly. Traffic patterns should be planned to avoid cross traffic between customers and service personnel and among the service personnel. Service personnel must be able to move freely and conveniently within the facility. In some places, this means, for example, that servers must be able to move into and out of a serving area to pick up food orders and to deposit soiled china and flatware for washing. In other kinds of establishments, it means that employees must be able to move about the dining area to clean tables and get rid of disposable paper and plastic food packaging.

The measures taken to facilitate free movement vary from one type of operation to another. In table service restaurants, for example, the servers' exit from the dining area to the kitchen is typically located some distance away from the street entrance used by customers. In establishments that do not provide table service, the area where customers order or select foods is typically near the street entrance. In part, this is to facilitate freedom of movement for customers carrying foods to their tables. If servers are required to pick up plates of food in a kitchen, it is important to have two doors between the kitchen and dining areas—one for traffic going into the kitchen, and the other for traffic coming out. This is illustrated in Figure 5.1, showing the floor plan of the Steak Shack. If only one door were provided, accidents could result from service staff coming and going into the kitchen at the same time. The farther apart the two doors are placed, the better the traffic flow. Similarly, lavatories should be installed in locations such that related traffic does not interfere directly with servers or other customers. Note the locations of rest rooms in the Steak Shack and in the Mountain Bank Staff Dining Room.

In planning a dining area, then, adequate space and suitable equipment must be provided for efficient and orderly service of food and beverage products to customers. Knowledge of the type of service, the variety and mix of table sizes, and management decisions about space between tables are critical to determining space requirements. As with food areas, adequate lighting and ventilation must be provided in all parts of the dining area. Finally, the dining area should be arranged to facilitate efficient movement of personnel and materials. Throughout, one must bear in mind that the ambience, or atmosphere—a critical factor in overall success—is determined largely by the layout and design of the dining area.

The Beverage Area

The beverage area is that part of the facility where beverage products are prepared and served. The following activities take place within the beverage area.

Purchasing

Beverage purchasing requires making decisions about the quantities and kinds of beverages to be purchased. Orders for beverages are often placed from the purchasing area by telephone or by direct contact with salespersons, if that is consistent with state law and the policies established by management for beverage purchasing.

Receiving

Receiving beverages requires verifying that beverages delivered conform to the orders placed. In many small establishments, the beverage receiving area is the bar; in larger establishments offering both food products and beverage products, one receiving area is likely to exist for both.

The beverage area is that part of the faciity where beverage products are prepared and served, as shown in this photograph of the Fairmont Copley Plaza Lounge.
(Photo courtesy of Fairmont Hotels and Resorts)

Storing and Issuing

Beverage storing and issuing activities vary greatly from one establishment to another. The variations stem from needs that differ with the size of the establishment, the number of customers served in a given period, and the complexity of the beverage product list. In a small neighborhood bar, the storing and issuing facility may be a small closet located near the bar; in a large hotel or restaurant doing high-volume business and offering a complex array of beverage products, at least two separate areas are used for storing and issuing beverages. One of these is a locked storeroom, maintained at normal room temperature, which is used for storing liquors and may be used for storing mixers and alcoholic beverages that are not refrigerated. Another is a locked, refrigerated room for the storage of beers, ales, and wines that require chilling.

Restaurants offering their guests choices from wine lists must keep reasonable supplies of bottled wine on hand. Some of the finer restaurants maintain wine inventories worth thousands of dollars. These are typically kept under secure conditions in climate-controlled storerooms known as **wine cellars**. Wine cellars should be maintained in an organized manner so that particular wines can be located quickly when ordered by customers. To accomplish this, wines are normally classified by type, and each individual wine is given a number. The still wines and sparkling wines are stored on their sides in specially designed racks or bins. The number assigned to each wine is both printed on the wine list and posted on the bin or rack where the corresponding wine is stored. This makes it easier to find any wine ordered by a customer.

Producing

Beverage production activities typically take place at bars, where drinks are made by bartenders. There are three types of bar: front bar, service bar, and special-purpose bar. An understanding of beverage facilities requires that one know about them and comprehend their differences.

Front Bar. A **front bar** is a fixed counter for beverage service, open for business on a regularly scheduled basis and directly accessible to customers. Front bars are permanently fixed in particular locations within establishments. Many such establishments are open long hours daily, but the days and hours of operation are determined by owners within the parameters of state and local laws.

The three parts of a front bar are bar, back bar, and under bar. The term **bar** is used normally to refer to a physical device in a barroom or taproom that fills several purposes. It is a counter where bartenders can serve drinks to customers, a convenient surface used by customers who consume drinks, a surface on which bartenders may prepare drinks, and a serving station where servers may pick up drinks for consumption elsewhere.

A **back bar** is a storage and display facility located behind a bartender. The top surface is used to hold shelves on which are displayed bottles of some or all of the wines and liquors available at the bar. Glassware may be displayed here as well. The compartments underneath are used for storage of bar supplies, which may include beers, wines, liquors, mixers, paper supplies, and any other item used at the bar. If the facility is refrigerated, it may be used to store bottled beers and food supplies used in beverage production, such as milk, cream, lemons, limes, and fruit juices.

An **under bar** is a work area under the bar surface that contains equipment and supplies used by bartenders. Its work area has stations—one for each bartender. The number of stations governs the number of bartenders who can conveniently work at the bar at any one time. A station consists of a steel sink for ice surrounded by wells to hold bottles of frequently used liquors and mixers. In addition to these stations, the under bar has sinks or a machine for washing glassware and a sink for disposing of liquids and washing bar equipment. There may also be work space for preparing drinks, for storing supplies and equipment, and additional refrigeration facilities.

Front bars are the most common of the three types of bars. At the typical front bar, customers walk to the bar, where they are greeted by a bartender who takes their orders and prepares and serves their drinks. This is the type of bar found in the Frog's Pub, illustrated in Figure 5.3. Beyond the point at which the drink is served are many possible variations. Customers may or may not consume their drinks at the bar. In some establishments, customers can remain at the bar, sitting on stools or standing as they drink. In others, customers may carry their drinks elsewhere. Sometimes the bartender acts as a cashier, collecting for each drink as it is served. Sometimes the bartender records a given customer's drinks on a paper form called a **guest check**, which the customer settles before leaving. Occasionally, there is an employee at the bar who does not act as a bartender but who serves as cashier for the establishment.

Service Bar.   A **service bar** is a counter at which a bartender prepares drinks but does not serve them directly to customers. Drink orders are given to the bartender by servers who take the orders from customers and serve the drinks when ready. Service bars are frequently located in kitchens and similar areas that are neither visible nor accessible to customers. In other instances, a service bar may be visible but not accessible. Some service areas are too small for customer access to be feasible; others are behind glass walls; some are in establishments in which the level and extent of service is such that any appearance of self-service would be unseemly.

Some service bars are permanently located in fixed positions. Others are mobile, such as bars on wheels that can be moved from one location to another. Still others are temporary—folding tables set up quickly, possibly draped or otherwise covered, then dismantled when no longer needed. What differentiates service bars from others is not the degree of permanence but that customers are not permitted access to them. Customer access is not a characteristic of a service bar.

Special-Purpose Bar.   A **special-purpose** bar is one that, although directly accessible to customers, is open only for a defined period to accommodate a special need. Special-purpose bars are most commonly used in banquet or catering businesses to accommodate guests at special functions—parties, dances, or the receptions preceding special events. At special-purpose bars, customers have direct access to a bartender. They order and receive drinks just as at a front bar. Whereas a front bar is open on a regularly scheduled basis, the special-purpose bar is open only to accommodate the beverage service requirements of people present at the event. When the event is over, the special-purpose bar is closed. Thus, special-purpose bars are open for varying periods—some long, others short, depending on the length of the event.

Special-purpose bars can be permanent, mobile, or temporary. Some are built into the physical structure of a banquet room. Mobile bars on wheels can be moved from one location to another. Still others are merely tables or counters, folding or otherwise, that are fitted out for use as bars when required.

Bars can be built in various shapes and in any desired size. The layout and design are determined by the use that management plans for the bar. If the bar is to be used only as a service bar, it probably will be compact—no larger than required to prepare and serve a projected number of drinks in a given time period, with space allocated for storage. In contrast, if it is to be a front bar used in a cocktail lounge that also serves as a holding area for customers waiting to be seated in a dining area, it probably will be considerably larger, providing work space for several bartenders and counter space to accommodate a substantial number of customers seated at the bar. The sizes of special purpose bars vary with the number of customers to be served.

Serving

This activity involves transferring finished beverage products from the bartender to servers, to customers, or to both. These transfers take place at front bars, service bars, and special-purpose bars.

Layout and Design Considerations in a Beverage Area

Space

If the facility is to run efficiently, adequate space should be provided for the activities associated with the beverage area. The amount of space allocated to the beverage area varies from one establishment to another, depending on such considerations as product line, type of service, type and amount of equipment, and number of personnel required to work in the area. For example, an upscale cocktail lounge advertising the ability of its bartenders to make any drink requested is likely to require more preparation space than a neighborhood tavern offering nothing other than five brands of bottled beer. While it may be possible to plan sufficient space for every need in a new facility, older facilities being converted to bar use may lack the ideal amount of space for a specific use. In such circumstances, compromise may be necessary.

Equipment

Many considerations determine the equipment required in a beverage area. The two most important are product line and preparation methods.

Product Line. Product line is a key determinant in equipment selection. If the line is to include mixed drinks, the equipment needs are different than those in operations featuring imported beers on tap. Similarly, operations offering drinks requiring shaved ice require different equipment than those that serve straight shots of blended rye. In the Steak Shack, for example, an ice machine is an important piece of bar equipment. At Frog's Pub, there is an ice machine in the kitchen but not at the bar; most of the beverage orders are for the featured imported beers and ales, and the bartender has little need for ice.

Preparation Methods. Preparation equipment in beverage areas varies considerably from one establishment to another. In some, one might find **pourers**— measuring devices that hold a precise amount of liquor each time a drink is poured. In others—those with automated equipment for measuring drink quantities—few bottles may be in view and no pourers at all. Needs vary by operation, and choice of equipment should be based on the beverage products prepared.

Lighting

The primary consideration in beverage area lighting is the atmosphere management intends to create. Lighting is a critical element in this area. Some establishments—Frog's Pub, for example—keep lighting levels low to create an intimate atmosphere. By contrast, the bar in the Steak Shack has a higher level of lighting.

In designing a beverage area, the planner must include adequate and suitable equipment for purchasing, receiving, storing, issuing, producing, and serving activities associated with the beverage product list. Just as in the food area, adequate lighting and ventilation must be provided in all parts of the beverage area. Finally, the beverage area should be arranged to facilitate efficient movement of personnel and materials.

The key factors in food and beverage facilities discussed in this chapter— concept, legal requirements, product line, and layout and design—are major elements that lie at the heart of food and beverage operations. Obviously, many other aspects to planning and operating a food and beverage enterprise exist. Other topics requiring close attention include menu, organization plan, marketing plan, and budget. These are topics for discussion in the next chapter and Chapter 10.

SUMMARY

In this chapter, concept, legal requirements, and product line are introduced as fundamental to the layout and design of food and beverage facilities. Product line is described as having three components: food and beverages, services, and ambience. Case studies describing three foodservice facilities—Steak Shack, Mountain Bank Staff Dining Room, and Frog's Pub—are presented as aids to understanding facilities layout and design. Six key considerations in food and beverage facilities layout and design are identified as space, equipment, lighting, ventilation, materials flow, and traffic flow. These considerations are discussed as applicable to the three main areas of a food and beverage facility, identified as the food area, dining area, and beverage area. Front bars, service bars, and special-purpose bars are identified as three types of bars that may be found in beverage facilities. Finally, the three specific parts of a front bar are identified as bar, back bar, and under bar.

KEY TERMS

Back bar	Issuing	Service bar
Bar	Lumen	Serving
Concept	Pourer	Special-purpose bar
Feasibility study	Producing	Storing
Foot-candle	Product line	Under bar
Front bar	Purchasing	Wine cellar
Guest check	Receiving	

DISCUSSION QUESTIONS

1. The authors state that every food and beverage facility begins with a concept. In this context, define the term *concept* and describe its purpose.

2. Owners and managers of food and beverage facilities are said to require some knowledge of various laws and regulations. What types of laws and regulations should they know about?

3. Define the term *product line* as it is used in food and beverage operations.

4. What are the three elements in the hospitality service product line offered by food and beverage operations?

5. Identify the three main areas in a food and beverage facility, describing the principal activities that take place in each.

6. List the six considerations that should be taken into account in the layout and design of food and beverage facilities. Describe the importance and significance of each to efficient day-to-day operation.

7. What is a lumen? a foot-candle? How many foot-candles do experts suggest for normal kitchen work? for detailed work?

8. Distinguish between traffic aisles and working aisles.

9. Explain the importance of space, traffic flow, and lighting in the layout and design of a dining area.

10. In what ways do the arrangement and size of tables in a dining room influence the amount of space required for a given number of customers?

11. Distinguish between direct lighting and indirect lighting. Why might food and beverage operators choose to use each?

12. Why is it necessary that air pressure in a dining room and in other rooms adjoining the kitchen be greater than that in the kitchen itself?

13. Three types of bars are described in the chapter. Identify them and discuss their differences.

14. List and describe the three principal parts of a front bar.

MOMENTS OF TRUTH

1. Describe a restaurant that you recently visited. Can you identify the concept of the establishment?

2. For the restaurant identified above, describe its product line as completely as you can. Include in your description a summary of the foods and beverages offered, the services offered, and the ambience of the establishment.

3. Does the layout and design of the restaurant identified above follow the principles described in this text? If not, where does it differ?

INTERNET EXERCISES

1. Go to Avon Old Farms Inn (www.avonoldfarmsinn.com). Write a paragraph about the inn, outlining its concept and product line.

2. Go to Shoneys Restaurants (www.shoneysrestaurants.com/). Write a paragraph about the chain, outlining its concept and product line.

Food and Beverage Operations

▶ Learning Objectives

After reading and studying this chapter, you should be able to:

1. List and describe the seven basic steps common to food and beverage operations of all types.

2. List and explain the four critical issues that purchasing procedures must address.

3. Distinguish between perishables and nonperishables.

4. List the three primary goals of the receiving procedure and explain the importance of each.

5. Identify the four goals of the storing procedure.

6. Describe the two goals of the issuing procedure.

7. Name the four goals of food or beverage production procedures.

8. Identify the purposes of each of the following: sales histories, production sheets, and standard recipes.

9. Compare the goals of sales procedures in profit-oriented operations with those in not-for-profit operations.

10. List and describe three common means used to help sell food and beverage products.

11. List and describe eight styles of foodservice.

12. List and describe three types of wines.

13. Illustrate the interdependence of the seven steps common to all food and beverage operations.

INTRODUCTION

The previous chapter examined the common components of food and beverage facilities. We now turn to a subject that is typically of the greatest interest to those preparing for careers in the foodservice industry: food and beverage operations.

Given the array of types of food and beverage establishments discussed in Chapter 4, it should be apparent that operational details differ greatly from one type to another. The operational details relating to a college cafeteria are not the same as those relating to a sophisticated city restaurant dedicated to fine dining. Similarly, operational differences are apparent among types of beverage enterprise. For example, the neighborhood bar focused on beverages differs from the fine restaurant focused on food. These differences include the manner in which the organizations are structured, the titles of the personnel, the duties of each worker, and the manner in which food and beverages are prepared.

Many of these differences are discussed in Chapter 10. In this chapter, we focus our attention, instead, on similarities—the many steps of food and beverage operations that are much the same from one enterprise to another. We believe strongly that it is much easier to understand the differences among operations if one comprehends their underlying similarities—the basic operational activities and principles that are common to all.

The purpose of this chapter, then, is to identify important points of similarity. We identify and describe basic steps that all food and beverage enterprises share.

BASIC ELEMENTS OF FOOD AND BEVERAGE OPERATIONS

All food or beverage operations have the following basic steps in common:

- Purchasing
- Receiving
- Storing
- Issuing
- Producing
- Selling
- Serving

Many readers will recognize that these basic steps are familiar, largely because they seem much the same as the parts of a food and beverage facility discussed in the previous chapter. These basic steps are essential for all food or beverage operations, from college cafeterias to national fast-food outlets, from neighborhood taverns to hotel cocktail lounges, from nursing home foodservices to catering halls. They are the sequential steps necessary for preparing and serving portions of food or beverages. We describe each of these in detail and explore their inter-relationships.

Purchasing

The first of the basic steps of a food and beverage operation is purchasing, a necessary first step in any production process. All food or beverage enterprises must establish procedures for purchasing.

The primary objective of purchasing foods or beverages for production is to ensure the availability of suitable materials for preparing food or beverage products and for related uses. These materials must be available when needed, they should be in sufficient but not excessive quantities and of appropriate quality, and they should be purchased at suitable prices.

Four critical issues that any purchasing procedure must address are:

1. Quantity
2. Quality
3. Price
4. Space

Quantity

Food and beverage operators cannot ask customers to wait for deliveries. When a customer reading the menu in Frog's Pub requests a glass of Bass ale or an order of shepherd's pie, the owner is expected to have the items on hand. The purchasing procedure must be designed to ensure that foods, beverages, and other necessary materials are available when needed so that menu items can be produced on demand. One means for accomplishing this is to establish daily routines for evaluating existing supplies of raw materials, assessing needs for the upcoming period, and placing orders as required.

For the Steak Shack, it is obviously important to maintain adequate supplies of steak. This can be accomplished by establishing daily routines for evaluating existing supplies and by placing regular orders with a supplier. Assuming that the supplier delivers only on Tuesdays, it is necessary to order a sufficient quantity to last for one week. Purchasing food can be the job of any of several people in a foodservice operation. Some restaurant managers do their own food purchasing. In other restaurants, the chef does it, and in some larger operations, the purchasing is done by a purchasing steward. At the Steak Shack, the chef purchases all food for the establishment. The individual responsible for ordering must know the quantity used in a normal week and when larger or smaller amounts than normal may be needed. A good purchasing procedure is designed to help determine proper quantities for purchase.

Quality

Product quality is another critical purchasing issue. The food and beverages must be consistent and of a quality acceptable to customers. There are degrees of quality, and products need not always be of the highest quality obtainable, but they should be of the quality that meets customers' needs and preferences. Some experts would add that the quality should always match the image the establishment attempts to convey. If, for example, the Mountain Bank is attempting to convey to its employees the image of a caring employer, foods available to them in the dining facility—even the simplest foods—should be of consistently good quality. The purchasing procedure should be designed to ensure the purchase of products of consistent quality each time the food and beverages are ordered.

The quality of any item purchased should also be appropriate for its intended use. For example, when the steward in the Mountain Bank Staff Dining Room buys oranges for fresh orange juice, she buys Valencias or Temples, which are juice oranges, rather than California navels, which are eating oranges. The latter are more expensive and yield less juice. If someone were mistakenly to purchase the California navels, the bank's operating costs would be higher than necessary and the quality of the orange juice would be lower than desired.

Any procedure designed for food purchasing must take into account the two categories into which all food purchases are divided: perishables and nonperishables.

Perishables are foods that keep for only short periods of time before they begin to lose their quality. These foods spoil and become unusable. Such foods are typically fresh, including meat, fish, fruit, and vegetables. Fresh vegetables retain sufficient freshness for several days; fresh fish, in comparison, does not, and must be used much sooner. Perishables must be ordered frequently, sometimes each day. The quantity ordered is limited to anticipated demand.

Nonperishables are foods that keep for extended periods before spoiling. They typically come in cans, jars, bags, bottles, and boxes. Some are dried or frozen. Nonperishables are ordered infrequently and in larger quantities because they have a longer shelf life than perishables.

The terms *perishable* and *nonperishable* are not normally used in beverage purchasing. This does not mean, however, that shelf life for beverage products is unlimited. Some beverages—draft beers, for example—have a limited shelf life and must be kept refrigerated. For bottled beer, shelf life is considerably longer, but not unlimited. By contrast, spirits can be kept indefinitely.

Questions of quality should not be left to chance. Beef tenderloin, the commercial cut of beef used in the Steak Shack to prepare special steaks called *filets mignons*, is available at several levels of quality, known as *grades*, and someone must determine which grade is appropriate for the intended use in a given establishment. In addition, if customers ordering filet mignon are to receive steaks of the same quality on each visit to the establishment, provision must be made for ordering the same grade each time beef tenderloins are purchased.

One means for ensuring consistency in the quality of items is to prepare a carefully considered written description of each item to be purchased. This could include such information as grade, size, count, color, type and size of container, degree of freshness, and other characteristics, which vary with the product to be purchased. These descriptions are known as *standard purchase specifications* and are commonly used in most well-managed food or beverage operations. In the Steak Shack, all beef is purchased to match carefully written standard purchase specifications.

Price

Price is always a critical issue in food and beverage purchasing. The higher the purchase price for raw materials of a given level of quality, the higher is the cost of the food and beverage products an establishment offers its customers. The purchasing procedure should facilitate the purchase of the needed quantity of an item at the most favorable price for the quality selected. For example, while the Mountain Bank may be willing to subsidize the cost of its employees' meals, it is certainly unwilling to spend money wastefully.

Purchasers use several methods to determine the best price for the desired quality. Most commonly, purchasers obtain several quotations for desired products, then select the dealer offering the best price. A good purchasing procedure makes provision for comparing the prices offered by various dealers for a given item and selecting the best price. Before purchasing meats for the Steak Shack, the buyer obtains price quotations from three dealers, each of whom has a copy of the standard purchase specifications.

Storage Space

The final critical issue that the purchasing procedure must take into account is storage. Storage space is always limited, and decisions must be made as to its allocation to particular uses. Marecki Foods must determine the maximum quantity of each food item used in the Mountain Bank Staff Dining Room facility that can be stored in the limited space available. When storage space is severely limited, it clearly becomes necessary to place orders for some items more frequently than would be necessary otherwise. Thus, storage space can affect the timing of purchases. Quantities of any item purchased should never be greater than the storage space available for that item.

If an establishment lacks proper quantities of food or beverage ingredients to produce for customer demand, or if the food or beverage ingredients are of improper quality because the purchasing procedure malfunctions, other parts of the operation will not be able to function properly. The entire operation may be unable to achieve its goals.

Receiving

The second important step in food or beverage operations is receiving. The procedure for receiving has three primary goals. It must be designed to verify that:

1. The quantity delivered is the same as the quantity ordered.

2. The quality of the items delivered conforms to the quality specified in the order.

3. The price on the invoice is the same as the price quoted by the dealer when the order was placed.

Receiving clerks in many food-service establishments regularly receive deliveries from Sysco, one of America's leading foodservice suppliers. Here, an employee of Sysco is filling an order for a restaurant.
(Photo courtesy of SYSCO Corporation)

Food and beverage orders must be received by someone with sufficient knowledge to check carefully and accurately for quantity, quality, and price. Ideally, the person receiving the order should not be the person who places the order. Each delivery must be counted or weighed, and the quality and price of each item must be verified. Finally, after the verification process is completed, the food is sent to the appropriate storage facility—dry storage, refrigeration, or freezer.

For example, assume the Steak Shack placed an order for 15 beef tenderloins, U.S. prime grade, weighing approximately 8 pounds each, at a price of $9.60 per pound. When the delivery is received, it is necessary to verify that the beef is prime quality, that the invoice indicates a price of $9.60 per pound, and that the total weight for all 15 pieces equals the weight shown on the invoice. Experienced receivers would also be certain to check other attributes listed in the purchase specifications, such as packaging, freshness, and thickness of fat cover, for example. If the delivered beef conforms to the order, it is moved to refrigerated storage.

Should the delivery fail to conform to the order placed, there are likely to be problems in other parts of the operation, which could have a negative impact on the success of the overall operation. For example, if the Steak Shack receives only 12 pieces of beef tenderloin, some customers might not be able to have filet mignon. If the beef is of a lower grade than ordered, the steaks will be less acceptable to customers and the reputation of the restaurant may be negatively affected. If the invoice price is higher than quoted, the profit of the restaurant will be somewhat lower than anticipated.

The receiving procedure must be able to determine that items ordered are received at the quoted prices, and it must provide for ways to make the necessary adjustments when incorrect items are sent to the restaurant.

Storing

The third important step in food and beverage operations is storage of purchased items. The procedure for storing must satisfy four primary goals:

1. Ensuring the security of purchased materials

2. Preserving the quality of those materials

3. Providing ready access to available materials

4. Facilitating the determination of quantities on hand

All purchases are stored in one of three places: food or beverage items that can be stored at room temperature should be placed in dry storage areas, items that require chilling should be placed in refrigerators, and frozen foods should be stored in freezers. All storage areas should be locked to prevent **pilferage**—an industry term for theft—and it is essential that the storing procedure make provision for safeguarding all food and beverage supplies. Pilferage is a major cause of unwarranted costs and must be prevented.

The storage procedure must also ensure that the quality of supplies is maintained. Therefore, to preserve quality, rooms used for dry storage should be maintained at reasonable levels of temperature and humidity; if either or both become excessive, the shelf life of all foods and some beverages is negatively affected. Refrigerators must operate at the proper temperatures—33 to 40 degrees Fahrenheit for chilled foods, and slightly higher temperatures for draft beers—45 de-

Some foods require extensive preparation by kitchen staff. Shown in this picture are chefs preparing food in a Four Seasons kitchen.
(Photo courtesy of the Four Seasons Hotels, © 2000 Four Seasons Limited. Used by permission.)

grees Fahrenheit. Frozen foods belong in freezers that maintain temperatures of 10 degrees below zero Fahrenheit.

Another consideration in preserving the quality of food items is the potential for odors and flavors from some food products to affect other foods stored nearby, particularly if they are improperly wrapped or covered. In the Mountain Bank Staff Dining Room, employees of Marecki Foods store eggs and other dairy products in a different refrigerator from that used for fish because these products would take on the odors of the fish quickly.

One final consideration in preserving the quality of food in storage is taking all necessary steps to see that foods in dry storage are secure from contamination by rodents and other vermin. The manager of the Steak Shack, for example, must be careful to see that items in bags and boxes are carefully protected from invasion by these perennial pests.

Providing ready access to stored food and beverage supplies is another key aim of the procedure for storing. When a food or beverage item is needed from storage, it is clearly important that the storage facility be organized so that it can be obtained quickly and easily.

In most establishments, items are stored by category. In a food storage facility, canned fruits are stored together. So are meats. In beverage storage, spirits are stored together. The Scotch whiskeys, for example, are separated from the ryes and the bourbons. Each item has a predetermined location, and supplies are placed in these locations after they are properly received. When an item is needed, an employee familiar with the storage facility goes to the location of the needed item and gets the desired quantity. Thus, the owner of the Frog's Pub can quickly and easily obtain a bottle of dry gin to replace one that has just been emptied at the bar.

When all stored items are kept in predetermined locations, it is easier to assess the quantity on hand of any food or beverage item and to make a judgment about whether to place an order for an additional quantity. Thus, the procedure for purchasing is closely linked to that for storing. It is necessary to obtain accurate data from the storage procedure concerning quantity on hand if the purchasing procedure is to function properly.

Issuing

The fourth important step in food and beverage operations is issuing. The procedures for issuing are designed to ensure that materials for production are released to authorized personnel in the correct quantities and at suitable times. These two goals can be accomplished in any of several ways. For example, the owner of the Steak Shack may limit access to food storage to the chef, who would be the only individual with keys. Another possibility is to have one employee whose workstation is the food storage area and who gives supplies only to those requesting them on special forms bearing the chef's signature.

Accurate records of issues maintained by employees of Marecki Foods, on paper forms or by some other means, may provide data that can be useful in other parts of the operation. With data from both the receiving procedure about goods received and from the issuing procedure about goods issued, methods can readily be devised for maintaining perpetual inventories of goods. The value of that inventory at any given time, the cost of the foods or beverages issued, and considerable additional information can also be determined.

Producing

The fifth important step in food and beverage operations is producing, or production, as it is better known. Production has four primary goals aimed at producing food products and beverage products:

1. In suitable quantities

2. Of appropriate quality

3. In a timely manner

4. With minimal waste

The production of a menu of food or beverage products is a complex business. Some items are simple to prepare—merely placing bottles of beer in a refrigerator to chill or arranging portion packs of breakfast cereals on a breakfast buffet. Others are equally simple, but most require additional preparation—sometimes quite extensive preparation. The extent of complexity varies from item to item and from one establishment to another.

Every establishment does some daily preparation before opening for business. For example, the owner/operator of a simple hamburger stand must do some basic work before he can produce hamburgers. He moves several boxes of frozen hamburger patties from a freezer to a convenient location next to the grill, then places a corresponding number of packaged sliced rolls nearby. Both hamburger patties and rolls must be handy when the stand opens and customers begin to order hamburgers. He may even open several packages of rolls and place a few open rolls on plates just before opening. If this basic work is not done, service is slow, and both sales levels and revenues are likely to be lower than desired.

In the Steak Shack, prime ribs of beef and baked potatoes must be cooked in advance because of the length of time the cooking process requires. The steaks must be portioned in advance as well because they should be ready for broiling when customers' orders reach the kitchen. Similarly, the chef in the Mountain Bank Staff Dining Room prepares the tuna salad for sandwiches before the lunch hour begins. At Frog's Pub, the bartender cuts pieces of lemon peel and sections of lime as garnishes for drinks, then fills several bar containers with ice from the kitchen and places opened bottles of spirits and mixers in predetermined, easy-to-reach wells located under the bar. Employees producing food or beverage products do such work in advance so that guests may be served quickly and efficiently.

Many food and beverage employees commonly describe this as preparing their **mise en place**. This French culinary term means having everything in place. Thus, with the mise en place ready, the bartender in Frog's Pub and the chef in the Mountain Bank Staff Dining Room are ready to serve customers the foods and drinks of their choice without unnecessary delay.

A significant problem with many food items is determining the quantities to prepare in advance. The proper quantity of any item is that amount that enables the establishment to serve each customer who orders it without delay and without leftovers at the close of business. Ideally, the last portion of any item prepared for any given day is served just as the establishment is about to close for the day.

At best, this is difficult. Most chefs would say it is next to impossible. Chefs normally do not know the precise number of customers who will order a given menu item. Without a precise number, they are likely to prepare too much or too little. If too little is prepared, some potential customers are disappointed, and sales revenues may be less than would otherwise have been possible. If too much is prepared, unsold quantities may be unusable for their originally intended purposes. For example, the chef in the Steak Shack must prepare roast prime ribs of beef in advance. If too much is cooked, it is difficult to use the remaining amount the next day, and if too little is cooked, some customers are disappointed when told that none is left. Unless the chef can find some suitable alternative use for the leftover beef, it may go unused, then spoil and be discarded.

Because of their need to set production targets in advance, many foodservice operators incorporate into their production procedures useful techniques adapted from the manufacturing sector. These are sales histories and production sheets.

Sales Histories

As the name implies, **sales histories** are records of the number of customers served during past periods and the number of portions sold of each menu item. Some establishments maintain records of portion sales by day of the week, whereas others find alternative approaches preferable. The data may be obtained from a cash register that keeps track of items sold, a computerized management procedure, or by manual means. A sales history should include additional important information, such as inclement weather and out-of-the-ordinary events such as holidays, strikes, special sales in nearby stores, and nearby road construction. Any data that sheds light on the sales records for a given meal, day, or other period should be included.

It has often been said that the best indicator of future human behavior is past human behavior. Thus, the sales history for a given establishment provides the foodservice operator with a rational basis for predicting the total number of customers likely to patronize the establishment on a given day and for making reasonable assumptions about which menu items they are likely to order. The collection of such assumptions for a given day becomes the basis for judgments about the quantities of particular menu items to prepare for the day.

Production Sheets

A **production sheet** is a list of menu items to be prepared for a specific day or meal period, along with the amount of each item for production personnel to

EVERY BITE YOU TAKE, ← THEY'LL BE WATCHING YOU

As you savor the beef bourguignon at your table in an elegant restaurant, someone in the kitchen may be watching your reaction. Overhead may be a video camera hooked up to a screen in the kitchen so that the chef can determine if you are pleased with the dish.

Greater numbers of restaurants are having video technology installed so that the kitchen can observe what goes on in the dining room. In addition to watching customers' reactions to food served them at their tables, chefs also may want to observe the progress of the meal so that he can get the next course started.

Video systems cost from $15,000 to $100,000. However, restaurants that can afford them are pleased with the information.

Source: Adapted from an article in the *New York Times*, 1 March 2000.

prepare. Some production sheets also indicate particular recipes to be used in preparation. The initial entries on a production sheet are normally made by a foodservice manager after the sales history is reviewed and evaluated. When completed, the form is given to the kitchen staff as a work plan for the day. It provides cooks with essential information for their work.

In both food production and beverage production, product quality and cost are established by means of the recipes selected for cooks and bartenders to use in preparing food and drinks. The recipes are normally selected with great care after comparison with a number of similar recipes. The recipe selected for the preparation of any food or beverage is that which management believes produces a desirable product at a satisfactory cost. It must be of suitable quality and acceptable to customers. The recipe finally selected for producing a given menu item is known as a *standard recipe*.

Standard Recipes.   The **standard recipe** is established as the correct recipe to use each time a given item is prepared. This is an important element in the production procedure. Standard recipes ensure that menu items are prepared the same way each time, using the same ingredients, proportions, and methods. This provides consistent quality and does so at a cost that can be planned.

Many menu items, both food and beverages, can be prepared several ways. Each variation results in a product of different quality, taste, and cost, yet each could be listed on a menu by the same name. For example, a seafood Newburg can be prepared using many expensive ingredients such as lobster, shrimp, and scallops, or it can be done cheaply using inexpensive fish and very little of the more expensive ingredients. In the first instance, the cost and quality are obviously higher than in the latter. It is important for managers to determine the standard recipe for each item produced. In establishments that use standard recipes, customers can reasonably expect food and drinks to be of the same quality and taste the same every time they come to the establishment.

Selling

The sixth important step in food and beverage operations is selling, or sales, as it is better known. One of the principal aims of selling food and beverage products is maximizing customer satisfaction. In such not-for-profit establishments as the Mountain Bank Staff Dining Room, this is likely to be the sole purpose of selling menu items. In the Steak Shack, Frog's Pub, and other profit-oriented enterprises, selling has a second goal: to maximize revenue.

The difference between the goals of the selling in these two types of establishments has to do with the difference between the noncommercial goals of one type of procedure and the commercial goals of the other. Therefore, two possible goals of selling are to maximize customer satisfaction and revenues.

To help sell food and beverage products, food and beverage operators often use:

- Sales-oriented menus
- Visual sales materials
- Personal selling

Sales-Oriented Menus

A menu is a list of the items offered for sale in a food or beverage enterprise. Food menus normally list these items by category and in the same sequence in which they are customarily ordered. A dinner menu for the Steak Shack lists appetizers first, followed by soups, salads, entrées, vegetables, desserts, and the usual nonalcoholic beverage accompaniments for meals: coffee, tea, and milk. By contrast, beverage menus normally list contents by category alone. Typical categories include aperitifs, cocktails, spirits, wines, beers and ales, cordials, and dessert wines.

A good menu, however, is much more than a simple list of food or beverage items for sale; it is a sales tool that influences customers' orders and the dollar amounts they spend. Menus are carefully designed to be attractive and are written in language intended to promote sales. Some menus give special emphasis to the items that yield the greatest profit per sale.

Developing successful menus is a complex process. Many food and beverage operators use professional consultants, whose many years of experience are of invaluable assistance in preparing this important sales aid. Important considerations in menu making include:

- Selecting which food/beverage items to include
- Determining the best location for each category/item
- Writing sales-oriented item descriptions
- Making numerous art and design decisions

Best Sellers

Eggplant Pirogue Louis
Half an eggplant, lightly breaded & fried, filled with shrimp, crawfish & crab and topped with creamy sauce Louis.
Served with dirty rice and corn macque choux. $16.95

Prejean's Seafood Platter
Fried frog leg, shrimp, oysters, catfish, alligator, stuffed shrimp & stuffed crab. Served with dirty rice, french fries,
and corn macque choux. $16.95

Grilled Seafood Platter
Grilled frog leg, shrimp, oysters, catfish, alligator, stuffed shrimp & stuffed crab. Served with dirty rice, baked
potato and corn macque choux. $16.95

Catfish Catahoula
Fresh filet, stuffed with Louisiana shrimp, crawfish & crab. Baked & served in a pool of crawfish & tasso cream
sauce. Served with dirty rice, and corn macque choux. $16.95

Pepper Jack Shrimp
Gulf shrimp, stuffed with Jack Cheese and Tasso, wrapped with applewood-smoked bacon and topped with crawfish cardinale, served with dirty rice and corn macque choux. $16.95

Red Snapper Pontchartrain
8 ounce filet of fresh Gulf red snapper, pan sauteed and topped with a crawfish & brown butter sauce. Served with
a baked potato, dirty rice and corn macque choux. $16.95

Yellow Fin Tuna Rockefeller
Mesquite grilled Tuna tenderloin, recommended medium rare and set in a pool of creamed spinach, etched with lobster sauce &
3 blackened shrimp. Served with a baked potato. $17.95

Catfish Oscar Prejean
Crispy fried Mississippi catfish topped with jumbo lump crab and mesquite-grilled asparagus, set over a black
butter wine sauce, served with Paris potatoes and drizzled with Béarnaise. $17.95

Crispy Cajun Duckling
1/2 deboned duck fried crispy and fanned around Cajun fried rice with a sweet and hot spicy drizzle. $17.95

Spec Sea Trout
Florentine seasoned filets of spec trout fried golden, set in a pool of creamed spinach, topped with a light shrimp butter lemon
sauce and served with Paris potatoes. $17.95

Veal Sweet Breads La Rochelle
Delicate, succulent veal sweet bread, pan sautéed golden, topped with wild mushroom cognac reduction, served with grilled
asparagus and Paris potatoes. $17.95

Stuffed Red Snapper
Stuffed with shrimp & crabmeat, seasonal & grilled. Served with a baked potato, dirty rice and corn macque choux. $15.95
Smothered with étouffée - add $2.00

Southern Fried Catfish
Fresh Mississippi catfish seasoned and fried golden. This is the talk of the south! $14.95

Bon appétit!

A good menu is much more than a simple list of food or beverage items. The menu shown in this photograph is sales oriented, and is designed to influence customers' orders and the dollar amounts they will spend.
(Menu courtesy of Prejean's Restaurant)

Customers tend to read menus from top to bottom and from left to right. Thus, a one-page menu lists appetizers at the top and desserts and beverages near the bottom. Two-page menus tend to list appetizers at the top of the first page, followed by soups, salads, entrées, and any other items in sequence, carrying over to the second page. Because the menu is a critical factor in food and beverage operations, it is useful to present and discuss seven principal considerations in menu development. These are:

1. Product suitability
2. Product variety
3. Ingredient availability
4. Staff time and capability

5. Equipment capacity

6. Product salability

7. Item profitability

Product Suitability. This consideration refers to the need to see that each item on a menu is suitable for the clientele, the time of day, and the season of the year. One assumes, of course, that a feasibility study and other preliminary work have established an acceptable concept for an intended market and that the question of product suitability has thus been addressed. Beyond that, it is necessary to refine the list of items offered according to time of day and season. Breakfast items, after all, are normally quite different from dinner items. Less obviously, such items as hearty beef stew and warm apple pie are likely to be more popular on winter rather than summer menus.

Product Variety. To obtain the broadest appeal, menus should include a sufficient variety of items to attract the greatest possible number of customers. The extent of the variety required to do this varies from establishment to establishment. Even a specialty restaurant usually offers variety within its specialty. It also offers items outside the specialty so that those who do not care for the specialty items have alternatives. Even units in the nationwide hamburger chains, which formerly sold only hamburgers, now have such other items as chicken, pizza, fish, and salad.

Ingredient Availability. All restaurants must limit their menu items to those that are available in the marketplace. It is true that most menu items are available year round but, during parts of the year, some fresh vegetables and fruits are not available, are available in limited quantities or at high prices, or are of inferior quality. For example, in New England, fresh corn is unavailable in January and, during that month, blueberries are available only at very high market prices because they must be imported from other countries. During some periods, the only tomatoes available at reasonable prices come from hot houses, and their quality is inferior to those available during the normal growing season.

Staff Time and Capability. Because of the high cost of skilled labor, many restaurants employ cooks whose training and skill are limited. In such instances, management is wise to avoid offering menu items requiring special skills to prepare. Management must be careful to choose items that the kitchen personnel can prepare within the limits of their skill. Similarly, if staff members have the requisite skills but cannot prepare a given item within the time available, it is best to leave it off the menu.

Equipment Capacity. Although establishing the food product list makes it possible to select the equipment for an establishment, the equipment selected serves to limit the items that can be included on a menu (see Chapter 5). In fact, available equipment often determines which of the specific items from the complete list are actually offered at any one time. For example, a kitchen with one deep-fat fryer is unable to produce french fries, deep-fried chicken, and deep-fried fish during the course of one meal. The reason is that fat transfers odors and flavors from one item to another, thus affecting the taste of all products cooked in it. Similarly, a kitchen having limited broiler space or oven space must be careful not to offer too many menu items at once that require the use of these pieces of equipment.

Product Salability. The location of items on a menu greatly influences their sales appeal. Studies show that consumers who have not come to restaurants with particular menu items in mind tend to select the items that first catch their eye. Because of this, foodservice operators often emphasize menu items in such a way as to capture the customer's attention quickly and to sell the featured item. One way is to print these items in larger or bolder type. Another is to enclose the item in a box on the menu and position it in a place that customers see first. On a one-page menu, this is typically in the upper center, where customers' eyes usually focus first. Other studies show that customers tend more to purchase items appearing at the top of a list than those near the bottom. Thus, managers commonly list their most profitable items first or nearly first on the list of entrées, and those that are least profitable near the bottom. Another useful sales technique employed by the operators of many chain restaurants is to display pictures of items on the menu. These may be either photographs or artists' renderings. Colorful and appealing, they tend to increase sales of the items pictured.

Most managers agree that as much time should be devoted to writing menu descriptions as might be spent writing an expensive advertisement to place in a newspaper or a magazine. Each item description should be thought of as an advertisement; if the description makes the item sound appetizing, it will increase sales. After all, it is more probable that a customer will order a "U.S. Prime filet mignon: eight ounces of America's finest beef, broiled to perfection the way you want it done, then topped with a giant mushroom cap and served sizzling on one of our hot steak platters" over a simple menu listing of "broiled steak." Menu descriptions should always be honest and accurate and include information about method of cooking, major ingredients, and presentation. Menus are designed to tempt the appetite, and a customer should be able to visualize an item by reading the menu description.

Item Profitability. In foodservice, one measure of profitability is the difference between the selling price of an item and its food cost—the cost of the ingredients in that item. The resulting figure can be called *item gross profit*. The item gross profits from all item sales in a given period go toward meeting other costs of operation for that period, including labor costs, rent, and insurance. If the sum of the item gross profits for a period is greater than these other costs, the operation earns a profit for that period. If the costs are greater, a loss results. In general, it is advisable to price menu offerings at levels that ensure suitable item gross profits. By doing so, managers ensure the profitability of each individual item. Then, provided the establishment sells a sufficient number of portions of each item, management may achieve its financial goal for the period. In commercial operations, the financial goal is usually profit; in not-for-profit operations, it is more likely to simply meet all expenses for the period. If it is not possible to price a menu item accordingly and still sell an acceptable quantity of it, the item should probably be removed from the menu.

There is no more important selling device in any foodservice operation than its menu. A good menu requires considerable time and effort to produce, but the investment is well worth it. Menu development is an interesting combination of art and science and, clearly, one of the keys to successful foodservice operation.

Visual Sales Materials

In addition to the menu, there are other visual means for increasing food and beverage sales. Small signs, colorful pictures, tent cards, and other printed items for tables or counters can make customers aware of menu items that they might not otherwise consider. So can posters on walls or windows. Visual displays of desserts on a cart, lobsters in tanks, or racks of wine bottles provide similar suggestions to customers.

Another useful approach is to use service techniques that draw the attention of customers to items being artistically prepared or served. In some fine restaurants, the preparation at tableside of such foods as Caesar salad, veal piccata, or cherries jubilee by thoroughly professional servers may provide visual suggestions to other diners. Similarly, sales can be influenced by skilled servers trained to carry attractive plates of food so that they are easily viewed by customers.

Personal Selling

Personal selling requires that servers be trained to do more than simply take orders for food and beverage products. Servers in a food or beverage enterprise are the sales force of the establishment and have the potential to influence the number of sales and the particular items sold. In the Steak Shack, servers who are properly trained can often sell appetizers, soups, wines, or desserts to customers who might otherwise order entrées alone. In addition, servers can influence customer choices by suggesting items that provide higher profit.

Servers adept at personal selling usually provide greater customer satisfaction. Satisfied customers who enjoy the food and beverages suggested by their servers typically leave larger tips—partially because they are satisfied and partially because their checks are higher. After all, tips are commonly calculated as percentages of customers' total checks.

Serving

The seventh important step in a food and beverage operation is serving, or service, as it is better known. The goal of service is to deliver portions of food or drink to customers in a manner consistent with the objectives of the establishment. For some restaurant operators, the primary objective of service is to perform it as quickly as possible. Servers appear at the table promptly to take orders,

> ## COMMIT FIRST TO BASICS ◀
> ## OF CUSTOMER SERVICE
>
> Conventional wisdom says that customer service is about quality. But I say that while quality is certainly a large part of service, it isn't the only part. No, customer service also requires a commitment to quantity if it is to be effective.
>
> "Quantity," in this sense, refers to having the right amount of staff on hand. It is difficult to take commitment to customer service seriously when customers can't place orders or have to wait in spite of obviously empty tables, or when we give our servers too many tables and try saying it's just an exception.
>
> The commitment to staffing is expensive, but it is vital if you are to provide excellent customer service. Training staff is vital. Attitude, caring, attentiveness, courtesy, and a sense of urgency all can make a significant improvement in your level of customer service.
>
> *Source:* Adapted from an article by John T. Self, PhD, in *Nation's Restaurant News,* 13 March 2000.

deliver the food to customers quickly after the order is placed, and clear the table and present the check as soon as customers are finished with their meals. At fine restaurants, service objectives are considerably more complicated. Servers are expected to know ingredients of menu items and how they are prepared. Service techniques are important, and professionalism is a key element.

Styles of Foodservice

Professional foodservice managers should be familiar with a number of styles of service. Each has specific characteristics and is more suited to achieve some goals than others. An operator must determine which one, if any, best achieves the goals of the food or beverage facility. One can choose to adopt one of the styles of service identified below or to develop a hybrid based on these:

- American service
- Russian service
- French service
- English service
- Cafeteria service
- Buffet service
- Take-out/delivery service
- Room service

American Service

American service is characterized by food portioned and plated in the kitchen and carried by servers to diners. Virtually everyone has experienced some form of American service. In too many cases, it has come to mean simply transporting plated food from the kitchen to the dining room and placing the plates in front of diners in any manner that suits the server. Sometimes the food is served from the right, sometimes from the left, and occasionally from across the table. In some establishments, plates of food are even passed from one diner to another until they reach the individuals who ordered them. Empty plates are removed as soon as a person has finished, even though others at the table are still eating.

In our view, none of these methods of delivering food should really be called American service. These are simply ways of transporting food expeditiously; it is similar to placing cartons of goods on a warehouse conveyor belt, and just about as inviting. True American service involves a great deal more than that.

In proper American service, plates of food are placed before diners from the left. To do this correctly, servers use their left hands. Beverages are served from the right with the right hand. Plates and glassware are removed from the right. When a course is removed (but not until everyone at the table has finished that course), the flatware for that course is also removed, even if it has not been used. At the conclusion of the main meal, prior to coffee and dessert, all plates, glassware, and salt- and pepper shakers are removed and the table is crumbed. Appropriate silver is served with dessert. American service has the advantage of being relatively simple, and comparatively little training is required for servers to achieve proficiency.

Russian Service

Russian service is characterized by food arranged on serving platters in the kitchen for maximum eye appeal, then carried to a serving stand near the table. The server uses the right hand to place empty warm plates in front of each diner from the diner's right. The platter of food is shown to diners for their visual delight, then transferred to their plates. To do this, the server balances the platter on the left hand and uses a fork and spoon with the right hand to serve the food from the diner's left. Beverages are served from the right. All dishes, glassware, and flatware are removed from the right.

Russian service, sometimes mistakenly called French service, is used in many of the finer restaurants of Europe. It is elegant; food arrives at the table beautifully arranged on silver serving platters and is presented to diners prior to being transferred to their plates. It also has the advantage of facilitating the delivery of food at the correct serving temperature—a common problem with American service. The serving platters are very warm, and the plates set in front of diners are also warm. Both contribute to maintaining the proper temperature for the food ordered. Russian service is particularly well suited for serving soups, which come to the table in hot tureens and are served into warm bowls.

A variation on Russian service is often used at large banquets. Servers wearing white gloves carry large silver serving trays, each of which is used for a single menu item—filet mignon, for example. A server proceeds around a table placing single portions of meat before diners on plates previously set in place. That server is followed by others who have food to accompany the meat—potatoes and

Restaurants adopt one or another of several specific styles of service, some of which require considerable staff training. Pictured is Russian service at The Manor Restaurant in West Orange, New Jersey, one of the finest restaurants in the New York metropolitan area. *(Photo courtesy of The Manor)*

vegetables, most commonly. In this fashion, large numbers of people can be served quickly with both elegance and grace.

French Service

The most expensive and most elegant service used in restaurants is **French service**. It is sometimes called gueridon service, named after the specially equipped cart or trolley on which food is transported from kitchen to dining room: a **gueridon**, equipped with a gas burner for tableside cooking.

French service usually requires a staff of four:

The chef de rang, who is in charge of the service staff. A chef de rang takes diners' orders, supervises the service, finishes the preparation of some foods on the gueridon at tableside, and attends to carving, slicing, or boning of meat, fish, or poultry.

The demi-chef de rang, who assists the chef de rang, takes drink orders, and serves food under the chef de rang's direction.

The commis de rang, a waiter in training who serves some items, clears the tables, and performs other duties as directed.

The commis de suite, who takes orders to the kitchen and brings food from the kitchen on the gueridon. He assists in clearing tables and performs other duties as needed.

In French service, the gueridon is wheeled to a position close to the diners' table and is used by the chef de rang to complete the cooking of food. He expertly carves or slices the meat, fish, or poultry, then places the food on plates. It is served from the diners' right. Beverages are also served from the right, and all plates and glassware are removed from the right. One can appreciate the great expense, skill, and time required to perform this kind of service. For that reason, it is used only in the most expensive restaurants.

Additionally, French service requires more square feet of floor space per seat than other types of dining room service. Aisles must be wider than normal to accommodate the gueridon, and tables must be placed farther apart to provide room for the chef de rang to finish the preparation of the food.

French service takes a considerable amount of time compared with other forms of service. For that reason, establishments that use it must charge high prices to compensate for the relatively fewer number of customers they can serve in the course of a meal period.

English Service

English service is seldom, if ever, used in restaurants. It is used only in those few private homes that employ a staff of servants, or in one of a select few catering establishments. English service is often thought of as "mine host" service because the main entrée—a roast of beef or lamb, or a turkey, for example—is placed in front of the host, who carves and plates it at the head of the table. A server then takes each plate and sets it in front of the diner from the diner's right. Beverages are also served from the right.

Vegetables, potatoes, and other foods are either put on plates from a side stand prior to service or passed from one diner to the next in bowls, family style. All dishes and glassware are removed from the right. As with American service, the table is cleared of flatware, glassware, and salt and pepper, and the table is crumbed prior to dessert.

Cafeteria Service

Cafeteria service is characterized by prepared foods displayed so that customers can view the array of offerings prior to making selections. Hot foods are in warmers and cold foods are packed in ice or stored in reach-through refrigerators. Many foods are already plated for the convenience of diners selecting those items. Diners typically have trays and proceed to the area where the kinds of foods they want are displayed. If a customer wants a sandwich, he goes to the area where prepared and wrapped sandwiches are displayed and takes the one he chooses. If he wants a hot entrée, he goes to that part of the display where they are kept and a server plates the item he selects. Each item is usually priced separately. After the customer finishes making selections, he proceeds to a cashier, who adds the prices of all items selected. The customer pays the cashier and takes the tray to a table.

Variations of this procedure are common. In some cafeterias, customers receive a bill at the cashier's station but do not pay until they exit the restaurant. In others, employees may carry customers' trays to tables.

The several types of cafeteria service are:

- Straight line
- By-pass line
- Shopping center

Straight Line.   As the name suggests, in straight-line service, customers follow one another along a long line of displayed foods. Each customer reaches the cashier in turn at the end of the display. This form of service is perhaps the easiest to set up but has the disadvantage of providing the slowest service. The speed of the line matches that of the slowest customer.

By-Pass Line.   To speed service, many cafeterias establish by-pass lines. These enable customers to skip a section of the cafeteria line and proceed to the section where the foods they wish to buy are displayed. For example, many cafeterias have separate sections for salads and hot items. Customers who want only salads go to that section of the display, select their salads, and get back in line at a point beyond the hot food section. Those seeking hot foods go to the hot food section, make their selections, then proceed to the cashier.

There are several variations on the by-pass line. One resembles the teeth in a saw, with foods displayed on counters set at angles to one another. Another variation has recessed sections in the line so that individuals who do not want any foods in the recessed section pass it by, proceeding to another part of the line.

Shopping Center.   The shopping center approach is to arrange foods by type at islands or freestanding stations. This approach eliminates the appearance of a single line. Customers take trays to the stations containing the foods they wish to buy, make their selections, then proceed to a cashier to pay. This approach is becoming increasingly popular, particularly in establishments where many customers arrive at one time.

Cafeteria service has several advantages over table service. Customers can obtain their food selections quickly and consume their meals in a short time. Large numbers of people can be served quickly in a cafeteria setting. Customers can select whatever they wish—anything from a full meal to a cup of coffee. There is no pressure to take a great amount of food, although the better cafeterias have attractive displays and, frequently, customers take more food than they intended because it looks so appealing. Because customers serve themselves, they typically do not have to tip servers.

Cafeterias also make it possible for people with limited incomes to eat out more frequently. Cafeterias are particularly popular in the southern part of the United States, where a large number of retired people are on limited budgets, and in schools, where large numbers of students must be served at one time.

Buffet Service

Buffet service differs from cafeteria service in several ways. Trays are not used. Customers take plates and proceed to select and place on their plates foods displayed on the buffet. Items on the buffet are not individually priced. There is one fixed price for the meal regardless of the items selected or the quantities of food taken by customers.

Restaurants often use buffet service, either for such functions as wedding receptions or for specific meals—breakfast or Sunday brunch, for example. Buffet service is sometimes used in restaurants as the primary means of serving food. This type of service has the advantage of minimizing the service staff required and offering faster service. Because diners do not have to study menus, wait for a server to take the order, and wait for food to be prepared and delivered, it can be much faster than table service. Patrons merely go to the buffet when they are ready, make their selections, and return to their tables to eat the food selected. One disadvantage is that management has less control over the amount of food consumed. Typically, customers help themselves and go back to the buffet as many times as they like.

Many hotels and restaurants schedule buffets frequently to use up excess food. After all, buffets typically do not have set menus, except for a few specific items, and this allows the chef considerable latitude to prepare many items—and even to use up leftovers.

Take-out and Delivery Services

Take-out and delivery services are becoming increasingly popular. These forms of service are characterized by food being consumed off premises. In many establishments, customers are given a choice of coming to the establishment to pick up food or of having it delivered to their homes or offices. Many restaurants offer take-out or delivery services, or both, in addition to their regular table service. Although there may be some extra cost to the establishment associated with packaging foods for consumption off premises, take-out and delivery services effectively increase the sales capacity of the establishment without necessitating an increase in its physical size.

Perhaps the most popular types of take-out and delivery establishments are associated with common ethnic foods—Chinese food and pizza. Many foodservice establishments featuring these foods do not even have seating for customers. Because of this, they find it possible to operate in relatively small quarters and thus keep their operating costs to a minimum.

Room Service

Although **room service** is most commonly associated with hotels, hospitals also provide room service for their patients. This type of service differs from others in one major way: Food is moved to and served in the room of the guest or patient.

Room service is not classified as take-out or delivery service. The food does not leave the premises, and it is served in a guest's or patient's room rather than in a traditional dining facility. This type of service is particularly labor intensive, typically requiring a greater number of servers per meal than other forms of service. In hotels offering room service on a 24-hour schedule, both kitchen and service staff must be on hand to prepare room service orders when the dining room is normally closed. Hotels charge higher prices for items on the room service menu than for equivalent items served in traditional dining rooms. Although they charge higher menu prices, however, hotels often lose money on room service, offering it merely as an accommodation to guests. The higher labor costs associated with room service operation commonly make it unprofitable.

Styles of Beverage Service

The term **beverage** was previously defined as those alcoholic and nonalcoholic drinks typically prepared by bartenders rather than the items listed as beverages on food menus—coffee, tea, and milk among them. As indicated in the previous chapter, three types of bars are used in beverage operations: front bars, service bars, and special-purpose bars. At front bars, drinks are normally served by a bartender to customers seated at the bar. If there are tables or booths for customers in the bar area, three common approaches to service are used. One is to employ a server and to have a service bar, which may be a small section of the front bar, commonly at the end of the bar. A second is to require the bartender to act as a server, going to the tables to take orders and serve drinks. The third is to require customers to place drink orders at the front bar, then carry their own drinks to the tables. By contrast, service bars, as the term implies, provide servers to take drink orders and serve drinks. At special-purpose bars, customers act as servers, placing drink orders with bartenders and carrying their drinks from the bar.

In planning beverage service, it is necessary to consider what purpose a bar or bars serve in the establishment. In some establishments, managers consciously decide to restrict beverage service to a service bar located in the kitchen. One possible reason is that they do not like the physical appearance of a front bar in the establishment. Another is to reduce the noise level in an establishment; bars are typically noisy. Still another is to discourage patronage by customers interested only in sitting at a front bar. In contrast, some restaurant operators elect to have both front bars and service bars. This arrangement makes it possible to provide beverage service in the dining room without placing unwarranted demands on the front bar and also to use the front bar as a holding area for customers waiting to be seated. Many of these establishments provide tables in the front bar area to facilitate its use as both cocktail lounge and waiting area for diners. Establishments with side rooms that can be used to accommodate groups for functions often use special-purpose bars to serve the guests attending these functions. Some, in fact, have a front bar, a service bar, and special-purpose bars, the number of which is limited only by the number of functions that can be accommodated at one time.

It is important to note that laws regarding service of alcoholic beverages vary from state to state. In several states, for example, drinks must be served to customers by servers, which makes it illegal for customers to carry drinks from front bars to their tables. In these states, it is clearly illegal to set up special-purpose bars where customers or guests can place drink orders and carry drinks elsewhere to consume.

Another consideration in planning beverage service is the type of service used for wines served to guests in a dining room. Essentially, wines are the fermented juices of fruits—grapes, principally—although exceptions exist. The three types of wines are still, sparkling, and fortified.

Still wines do not continue to ferment after the wine is bottled. Cabernet sauvignon and Chablis are two of the better-known still wines. Sparkling wines are those in which the fermentation process continues after bottling. This produces the carbon dioxide that gives sparkling wines their characteristic fizziness. Champagne is the best known of the sparkling wines. Fortified wines are still wines to which brandy is added, thus increasing the alcoholic content. Sherry is among the best-known fortified wines.

Proper planning for beverage service requires knowledge of the techniques for serving wines. These are described as follows:

Still Wines

Still wines may be sold by the glass or by the bottle. The finer the wine, the more likely it is to be sold by the bottle. When wine is sold by the bottle, the following is a commonly used serving procedure:

After taking the order, the server brings the wine to the table and presents it for approval to the guest who placed the order. The server holds the bottle in a manner that facilitates inspection of the label. When the bottle is approved, the server opens it, which normally entails removing the cork with a corkscrew. The server inspects the cork to be sure that it remained moist and that its odor indicates a good wine—one that has not spoiled. The server then presents the cork to the guest for inspection. Next, the server pours a small amount of the wine into the guest's glass to be examined for clarity, color, and aroma. If these are satisfactory, the guest sips the wine. If the taste is satisfactory, the guest approves the wine and the server pours for those at the table who will be drinking it. If the bottle is not empty, the server leaves it on or near the table for refilling glasses later in the meal.

Sparkling Wines

Sparkling wines are not normally sold by the glass because opened bottles lose their effervescent character. When they are sold by the bottle, service technique is essentially the same as that for still wines. The major exception is in the removal of the cork, which never entails the use of a corkscrew. The corks in bottles of sparkling wine are removed by hand, very carefully, to prevent the cork from being projected some distance by the pressure in the bottle. As the cork is removed, it produces the pop that is characteristic of sparkling wines.

Fortified Wines

As the name implies, **fortified wines** are wines to which small quantities of brandy or spirits have been added to increase the alcoholic content. They are not normally sold by the bottle. They are sold by the glass and poured at the bar by a bartender.

Serving Procedures at the Steak Shack, Mountain Bank, and Frog's Pub

As you learned in Chapter 5, it is important, in planning food or beverage operations, to determine in advance the type of foodservice and beverage service that will be offered so that equipment and space needs can be factored into the planning.

Because the goals of the Steak Shack, the Mountain Bank Staff Dining Room, and Frog's Pub are quite different from one another, the three facilities established different procedures for serving customers.

Service in the Steak Shack is typical of that found in many American restaurants. Once customers are seated, a server appears promptly to suggest drinks and distribute menus. The server takes dinner orders when drinks are served, offering suggestions for appetizers, soups, and dinner wines. Entrées are served using American-style service. After clearing the entrées and taking the dishes to the kitchen, the server presents dessert menus and suggests after-dinner drinks. Finally, the server places the checks on tables as soon as she serves the last items and asks the customers to pay the cashier as they leave.

In contrast, employees of the Mountain Bank pay as they enter, then serve themselves by selecting from the array of food displayed. Employees are expected to clear their own dishes by placing their trays on a conveyor belt located near the exit. One person is employed to clean the tables. Marecki Foods chose this method of serving to meet the bank's objective of quick, efficient service within the planned meal periods.

At Frog's Pub, the primary emphasis is on beverages rather than food. Customers choosing tables can either obtain their own drinks quickly from a bartender and carry the drinks to tables or wait to order from a server. Customers at tables order foods from servers; those seated at the bar order food and drinks from a bartender. At lunch, extra servers are on duty to provide very fast foodservice. The servers are responsible for clearing all tables.

In all three establishments, washing dishes, glasses, and flatware is an important adjunct to the serving procedure. Dirty dishes, glasses, and utensils are returned to the kitchen, separated into appropriate racks, then sent through a dishwashing machine. When clean, they are placed where needed to serve additional customers—clean dishes in the food preparation areas, glasses at the bar, and flatware in the dining room.

THE INTERDEPENDENCE OF FOOD AND BEVERAGE ELEMENTS

All steps of a food or beverage operation must work well together if the goals of the operation are to be achieved. When preparing and serving portions of any food or beverage product, purchasing and receiving must work together to provide the necessary materials. If they do not, unfortunate consequences may result.

For example, the kitchen might be unable to prepare the proper quantity of food or beverage products or to prepare products of the proper quality. This, in turn, could result in customer dissatisfaction, or loss of revenue, or both of these consequences. Similarly, spoilage and theft of materials in storage can lead to problems. In production, for example, this could result in an inability to produce the required products because of inadequate supply of the necessary ingredients. If production does not turn out the necessary menu items at appropriate levels of quality and cost, sales goals may not be met and profits suffer. If sales volume is lower than planned, materials purchased in quantities suitable for the planned higher levels of sales may spoil, leading to unwarranted costs. For the basic steps to work together in a coordinated way, effective management is necessary.

While management of the basic operational steps discussed in this chapter is clearly one requirement of successful operation, many other tasks are required as well. These include promoting sales in the establishment through advertising and other means, preparing and following budgets, and training members of staff to do their jobs correctly. These are addressed in Chapter 10.

SUMMARY

In this chapter, food and beverage operations are examined in detail. The steps of food and beverage operations—purchasing, receiving, storing, issuing, producing, selling, and serving—are identified, and the necessary procedures for preparing and serving portions of food and beverages are examined. Procedures for each of these food and beverage steps are illustrated in terms of the three case studies introduced in Chapter 5: the Steak Shack, the Mountain Bank Staff Dining Room, and Frog's Pub. Finally, the way in which these steps are interrelated is emphasized and offered as a basis for understanding the complexity of food and beverage operations.

KEY TERMS

American service	Gueridon	Russian service
Beverage	Mise en place	Sales history
Buffet service	Nonperishable	Sparkling wine
Cafeteria service	Perishable	Standard recipe
English service	Pilferage	Still wine
Fortified wine	Production sheet	Take-out/delivery service
French service	Room service	

DISCUSSION QUESTIONS

1. Define each of the following terms:
    a. Procedure
    b. Perishable
    c. Nonperishable
    d. Sales history
    e. Production sheet
    f. Standard recipe
    g. Beverage

2. Identify the seven basic steps that all foodservice operations have in common.

3. Identify the four critical issues that any purchasing procedure must address and describe the significance of each.

4. List the three primary goals of the receiving procedure and explain their importance.

5. Identify the four goals of storing procedures for foods and beverages.

6. Describe the two goals of issuing procedures for foods or beverages.

7. Name the four goals of procedures for producing portions of food and beverage products.

8. Compare the goals of procedures for selling portions of food or beverage products in profit-orientated operations with those in operations that are not profit oriented.

9. List and describe three common means used to help sell food and beverage products.

10. Identify the goal of service in food and beverage operations.

11. List the eight styles of service described in the chapter and identify the distinguishing features of each.

12. Name and describe the three types of cafeteria service identified in the chapter.

13. List and describe the three types of wines identified in the chapter.

14. Describe the interdependence of the seven steps common to all food and beverage operations.

MOMENTS OF TRUTH

1. Visit a food or beverage operation that you are completely unfamiliar with. Have the seven basic elements of foodservice operations clearly in mind when you do so. Identify the procedures used in the operation that deal with as many of the elements as you can. State the goals of these procedures, from your point of view. Are the procedures achieving these goals? Why or why not?

2. You have been appointed assistant manager of a new cafeteria scheduled to open in a busy ski area. You expect that there will be a rush of business over the luncheon hours and have been asked by the manager to suggest the best service arrangement for the cafeteria. Which of the types of cafeteria service described in this chapter would you suggest to accommodate the greatest number of people in the shortest time? State the reasons for your choice.

3. You are the assistant manager in a family restaurant. A variety of equipment in the kitchen is used to produce the menu, including two ovens, one deep-fat fryer, and two broilers. The manager wants to offer more fried foods and has suggested adding to the menu five more items requiring deep-fat frying. Five current items prepared in the ovens would be dropped from the menu. Given the type of restaurant and the kitchen equipment available, what do you think about making these menu changes?

INTERNET EXERCISES

1. Go to Culvers (www.culvers.com). How would you characterize the restaurant operation? Would it be considered a fast-food establishment? Would it be considered a table service operation?

2. Go to http://www.food-dudes.com. What kind of service to they provide? How many types of cuisine does the organization handle?

PART IV
Lodging
Perspectives

Dimensions of Lodging

▶ Learning Objectives

After reading and studying this chapter, you should be able to:

1. Define the term *lodging property* and identify several types of properties covered by the definition.

2. Discuss the size and scope of the commercial lodging industry in terms of numbers and types of properties of various sizes.

3. Identify the approximate number of persons employed in commercial lodging and the annual sales volume generated.

4. List and discuss five key elements in a lodging operation that differentiate one lodging establishment from another.

5. Describe the characteristics commonly associated with each of the following terms: inn, hotel, motel, lodge, tourist home/guest house, bed-and-breakfast, hostel, condominium, and hospital.

6. Identify the principal characteristics of each of the following specialized types of lodging establishments: motor inn, transient hotel, residential hotel, resort hotel, traditional resort, all-inclusive resort, resort condominium, resort motel, guest ranch, commercial hotel, convention hotel, all-suite hotel, extended-stay hotel, conference center, casino hotel, health spa, boardinghouse, lodging house, dormitory, and nursing home.

7. Identify ten lodging operations that are directly or indirectly associated with transportation.

8. List three methods used to classify commercial lodging establishments.

9. Name and describe the four rate plans that include food and the one rate plan that does not.

10. Identify the two national organizations that rate commercial lodging establishments and list five factors used by one organization in making their ratings judgments.

Previous chapters described the historical development of the lodging industry, but a recap here is useful. Clearly of ancient origins, the lodging industry dates to the beginnings of trade nearly 5000 years ago. Its development paralleled the development of trade, travel, and transportation throughout civilization.

But the modern age of travel and trade can really be traced to the Industrial Revolution in the mid-eighteenth century. The development of railroads and the increasing prosperity brought by industrial growth contributed greatly to making travel more common. The comparatively small coaching inns of the earlier era were replaced by larger properties—hotels—which were typically located near railroad stations.

Innkeeping in the United States developed in a similar manner. However, unlike his European counterpart, the American innkeeper was always a respected member of the community. Although many rural American inns of the seventeenth and eighteenth centuries were uncomfortable and somewhat primitive by modern standards, those located in cities and towns were generally better. Laws and societal values in many communities regulated eating and drinking in taverns.

In America, as in Europe, the Industrial Revolution was responsible for a period of unprecedented growth in the number of people traveling and in the distances they traveled. By the early 1800s, grand palaces of the public were being constructed in the developing cities. Unlike hotels in Europe, American hotels were community centers for local parties, dinners, receptions, and political events. They were often the most elegant and impressive structures in cities. By the third quarter of the nineteenth century, cities across the country were linked by a network of railroads, and many of them boasted of the quality of their luxury hotels.

In the twentieth century, mass production of automobiles and a developing system of paved roads began to make travel easy for Americans. Eventually, the federal government sponsored the development of a coast-to-coast network of roads, which facilitated the transportation of goods around the country. With the resulting economic growth, the United States grew strong in the world economy, and Americans became prosperous. Many American businessmen found it necessary to travel in the course of their work, and some Americans had sufficient disposable income to travel for pleasure. This increase in travel for business and for pleasure led to an expansion of the lodging industry that continued until the Great Depression of 1929, the most severe shock in history to the nation's economic system. During the depression, the number of people traveling declined dramatically, leading to numerous bankruptcies and general economic hardship for the lodging industry.

In the early 1940s, business and military travel associated with World War II brought renewed demand for lodging services, and the industry experienced a period of great prosperity. After the war, Kemmons Wilson charted new directions for the industry with his Holiday Inn concept. During the 1960s, new large hotels were constructed by growing organizations such as Hilton, Sheraton, and Marriott. Although the automobile had become America's favorite vehicle for travel, the airplane replaced the railroad as the primary means of public transportation for long-distance travel. By the time commercial jet aircraft were introduced in 1958, airports were becoming favorable locations for lodging establishments.

The lodging industry continues to evolve, seeking new customers by offering new and different kinds of lodging establishments each year. Increasing amounts of travel continue to create opportunities for imaginative lodging developers.

Lodging Properties Defined

Lodging properties may be defined as establishments that charge fees for providing furnished sleeping accommodations to persons who are temporarily away from home or who consider these accommodations their temporary or permanent homes. Many of these establishments also provide food, beverages, cleaning services, and a range of other services normally associated with travel and commonly sought by travelers.

The above definition includes transient and residential hotels, motels, and inns as well as resorts, college dormitories, hostels, boardinghouses, condominium rentals, and related establishments. It even includes the accommodations aspect of hospital operations. The definitions and distinctions between these lodging properties are discussed later in this chapter.

Many lodging properties provide accommodations to both travelers and non-travelers. The Plaza Hotel in New York City is an excellent example. Shortly after it opened, up to 80 percent of those staying in the Plaza considered it their permanent home. Many properties cater almost exclusively to permanent guests, providing them with many of the same services that other properties offer to travelers and temporary guests.

The Commercial Lodging Industry

The **commercial lodging** segment is a major part of the lodging industry. It is the group of profit-oriented lodging properties and includes hotels, motels, inns, and similar establishments that provide transient accommodations and operate as businesses.

At the end of the twentieth century, the American Hotel and Motel Association AH&MA reported that the commercial lodging industry in the United States consisted of approximately 51,000 properties ranging in size from small inns with fewer than 10 rooms to giant hotels with over 3000 rooms. About 65.3 percent of the properties have fewer than 75 rooms. These small establishments account for approximately 25.7 percent of the 3.9 million rooms available in commercial lodging establishments in the United States. At the other extreme, only about 2.9 percent of the properties have 300 or more rooms, but these establishments account for 20.4 percent of the total number of rooms available. The remaining 31.8 percent of the properties range in size from 75 to 300 rooms and account for 53.9 percent of the rooms available. It is apparent that typical commercial lodging establishments are quite small and tend to be owned by individuals, partnerships, or small corporations. Their owners manage many of these small properties.

In total, the commercial lodging industry in the United States generates about $93.1 billion in sales, representing more than 1 percent of the gross domestic product. The industry employs 1.16 million people, full time and part time.

In the same report, AH&MA reports that 30 percent of today's lodging customers are traveling for business purposes, 25 percent are attending conferences, and 24 percent are vacationing. Another 21 percent are traveling for personal reasons.

VARIATIONS IN LODGING ESTABLISHMENTS

Any keen observer of lodging establishments is certain to note significant differences among them. These differences are a result of decisions made by owners and managers about five key elements in a lodging operation:

1. Services

2. Accommodations

3. Decor

4. Rates

5. Target clientele

These elements are generally used to define and differentiate among lodging establishments. Each is discussed in the sections that follow.

Services

The range of services offered to guests varies considerably from one lodging establishment to another. At one end of the scale are guest houses that offer little more than a bed in a room and bathroom facilities down the hall. At the other end of the scale, luxury properties offer a complete range of services. These include 24-hour room service, valet and laundry service, secretarial service, hair stylists, health clubs, pay-per-view sporting events and films, in-room bars stocked with a selection of beverages, in-room safe boxes, concierge service, and extensive maid service that incorporates placing fresh towels twice a day, turn-down service at night, and wake up coffee or tea in bed in the morning. Most lodging operations fall between these two extremes and provide full or limited food and beverage service, color television, telephone, and private bath. Many motels limit their services to a private room with bath, telephone, and television. Ice and snacks may be available in a vending machine located in the hallway.

Accommodations

The types and sizes of accommodations also differ from one lodging property to another. The types of rooms vary from the bunk room with bath down the hall, provided by some inexpensive ski lodges, to the elegant suite with bedroom, private bath, living room, dining area, and small kitchen, offered by many luxury hotels. The most common type of accommodation is a bedroom with private bath. The room contains one or two beds, each of which is designed for one or two people. Other furnishings depend on the nature of the property and the size of the room.

Room sizes for the typical bedroom and private bath vary considerably. In the United States and Europe, the smallest may have 150 square feet or less. These properties are designed to operate profitably at rates even lower than those of the lower-priced motels. The minimum number of square feet for lower-priced motels ranges from about 175 to 250 square feet. Mid-priced hotels generally allocate 250 to 325 square feet, and fine hotels may allow 450 square feet or more.

Many properties provide accommodations other than the typical unit of bedroom and bath. The size of these also varies, both with the type of property and the nature of the accommodation. It is possible, for example, for a unit with two bedrooms, two baths, and a living room in an inexpensive hotel to contain fewer square feet than a unit with one bedroom, one bath, and living room in a luxury property.

Decor

The decor of a lodging establishment refers to the style and layout of its interior furnishings. The decor determines its atmosphere. The higher the quality of the furnishings, the higher the degree of luxury the establishment is perceived to offer. At one end of the spectrum are lodging establishments with simple, plain decor and inexpensive furnishings. At the other are the elegant luxury accommodations, where highly skilled interior decorators are hired to plan the decor and to select each item with great care, from fine period furniture to the simplest ashtray.

Lodging establishments belonging to a given chain are often noted for a particular style and type of decor. They may feature the same color scheme and style of furnishings in all their properties, so that customers in these properties may not be able to distinguish between the rooms in the chain's Boston unit and those in its Los Angeles unit.

Rates

The fees charged by lodging operations for the sleeping accommodations they provide are commonly known as **rates**. In hotels and motels, one speaks of room rates, for example, as the fees charged guests who rent rooms. Rates for rooms vary by locale and by property, as do the charges for additional services a lodging facility may offer.

Generally, room rates are much higher in major cities than in suburban locations because of the higher costs of construction and operation. Some cities are well known for their high room rates. New York, for example, has traditionally been the most expensive city in the United States for hotel rooms; and London, Paris, and Tokyo are expensive cities for lodging accommodations in their respective countries.

Target Clientele

Throughout history, people opening lodging establishments have always attempted to attract particular types of customers. Four thousand years ago, lodging operators had caravans of traders in mind and set up their establishments on trade routes. In seventeenth-century England, lodging operators had stagecoach passengers in mind when opening their coaching houses. In the early part of the twentieth century, American companies opening hotels in major cities near railroad terminals targeted railroad travelers. Today, we see lodging operators building properties along highways and at airports for much the same reason. Targeting particular groups of potential customers has become a sophisticated endeavor. Properties are designed and built to accommodate travelers at a number of price levels, from low to high. Others are designed and built to accommodate the needs of a particular clientele—ski lodges, for example.

Taken together, the five elements just discussed—services, accommodations, decor, rates, and target clientele—determine the nature of the lodging property. Major metropolitan centers tend to have numerous lodging properties of widely varying types. These range from limited service to full service, from simply furnished small rooms to luxuriously furnished large rooms, from the simplest to the most ornate decor, from cheap to extraordinarily expensive, and from those targeting bus travelers to those catering to corporate executives and show-business personalities. Smaller communities also have variety, of course, but tend to have less of it.

CHARACTERISTIC TYPES OF LODGING ESTABLISHMENTS

As in the case of food establishments, the number of possible variables in lodging establishments makes attempts at classifying them difficult. Most classification systems are either too simple—urban, suburban, and rural, for example—or too complex to be useful. It can take dozens of categories to account for the variations from one operation to another in services, accommodations, decor, rates, and target clientele.

Nevertheless, owners and operators of lodging establishments do select terms to identify their establishments to the public. A lodging property that is about to open in a community may be described in local newspapers by such terms as motel, lodge, or inn. Because the public tends to associate different characteristics with each terms use and to select or avoid lodging establishments on the basis of their interpretation of the terms, it is useful to list and discuss the most common. One must remember that this list does not constitute any real system of lodging classification because the terms do not represent mutually exclusive categories. Two or more of these terms can describe many lodging operations.

Most people have heard the names used to identify lodging establishments—hotel, motel, inn, motor inn, resort hotel or motel, condominium, lodging house, residential hotel, tourist home, guest house, bed-and-breakfast, guest ranch, hostel, hospital, and dormitory among them. Each of these conveys an impression. No one believes that a hotel is the same as a dormitory, for example. These are clearly very different from one another, and someone opening a hotel would be making a terrible mistake to identify it as a dormitory; the facility would not appeal to those seeking traditional hotel accommodations. The following is an examination of the characteristics commonly associated with lodging establishments identified by each of these terms.

Inn

The term **inn** was brought to the United States from England in the early seventeenth century. Originally, the word referred to an establishment that provided rooms, food, and entertainment to both travelers and residents of the local community. Over the years, the term came to be used to describe three types of hospitality enterprises:

1. A small, typically rural lodging establishment that may or may not serve food

2. A larger property—or one that was once known as a hotel—that wishes to convey an image of smallness and caring for their customers

3. A restaurant or bar without sleeping accommodations

Hotel

The term **hotel** was used traditionally to identify a lodging facility of two stories or more that provided sleeping accommodations and other services for its guests. In the United States, hotels are often built in or near the business centers of cities, towns, and villages and regarded as centers of social and political activity.

Hotels have commonly offered housekeeping services and luggage-carrying assistance as well as food, beverages, telephone, and other services. The extent of these services varies from property to property. Some hotels provide the full range: restaurants; bars; cocktail lounges; room service; hair stylists; exercise salons; computer, photocopy, and fax facilities; laundry; dry cleaners; gift shops; check cashing and other financial services; newsstands; travel agencies; drugstores; and others. Other hotels provide nothing beyond the basics: sleeping accommodations and housekeeping services.

Motel

The term **motel** traditionally described a special variety of lodging establishment that catered to travelers with automobiles and provided self-service parking on premises. The original motels, built in the 1950s, were single-story properties providing basic sleeping accommodations to overnight travelers. They were inexpensive, offering free parking and housekeeping service but little else. Staff was kept to a minimum to keep costs down. Motels offered none of the services normally associated with hotels—room service, bellmen, restaurants, and the like. Motels were located on the outskirts of cities and towns and catered to those who did not want the expense and formality of a hotel. Later, many had adequate land to expand and to add swimming pools, which helped differentiate motels from hotels and attract new customers.

Over the years, many motels evolved into properties that so resemble hotels that it is impossible to identify differences. Many are multistoried, provide full services, and are located in the centers of cities. They continue to characterize themselves as motels for a variety of reasons, the most common being to suggest that they are not expensive.

Lodge

The term **lodge** was traditionally used to describe a lodging establishment associated with a particular type of outdoor activity, such as ski lodge or hunting lodge. The typical lodge was a small establishment, usually in a rural setting, that provided food and housekeeping services to guests who came to be with others engaging in the same activity. Over the years, many lodging proprietors have used the term *lodge* instead of *inn* or *motel*, presumably because it sounds better. A substantial number of properties are known as **motor lodges**. For all practical purposes, this is merely another name for a motel.

The San Francisco Fairmont Hotel contains 591 rooms and is perched atop Nob Hill, providing a panoramic view of the city.
(Photo courtesy of Fairmont Hotels and Resorts)

SAN FRANCISCO'S FAIRMONT HOTEL ◄

The historic Fairmont Hotel in San Francisco has been renovated. Its interior has been changed to look exactly the way it was when Julia Morgan, the celebrated architect of a century ago, designed it following the 1906 earthquake.

The centerpieces of the $72 million project are the Lobby, Laurel Court, the Venetian Room, and the guest rooms. The lobby has been restored with its original white and gray marble floors. The Laurel Court has been recreated as a beautiful bar and restaurant. The Venetian Room has been renovated to emphasize its original Beaux-Arts design, and each of the guest rooms and suites renovated with classic elegance complete with marble bathrooms.

This world-renowned hotel contains 591 rooms and offers three restaurants and four lounges. It is perched high atop Nob Hill and provides a panoramic view of the city and San Francisco Bay.

Source: Adapted from the Web page of the San Francisco Fairmont Hotel, 1 June 2000.

Tourist Home/Guest House

Tourist home and **guest house** are terms that were developed to describe private homes in which the owners rented spare bedrooms to transient guests. Few remain in operation today. In these establishments, no meals were served to guests. They were not normally run as business ventures in the usual sense; they were more often sources of extra income for those whose primary income was derived from some other source. Bed-and-breakfast establishments, described below, have largely replaced tourist homes and guest houses.

Bed-and-Breakfast

Bed-and-breakfast establishments have long been popular in Europe. In recent years, they have been gaining popularity in the United States. They are close relatives of the tourist homes and guest houses that they have tended to replace. Owners of private homes rent rooms to overnight guests. They differ in one important respect: A full breakfast is included in the rate. Some travelers prefer to stay in bed-and-breakfast establishments because they are smaller, more intimate, and frequently less expensive than hotels and motels and because the proprietors of many offer a degree of hospitality seldom equaled in commercial properties. The bed-and-breakfast industry has developed a wide variety of establishments ranging from simple accommodations with bath down the hall to elegant accommodations costing as much as luxury hotels.

Hostel

Hostels are very inexpensive lodging establishments that typically cater to young, transient customers. They provide little or no service, and many offer little privacy. The typical hostel provides a bed for the night and offers no frills. Some provide a community kitchen in which guests may prepare their own meals. Everyone staying in a hostel is expected to participate in keeping it clean. The number of nights an individual is allowed to stay is usually limited.

Condominium

Condominium is a term that identifies a furnished housing unit with kitchen area, living room area, sleeping area, and bath. Condominiums are distinguished from other types of lodging establishments by their ownership characteristics. Each condominium unit in a complex is independently owned, but the management of the complex provides maintenance for the outside and the common inside areas of the facility for a monthly fee. In addition, the grounds and other facilities are usually owned jointly by all of the condominium owners.

Many owners rent their units to permanent or transient guests. Those located in resort areas are called resort condominiums. Major corporations—Marriott, for example—have built large condominium developments in recent years, sold the individual units, and retained the management of the condominium development.

Condominiums take many forms. They can be free standing single units, individual units among several built as a single structure, sections or segments of hotel facilities, or units in a residential apartment facility.

Hospital

In many respects, a **hospital** can be regarded as a specialized lodging facility. Hospitals provide sleeping accommodations and many of the same services provided by hotels—including housekeeping, room service, telephone, television, and a pharmacy—and often such additional services as hair stylists, gift shops, and lending libraries. A principal difference is in the clientele: Hospital guests are known as patients, and are normally resident in the facility for medical reasons.

Motor Inn

Motor inn is a term that came into use as an alternative to the term *motel* and originally described a motel property whose proprietors wished to convey the concept of free parking and the traditions of an inn—a kind of modern inn. During the 1950s and 1960s, when older hotels were no longer in favor because of competition from motels, many hotel properties that had parking facilities on premises or nearby changed their names from hotel to motor inn in order to compete with motels.

Transient Hotel

A **transient hotel** is designed to cater to temporary guests—people who have need of accommodations for a comparatively few nights. The guests may be businesspeople, groups of sightseers, government employees, members of the armed forces, students, or any persons seeking temporary lodging.

Residential Hotel

In contrast to transient hotels, some hotels have traditionally provided accommodations for long-term guests—individuals who consider the hotel their temporary or permanent home. Establishments that offer traditional hotel services—food and beverages, laundry and dry cleaning, telephone, and the like, for those who choose to live there permanently—are known as **residential hotels**. A considerable number of people stay for long periods in these hotels, some for many years. They enjoy and are willing to pay for daily maid service and other services that their hotel may offer.

Some transient hotels emulate residential hotels. They set aside a number of rooms or suites for permanent guests. Many well-known hotels have permanent guests, and some have whole sections of the hotel building set aside for resident guests. Perhaps the most famous of these is New York's Waldorf-Astoria. One section of the hotel, known as the Towers, caters to permanent guests. The Towers has a separate entrance for its guests and provides a full range of the finest hotel services for them.

Resort Hotel

The term **resort hotel** is commonly used to describe lodging establishments that feature recreational activities for their guests. These activities may be strictly for enjoyment, for health purposes, or both. Swimming, tennis, and golf are among the most common activities, although many others are possible. Some resorts have all the necessary facilities for these activities on premises. Others have limited recreational facilities on premises and provide their guests access to other facilities nearby.

Resorts have traditionally catered to customers who stayed for several days or several weeks. In past generations, many resorts had guests who stayed for an entire season. While this is no longer common because transportation to the resorts has improved so dramatically, some resorts still have guests who stay for extended periods.

As discussed in previous chapters, the United States had a tradition of developing resort accommodations in rural areas. Today, many resort properties that were once in rural settings find themselves situated in suburban or urban areas. Older resort hotels in Miami Beach, Phoenix, and San Diego, for example, are actually located in or near city centers; metropolitan centers have grown up around the resort properties. Many resort hotels that once catered exclusively to vacationers now cater to people attending meetings and conventions. Thus, it is becoming increasingly difficult to distinguish between resort hotels and other kinds of hotels.

Various types of resort properties exist. These include:

- Traditional resort
- All-inclusive resort
- Resort condominium
- Resort motel
- Guest ranch

Traditional Resort

A **traditional resort** has recreational facilities on its premises. The rates include some or all of the meals. Entertainment is usually free, but liquor, gratuities, and many recreational activities are extra. Rates are charged on a daily or weekly basis.

All-Inclusive Resort

An **all-inclusive resort** includes everything in one weekly rate—airfare to the resort, sleeping accommodations, all meals, liquor, gratuities, entertainment, and activities. Many all-inclusive resorts charge extra for some recreational activities—golf, for example. The best known of these is Club Med.

Resort Condominium

A **resort condominium** is located in a resort area or on a resort property. Some resort hotels have resort condominiums on their properties. The condominium

Marriott's Ihilani Resort on the Hawaiian Island of Oahu is an excellent example of a modern resort hotel. It offers almost all of the amenities a traveler would want. *(Photo courtesy of McNeil Wilson Communications)*

JW MARRIOTT RESORT IHILANI ←

JW Marriott Ihilani is located on the first of four magnificent lagoon sites on the Hawaiian Island of Oahu. This five-diamond, 387-room, 36-suite resort and spa is a brief 25-minute drive from Honolulu International Airport. It is situated on a 640–acre resort and offers almost all of the amenities one would want. It features a 35,000-square-foot state-of-the-art spa and fitness center that includes a health club, sauna, and whirlpool.

An 18-hole championship golf course is available to guests. The resort has four restaurants offering Mediterranean, Continental, and Japanese cuisine. Guest rooms average 680 square feet in size and feature lanais, deep-soaking European tubs, and custom-designed furniture.

For meetings and conferences, the Ihilani has nine meeting rooms with 16,000 square feet of meeting space.

Source: Adapted from the Web site of JW Marriott Resort Ihilani, 1 June 2000.

---

units differ from regular guest rooms; they have kitchen and living room facilities as well as the traditional sleeping accommodations. Customers may prepare their own meals in the condominium kitchen or dine in one of the restaurants operated by the resort. In addition, guests have access to all the recreational facilities of the resort. Many older resort hotels that were lacking business have been transformed into resort condominiums. This is done when hotel rooms are sold to investors and the funds are used to develop the property.

Resort Motel

Resort motels are simply motels located in resort areas. Many of them serve food and most have limited recreation facilities.

Guest Ranch

Guest ranches are resort properties that emphasize horseback riding and related activities. They are typically small properties of fewer than 100 rooms. They provide housekeeping services, food, and other seasonal recreational facilities such as swimming pool, tennis court, and hunting. Guest ranches are typically very informal and attempt to suggest the rough and ready, informal democratic spirit that we have come to believe was characteristic of the old West.

Commercial Hotel

Commercial hotel is a term that refers to a specialized property that caters to business travelers, such as executives and sales personnel, in need of transient lodgings. The term dates from the early twentieth century, when a number of newly constructed hotels—Statler's Buffalo property was among them—were designed to accommodate single business travelers, providing the types of rooms and services that would appeal to these anticipated guests.

In recent years, as the mix of travelers has changed, the term has come to have less significance. Today, probably no hotels accommodate only commercial guests; most cater to a more varied clientele.

Convention Hotel

A **convention hotel** refers to a specialized type of hotel that focuses on conventions as the primary source of business. A **convention** is a gathering of people sharing some business, professional, social, or avocational interest; it is characterized by meetings, exhibits, and related activities regarding that interest.

Some convention hotels were specifically designed to accommodate convention business; others set their sights on conventions only after newer properties—motels, for example—began to capture their regular transient business.

The principal difference between convention hotels and other hotels is in specific facilities available for convention groups. These include at least one large ballroom or similar meeting room and a reasonable number of other meeting rooms nearby. Convention hotels also have the capacity to prepare and serve food and beverages to large numbers of people in their ballrooms and meeting rooms as well as in several public dining rooms and bars. Convention hotels normally do not limit their business to convention groups; they routinely accommodate individual reservations to maintain the highest possible level of occupancy.

All-Suite Hotel

Suite is a term commonly used in lodging operations to describe an accommodation consisting of two or more rooms, one of which is a living room—sometimes called a parlor—plus one or more than one bedroom and bathroom. Many have some type of kitchen facility. Some properties offer suites that have several bedrooms and baths. Sometimes the term is used to describe a one-room accommodation with a living room area and a bedroom area rather than separate rooms.

All-suite hotels do not offer the traditional bedroom and bath accommodations provided by most hotels. They offer only suites. These include facilities for limited cooking. Most all-suite hotels lack traditional restaurants or bars, and most have no public meeting rooms. Free breakfast buffets in the lobby, food vending machines in designated areas, and in-room bars are some of the possibilities. The elimination of restaurants, bars, and public meeting rooms reduces construction and operating costs and enables the owners of all-suite properties to offer guests larger accommodations at competitive rates.

However, in recent years, many all-suite hotels have been constructed that provide food service and beverage service as well as meeting space. Marriott All-Suite hotels are a good example. They are first-class and luxury properties offering all the services of traditional hotels.

Extended-Stay Hotel

A relatively new term, **extended-stay hotel**, is used to describe a property that caters to people who intend to stay longer than typical transient guests and who

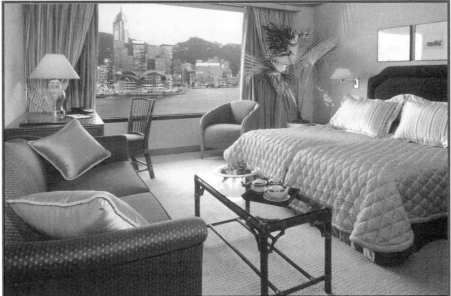

All-Suite Hotels contain only suites. Shown in this picture is the Chateau Whistler Resort Suite Hotel.

(Photos courtesy of Fairmont Hotels and Resorts; and of Regent International Hotels)

seek accommodations other than the traditional hotel accommodation of bedroom and bath. The typical extended-stay hotel provides a homelike environment and attempts to minimize the resemblance to other commercial lodging facilities. Accommodations in extended-stay hotels tend to resemble those in a fine garden apartment complex—a suite consisting of a kitchen, living room, bedroom, and bath, plus recreational facilities for swimming and other forms of exercise. Suites in extended-stay hotels commonly feature exterior entrances with parking by the door.

Conference Center

Conference centers are facilities designed especially to accommodate meeting and conference business. They are typically located in suburban and rural areas and provide a setting that is comparatively free of distractions. Thus, conference centers tend to be conducive to concentration and learning and are selected by groups that require such settings for productive work.

Conference centers typically accept group business only. Given high operating costs in some regions of the country, however, some conference centers accept individual reservations during slack periods in order to maximize revenues.

Casino Hotel

Casino hotel is a term used to refer to transient hotels that house gaming casinos. These hotels allocate major amounts of space to casino gaming, which includes games of chance using cards or dice—blackjack, roulette, and poker, for example—and slot machines. Casino gaming, illegal in most parts of the United States, is a major attraction for many Americans, and casino hotels are popular with vacationers and conventioneers. Casino hotel operators also provide lavish entertainment—nationally known artists and professionally staged shows—as added attractions.

Until recently, casino hotels in the United States were limited to the state of Nevada and the city of Atlantic City, New Jersey. Now, however, casino gaming has spread far and wide to several jurisdictions in Colorado, Mississippi, and South Dakota; to riverboats licensed by the states of Illinois, Iowa, Louisiana, and Mississippi, among others; and to growing numbers of Indian reservations in Arizona, California, and Connecticut as well as other states. Newspapers across the country carry stories daily about consideration being given by state legislatures to the legalization of gambling within their borders. With an increase in the number of legal sites for casino gaming, it is likely that casino hotels will be constructed in other states in the near future.

Because casino gaming is very profitable, casino hotels can be desirable properties to own. In successful casino hotels, the major share of revenues and profits comes from gambling operations rather than from lodging or from food and beverage. Casino hotels commonly offer free lodging, food, and drinks to guests who routinely wager large amounts of money—the so-called high rollers. Obviously, this is done to attract their continuing patronage.

Health Spa

Health spa is a general term given to lodging establishments that focus on providing some form of beneficial, health-related services. Many specialize—some in weight reduction, other in cosmetic therapy or drug or alcohol rehabilitation, among many others. The newest form of health spa provides a holistic approach, emphasizing relaxation and well-being, as well as providing healthy food and exercise. For obvious reasons, health spas typically do not accept guests other than those seeking the health-related services in which they specialize. Some even restrict admission to people referred by physicians.

Boardinghouse

A **boardinghouse** is a residential facility that provides lodging and meals for guests who normally consider the facility their home, whether temporarily or permanently. Boardinghouse services are typically restricted to limited housekeeping and meals; these characteristics tend to distinguish boardinghouses from residential

At Casino Hotels, gaming is the primary attraction. Shown here is the world's largest hotel, the MGM Grand Hotel, which also is a casino hotel in Las Vegas, Nevada.
(Photo courtesy of MGM Grand)

HOLISTIC SPAS: THE TREND OF THE FUTURE

A holistic approach emphasizing relaxation and well-being is a trend at many of the estimated 1600 spas around the United States.

Holistic spas treat the whole person—mind, body, and spirit. The prototype calls for a diet of organically grown food; generous exercise with emphasis on strength training, hiking, and yoga; and exotic pampering treatments using techniques and natural ingredients from the Far East or ancient India.

The philosophy is that physical fitness is not enough. One needs to nourish and refresh the mind to be completely relaxed. In a recent survey, 61 percent of those surveyed said that they went to spas to relax.

Prevailing treatments include shiatsu massages, reiki and Thai yoga massages, and watsu, a type of massage performed while you float in a pool. Another treatment purported to make the skin look younger uses herbal medicine made of fresh herbs harvested in Hawaii and India during the monsoon season.

Industry observers expect the growth to continue, particularly as the health-conscious baby-boom generation ages. However, such spas are labor intensive and costly to run.

Source: Adapted from an article in the *New York Times*, 5 March 2000.

hotels. Such establishments are inexpensive, compared to residential and other hotels. In the past, boardinghouses were much more common than they are today.

A boardinghouse may be as small as a private home, or it may be a larger facility resembling a small hotel. Rates are commonly charged on a weekly or monthly basis. Housekeeping services in a boardinghouse are typically limited; daily maid service is unlikely, and cleaning services may be restricted to once a week. In some facilities, guests clean their own rooms and exchange soiled for clean linens in an office on the main floor. Foodservice is typically two or three meals a day served at specified hours or during specified time periods.

Lodging House

Essentially, a **lodging house** is a boardinghouse that does not provide meals. The weekly or monthly rate is for the lodging alone. Lodging houses, also known as rooming houses, were more common in the past. Some lodging houses offer kitchen privileges—free use of a common kitchen, provided the user leaves the facility clean after each use.

Dormitory

Typically, the term **dormitory** is used to refer to a lodging facility affiliated with some educational or other institution that provides sleeping accommodations for those in residence. The institutional affiliation differentiates a dormitory from a lodging house.

The characteristics of dormitories are extremely varied. Some have daily maid service; others have none. Some have private rooms with private baths; others have rooms shared by several people and bathrooms shared by all residents of one floor. Some have kitchen facilities; others prohibit cooking. In most, foodservice is available, often in a separate facility. If food is available, it may be provided only to those who pay extra for it. In some instances, the fee charged includes both room and board, in which case residents usually eat in a foodservice facility.

Nursing Home

A **nursing home** is a residential facility that provides lodging and food service for people requiring nursing or related care. People residing in nursing homes tend to be temporarily or permanently infirm, physically or mentally.

Some nursing homes cater to the elderly; others assist patients recovering from major surgery. Some specialize in the care of chronically ill children; others, called **hospices**, deal with the terminally ill. The services provided vary from one establishment to another and are closely linked to the needs of the residents.

Other Lodging Operations

One collection of lodging operations, loosely related by their direct or indirect association with transportation—water, rail, air, or highway—comprises cruise ships; freighters that accept passengers; riverboats; overnight passenger ferries; specialized commercial sailboats, or windjammers; railroad sleeping cars; planes with sleeping accommodations for passengers on long international flights; specially fitted charter buses used for golf tours and similar purposes; completely furnished and outfitted motor homes, campers, trailers, boats, or barges rented on a daily or weekly basis; and lodging facilities known as boatels, located at marina developments. None of these constitutes a major segment of the lodging industry.

CLASSIFICATION OF LODGING ESTABLISHMENTS

It is important to recognize that many of the transient lodging establishments listed and discussed above cater to more than one type of business. In major cities, many accommodate residential guests at weekly or monthly rates because they are not able to maintain a sufficiently high level of occupancy with transient trade alone. In contrast, some transient hotels do not accommodate residential guests but maintain high levels of occupancy by attracting several types of transients—business travelers, vacationers, and those attending conventions, for example. It is common to find a single hotel property that has characteristics of two or more of the many types that one encounters in this dynamic industry. This has been a major difficulty to those attempting to develop useful classification systems for lodging properties.

Many attempts have been made to classify lodging properties. Some have classified them by location; other have attempted various other approaches, including size:

Under 75 rooms

From 75 to 149 rooms

From 150 to 299 rooms

Over 300 rooms

One classification system of interest is that used by the Bureau of the Census, a branch of the United States Department of Commerce. Because this is the system used by the government to report industry statistics, others have adopted it. This system separates properties into four categories:

1. Full-service

2. Economy

3. All-suite

4. Resort

The following language for three of the categories accompanies the table that lists statistical data about these properties.

An economy property is defined as one that offers clean, standard-sized, fully furnished modern rooms at usually $10.00 to $20.00 per night below the rate of typical full-service motor hotels. Their customers do not need food facilities, banquet rooms or meeting facilities, indoor recreation areas, or entertainment.

An all-suite hotel doesn't have rooms, only suites. A suite differs from a hotel room by several characteristics. Generally, there is a separate bedroom, and guest amenities often include "extras," such as a wet bar or microwave and in some cases a full kitchen.

A resort hotel is a lodging facility providing an environment conducive to leisure and recreation and an ambiance of isolation/destination while providing a full range of leisure-oriented amenities.

This system is intended to be used for reporting data obtained from surveys—rates, averages, and similar variations—of characteristic types of lodging properties. Some lodging properties are not included—bed-and-breakfast establishments, hostels, and others.

Travel Research Firms

Travel research firms categorize lodging operations according to the purposes of their research. For example, Smith Travel Research categorizes firms according to prices charged by lodging establishments in 162 market areas in the United States. Within each market area, lodging properties are classified as:

- **Luxury:** Top 15 percent in the market area
- **Upscale:** Next 15 percent in the market area
- **Midprice:** Middle 30 percent in the market area

- Economy: Next 20 percent in the market area
- Budget: Bottom 20 percent in the market area

The purpose of this classification is to record changes in price levels over time. With this classification, it is possible for hotels of the same quality to be classified in more than one category if they are located in different market areas.

In light of the foregoing discussion, a person attempting to learn about the lodging industry will find no single classification system for lodging properties that is both useful and includes all properties. Some are useful but leave out large numbers of properties; others include all properties but are not particularly useful; still others are useful, but only for specific purposes.

MEAL SERVICE IN LODGING ESTABLISHMENTS

As indicated above, many lodging establishments provide foodservice to guests. Some offer limited food service—vending machines, for example—while others provide room service and several public restaurants. Some hotels quote room rates that include foodservice, some do not include foodservice with the room rates, and others offer their guests a choice. The following are the accepted terms used to describe the various arrangements:

American Plan (A.P.)

American Plan rates include three meals daily: breakfast, luncheon, and dinner. In some properties, these meals may include a full choice of the menu; in others, choices may be restricted to certain menu items, with other, more expensive items available at an extra charge. In some, it can mean unlimited quantities of unlimited selections—anything the guest chooses from the menu. More commonly, it means a choice of one item in each menu category: one appetizer, one entrée, and so on. In years past, many resort hotels offered American Plan rates. In recent years, the popularity of the American Plan has decreased markedly, except in those hotels in which alternative foodservice is not readily available.

Modified American Plan (M.A.P.)

Modified American Plan rates include breakfast and dinner. Luncheon is available, but for an extra charge. This plan has become popular at resort operations. It was devised to satisfy guests who objected to being charged for luncheons they did not eat, either because they were sightseeing and found it inconvenient to return to the dining room for lunch or because they finished breakfast late in the morning and were not hungry at lunchtime. Other guests were weight conscious and did not want to consume three hearty meals in any one day. Resort owners responded by offering rates that did not include lunch.

Breakfast Plan (B.P.)

The **Breakfast Plan**, sometimes called the **Bermuda Plan**, includes a full breakfast with the quoted room rate. Although the term was not used, this plan has been common and popular in many parts of Europe for years. However, rising operating costs have made it necessary for many European hotels to impose a charge for the full breakfast. In the United States, the Breakfast Plan survives as the standard in bed-and-breakfast establishments and a few other properties. Many all-suite hotels serve full breakfast; some impose the extra charge, just as in the European hotels.

Continental Breakfast Plan

The **Continental Breakfast Plan** includes a light breakfast with the room rate. The composition of the light breakfast varies from one establishment to another. In some, it is limited to juice, Danish pastry—also known as sweet rolls in some parts of the country—and a choice of coffee or tea. In others, it can include an array of juices, fruits, pastries, croissants, rolls, bagels, and doughnuts, and a choice of regular and decaffeinated coffee and tea.

A large number of hotels and motels offer this plan to attract business travelers and other guests accustomed to having light breakfasts—possibly just juice and coffee—in the morning. When some operators in an area do this, others have to do it also in order to remain competitive; continental breakfasts are very popular.

European Plan (E.P.)

Rates quoted under the **European Plan** include no meals. Ironically, the European Plan has become the standard in most American transient hotels; this was not the case through most of the nineteenth century.

Although many hotel guests choose to dine in the restaurants operated by hotels, many do not. Hotel-keepers have found that guests staying for two nights commonly have one evening meal in the hotel restaurant and the other away from the hotel, depending on their sense of security about the area in which the property is located.

The weather often plays an important part in helping a guest decide whether or not to patronize the hotel's restaurant. If the weather is poor—rain or snow, for example—guests often stay in; if the weather conditions are good, they are more likely to go out.

Some resort hotels with long traditions of offering American Plan rates alone are now giving their guests a choice of American Plan, Modified American Plan, Breakfast Plan, or European Plan. Guests who select any of the latter three can still order other meals in the hotel restaurant. However, they must order from the menu and pay separately for meals not included in the plan they have selected. Prices for these meals are normally somewhat higher than for the same meals taken as part of a meal plan.

RATINGS OF LODGING ESTABLISHMENTS

Another method of differentiating among lodging properties is to consult a guide that rates hotels and motels. Because quality of lodging operations varies from one establishment to another, in some parts of the world, including some European countries, lodging establishments are rated for quality by government agencies. In the United States, no government agency performs this service for the traveler. However, two well-known private organizations judge the quality of lodging operations and publish rating guides based on these judgments. The first of these is the Mobil Corporation which, in collaboration with the trade division of the publisher Prentice Hall, publishes the *Mobil Travel Guide*. The second is the American Automobile Association (AAA), which publishes the *Tour Book*. The *Mobil Travel Guide* is sold through many commercial outlets and may be purchased by anyone; the *Tour Book* is distributed to members of the American Automobile Association only.

Neither of these guides lists all lodging establishments. The publisher of each reserves the right to determine which to include. All properties listed are recommended by the rating organization. Unlisted properties are merely unlisted; they may be superior, equal, or inferior to a listed property. In every region of the country, one can identify numerous small properties with fine accommodations, food, and service that are not listed in the rating guides.

The following is the rating scale used in the *Mobil Travel Guide*:

    ★   Good; better than average

    ★★   Very good

    ★★★   Excellent

    ★★★★   Outstanding—worth a special trip

    ★★★★★   One of the best in the country

The principal areas evaluated by Mobil include quality of physical structure, furnishings, maintenance, housekeeping, and overall service. Each property listed in the Mobil guide must undergo an annual review, so no rating is ever final.

The five-star rating is awarded by Mobil to a comparatively small number of properties, which represent the finest in the United States. This top rating is extremely difficult to achieve; cities with many excellent hotels may have only one with the five-star rating, and most cities have no five-star properties.

The tour books published by AAA use a rating scale based on diamonds rather than stars. Rated establishments can be awarded as many as five diamonds. The five possible ratings signify the following:

      ◇   Properties meet all listing requirements. They are clean and well maintained.

    ◇◇   Properties maintain the attributes offered at the ◇ level while showing noticeable enhancements in decor and/or quality of furnishings.

◇◇◇   Properties show a marked upgrade in physical attributes, services, and comfort. Additional amenities, services, and facilities may be offered.

◇◇◇◇   Properties reflect an exceptional degree of hospitality, service, and attention to detail while offering upscale facilities and a variety of amenities.

◇◇◇◇◇   Property facilities and operations exemplify an impeccable standard of excellence while exceeding guest expectations in hospitality and service. These renowned properties are both striking and luxurious, offering many extra amenities.

As with the five-star Mobil rating, the top rating is very difficult to earn, although AAA typically awards more top ratings than Mobil. Interestingly, the guides often differ in their judgments about specific properties. As with Mobil, no AAA rating is ever final. Field representatives annually reinspect all properties listed in the *Tour Book*.

SUMMARY

In this chapter, the term *lodging property* is defined. Data are provided to illustrate the size and scope of the commercial lodging industry, including number of properties, number of employees, and total annual sales. Five key elements of lodging operations that differentiate one lodging establishment from another are listed and discussed. Numerous characteristic types of lodging establishments are described—commercial and noncommercial, generic and specialized. Three classification methods for commercial lodging properties are identified, including one used by the Bureau of the Census and another used by a travel research firm. Various rate plans are identified; several include food with room rates, and one does not. Finally, the two national organizations that rate the quality of lodging operations for consumers are identified and their rating scales illustrated.

KEY TERMS

All-inclusive resort
All-suite hotel
American plan
Bed-and-breakfast establishment
Bermuda plan
Boardinghouse
Breakfast plan
Casino hotel
Commercial hotel

Commercial lodging industry
Condominium
Conference center
Continental breakfast plan
Convention
Convention hotel
Dormitory
European plan
Extended-stay hotel

Guest house

Guest ranch

Health spa

Hospice

Hospital

Hostel

Hotel

Inn

Lodge

Lodging house

Lodging property

Modified American plan

Motel

Motor inn

Motor lodge

Nursing home

Rate

Residential hotel

Resort condominium

Resort hotel

Resort motel

Suite

Tourist home

Traditional resort

Transient hotel

DISCUSSION QUESTIONS

1. Define the term *lodging property* and list ten types of lodging properties that fit the definition.

2. Briefly describe the size and scope of the commercial lodging industry. Include data in your response to indicate number of properties, number of persons employed, and approximate gross sales annually.

3. What percentage of guests in commercial lodging establishments are:
   a. Traveling for business purposes?
   b. Attending conferences?
   c. Vacationing?
   d. Traveling for personal reasons?

4. List five key elements in a lodging operation that differentiate one lodging establishment from another.

5. Describe the impressions lodging property owners tend to convey to the public by selecting the following terms to identify properties.
   a. Inn
   b. Hotel
   c. Motel
   d. Lodge
   e. Guest house
   f. Bed-and-breakfast
   g. Hostel
   h. Condominium
   i. Hospital

6. Identify the principal characteristics of each of the following:
   a. Motor inn
   b. Transient motel
   c. Residential hotel

    d.   Resort hotel
    e.   Traditional resort
    f.   All-inclusive resort
    g.   Resort condominium
    h.   Resort motel
    i.   Guest ranch
    j.   Commercial hotel
    k.   Convention hotel
    l.   All-suite hotel
    m.   Extended-stay hotel
    n.   Conference center
    o.   Casino hotel
    p.   Health spa
    q.   Boardinghouse
    r.   Lodging house
    s.   Dormitory
    t.   Nursing home

7. The chapter discusses a number of lodging operations thought of more commonly as modes of transportation. Cruise ships are one example. Name ten others.

8. Identify the specific categories used to classify commercial lodging properties by:
    a.   Number of rooms
    b.   Types of properties

9. Identify the inadequacies inherent in each of the classification systems identified in question 8.

10. Define each of the following:
    a.   European plan
    b.   American plan
    c.   Modified American plan
    d.   Breakfast plan
    e.   Continental breakfast plan

11. Given a 200-room commercial hotel in the business center of one of America's ten largest cities, which of the five plans identified in question 10 would be appropriate to offer transient guests? Why?

12. Given a 350-room beachfront resort property located in Miami Beach, Florida, which of the five plans identified in question 10 would be appropriate to offer transient guests? Why?

13. Identify the two national organizations that publish widely recognized ratings of commercial lodging establishments.

MOMENTS OF TRUTH

1. A particular lodging operation in your community has the following characteristics. It is two stories tall, has 300 guest rooms with bath, a restaurant, a swimming pool, an exercise room, meeting space for 400 persons, a large parking lot, and a location on the outskirts of town. Which of the characteristic types of lodging establishments presented in this chapter could be applied to the operation?

2. In the center of a medium-size city near you is the Hotel Astor. It is rated by the American Automobile Association with 4 diamonds. The hotel has 350 rooms, two fine-dining restaurants, a coffee shop, extensive convention facilities, a ballroom, a separate banquet kitchen, and various shops such as barber shop, beauty salon, newsstand, and travel agency. Which of the characteristic types of lodging establishments presented in this chapter could be applied to the operation?

3. The resort hotel at which you work as assistant food and beverage manager has traditionally had only American plan rates. In recent years, several fine restaurants have opened in the immediate area and, last year, the resort added a golf course to the recreational activities available to guests. Many of your guests have dined at these new restaurants or played golf. However, they have still had to pay for the meals they missed at the resort when they went to one of the restaurants or missed lunch during the time they were on the golf course. What would you recommend to management?

INTERNET EXERCISES

1. Go to http://www.bedandbreakfast.nu. Find two historic bed-and-breakfast establishments near your home. Write a paragraph describing each.

2. Go to http://las-vegas.hotelaccommodations.com. List all of the five-star and four-star hotels located in this city.

Lodging Facilities

▶ Learning Objectives

After reading and studying this chapter, you should be able to:

1. Define the term *product line* as used in lodging operations.

2. List and discuss the three elements in the service product line of a lodging enterprise.

3. Identify the activities common to all front-office operations that must be taken into account in their layout and design.

4. Identify by name and size eight types of beds commonly used in lodging properties.

5. Provide the size range in square feet for each of the following: sub-budget motel room, budget motel room, commercial hotel/motel room, luxury motel room, hotel junior suite, hotel standard suite, suite in an all-suite property.

6. Compare and contrast the size and furnishings of a budget motel room with those of a luxury hotel.

7. List and discuss ten engineering systems found in lodging facilities.

8. Distinguish between centralized and decentralized air-conditioning systems.

9. List four possible sources of water for lodging operations having no access to a public water supply.

10. Identify the principal components of a fire safety system.

11. List and describe four common types of energy control systems.

INTRODUCTION

The previous chapter was devoted to examining the size and scope of the lodging industry. We identified characteristic types of lodging establishments and discussed three classification systems. In addition, we identified several rate plans that include food and described two rating systems used for lodging properties. With that as background, we now turn to the subject of lodging facilities.

As indicated in the previous chapter, lodging establishments may offer any number of services to guests. Some lodging operations offer very few—simple guest houses offering rooms with a bath down the hall, for example. Others present a full range—elegant luxury hotels, for example, offering 24-hour service, laundry and valet services, concierge service, 24-hour maid service, secretarial services, hair stylists, and many other services.

Lodging establishments also vary greatly in size and in target clientele. The simple guest house may have only one or two rooms to rent, whereas the large, complex hotel may have over 3000 rooms. Similarly, some lodging operations cater to business travelers, while others specialize in convention business. Still others offer permanent accommodations to people who consider the hotel their home, while some provide temporary accommodations to people on vacation. It should be apparent from the broad range of possibilities for service, size, and target clientele that lodging facilities differ considerably from one another. For example, compare a resort property to a city hotel. The resort is likely to provide recreational activities—golf, tennis, and swimming, for example—requiring specialized facilities and equipment. In contrast, the city hotel might offer specialized services to appeal to high-level business executives—in-room computers and fax machines on each floor, possibly—requiring specialized facilities and equipment. While there are obvious differences between these two—and between any two different types of lodging properties—there are also important similarities. All lodging properties provide accommodations for guests, and all provide some services—although the services may be very limited in some properties. The points of similarity are of far greater importance than the many apparent differences.

As we proceed with a discussion of lodging facilities, it is important to remember that the typical lodging facility is likely to be far more complex than the typical food and beverage facility. In addition, the amount of money and the length of time required to plan and open a food and beverage operation is far less than that needed to plan and open a lodging operation. These realities clearly help explain why comparatively few people develop their own commercial lodging operations. Most are planned and developed by corporations.

Prior to a discussion of lodging facilities, it is necessary to address three key topics fundamental to the layout and design of a lodging facility:

1. Concept

2. Legal requirements (local, state, and national)

3. Product line

These are the same key topics that were addressed before the discussion of foodservice facilities in Chapter 5. However, while the topic areas are the same, the details differ considerably.

Concept

Every lodging operation is, or should be, established around a **concept**—an imaginative, unifying idea of the operation that serves as the focus for the people, energies, and other resources required to convert it into reality. This concept originates with the person or company that owns the property or with some other person or firm that develops it under commission.

We begin with one fairly obvious element in this concept: the type of lodging operation to be developed. The person or company responsible for the concept must have in mind an idea of the type or types of lodging operations that might be developed—motel, convention hotel, resort hotel, or some other. A new property is likely to resemble one of the characteristic types discussed in Chapter 7, or some combination of these. The people responsible for the concept must clearly understand the nature of the hospitality service products to be offered in the lodging operation they are developing.

Legal Requirements

The laws and regulations—federal, state, and local—that an owner faces in operating a lodging facility must be taken into account. Building codes, fire codes, health codes, zoning regulations, environmental regulations, and licensing requirements are among the most common. Each of these provides specific direction about what an owner can and cannot legally do in planning, designing, and operating a lodging enterprise.

Laws and regulations vary considerably from one state to another and even from city to city within a given state. For example, zoning regulations in some areas limit the height of new buildings constructed in the area. Plans for a facility that failed to comply with these regulations do not receive approval from local authorities. Consequently, it is impossible to obtain a building permit until architects and engineers redesign the building to comply with the regulations. This is just one example of the many possibilities.

Before proceeding with plans for lodging facilities, owners lacking full knowledge of the laws and regulations that apply in given locales must have advice from lawyers, architects, engineers, professional lodging consultants, and others with necessary expertise. Failure to take these details into account can lead to costly errors.

Product Line

As indicated in Chapter 5, the term **product line** is used in marketing to refer to a group of products with similar characteristics. We borrow the term from marketing once again and use it to mean the service products that a lodging operator intends to offer, based on the concept developed for the establishment. For example, if one intends to operate a budget motel, the service products are significantly different than those offered by a developer who intends to operate a luxury resort. Each lodging establishment offers its own distinct product line.

The hospitality service product line offered by lodging operations has three elements:

1. Accommodations

2. Services

3. Ambience

Accommodations

Lodging establishments offer **accommodations**—the most basic element in their service product line. The accommodations are the specific rooms, suites, or other sleeping facilities to which guests are assigned. All of these, taken together, are defined as the accommodations element in the service product line.

Many lodging operations offer specialized accommodations. Some, for example, feature only one type: suites. Any number of specialized accommodations can be found in the lodging industry today. Two of the characteristic types of properties discussed in the previous chapter offer good examples: budget motels and residential hotels. In contrast, other lodging operations offer a broader range of accommodations, which may consist of both rooms and suites of varying sizes and types.

Services

The second basic element in the hospitality service product line offered in a lodging enterprise consists of the **services** available to guests. Again, the type of establishment strongly influences the nature and extent of the services offered. Housekeeping service is the basic service offered by transient hotels, motels, and similar lodging enterprises. Other common services include security, parking, valet and laundry, and bell services. Additional services include information about goods and services available in the geographic area and assistance in making reservations in affiliated properties in distant locations for future nights.

Many operators offer such additional services as entertainment and recreational facilities—common hospitality-related services that are central to specific types of lodging operations and expected by guests in these operations. Again, the characteristic type of lodging facility established strongly influences the nature and extent of additional services offered. Thus, entertainment and recreational facilities are central to resort hotel operations.

Ambience

The third basic element in the hospitality service product line in lodging operations is **ambience**. This element comprises a vast array of tangible and intangible features that give a lodging operation its special and distinctive character. These include theme, lighting, uniforms, furnishings, cleanliness, wall coverings, fixtures, fabrics, feelings, decorations, and any other related features that customers see or sense and that help to form their impressions of the establishment. For example, when an arriving guest walks through the front door of a lodging facility, she gets an impression of the property from the lighting, furniture, carpet, wall coverings, works of art, and other coordinated elements that make up the lobby area. Similarly, after being assigned to a particular accommodation, the guest gets additional impressions from the elevator, the elevator foyer on her floor, the general appearance of the corridor leading from the elevator foyer to her room, and so on. To a guest, the sum of these and many other tangible and intangible features constitutes the property's ambience or atmosphere.

The discussion above does not take into account that many lodging operations also offer food and beverage products. Some say that the lodging enterprise that offers food and beverages is offering a second product line. Others disagree, arguing that if food and beverages are offered because of guests' expectations, the food and beverage operations should be thought of as additional services, akin to the recreational facilities discussed above. One can agree or disagree with either point of view.

In summary, the service product line offered by a lodging establishment consists of three basic elements—accommodations, services, and ambience. Some operators choose to add other possible product lines by including boutiques, jewelry shops, gift shops, souvenir stands, and other retail shops on premises. Although these are interesting and often desirable additions to a property, they are not essential to the basic lodging enterprise. Therefore, we limit the following discus-

Ambience is the third element in the hospitality service line. Shown in this picture is the lobby of a Bass Hotel. One gets a distinct impression of the hotel when entering the lobby.
(Photo courtesy of Bass Hotels and Resorts, Inc.)

sion to the facilities required for the basic service product line of a lodging enterprise. Discussion of food and beverage facilities appeared in Chapter 5.

In the present chapter, we assume that the owner has attended to the necessary preliminaries and decided to proceed. At this point, we turn our attention to the specifics of lodging facilities.

The student reading about lodging facilities may find it useful to refer to particular lodging properties. Therefore, in order to describe the various facilities and to point out differences from one property to another, we refer to the three distinctly different types of lodging properties described in case studies 8.1, 8.2, and 8.3. The first of these is a limited-service budget motel catering to economy-minded transient travelers. The second is a full-service, upscale resort hotel that provides accommodations and services primarily for vacationers. The third is a luxury hotel located in a major cosmopolitan city; it offers the services usually associated with this type of property.

CASE STUDY 8.1

The Value Lodge

The Value Lodge is a 50-room property located in a small midwestern town adjacent to an exit on Interstate 80. It is owned and operated by a couple named Goodson—Roger and Janet. It is part of a chain called Value Lodges, Inc. Roger and Janet were both executives for major companies for many years. Eventually, they both began to dislike their work and felt they were wasting their lives, so they decided to open their own business. They had always been fascinated by innkeeping and felt they had the talent for it. Because they had no formal training in the business, they decided to work with a chain to receive the necessary training and to reduce risk. The Goodsons sold their home and as many other assets as they could. Because they had limited funds, they could afford only a relatively small property. They answered an advertisement in the *Wall Street Journal* placed by Value Lodge, Inc. After thorough investigation, they agreed to an arrangement giving them a motel in an excellent location, a Value Lodge sign, a large mortgage, and an obligation to pay various fees to the chain.

The Value Lodge is a fairly simple operation. Roger and Janet, as owner-managers, live in quarters connected to the office where guests check in and out. The 50 units are modern and comfortable—pleasantly decorated, yet simply furnished. Each unit contains two queen-size beds, a private bath, a color television, two lounge chairs, a dresser with mirror, and a telephone, among other items. The motel does not have a restaurant, a meeting room, a swimming pool, or recreational facilities. It does have a small dining area with tables, chairs, and vending machines from which guests may obtain ice, beverages, sandwiches, and snacks. The motel caters almost exclusively to travelers—motorists from Interstate 80 looking for clean, comfortable overnight accommodations. Most guests check in by late afternoon and are back on the road again early the following morning.

A fast-food restaurant is located across the road and a family restaurant nearby. Value Lodge Inc. has a central system that takes reservations for all units in the chain. Roger and Janet receive about 25 percent of their business from the reservation system.

Roger and Janet take turns in the office during the day. Roger is usually there during morning hours, doing the bookkeeping and ordering supplies, while Janet supervises the housekeeping. During the afternoon, Roger sees to the maintenance of the grounds and rooms while Janet takes her turn in the office. In the evening, neither stays in the office, but the door to their quarters is open so they can attend to any needs of the guests and to check-ins.

CASE STUDY 8.2

The Mountain Inn

The Mountain Inn is a 400-room, three-star resort hotel located in a major ski area in Colorado. It is owned by the Mountain Inn Corporation, a company formed by the group of investors that built the property. They hired the Preferred Management Company to run it. The agreement calls for Preferred to receive 3 percent of gross room sales and 10 percent of profits.

The Mountain Inn is a seasonal resort hotel. During the winter months—early November to mid-April—the hotel is a ski resort, catering to vacationers who come for winter sports. During the summer months—from 1 June to 30 September—it is a summer resort catering to individuals and groups that come for summer recreational activities and meetings. The hotel closes during the months of October and May.

The hotel has two dining rooms, one for individual guests and families and the other for groups. It has one large meeting room that can be divided into several smaller ones, plus a coffee shop, a pharmacy, a hair stylist, several boutiques, indoor pool and exercise room, two racquetball courts, and four outdoor tennis courts.

The hotel is located at the base of a ski slope within 1 mile of an excellent golf course. Mountain Inn guests receive special consideration at the golf course. There is an excellent stable nearby for horseback riding. Additional services offered guests include room service from 7:00 A.M. to midnight as well as tennis and swimming instruction.

CASE STUDY 8.3

The Kensington Hotel

The Kensington is a 350-room four-star luxury hotel located in the center of a major eastern city. It is a classic hotel, owned and operated by a nationally known chain, but the name of the chain is not used on any signs, linen, literature, or other matter that would be noticed by guests. Management decided that the image of the property would not be improved by being linked with this particular chain.

All guest rooms are furnished with reproductions of antique furniture. A doorman is on duty at the front door at all times to welcome guests, take charge of their cars, and obtain transportation for them. The lobby is finished in marble and brass. Elevators are operated by an attendant, even though they can be operated automatically.

The Kensington has a large ballroom with its own kitchen and a separate entrance from the street for guests attending weddings and similar formal functions. The hotel does not have the number of meeting rooms that one would find in a convention hotel. It does have three small meeting rooms that can be used by guests—usually business executives—for small meetings.

Other services offered to guests include 24-hour room service, concierge, secretarial service, hair stylist, gourmet dining in the Empire Room, cocktails in the Kensington Lounge, pharmacy, indoor pool and exercise room, and extensive housekeeping service that includes the service of early morning tea or coffee, fresh towels twice each day, and turn-down service in the evening.

Seventy-five of the Kensington's 350 rooms are presently occupied by permanent guests. The remaining rooms are available for transient business. Guests are served by a staff of 500 employees, half of whom have worked in the hotel for over ten years. The Kensington emphasizes personal service. All staff members—desk clerks, elevator operators, bellmen, doormen, among others—make special efforts to know guests by name. Staff members are expected to be friendly and courteous at all times and to attend quickly to all reasonable requests made by guests.

These three lodging properties, although they appear, at first glance, very different from one another, really have much in common. In fact, they have the same basic facilities that any property must have to be called a lodging facility:

- An area for activities and records associated with guest reservations, check-in, and check-out: the front office
- The accommodations themselves: guest rooms
- An area for attending to housekeeping activities, including the storage of linens, uniforms, and cleaning supplies and equipment: housekeeping

In the following discussion, we focus our attention on the layout and design of these three basic elements found in all lodging facilities.

FACILITY LAYOUT AND DESIGN

Because the front office, guest rooms, and housekeeping area are so different from one another, the layout and design of each are addressed separately.

Front-Office Layout and Design

Front office layout and design tends to be determined by the size of the lodging establishment. In smaller properties, for example, front-office areas tend to be small, simple, and compact because there is no need to have more than one clerk on duty for each shift. By contrast, larger properties tend to have large front offices because they need more people on duty simultaneously to deal with the large number of guests.

A lodging enterprise needs a facility to handle **front-office** activities, which are traditionally separated into several categories of work known by the terms *reservations*, *check-in*, *information*, and *checkout*. These four terms require simple explanations.

Reservations refers to a process for holding accommodations for future guests. **Check-in** is the process by which people become guests. *Information* refers to providing guests with advice and directions relating to shopping, dining, entertainment, local transportation, and a range of other possibilities. **Checkout** is the process by which guests terminate their status as guests.

The layout and design of the front office of a hotel tends to be determined by the size of the hotel. Shown here is the Four Seasons George V in Paris. *(Photo courtesy of the Four Seasons Hotels, © 2000 Four Seasons Limited. Used by permission.)*

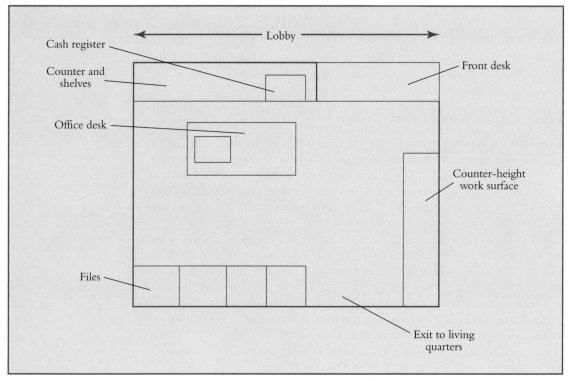

FIGURE 8.1
Layout of the front office
of the Value Lodge

Further discussion of front-office work is deferred to the following chapter on lodging operations.

The facilities in which front-office activities take place vary greatly from one property to another. In a 50-room motel, such as the Value Lodge described above, the front-office facility is normally quite small. Figure 8.1 is a layout of the front office of the Value Lodge.

In a larger property, such as the 350-room Kensington Hotel, the amount of work and the number of employees make a larger front-office facility necessary. Figure 8.2 is a layout of the front office of the Kensington.

Note that both facilities are designed to deal with the same activities—those associated with reservations, check-in, information, and checkout. As previously noted, these activities are common to all front-office operations, and every lodging establishment has some form of front office designed to accommodate the level of activity anticipated in each of those four areas. To that extent, the front offices of the Value Lodge and the Kensington hotel are the same. There are obvious differences, however, between the two front offices, and these differences reveal much about the differences between the two properties. The principal differences are in size, space allocation, and equipment.

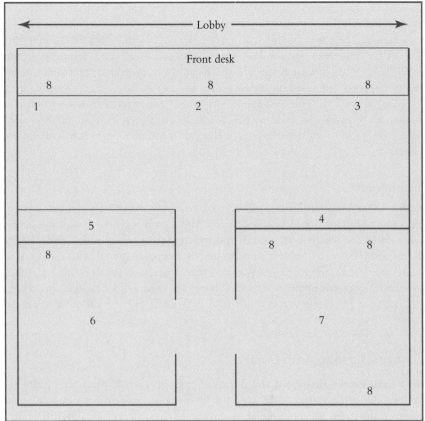

FIGURE 8.2
Layout of the front office of the Kensington

Key:
1. Cashier's area
2. Information area
3. Room clerk's area
4. Wall of mailboxes for keys, mail, and messages
5. Counter-height bank of safe deposit boxes
6. Office for front office manager
7. Reservations office
8. Locations of computer terminals and printers

Size

In the Value Lodge, the volume of front-office work can be handled by one individual in a single small area. The entire front-office area, including the front desk, is only 54 square feet—6 feet by 9 feet. In contrast, the front-office area at the Kensington is quite large, encompassing 540 square feet: 18 feet by 30 feet.

Space Allocation

The Value Lodge has one single area in which all front-office activities take place. In the Kensington, however, some front-office activities occur in sufficient volume to require that some employees dedicate their time to specialized work. For example, the volume of financial activities—updating guest accounts, processing guest checkouts, cashing checks, and making change—make it desirable to assign specialists (cashiers) to the work and to allocate one specific area for their work. The same is true for the specialist employees assigned to deal with reservations, information, and check-ins. In the Kensington, the front-office staff is large enough to require supervision by a front-office manager, for whom a separate office area is allocated.

It should be noted that not all large lodging operations follow the Kensington's system for functional division of front-office work. In many lodging operations with front offices similar to that of the Kensington, the three front-office computer terminals are used interchangeably for check-in and checkout. During evening hours, when the number of arrivals in commercial hotels tends to be higher, all terminals are used to handle check-ins. By contrast, in the morning, when the number of departures is higher, all terminals can be used to process checkouts.

Equipment

In the Value Lodge, the front office requires simple manual equipment: a room rack that also holds room keys and guests' bills, a cash register, a telephone, and a file cabinet for reservations records and for storage of forms and records. In the Kensington, the front office has an integrated computer system with terminals in each area. For example, the reservations office has a workstation with a terminal at which all reservations are input. A telephone and a fax machine are within reach, as are file cabinets and other storage facilities for reservations and related forms.

Rooms Layout and Design

To a great extent, the layout and design of guest accommodations in a given establishment are determined by its type. In economy motels, for example, guest rooms tend to be smaller, simpler, and more compact than in traditional luxury hotels.

Because beds, the principal furnishings in most guest accommodations, vary considerably in size, it is useful to know the dimensions of beds most commonly found in lodging establishments (see Table 8.1).

TABLE 8.1

Dimensions of Beds in Lodging Establishments

Bed Type	Width
Rollaway/cot	30 inches
Studio	33 inches
Single	36 inches
Twin	39 inches
Three-quarters	48 inches
Double	54 inches
Queen	60 inches
King	78 inches

Bed sizes in guest rooms can include twins, doubles, queen, king, or some other size. Shown here are housekeeping personnel preparing a guest room for new occupants. *(Photo courtesy of the Four Seasons Hotels, © 2000 Four Seasons Limited. Used by permission.)*

Most beds are 75 inches long. Some guests however, prefer longer beds, and these are readily available to lodging operators who choose to buy them. Some are 78 inches long; others may be 80 or 82 inches. The latter are often called California lengths.

Table 8.2 indicates typical sizes of guest accommodations in seven types of lodging operations. Note that the number of square feet in each accommodation includes bedroom, parlor or living room (if any), bathroom, and entry area, as well as closets and hallways.

Figure 8.3 illustrates typical floor plans for guest accommodations in the seven common types of lodging establishments listed in Table 8.2.

The layout and design of guest rooms in the Value Lodge closely resembles that for the budget motel room in Figure 8.3. Each unit has a private bath, two queen-size beds, a color television, two lounge chairs, and a dresser with mirror, among other items. Units in this property are of uniform size: 236 square feet.

Guest rooms in the Kensington more closely resemble those for the luxury hotel room in Figure 8.3. Some, like that in the diagram, have a private bath, one king-size bed, two nightstands, a desk/dresser with mirror, and a lounge area consisting of corner table, loveseat, lounge chair, and coffee table. Units in the Kensington hotel are of differing sizes but average approximately 400 square feet. That illustrated is among the largest the property offers.

Note that both guest rooms are designed for the same basic purpose—to provide accommodations for travelers. Every lodging establishment has guest rooms designed to accommodate the needs and desires of the kinds of travelers management intends to attract to the establishment. To that extent, the guest rooms

---

→ **SWEET DREAMS ARE MADE OF THIS**

Westin Hotel has spent over $30 million to provide a good night's sleep for its guests by adding new beds to its properties. The new bed at Westin is called a "heavenly bed." It is a king-size bed that is valued at $1940 and designed to give maximum comfort to the guest. The bed is an elaborate construct of sheets, comforter, duvet, and pillows. The mattress is nearly a foot thick, and the bed measures 29 inches from the top of the comforter to the bottom of the bed. It is 10 inches higher than the bed it is replacing.

Luxury hotels have always purchased the finest-quality beds available. For example, the Ritz-Carlton installs feather bed inserts and 300-thread Italian sheet sets. Guests at the Four Seasons like their beds enough that they buy about 100 mattress sets each year from the hotel. But this is the first time first-class hotels have spent large amounts of money on beds.

Source: Adapted from an article in *USA Today,* 31 August 1999.

---

in the Value Lodge and the Kensington hotel have the same general purposes. Obvious differences do exist between the two guest rooms illustrated, and these differences reveal much about the differences between the two properties. The principal differences are in size, space allocation, and furnishings.

Size

The typical room in the Value Lodge is approximately 150 square feet smaller than that in the Kensington.

Space Allocation

In the Kensington, space is allocated to furnishings not found in the Value Lodge. In addition, the Kensington Hotel room appears to be more open and uncluttered. Some of the extra space is used, quite simply, as space, affecting the ambience of the lodging product.

TABLE 8.2

Typical Size Ranges of Lodging Accommodations

Type of Lodging Accommodation	Common Sizes of Guest Accommodations (in sq ft)
Subbudget motel room	175–200
Budget motel room	225–250
Commercial hotel/motel room	250–325
Luxury hotel/motel room	350–450
Hotel junior suite	400–475
Hotel standard suite	450–550
Suite in an all-suite property	450–700

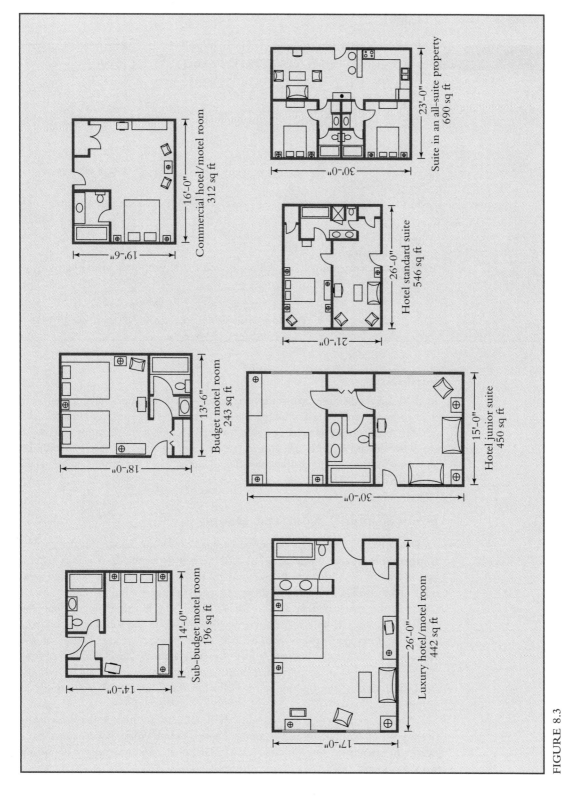

FIGURE 8.3
Typical floor plans for guest accommodations in lodging establishments

Commercial hotel/motel room
312 sq ft
16'-0"
19'-6"

Suite in an all-suite property
690 sq ft
23'-0"
30'-0"

Hotel standard suite
546 sq ft
26'-0"
21'-0"

Budget motel room
243 sq ft
13'-6"
18'-0"

Hotel junior suite
450 sq ft
15'-0"
30'-0"

Sub-budget motel room
196 sq ft
14'-0"
14'-0"

Luxury hotel/motel room
442 sq ft
26'-0"
17'-0"

➤ ONE OF THESE POSH POWDER ROOMS MAY FILL YOUR FANTASY

High-tech bidet-toilets at the RIHGA Royal Hotel in New York City take care of guests from the bottom up with heated seats, twin warm-water nozzles, and safety sensors that eliminate water spillage.

Bathtubs at the Four Seasons New York Hotel fill up in 60 seconds. In Milan, Italy, heated marble floors, heated towel racks, and steam-resistant mirrors at the Four Seasons Hotel keep out chill.

At the Saratoga Arms in Saratoga Springs, New York, handwritten tiles in each shower tout facts about the hotel.

The Abendblume Pension in Leavenworth, Washington, has a 204-square-foot bathroom with a fireplace, wet bar, sitting area, and CD player.

Simulated sounds recreate the ocean, rainfall, a babbling brook, or tropical birds in the bathrooms of the Hotel Metropolis in San Francisco.

These are just a few of the innovative ideas found in hotel bathrooms today.

Source: **Adapted from an article in** *USA Today*, **17 December 1999.**

Furnishings

In the Value Lodge, the furnishings are better suited to people staying overnight than to those remaining for longer periods. They are not quite as attractive and comfortable as those in the Kensington, which features reproductions of classical antiques. However, the Kensington caters to guests seeking attractive furnishings and who are both willing and able to pay higher rates for more luxurious accommodations.

Housekeeping Layout and Design

As in front-office and guest accommodations layouts, the layout and design of a **housekeeping area** in a lodging establishment is determined, to a great extent, by the type of establishment. In economy motels, for example, housekeeping areas tend to be smaller, simpler, and more compact than in traditional luxury hotels found in the more affluent areas of major cities. The housekeeping area in the Value Lodge, for example, is quite small and compact. In the Kensington, by contrast, housekeeping requires considerable space because of the nature of the Kensington as a luxury enterprise and the comparatively large number of employees required to maintain such a property.

The layout of the housekeeping facility in the Value Lodge is illustrated in Figure 8.4.

Note that the facility is comparatively simple, having storage space for laundered bed and bath linens and cleaning supplies and providing floor space for the overnight storage of three mobile carts used by the housekeeping staff during working hours.

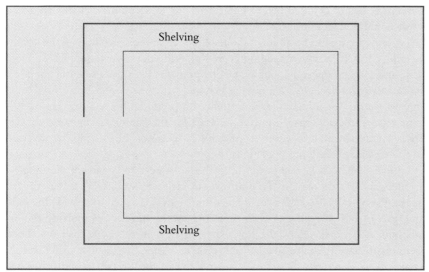

FIGURE 8.4
Layout of the housekeeping facility in the Value Lodge

Figure 8.5 illustrates the layout of the main housekeeping facility in the Kensington.

The housekeeping area in the Kensington includes an office for an executive housekeeper as well as considerable space for storing bed linens, bath linens, and cleaning supplies. A separate room is set aside for soiled linens. Here, soiled linens

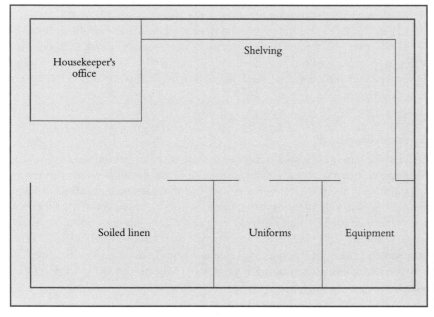

FIGURE 8.5
Layout of the housekeeping facility in the Kensington

are separated and counted before being sent out to a commercial laundry to be washed and folded or ironed.

Caring for bed and bath linen is one of the major responsibilities of the housekeeping department in any lodging operation. Without adequate supplies of linen, it is impossible to operate a lodging facility properly. Essentially, one can adopt either of two approaches to laundering bed and bath linen: send it out to a commercial laundry or install a laundry facility on premises. If the latter approach is adopted, considerable space must be set aside for the laundry facility and considerable funds allocated to equip it. Additional discussion of this topic is deferred to the chapter on lodging operations.

Note that housekeeping areas in both the Value Lodge and the Kensington are designed for the same basic purpose—to facilitate housekeeping services for guests. Every lodging establishment has a similar area designed to provide the kind and level of housekeeping services preferred by the travelers patronizing the establishment. To that extent, the housekeeping areas in the Value Lodge and the Kensington have the same general purposes. However, the obvious dissimilarities between the two areas illustrated suggest some of the overall dissimilarities between the two properties. The principal differences are in size, space allocation, and equipment.

Size

Two major factors account for the differences in size between the housekeeping areas of the Value Lodge and the Kensington. The first is the number of rooms to be serviced—50 in the Value Lodge versus 350 in the Kensington. Thus, the Kensington must have at least seven times the amount of bed and bath linen. The second reason is the need to store uniforms in the housekeeping area of the Kensington—a need that does not exist at the Value Lodge.

The diagram of the Kensington housekeeping area does not show the additional housekeeping storage facilities located throughout the hotel. Each floor has a housekeeping closet used for storing small amounts of cleaning supplies, guest room supplies, and linens, and for housing mobile carts when not in use by the housekeeping staff.

Space Allocation

Besides the space allocated for an office in the housekeeping area of the Kensington, there is also space for storing uniforms for all hotel employees required to wear them. This is not necessary in the Value Lodge, as noted. Because the Kensington is an older property, some of the side rooms now used for storage were once used by housekeeping employees with job titles no longer found in most hotels—upholsterers and seamstresses, for example. Work formerly done by people in these job classifications is now typically done outside the hotel by independent contractors, making it possible to allocate this space for additional storage.

Equipment

Because it is a luxury property with a large lobby and considerable public space, the Kensington uses heavy, specialized cleaning equipment to maintain these areas. Because the Value Lodge has no comparable space, it has no such equipment. In addition, the Kensington, as a luxury enterprise, makes available to its guests various kinds of equipment not offered to guests in the Value Lodge. Guests in the Kensington can telephone the housekeeping office to obtain such common items as steam irons and ironing boards, and guests visiting from other parts of the world can borrow conversion devices that enable them to use their electrical appliances.

From the foregoing discussion, it should be apparent that lodging facilities are relatively complex physical structures. Because of this, students of lodging management need some basic knowledge of the complex physical systems required to make them operational. These are the systems designed to provide the basic requirements that make it possible for people to inhabit buildings in reasonable comfort and safety. They are commonly referred to as engineering systems.

ENGINEERING SYSTEMS

The following are brief descriptions of the basic engineering systems common to most lodging properties. These discussions suggest the degree of complexity inherent in the layout and design of a building constructed for use as a hotel, motel, or similar lodging enterprise.

The engineering systems in a building may include all of the following:

- Heating
- Air conditioning
- Ventilation
- Electrical
- Water
- Transportation
- Waste
- Fire safety
- Energy control
- Communications

Heating Systems

In the United States, lodging facilities have **heating systems** to raise the temperature of air and water in the building, thus providing warm rooms and hot water. Heating systems accomplish this by converting energy resources to heat. Common energy resources include oil, gas, electricity, steam, coal, and solar energy. The selection of one of these over another depends on availability, relative cost, and the preferences of the owner/operators of the facility.

Air-Conditioning Systems

Technically, **air conditioning** is any treatment of the air in a building that changes that air in any way. Thus, heating, cooling, humidifying, dehumidifying, and filtering are all air-conditioning processes. However, the term *air conditioning* is commonly taken to mean the improvement of the comfort level in a facility by reducing the temperature of air, by controlling the level of humidity in the air, or by doing both of these. Two types of air-conditioning systems are used in lodging facilities: centralized and decentralized.

Centralized Air-Conditioning System

A central system services guest rooms and other facilities, treating the air in one large unit and distributing the treated air through ducts.

Decentralized Air-Conditioning System

A decentralized system relies on individual units in each room or part of the facility to treat the air. In some properties, these are built into the walls of the rooms they serve; in others, they are installed in windows.

Ventilation Systems

Ventilation systems provide fresh or recirculated air and control the volume of air. They ensure an adequate supply of air with sufficient oxygen for human activity. Some ventilation systems also filter air to remove dust and other particles and such undesirable properties as cigarette smoke and cooking odors. Lodging facilities in the centers of major cities commonly install air filtration equipment to remove the pollutants from automobile, truck, and bus traffic.

Ventilation systems are designed to remove and replace all the air in a given space or room a number of times each hour. That number varies from a few times per hour—possibly six, for example, in a large hotel ballroom—to a great many times per hour—up to 50 in a large hotel kitchen, according to one authority. Ventilation systems are typically linked to heating systems, air-conditioning systems, or both.

It should be noted that heating, ventilation, and air-conditioning systems are typically combined into a single unit and called an **HVAC** system. Thus, if the system is centralized, the same ducts that carry heat also carry air conditioning and fresh air for ventilation. If the system is decentralized, each unit provides heat, air conditioning, and fresh air as needed.

Electrical Systems

Electrical systems are designed to provide electric power wherever it is needed as an energy source in the building. Electrical systems consist of wires of various sizes as well as the circuit breakers or fuses, switches, and outlets that facilitate the safe use of electric power. Electricity is used for three primary purposes in lodging facilities: lighting, heating, and operating equipment requiring electric power.

Because of their public nature, many lodging establishments are required to maintain emergency systems to use in the event of a power failure. The nature and extent of the emergency systems vary, depending on state and local regulations. Some are simple battery systems that provide emergency lighting in corridors and other public areas for limited periods; others are complex systems that include gasoline-powered generators to provide sufficient electricity for lighting, computers, and limited elevator service. Many operators install emergency systems that also provide power for refrigerators, freezers, and computer systems until the regular flow of power resumes. Frequently, these emergency systems automatically engage when there is a power failure. This prevents interruption of the computers and loss of data, allows sufficient light so that guests and employees can move around, and allows the elevators to continue working without interruption.

Water Systems

A **water system** consists of those parts of the plumbing system that provide fresh water to various parts of the lodging establishment, including guest rooms, food and beverage facilities, laundry facilities, and public bathrooms.

In many localities, the source of fresh water is a public supply whose pipes run under the streets. In many remote rural areas, however, absence of a public water system makes it necessary for lodging operators to use some alternative means to obtain fresh water. Most commonly, this means drilling a well. Another possibility is pumping the water directly from a nearby lake or river. Others, although rare, include collecting it from rainwater and processing seawater.

Sometimes incoming fresh water is processed before being distributed throughout a building so that its properties may be changed before use. There are various reasons for doing this. One is that the water is too hard, a term used to describe water containing excessive amounts of calcium and magnesium salts. Another is that the water may contain other minerals or impurities that must be filtered out. Still another is that the water may require the addition of chlorine to make it safe for human use.

Some fresh water—the cold water—is distributed directly to the areas in which it is used. The rest, the hot water, is diverted to the heating system, where its temperature is raised before distribution.

One of the significant engineering challenges in a multistory lodging operation is to design a water system that provides both of the following:

- Adequate water pressure on all floors during periods of peak use. If this is not addressed, guests in rooms on high floors may not be able to obtain adequate water at times.

- An adequate supply of both hot and cold water, so that each water user can maintain the temperature he selects for any given purpose. Failure to provide for this may result, for example, in sudden changes in shower water temperatures from comfortable to excessively hot or cold, either of which may be unpleasant or dangerous.

Transportation Systems

The **transportation system** in a lodging establishment consists of those facilities used to move guests, employees, equipment, and supplies from one level of the building to another. Its most common components are **elevators** and **escalators**.

Wherever feasible, planners of lodging facilities provide for an adequate number of elevators so that those used by guests need not be used for other purposes. Elevators used for other purposes are often called service elevators and are usually located some distance from the guest elevators. Service elevators are used for transporting employees, equipment, and supplies from one part of the building to another.

A small, specialized kind of elevator called a **dumbwaiter** is used for moving food, normally for short distances between floors. For example, if the main kitchen in a large hotel is one or two floors below the dining rooms and banquet rooms, a dumbwaiter may be installed to transport food and materials between kitchen and the foodservice facilities.

Dumbwaiters are not normally used to transport personnel and, consequently, lack the internal operating controls found in elevators. Staff members usually place food and other items in a dumbwaiter, close the door from the outside, and control it by depressing a button on the wall next to the dumbwaiter shaft.

Escalators are normally used to transport large numbers of people for short distances—one or two floors up or down. They are more commonly used at banquet and meeting facilities; the goal is for those attending meetings, dinners, and other events to get into and out of the facility quickly and easily. If it becomes necessary to move large numbers of people into or out of a facility quickly, all escalators can be made to move in the same direction—up or down. With this arrangement, greater numbers of people can be moved more quickly than would be possible using elevators.

Waste Systems

The **waste system** in a lodging property is designed to facilitate the removal of solid and liquid wastes produced in the property. Solid waste includes paper, glass, fabric, plastic, metal, wood, and food. Liquid waste is primarily wastewater being drained into a sewage disposal system.

Solid waste is normally collected throughout a lodging establishment by employees who transport it to a central area. From there, it can be put out for pickup in plastic bags, trash cans, or dumpsters, depending on type, volume, and local regulations. Alternatively, it can be compacted before being put out, or incinerated on premises. Many large hotels accumulate huge amounts of solid waste daily. Local regulations often identify certain solid wastes as recyclables and require that they be separated and made ready for special handling or collection.

In contrast, the disposal of liquid waste is normally quite simple. Areas with public water supply systems also have public sewer systems, and disposal is a simple matter of connecting to that system. Elsewhere, some other means must be found. The most common alternatives are treatment plants and underground drain fields.

Fire Safety Systems

A **fire safety system** is designed to detect, contain, or extinguish fires and to alert both guests and employees to the danger. Some are also designed to summon fire and police personnel to the scene. A fire safety system consists of:

- Sensing devices for detecting heat, smoke, flame, or some combination of these
- Devices for containing or extinguishing fires, such as doors that close automatically to prevent the spread of fire; sprinklers; and portable extinguishers containing water, carbon dioxide, foam, or other chemicals
- Warning devices for alerting guests and employees, such as fire horns, fire alarms, and flashing lights

Because of the public nature of lodging establishments, all but the smallest are required by law to have some type of fire safety system. The nature and extent of the systems required vary from one area to another and from one size and type of lodging facility to another.

Energy Control Systems

The **energy control system** in a lodging establishment is designed to manage the use of energy in the building efficiently, minimizing its use and consequent cost. It consists of devices that turn energy-consuming equipment on and off at optimum times or that prevent excessive use of energy in any system or subsystem. The four common types of systems are the time clock, the automatic sensor, electric demand, and computer.

Time Clock

This is the simplest and least costly of the systems. It uses time clocks to turn on and off the flow of electricity to such devices as exterior lights, lighted signs, and even swimming pool filtration systems, ensuring that they operate only when needed and for the proper length of time.

Automatic Sensor

Some lodging operators control energy costs by installing automatic sensors that detect the presence or absence of people in a room. These are used primarily to turn lights on and off, ensuring that lights are off when no one is in a room. They may also be used to turn off such appliances as television sets when guests leave a room.

Electric Demand

Electric demand systems are designed to limit the amount of energy of one type that can be used at one time. This may entail limiting the length of time that a given device can operate continuously or preventing the use of a given device while another is in use. These systems are more commonly used in large buildings where, say, three major air-conditioning systems serve different parts of the building. An electric demand control system may be used to prevent two or more from operating together and to limit the length of time that any of them can run before being automatically turned off to enable a second to operate.

Computerized System

Computerized systems are the most flexible, efficient, and effective in use today. These are the systems most commonly installed in newly constructed lodging facilities. They can be programmed to control energy use and are capable of all the controls exercised by the three systems described above.

Because proper use of an appropriate energy control system can result in considerable savings in energy costs—some manufacturers claim up to 40 percent—owners of lodging properties are normally interested in selecting systems that produce minimum energy costs for their facilities.

Communications Systems

Communications systems in lodging establishments are designed to enable guests, managers, staff members, and others outside the lodging property to communicate with one another. This system may be as simple as a telephone system used by guests, employees, and managers to speak to one another. This is the case in the Value Lodge, for example, where an overnight guest may use the telephone to call the front desk, request information, request a morning wake-up call, or to make a local or long-distance call. However, some communications systems in lodging properties today are far more complex.

A typical modern communications system may link telephones, televisions, computers, and audiovisual devices. The communications may range from telephone calls between front desk and guest room to interactive televised conferences linking groups in two or more cities via satellite transmission. They may involve business travelers using computers with modems in guest rooms or suites to communicate with their offices via telephone lines. They may even provide a means for guests to view and approve their room bills via the television sets in their rooms. The possibilities for developing increasingly complex telecommunications equipment for installation and use in lodging enterprises are growing with each development in this relatively new field. Therefore, people purchasing communications systems for lodging facilities are challenged to select systems and equipment that will not soon become obsolete as new systems are developed.

SUMMARY

In this chapter, concept, legal requirements, and product line are introduced as fundamental to the layout and design of lodging facilities. Product line is described as having three components: accommodations, services, and ambience. Case studies describing three lodging facilities—Value Lodge, Mountain Inn, and Kensington Hotel—are presented as aids to understanding facilities layout and design. The layout and design of three areas central to lodging operations are illustrated and discussed: front office, guest room, and housekeeping area. The layout and design of these three in the Value Lodge and the Kensington Hotel are described, compared, and contrasted. Finally, ten engineering systems are identified as the basic elements in lodging properties that make it possible for people to inhabit lodging facilities buildings in reasonable comfort and safety.

KEY TERMS

Accommodations
Air conditioning
Ambience
Check-in
Checkout
Communications system
Concept
Dumbwaiter
Electrical system
Elevator
Energy control system
Escalator

Fire safety system
Front office
Heating system
Housekeeping area
HVAC
Product line
Reservation
Services
Transportation system
Ventilation system
Waste system
Water system

DISCUSSION QUESTIONS

1. Define the term *product line* as used in lodging operations.
2. List and discuss the three elements in the service product line of a lodging enterprise.

3. What are the activities common to all front-office operations that must be taken into account in their layout and design?

4. How would you expect the front-office layout and design for a 75-room budget motel to differ from that for a 500-room luxury hotel?

5. Identify by name and size eight types of beds commonly used in lodging properties.

6. Provide the size range in square feet for each of the following: sub-budget motel room, budget motel room, commercial hotel/motel room, luxury motel room, hotel junior suite, hotel standard suite, suite in an all-suite property.

7. Compare and contrast the size and furnishings of a budget motel room with those of a luxury hotel.

8. How would the layout and design of the housekeeping area in a 50-room motel be likely to differ from that in a 500-room luxury hotel?

9. Why would there be great differences in the size, space allocation, and equipment found in the housekeeping areas cited in question 8?

10. List and discuss ten engineering systems found in lodging facilities.

11. Distinguish between centralized and decentralized air-conditioning systems.

12. How often should air be changed in the ballroom of a large hotel? in the kitchen serving the ballroom?

13. List four possible sources of water for lodging operations having no access to a public water supply.

14. What are dumbwaiters? For what purposes are they used in lodging facilities?

15. What are the principal components of a fire safety system?

16. Identify four common types of energy control systems.

MOMENTS OF TRUTH

1. Visit a lodging facility with at least 150 rooms. From your own perspective, describe the concept around which this operation is established.

2. Describe the product line of the lodging facility you identified above as completely as you can.

3. Describe the layout and design of the front office in the lodging operation you discussed above.

INTERNET EXERCISES

1. Go to http://www.telluride-lodging.com. Describe one guest room from each of three properties listed on this site. Explain the differences in the rooms you have described.

2. Go to http://www. atlanticoceanside.com. Reproduce a drawing of the layout of a suite shown on this site. How different is it from the illustration in the chapter text?

Lodging Operations

▶ Learning Objectives

After reading and studying this chapter, you should be able to:

1. Identify the four basic operations and services common to all lodging operations.

2. Identify six additional services offered by some, but not all, lodging operators.

3. List and state the goals of the four activities associated with front office operation and describe the functions of each.

4. List the advantages of using electronic locks rather than traditional locks with metal keys.

5. Describe three possible variations of the check-out procedure used by hotels, motels, and similar facilities.

6. Identify two common problems that have induced some lodging operators to overbook reservations.

7. Describe a minimum of ten tasks that may be assigned to the housekeeping operation.

8. List a minimum of ten tasks required to make a room ready for occupancy.

9. Identify three methods used to assign daily work quotas for room attendants in hotels, motels, and similar properties.

10. Discuss the key differences between security measures used in large center-city hotels and those used in smaller rural and suburban properties.

11. Identify the kinds of activities normally associated with front service.

12. List three services offered by the telephone system in modern lodging operations.

13. List and describe the three types of foodservice facilities found in lodging establishments.

14. Identify eight personal services offered by some lodging properties.

INTRODUCTION

In the previous chapter, the basic similarities of all lodging establishments were illustrated by means of case studies describing three properties: the Value Lodge, the Mountain Inn, and the Kensington Hotel. Chapter 8 is the foundation for this chapter, which identifies significant concepts that lie at the heart of lodging operations.

In this chapter, we point out similarities in lodging establishments that are sometimes obscured by the vast array of differences. We define and describe important operations—elements and services—that lodging establishments have in common.

BASIC OPERATIONS AND SERVICES OF LODGING OPERATIONS

The operations and services that one encounters in lodging can be divided into two groups:

1. Those found in all lodging establishments

2. Those found in some, but not others

Without those in the first group, an enterprise is not considered a lodging establishment. Those in the second group are used selectively, depending on the goals of a particular lodging establishment. Those goals can best be reached by including one or more of these operations.

Group 1 is made up of:

- Front office
- Telephone
- Housekeeping
- Security

Group 2 includes services not necessarily available in all lodging establishments. Their availability depends on the goals of the individual lodging operator. The following is a list of some of the services included in Group 2:

- Front service
- Food and beverage services
- Recreation/entertainment
- Parking
- Other personal services

Many lodging operators use their own employees to provide services. However, a large number hire outside contractors to provide some services. For example, many lodging operators have an outside firm manage their food and beverage operation. Some hire security firms to provide that service. Employing an outside contractor to provide a service is referred to as **outsourcing**.

For purposes of this text, we consider that either option results in the addition of an activity to the lodging facility—one devoted to providing the service. In addition, guests using the service consider that activity part of the lodging facility regardless of whether it is provided by employees of the lodging establishment or those of an outside contractor.

GROUP 1

As indicated above, the four operations and services in this group—front office, telephone, housekeeping, and security—are common to all lodging establishments. However, although this is true, discussion of housekeeping or security in a small boardinghouse would be much less enlightening than discussion of those activities in a large hotel, motel, or similar commercial lodging enterprise. Therefore, much of the following discussion relates to those kinds of properties—the kinds illustrated in Case Studies 8.1, 8.2, and 8.3.

Front Office

Front office is a term commonly used to refer to the location where the front desk is situated within a lodging property. To guests, the front office represents the lodging property. It is their first point of contact on arrival and last point of contact at departure.

Front-office operation consists of four primary activities known in the lodging industry by the following terms:

- Check-in
- Information
- Checkout
- Reservations

Together, these four activities comprise front-office operation.

Check-In

Check-in refers to a process by which people become guests in a lodging establishment. Check-in takes place in a reception area, another name for that part of a front office known as the front desk. Here, guests register, are assigned accommodations, and pick up keys for these accommodations. In the Kensington, the check-in process proceeds in the following manner.

Front Office is a term commonly used to refer to the location where the front desk is situated within a lodging property. Shown here is a party checking into a Radisson Hotel at the front desk. *(Photo courtesy of Radisson Hotels and Resorts)*

An arriving guest goes first to the front desk, located in the lobby near the main entrance. A **room clerk** (a job title for the person on duty at the front desk) greets and welcomes the arriving guest and asks if he has a reservation. The term *room clerk* is used by Kensington for the person stationed at the front desk. However, other titles are commonly used for that position. They include room attendant, desk attendant, desk clerk, receptionist, and room services attendant.

If the guest has a reservation, the room clerk asks the guest to register, which means to fill out a form known as a registration card. A registration card is a printed front-office form on which guests record their names, addresses, and other information. The clerk then updates information about the guest in the computer and confirms the number of nights he expects to stay. If the guest has no reservation, the room clerk describes available accommodations and rates, thus attempting to sell a room to the individual. If successful, the room clerk asks the individual to register. Once the guest is registered, the room clerk assigns a suitable accommodation.

In some operations, the guest does not write the necessary information on a registration card but dictates it to a room clerk, who inputs it into a computer terminal. After the information is entered, a form with this information is printed from the computer record and the guest is asked to sign this hard copy.

Today, most hotels, motels, and similar lodging establishments determine at the time of arrival how guests intend to settle their bills. In general, bills are settled by one of three means: credit, cash (or check), or billing to a third party. If a credit card is to be used, the guest is asked to produce the card so that a record can be made of the credit card number. This gives the lodging operator a means of verifying that the guest has sufficient credit available. If payment is to be with cash or check, the guest is likely to be asked for credit identification. Credit identification is verifiable proof that an individual has sufficient credit to cover the hotel bill. Without credit identification, guests are usually asked to pay cash in advance. If the bill is to be settled by a third party, a suitable arrangement has normally been made with the reservation. The Mountain Inn, for example, accepts both cash and national credit cards, but virtually all of its guests present credit cards at check-in and settle their bills at the time of departure. In contrast, the Value Lodge requires that all guests either pay for their accommodation in cash as they check in or sign credit card vouchers imprinted with their card numbers. Many of the guests pay cash.

In order to be able to assign guests to rooms, room clerks must be able to determine quickly which rooms are occupied, which have been vacated but not cleaned, and which are both vacant and ready. To enable room clerks to do this, lodging establishments use one of two means to maintain the necessary information: manual or electronic. The latter refers to computers, of course, and computers are fast becoming the preferred means in most properties. Computers used for guest check-in are typically part of an overall property management system—a term for a computer system designed to perform a variety of tasks formerly accomplished by manual means.

In some properties—the Value Lodge, for example—the information needed by room clerks is maintained manually in a device called a room rack; in more complex operations—the Kensington, for example—property management systems are used. Detailed information about specific equipment and techniques for registering guests is normally covered in a rooms management course. The important point to remember is that the check-in process in all lodging establishments has at least two goals: to assign guests to accommodations and to ensure payment.

After a room number is assigned and questions of billing attended to, guests are given access to their assigned accommodations in one of two ways. Either they are given keys to their assigned rooms or their keys are given to bellstaff, who accompany guests to their rooms. In the Value Lodge, there is no bellstaff; guests are simply given keys and directed to their rooms. In contrast, room clerks in the Kensington are required to give the keys to bellstaff, who always accompany guests to their rooms. At the Mountain Inn, guests are offered their choice of being accompanied by bellstaff or finding their own way.

Modern technology has changed the nature of the room keys used in most hotels and motels. Although some operations still use the traditional lock with metal key—the kind inserted into a lock, then turned to unlock the door—most hotels and motels now use new types of locks that open by means of cards or keys with magnetic strips rather than traditional metal keys. Two types of cards are common. The first has information electronically encoded on magnetic strips. To enter a room, the guest inserts the card or key into an electronic device that reads the code and opens the lock. The keys with magnetic strips work the same way as cards with magnetic strips. The second type is a thick card made of plastic or some other material in which round holes have been punched. With each type, the guest inserts the card in the lock to open the door.

These new types of keys have several important advantages over traditional metal keys, which have always given hotel and motel operators problems. When lost or stolen, traditional keys are sometimes used by burglars to enter rooms illegally and steal guests' money and valuables. In addition, lost keys must be re-placed, an expensive and time-consuming requirement in a large property. Some large hotels have traditionally employed full-time locksmiths to make duplicates of lost metal keys and to change locks in guest-room doors when necessary. The newer card keys eliminate many of the problems associated with metal keys. Frequently, no room numbers are visible, so a lost card is useless to the finder. In properties using cards with magnetic strips, the code is changed each time a guest checks out; this is the same as changing the lock. In properties using cards with punched holes, it is relatively easy to change the code in the door lock and pre-pare a new key if the card is lost.

Information

The goal of the **information activity** in a hotel or motel is to serve the special needs of guests and employees for information about guests and goods and services.

Guest Information. The front office serves as a center for guest information. In effect, it maintains a data bank with the names and addresses of current guests, their room numbers, the status of their accounts, and considerable additional in-formation. As guests check in, information about them is added to this data bank; as guests leave, the data bank is changed to keep it current. Thus, the front office of a hotel or motel always has up-to-date information about all current guests and about the status of each room, whether occupied or vacant. This information may be maintained in any number of forms; data in a computer, typewritten slips of paper, and handwritten sheets of paper are some of the possibilities. The infor-mation is used constantly.

Without this information, routine front-office matters would be difficult to handle. For example, in the Kensington, one of these routine matters is assisting guests who have forgotten their room numbers. When the guest goes to the front desk, the clerk on duty finds her name and room number in the data bank and is thus easily able to give the guest her room number. In the Value Lodge, a small property, the owners have the same need for information but maintain the records in a very different way. The registration cards are simply kept in a file box in al-phabetical order.

In front-office work, other tasks that require the use of this guest informa-tion include placing mail and messages for guests in numbered mailboxes that cor-respond to their room numbers; directing incoming telephone calls to guests' rooms; assisting visitors in finding the guests they have come to see; verifying the room numbers of guests who signed guest checks in the restaurant or bar; deter-mining the number of occupied rooms expected to be vacated by guests check-ing out on the current day; counting the number of rooms vacant at any given time during the course of a day; determining the house count, meaning the num-ber of guests registered in the property; advising housekeepers that a room has been vacated so that it can be cleaned; and calculating the percentage of guest rooms occupied.

HOTELS CHECK IN GUESTS ←
BEFORE THEY STEP INSIDE

Instead of checking in at the front desk, many hotels are allowing guests to check in outside their front door, on airport shuttle buses, or even at airports. Hotels are now accelerating express check-in by using wireless technology to program electronic card keys outside the hotel.

Hilton is using the technology to provide curbside check-in at many of its properties. The Fairmont Vancouver Airport Hotel accepts reservations, checks bags, and hands out keys from two satellite lobbies at the airport. Hilton Boston Logan Airport allows guests to register on the shuttle bus ride from the airport to the hotel. The Loews Portofino Bay Hotel in Orlando, Florida, provides curbside check-in. Employees greet guests outside the hotel, take their baggage, and register them on handheld computers.

Source: Adapted from an article in *USA Today*, 2 November 1999.

Information About Goods and Services. Many transient guests find themselves in strange surroundings when they have registered in a hotel or motel. Most are strangers to the community and need orientation and assistance. In many hotels and motels, the front office offers maps, guidebooks, and other sources of information to help guests. Room clerks and other employees may be asked to recommend restaurants, give directions to places of interest, or help guests find sources for goods or services that the community offers. The front office in the Mountain Hotel, for example, has maps of the surrounding region that it makes available without charge to guests interested in sightseeing. Similarly, the owners of the Value Lodge provide guests with free copies of a directory listing the locations of all other motels in the chain, from coast to coast.

In hotels, motels, and other lodging establishments that offer services beyond sleeping accommodations, guests normally ask many questions about these services. They may ask about the hours of operation of restaurants, bars, swimming pools, stables, or other facilities; regulations governing the use of the golf course; availability of child care services, hair stylists, or travel agents; and details about the kinds of exercise equipment, types of computers and printers, or hair dryers available. An unlimited number of questions can be asked about the facilities and services of the property itself. Consequently, room clerks and other employees are expected to provide all sorts of information to guests quickly and courteously.

Checkout

Checkout refers to a process by which guests terminate their status as guests of a lodging establishment. The goal of checkout activity in hotels, motels, and other lodging operations is to accomplish this process.

There are several variations of the checkout process. In the Value Lodge, overnight guests typically pay their bills in advance at check-in, so most simply leave their keys in the rooms and drive away. Because of the size of the property, the owners normally see or hear guests depart and thus know that the vacated room needs to be cleaned and made ready for its next occupant.

In the Mountaine Inn, the procedure is different. All guests are expected to stop at the front office to settle their accounts and leave their keys. As indicated above, these accounts are created and maintained in the front office. When guests leave, employees update the front-office data bank and make the room number available to housekeepers, who make the room ready for the next guests.

In the Kensington, in contrast, guests have access to advanced technology that enables them to check out before they leave their rooms by using the television screen to review and settle their bills. While the approaches differ from one establishment to another, the goal is the same in all three: to accomplish the check-out process.

Today, because so many lodging operations require that guests sign credit card vouchers or pay cash at check-in, fewer problems with unpaid and uncollectible bills occur than was the case years ago. Because credit cards can be verified as guests check in, hotels, motels, and similar lodging establishments do not have as many skippers, an old hotel term that refers to guests who leave without paying their bills.

Reservations

The term **reservation** refers to an arrangement by which lodging operators hold accommodations for guests who will be arriving at some later time. This may be later during the same day or at some date in the future. The reservations operation in a hotel or motel is designed to make such arrangements. There are two major goals of reservations activity:

1. To provide assurance to prospective guests that suitable accommodations will be available to them at a specific price for a specified period

2. To ensure that the greatest number of rooms possible is occupied each day and that the rates charged for those rooms are the highest possible

The first major goal is to serve the needs of people seeking assurance that accommodations will be available to them when needed. Individuals intending to travel to a distant location want to be certain that they will have rooms to stay in when they arrive. Reservation operations are intended to meet this need. A potential guest can call, write, fax, or e-mail the reservation office in a hotel, motel, or other lodging establishment to arrange for a room to be held for the necessary number of nights.

The reservations operation in a lodging establishment typically consists of an office with some number of employees, known as reservation clerks or reservationists, who respond to requests for accommodations from potential guests. Requests may be for the coming night, some date in the distant future, or any time in between. Each request for a room reservation must be answered promptly with a definite "yes" or "no." "Maybe" is never an acceptable response to a potential guest. In order to give a definite answer, reservationists must have access to information about the number of rooms already reserved for each night, the number of rooms remaining available for those same nights, sold-out dates for which no reservations can be taken, and rates for the rooms available for any given night.

Without such information, no reservationist can give a prompt response to someone calling on the telephone to ask about the availability of, say, a room for one person for three nights beginning next Tuesday. Potential guests need immediate, unequivocal answers to requests of this nature, and reservationists must be able to provide them.

Assuming that an appropriate room is available at an acceptable rate for the nights requested by a caller, the reservationist must record some information quickly. This normally includes name, address, dates for which the room is to be reserved, type of room required, rate, expected time of arrival, and intended method of payment. Some lodging operators require additional information—telephone number, for example. Many require deposits from guests before they confirm reservations. Others reserve rooms only for guests who provide national credit card numbers when they make their reservations.

The information taken from guests is recorded either on a paper form or in a computer terminal. If the paper form is used, additional processing is required to add the reservation to others for the same arrival date. If a computer terminal is used, the reservation is automatically added to the reservations database. The Value Lodge, for example, uses inexpensive paper forms for recording reservations and files all the reservations for one date in one folder. In contrast, the Kensington has a computerized system, and all reservations are recorded in terminals that add them to the reservations database.

Each day, the reservations taken for that particular day are given to the front desk so those on duty have the names, addresses, and other information about guests expected to check in during the course of the day. In the Value Lodge, the owner has a single folder at the desk that contains all reservations for the current day. In the Kensington, the morning desk clerk uses the computer system at the front desk to print the list of reservations for the day. In some hotels, no list is printed. Desk clerks use the computer system to look up arriving guests' reservations.

The second major goal of the reservations operation is to ensure that the greatest number of rooms possible is occupied each day and that the rates charged for those rooms are the highest possible.

The ideal situation for a hotel or motel is to have every room occupied every night at the highest possible rate. This is obviously the way to earn maximum revenue. Although it is desirable, however, it is nearly impossible to accomplish. In order to come as close to this ideal as possible, an owner or manager must establish a rate structure that enables reservationists to sell as many rooms as possible. Management must establish a range of rates that appeal to the target clientele— that group of individuals and businesses that management wants to attract to the property.

Yield Management.   In recent years, many hotels have instituted a reservation system taken from the airline industry: **yield management**. Although each hotel chain employs a different variation, the goal is always the same—to obtain maximum occupancy at maximum rates.

The yield management system at the Mountain Inn works as follows. A yield management team consisting of the reservation manager, front-office manager, and director of sales meet once each week to review current reservations and establish room rates for the future.

The Mountain Inn has three rates for its double rooms—A, B, and C. Rate A is the highest rate, B is the standard rate, and C is the lowest rate. During a future holiday period, the team expects demand for accommodations to be very high, and the Mountain Inn is expected to be sold out for the entire time. The team decides that only rate A will be quoted to potential guests seeking accommodations for that period. The week immediately after the holiday will be busy, but the Mountain Inn is not expected to be sold out. After discussion, the team decides to quote rates A and B for that week. Rate A is quoted first to all customers and rate B is quoted only if rate A is unacceptable to the person requesting a reservation. The team also decides to review room demand for that week at a future meeting. If reservations for that week are strong, they will continue to quote only rates A and B. If many rooms are still available for that week, they will open up rate C to customers who request a lower rate.

In the fashion described above, the Mountain Inn yield management team reviews all weeks for a six-month period. Demand for accommodations is assessed based on past occupancy and current conditions. During periods of low demand, all rates are available to potential guests. During periods of high demand, only the highest rates are quoted. In that way, only people willing to pay the higher rates are accepted during periods of high demand, and people seeking only low rates can be accommodated during slack periods. This method assures the Mountain Inn maximum revenue and maximum occupancy.

One of the more difficult and interesting problems of lodging operation results from customers who make reservations and either cancel at the last minute or fail to check in. Those who fail to check in are called **no-shows**. Last-minute cancellations and no-shows may result in vacant rooms and lost revenue. Potential guests whose requests for reservations were turned down when it appeared the hotel was sold out have gone to other properties and may be permanently lost.

Historically, lodging operators attempt to deal with this problem by **overbooking**, which means taking more reservations than the number of anticipated rooms available. Many transient hotels use this method with some success. They accept 10 to 15 percent more reservations than rooms are available, knowing from historical data that some customers will cancel and others will not arrive to claim their reservations.

Difficulties arise when the anticipated number of cancellations fails to materialize, or when more people than anticipated arrive to claim their reservations. On these occasions, some guests must be **walked**—a hotel term meaning to send guests with confirmed reservations to other lodging properties because their reservations cannot be honored.

A few lodging operators are guilty of serious overbooking. The vast majority are not. Nevertheless, almost all have found themselves in the unfortunate position of having to walk guests. When this happens, most lodging operators attempt to find suitable accommodations for the guest at other properties, then pay for the guest's transportation to that property. Some even pay for the first night's accommodation.

In recent years, lodging operators have developed new strategies for dealing with last-minute cancellations and no-shows. They include:

1. Confirming reservations with the provision that they will be held only until a specific time—5:00 P.M., for example. Thus, hotels do not need to overbook to any great extent because they can rent rooms to walk-in guests after that time.

2. Taking only **guaranteed reservations**, meaning that the lodging establishment will hold a room and charge the guest for that room unless the reservation is cancelled prior to arrival by a specified date or time. Properties taking guaranteed reservations require a deposit in the form of cash, a check, or a credit card number when the reservation is made.

Hotels will not accept guaranteed reservations without a deposit. Guests with guaranteed reservations are typically registered and charged for their rooms whether or not they actually arrive. Resort hotels have long required advance payment for accommodations. The typical resort hotel requires a substantial advance deposit, and some resort hotels require full payment in advance. All have refund policies for customers who must cancel, but they vary greatly. Some refund only a portion of the advance payment; others refund the entire amount if the reservation is canceled within two or three weeks prior to scheduled arrival. Some have a sliding scale that provides a percentage refund ranging from 100 to 0 percent depending on when the reservation is canceled. The closer the cancellation is to arrival time, the less of a percentage is refunded. No-shows are seldom a problem with resort hotels that require advance deposits. Thus, many of them do not overbook, and some overbook only slightly, knowing that a few cancellations will occur.

Telephone

In past years, telephone service was not included in all lodging operations. Some motels, guest houses, hostels, and dormitories had telephones for use by management only, and the service was not available to guests. Today, all lodging properties have telephone service. If it is not available in guest rooms, it is available at the front office. Telephone service has the obvious goal of providing a means for voice communication for guests and employees. Additionally, a telephone communication system may be used to provide guests with voice mail, wake-up services, and the means for sending and receiving fax messages. In some properties, guest rooms are equipped with the necessary jacks for linking laptop and notebook computer modems to the telephone system—a requirement of growing numbers of guests. Today, the telephone service in most lodging establishments is automated. Guests in many hotels and motels can dial local and long-distance calls directly. Charges are calculated by computerized call accounting systems and automatically charged to guest accounts. Telephone operators in major metropolitan hotels do not make individual wake-up calls to guests; this job is now accomplished by computer. In many properties, guest rooms are equipped with clock radios so that guests no longer need wake-up calls. In some properties—the Kensington, for example—the telephone system is operated as a separate department, with round-the-clock operator service available. In others—typically smaller establishments such as the Value Lodge—the telephone operation is actually part of the front-office operation. The desk clerk on duty serves as telephone operator in addition to other duties.

Housekeeping

The third major operation in lodging operations is **housekeeping**. The principal goal of housekeeping is to serve the needs of guests by providing appropriate care for their accommodations and for other areas in the lodging property. Although this may sound simple, it entails numerous tasks, large and small, many of which are easy for staff members to overlook. However, survey after survey shows that guests notice and rate overall cleanliness in hotels, motels, and similar properties. These surveys also reveal that positive or negative feelings about housekeeping in a given property play a pivotal role in determining whether or not a guest will return to stay in the property again. In housekeeping operations, even the smallest task can be of great importance to guests.

Providing appropriate care for guest rooms and other areas includes changing bed and bath linen, making beds, and cleaning rooms for current guests; doing the same in rooms vacated by guests who have checked out, thus preparing these rooms for new occupants; cleaning hallways and such areas as the lobby, meeting rooms, public bathrooms, and offices used by the management; and ensuring a supply of clean bed and bath linens either by operating an on-site laundry, using a commercial laundry to wash soiled linen, or making suitable arrangements with a linen rental company. In addition, the housekeeping departments in some properties are responsibile for looking after the supply of uniforms for uniformed employees in all departments, plus the food linen (the general term for all linens used in food and beverage departments). They may also have responsibility for redecorating and rehabilitating rooms; looking after articles in the property's lost-and-found area; maintaining floors throughout the property—washing and waxing floors and vacuuming and shampooing carpets, for example; washing windows; raising and lowering flags; moving furniture; repairing torn fabrics; attending to the rooms of employees who live in the property; and cleaning such outside areas as porches or sidewalks that surround the building. The tasks assigned to housekeeping are limited only by the imaginations of those who make the decisions in hotels, motels, and similar lodging properties.

The operation of the housekeeping operation can be complicated. Housekeeping is commonly the largest department in a lodging operation. It is managed by an individual who usually has a title such as head housekeeper, supervising housekeeper, or executive housekeeper. A head housekeeper manages a staff that may include people with such job titles as maid or housekeeper, room attendant, rooms inspector, houseman, laundry manager, linen room manager, assistant housekeeper, floor supervisor, among many other possibilities. Job titles vary considerably from one property to another.

While the responsibilities of housekeeping vary from one property to another, one major responsibility is common to all: giving daily attention to guest rooms occupied the previous night, whether or not the guests in those rooms check out on the current day.

Attending to Guests' Rooms

Each guest room in a property is monitored daily by the housekeeping department to determine whether it is occupied or vacant. In most major hotels and motels, daily comparison is made between housekeeping's determinations and front-office records of occupancy so that discrepancies can be identified and investigated.

When an occupied room becomes vacant because of a guest checkout, the housekeeping office is informed and a maid or room attendant is advised so that the room can be made ready for a new occupant. The room is considered **on change** until it is made ready for occupancy. This entails removing all soiled bed and bath linen from the room; replacing it with fresh, clean linen; making the bed(s), cleaning the bathroom; vacuuming the floor; dusting or polishing furniture; cleaning mirrors; emptying wastebaskets; replenishing supplies of tissue, toilet paper, matches, laundry bags, soap, and such amenities as shampoo, hair conditioner, and shower caps; and checking electric lights, televisions, clock radios, heating/cooling units, hair dryers, shoeshine machines, and other devices to be sure they are working properly. It may also require washing ashtrays; replenishing supplies for in-room coffee- and tea-making devices; restocking supplies for in-room bars; reporting items used from an in-room bar to the front office for billing purposes; checking the number of hangers in closets; and many other possibilities. There can be so much to do in every room that some properties give staff members printed checklists to help ensure that nothing is forgotten.

For rooms that will continue to be occupied by the current guests, the procedures may be essentially the same, although some properties do not change bed linens every day for guests staying several nights. It should be noted, as well, that it is probably not possible to do a thorough job of cleaning when guests' belongings are in the room. This is particularly true when clothes and other items are scattered around the room. If a room has remained vacant since it was last made ready for a new occupant, it is not normally necessary to do more than check it quickly, just to be sure it is still fresh and clean.

In order to have adequate supplies of linens and other materials available as they work, room attendants normally have mobile carts that can be pushed from room to room. Each of these carts typically has a canvas bag for storing the soiled laundry taken from guests' rooms. All soiled laundry collected in the course of one day is normally taken to a single area for processing, which may entail separating it by type and reloading it in other carts that will be collected by a commercial laundry or linen rental company, or preparing it for processing by the in-house laundry.

In the larger hotels and motels of major cities, the work of room attendants may be inspected by supervisors, who verify that rooms are properly cleaned and meet the standards established for the property. After a vacated room is made up and inspected, the supervisor may have responsibility for reporting it ready for occupancy—by informing the front office directly or reporting it via the housekeeping office. In smaller properties, room attendants may have little or no immediate supervision and may report directly to the front office.

The number of room attendants and the manner in which their work is assigned varies greatly from one property to another. In some, they are paid by the hour and expected to work at a reasonable pace, completing as many rooms as possible. In others, they are given a work quota for the seven-hour day that is stated in terms of number of rooms or beds that must be done. In still others, they are paid by the room. In most cases, they are assigned a station, a term used to describe the particular section of property or the group of rooms assigned to a room attendant. The station may be a complete floor or a specific number of rooms on one floor, for example. Some hotels, motels, and similar properties use a team approach, assigning more than one attendant per room. The amount of time required to clean a room depends on the number of attendants assigned to it as well as the size of the room, the number of beds, the extent of cleaning expected each day, and whether or not the room is a checkout. When a room is occupied by the same guests for several days, the amount of time attendants must spend in that room daily is somewhat less than the time they must spend in checkouts.

In hotels considered luxury properties, room attendants normally have more work to do in each room. In some properties, they must polish fine antique furniture; in others, they may be required to place arrangements of fresh flowers in rooms daily. In luxury hotels, standards of cleanliness are typically higher than in many other types of properties, so a greater amount of time is expected to be taken with each room. In many luxury operations, guests may be provided with services not provided in other types of properties. In some, room attendants visit each occupied guest room during the early evening to supply fresh towels, empty wastebaskets, and turn down bedding.

At the Kensington and many other similar properties, these services are routinely performed for each guest. It is necessary, therefore, for the hotel to employ additional room attendants for this purpose. They are supervised by an assistant housekeeper who works an afternoon and evening shift. The Kensington uses housekeeping teams to clean rooms. Two room attendants spend approximately half an hour working together to clean a typical room—one full hour of working time in each room. This is about 50 percent more time than is spent by room attendants at other hotels in the area.

The Mountain Inn and the Value Lodge assign specific rooms to each room attendant. In the Mountain Inn, each is assigned a permanent station consisting of ten rooms on one floor, which are to be completed in one seven-hour shift. In the Value Lodge, room attendants are expected to do 14 rooms in the seven-hour shift, and those who complete the work satisfactorily in less time are allowed to do additional rooms for extra pay. Thus, room attendants in the Mountain Inn complete each room in an average of 42 minutes, whereas those in the Value Lodge take about 30 minutes.

BUTLERS MAKE A COMEBACK ◀

Ring for a hotel butler these days and you're apt to get one savvier about your laptop dataport than about serving a glass of port. This new twist on an old idea is the "technology butler" on the club level of Atlanta's Ritz-Carlton Hotel. It is just the latest service offered by hotels on their premium floors.

Hotels are scrambling to outdo each other with upgraded amenities and service. In an effort to out-ritz the Ritz, premium floors are models of pampering, offering such features as complimentary breakfast, cocktails, and hors d'oeuvres; 24-hour concierge service; and rooms with plush terry-cloth robes, bottled water, and fruit baskets.

Guests at Boston's Ritz-Carlton enjoy six food and beverage servings a day, including a champagne and caviar hour. At the Empress Hotel in Victoria, British Columbia, you can have a foot massage delivered to your room. At the St. Regis Hotel in Washington, D.C., a *maître d'étage* caters to the needs of guests on his floor, providing clothes pressing, shoe shining, and custom-brewed coffee or tea throughout the day, and meeting guests' special requests.

Source: Adapted from an article in *USA Today*, 23 October 1999.

Caring for Linen

Caring for linen is one of the major responsibilities of the housekeeping department in any lodging operation. Without adequate supplies of appropriate linen, it is impossible to operate a lodging facility properly.

Linen—bed linen, bath linen, and, in some establishments, food linen—is one of the major problems and largest expenses in a lodging operation. Every bed in every room must be made up and ready for use at all times, whether or not the room is occupied. In addition, the property must have an adequate supply of linen on hand each day to change the linen on each bed, just in case the bed was used the previous night. Finally, some linen is always in the process of being washed and ironed or folded, whether in the property's own laundry or at an outside service. In effect, lodging operations must have at least three complete sets of linen for each bed and an additional quantity in inventory to replace items that are worn, torn, lost, or stolen. To make up a bed, one needs at least two sheets and one or more pillowcases, depending on the bed and the standards of the property.

In addition to bed linen, housekeeping should have at least three complete sets of bath linen for each guest that the property can accommodate. A set of bath linen consists of at least one bath towel, one face towel, and one face cloth. Most properties also supply one tub mat for each bathroom. Considerable money is invested in the bed linens and bath linens that lodging establishments need for operation.

Better lodging establishments typically change bed and bath linens for each guest daily. Others—some economy motels and inexpensive resorts—provide guests with changes of bath linens daily and changes of bed linens every two to three days. Still others—boardinghouses, typically—are likely to change all linens just once a week. Every responsible lodging establishment certainly changes all linens in any guest accommodation after each checkout.

In general, there are three possible approaches to obtaining clean linen. The lodging operator can:

1. Own linen and install a laundry on premises to wash, iron, and fold it.

2. Own linen and send it out to a commercial laundry to be washed, ironed, and folded.

3. Rent clean linen.

Each of these approaches has advantages and disadvantages.

Owning Linen and Installing a Laundry on Premises.   Many hotels and motels maintain their own laundry equipment on premises. Space is set aside for the specialized equipment needed to wash, dry, and iron linens, which may have the name of the property embroidered on or woven into the fabric.

Having one's own laundry has several advantages over other approaches. Linen does not leave the premises, so it is easier to control. If linen remains on the premises, it does not get lost as easily as when other methods are used, and personnel do not have to count linen leaving or returning to the building. The lodging operation is not dependent on an outside laundry, which can be late in returning clean linens, and, thus, is less likely to encounter the difficulties caused by linen shortages. Finally, maintaining an in-house laundry is often more cost-effective than the other approaches. In order for a lodging establishment to justify the expense of the investment in equipment and the ongoing cost of operating a laundry, however, the establishment must be large enough to keep the laundry operating several hours each day. Because of its remote location, the management of the Mountain Inn takes this approach.

Own Linen and Send It Out to a Commercial Laundry.   Many lodging operations prefer to own their own linen but are not large enough to justify the installation of laundry equipment on premises, or the cost of using their own employees to wash and fold linen is deemed excessive. In these cases, they must use the services of a commercial laundry. This choice still permits management to choose linen of the desired quality and inscribe it with the property's name, logo, or both. However, housekeeping departments that send out their laundry to a commercial establishment must separate and either count or weigh all sheets, pillowcases, towels, and other items going to and coming from the laundry. Billing is often a problem when the hotel's count or weight does not agree with that of the commercial laundry. In addition, commercial laundries may lose, tear, or otherwise destroy items sent out to be washed, and this can be a source of difficulty and misunderstanding.

The Kensington judges it less expensive to send its laundry to a commercial laundry located in a nearby suburb than to allocate space and pay the higher wages required to have it laundered on premises.

Rent Clean Linen.   Many lodging operators choose to rent clean linen rather than own it and have it laundered either on the premises or in a commercial laundry. This is the most convenient of the three approaches. There is no investment in either linen or equipment, and management does not have the problems associated with operating a laundry. Many rental companies do not keep accurate records of the amount of linen returned by lodging operators because the task is too time-consuming. Thus, lodging operators that rent clean linen may not have to account for it. They simply pay for the number of clean pieces they are sent and return the soiled linen. Laundries may not know how much linen they are losing to any one lodging operation, so they build the replacement cost of the lost linen into the rental prices charged to all lodging operators using their services.

Renting is typically the most costly of the three approaches, which is a distinct disadvantage. Another is that the lodging operator must accept the quality of linen supplied by the rental laundry, except when the rental laundry agrees to purchase higher-quality linens for a specific lodging operation.

For many smaller operations, renting clean linen is the most desirable of the three approaches. The Value Lodge uses this approach because the owners of the motel are satisfied with the quality of the linen supplied by the rental company. Also, they lack the time to deal with laundry, choose not to invest in linen or laundry equipment, and do not want to add laundry staff to their payroll.

Redecorating and Rehabilitating Rooms

An important function of the housekeeping operation is long-term upkeep. This is the process of maintaining the appearance of guest rooms by attending to the many items that make rooms attractive and appealing to guests, including paint, wallpaper, fixtures, carpeting, furniture, lamp shades, curtains, draperies, and other fabrics. All these must be kept in the proper condition. This may mean touching up the paint on one wall, patching damaged wallpaper on another, or replacing a burned patch of carpet, a damaged lamp, a tattered lamp shade, or a broken mirror—the list is endless. If the quality of guest rooms is allowed to deteriorate, they become less appealing to potential guests and fewer people are willing to stay in them. Over time, lodging operators who ignore this important element of housekeeping find that the establishment has deteriorated below the standards of the original property.

Many hotel and motel operators refurbish guest rooms regularly on a planned rotation system. Each year, a certain number of rooms are taken out of service to be completely refurbished. They are stripped, then redecorated and refurnished. One well-known hotel in New York completely refurbishes several floors each year. Over the course of several years, every room in the property is completely redone.

Security

The fourth basic element is providing security, one of the most important services. Hotels have both moral and legal obligations to protect guests from harm and to safeguard their property. The goal of the security system is to provide the necessary protection to keep guests and their property safe. The extent of this protection varies from establishment to establishment and from location to location.

Danger to guests may came from intruders, other guests, or such hazards as fire or unsafe conditions in the property.

Major metropolitan areas typically have greater crime problems than rural areas, and large hotels in the centers of cities tend to have greater difficulty with burglary and robbery than do small properties in outlying areas. Thus, major hotels in major cities both need and take greater security measures than their rural counterparts.

Hotels have always attracted thieves. Transient guests, after all, tend to have many of the items thieves seek—cash, credit cards, jewelry, and other valuables. Although all states have laws stating that lodging operators cannot be held responsible for losses of these valuables unless they are deposited in management's safe, many guests keep cash, jewelry, and other valuables in their rooms, where it is subject to theft either by professional thieves or even by unscrupulous employees of the establishment, although this is rare.

In some hotels, motels, and similar establishments, prostitution presents problems. Most major cities have prostitutes who find willing customers among hotel and motel guests. It is not uncommon for guests to meet prostitutes in bars and invite them to their hotel rooms. Sometimes guests give their room keys to prostitutes who promise to come to the hotel room. Often, they do. Sometimes, however, they merely give or sell the keys to professional thieves.

Major hotels, motels, and similar properties normally provide safe-deposit boxes for guests. In most establishments, these are located in the front office and are exactly the same as those used by banks. Increasingly, hotels provide in-room safes. In contrast, smaller and older properties, including small inns and motels, may provide nothing more than a single safe in the front office where valuables can be placed.

Fire and smoke represent continuing threats in most lodging operations. Sometimes guests accidentally start fires in their rooms. During the day, when people are awake, this is a difficult enough problem; at night, when guests are asleep, it is a terrifying threat to life. Newer establishments have smoke detectors and alarms to signal fire stations and to alert employees, but such systems are not universally required, and fire continues to be a danger. The security department of a large hotel in a major city may include personnel who patrol all floors of the building at night with watchmen's time clocks, looking for signs of smoke or fire as well as other potential threats to guests.

Unsafe conditions that exist within the lodging property present a serious threat to the welfare of guests and employees. Therefore, identifying, reporting, and remedying such conditions is of major importance in any lodging operation. Doing so is not the sole province of security, however; it is or should be one element in the job of every lodging employee. For example, room attendants who note frayed electric cords on hair dryers, lamps, televisions, or other appliances should be trained to report these so that repairs can be made. Similarly, instances of torn carpets, broken glass, burned-out lights in stairwells, broken chairs or other pieces of furniture, elevators that do not function properly—all such hazards should be reported immediately by the employees who spot them to prevent unnecessary harm or injury to guests and to other employees.

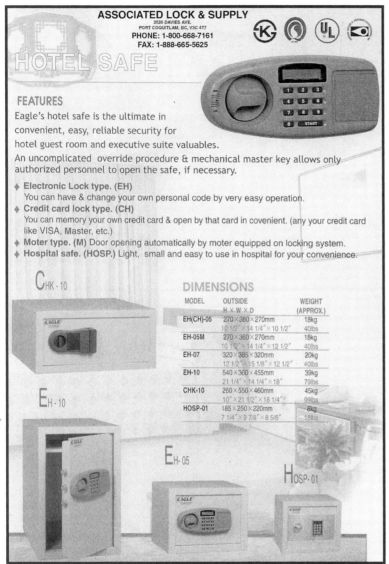

ASSOCIATED LOCK & SUPPLY
2528 DAVIES AVE.
PORT COQUITLAM, BC, V3C 4T7
PHONE: 1-800-668-7161
FAX: 1-888-665-5625

HOTEL SAFE

FEATURES

Eagle's hotel safe is the ultimate in convenient, easy, reliable security for hotel guest room and executive suite valuables.

An uncomplicated override procedure & mechanical master key allows only authorized personnel to open the safe, if necessary.

- ◆ **Electronic Lock type. (EH)**
  You can have & change your own personal code by very easy operation.
- ◆ **Credit card lock type. (CH)**
  You can memory your own credit card & open by that card in covenient. (any your credit card like VISA, Master, etc.)
- ◆ **Moter type. (M)** Door opening automatically by moter equipped on locking system.
- ◆ **Hospital safe. (HOSP.)** Light, small and easy to use in hospital for your convenience.

DIMENSIONS

MODEL	OUTSIDE H × W × D	WEIGHT (APPROX.)
EH(CH)-05	270×360×270mm	18kg
	10 1/2″×14 1/4″×10 1/2″	40lbs
EH-05M	270×360×270mm	18kg
	10 1/2″×14 1/4″×12 1/2″	40lbs
EH-07	320×385×320mm	20kg
	12 1/2″×15 1/8″×12 1/2″	40lbs
EH-10	540×360×455mm	39kg
	21 1/4″×14 1/4″×18″	79lbs
CHK-10	260×550×460mm	45kg
	10″×21 1/2″×18 1/4″	99lbs
HOSP-01	185×250×220mm	8kg
	7 1/4″×9 7/8″×8 5/8″	18lbs

CHK-10

EH-10

EH-05

HOSP-01

Traditionally, hotels have provided guests with safe deposit boxes in the front office. Today, many hotels are providing safes in guest rooms. Shown in this picture are various types and sizes of in-room safes.

(Photo courtesy of Associated Lock and Supply)

An important element in providing security for the guests of hotels, motels, and similar properties is that group of individuals known as the security staff. As indicated previously, they may be hotel or motel employees, or may work for an outside company that provides security services on contract.

Larger properties may have security personnel in uniform, while others work in plain clothes. Many people employed as security personnel have backgrounds in law enforcement and are trained to spot people who are likely to present problems—potential thieves, confidence artists, prostitutes, and others. Security per-

Many hotels employ closed-circuit television, as shown in this picture, to monitor a number of areas on their properties.
(Photo courtesy of Pinkerton Services Corporation, © 2001)

sonnel are often placed in locations from which they can observe everyone who enters and exits the property. Resort properties, such as the Mountain Inn, often follow this procedure. They employ a director of security who supervises several security guards in plain clothes. Some guards observe entrances and exits while others mingle with guests in bars, nightclubs, and other recreational facilities.

In contrast, the large transient hotels and motels in major cities may install closed-circuit television cameras to monitor entrances, corridors, storage facilities, and other important areas. Properties such as the Kensington commonly have modern closed-circuit television networks that are used to monitor a number of areas in these properties—particularly areas that are deserted at night and those from which food, liquor, and other hotel property may be stolen. In the Kensington and similar properties, employee entrances are typically locked during late evening and night hours, and security guards are posted at these entrances during the day to prevent their use by unauthorized individuals.

Small motels and similar properties cannot normally afford the number and type of security personnel employed in the larger operations just described. In the small property, the owner or manager, who is normally on premises most or all the time, typically serves as the security staff. On a small scale, he must attend to all the security routines for which major city hotels employ security staff. Typically, this means keeping watch for suspicious or unusual activities. In the Value Lodge, for example, the owner must note carefully who enters and leaves the rooms and watch for strangers attempting unauthorized entry. The owner of such a property normally walks throughout his property several times during the evening.

Most commercial hotels, motels, and similar lodging properties provide more than the basics, in keeping with the wishes of their guests. The majority provide additional services, some of which are listed above in Group 1. Because the number of possibilities is so great, we restrict the following discussion to those listed earlier in the chapter, which are those most often provided by lodging operators.

The extent to which these services are provided to guests varies. Some motels provide few, if any, of them, and some luxury hotels provide them all; other lodging properties offer a limited number. One of the most common and important of the services and operations offered in lodging operations is front service.

Front Service

Front service is a term used to identify the operation that provides a variety of useful and desirable personal services for guests. These include attended service at the front door for handling luggage, obtaining taxicabs, and opening doors; escorting guests from the front desk to the assigned accommodations, as discussed in the section on check-in; carrying luggage for guests; opening guest room doors for those having difficulty with their keys; delivering newspapers, mail, packages, or telephone messages to guest rooms; providing information about restaurants, theaters, shopping, and sightseeing (if this is not done at the front desk); and making reservations or providing tickets, or attending to both of these, for shows, tours, sporting events, and transportation.

The employees engaged in front service are normally uniformed and have such job titles as bellman or bellperson, doorman or doorperson, baggage porter, concierge, or superintendent of service. People in these positions are typically paid low hourly wages and receive gratuities or tips from guests for whom they perform services.

Food and Beverage

The food and beverage operation can be critical to the overall success of some lodging operations. For luxury establishments, the quality of the food and beverage products offered in the restaurants and bars are among their major attractions.

For those hotels, motels, and similar lodging operations that offer food and beverage services, the primary goal of the operation is to provide food and beverage products and services that meet the quality standards established by the owners and managers.

Food and beverage operations in lodging establishments offer their services in four distinct types of facilities:

1. Restaurants and bars
2. Vending areas
3. Guest rooms
4. Banquet rooms

Front service personnel are normally uniformed. Shown here is a doorman on duty at the Copley Plaza Hotel in Boston, Massachusetts.
(Photo courtesy of Fairmont Hotels and Resorts)

Restaurants and Bars

Many commercial hotels, motels, and similar lodging operations operate food and beverage facilities that are normally open to guests of the property and to the public at large. These facilities include formal and informal restaurants—specialty restaurants, coffee shops, snack bars, and cafeterias among them—as well as bars, cocktail lounges, and nightclubs.

Many luxury hotels take pride in providing the finest food and beverage products and services available. These properties have a talented staff of professionals in their food and beverage department, the equal of those in the finest restaurants. The majority of hotels, motels, and similar lodging establishments serve guests and customers from the surrounding community foods and beverages comparable to those served in most restaurants.

The Kensington employs a chef who was trained at the Culinary Institute of America, one of the leading culinary schools in the United States, and, thus, have superior cuisine. The Mountain Inn has a dining room that serves typical American fare of very good quality as well as a snack bar for skiers and people who want short-order foods.

Vending Areas

The type and quality of food and beverage products and services available to guests in lodging establishments vary, of course, from one establishment to another. Some properties—motels, most commonly—provide only vending machines with packaged foods. Other motels have vending machines that contain frozen meals, which can be cooked with microwave ovens installed in the lobby or near guests' rooms.

The Value Lodge has a room set aside for vending machines that are serviced by a local company. The room contains microwave ovens and tables for food dispensed in the vending machines. Customers cook the food themselves and eat at the tables or take the food back to their rooms.

Guest Rooms

Most first-class and luxury hotels provide **room service**, a type of service that provides guests with food and beverages ordered from and consumed in their rooms. The most popular meal for room service is breakfast, even though some hotels provide room service 24 hours a day. Room service menus typically include items that are similar to or the same as those offered on menus in the public rooms. However, the prices for items offered on room service menus are normally higher than regular menu prices.

Even with higher prices, however, room service is not always a profitable enterprise. One of the primary reasons is that room service is labor intensive and relatively inefficient. It is necessary to have a separate staff of servers for room service, and these individuals may have few orders and little work much of the time. In addition, delivering room service orders can be a slow and time-consuming business. Food that comes from the main kitchen often must be transported great distances to guest rooms. For all of these reasons, the labor cost associated with a given room service order is higher than that for the same item served in a public restaurant. Of the three properties illustrated in this text, the Kensington is the only one that offers room service, which it does 24 hours a day.

The most popular meal for room service is breakfast, even though some hotels provide room service 24 hours a day.

Banquet Rooms

Most establishments with extensive food and beverage facilities make concerted efforts to attract banquet business. The term **banquet** refers to the prearranged service of food and beverages to a group of people in a private room not in use as a public dining room. Banquet business is normally profitable—often more profitable than restaurant or bar operation—because exact numbers of guests are guaranteed in advance, making it comparatively easy to achieve planned food and labor costs.

The availability of food and beverage products and services in some or all of the above can increase the appeal of a given property to potential lodging customers. Some guests return to particular lodging operations time after time because of the excellent food offered in the dining room or because of the superior wine list available. Some enjoy the great luxury of having breakfast or some other meal served in the comfort and privacy of a guest room or suite. In some instances, people planning a banquet function reserve sleeping rooms in the hotel, bringing revenue that would otherwise not have come to the property. Sometimes groups select a particular hotel and reserve large numbers of rooms for a convention because the hotel has the capacity to provide banquet service for a very large group—500 or more people. The presence of a food and beverage operation can be important to a lodging operation and make a difference in the amount of revenue the property generates, both from food and beverage sales and from room sales.

Recreation and Entertainment

Recreation and entertainment can be major factors in attracting guests to a lodging operation. One of these may be the only reason for deciding to go to a particular property. Recreation and entertainment is a broad category that can include an array of activities and events that guests find appealing. One type includes well-known and popular athletic and sporting activities: tennis, skiing, horseback riding, golf, and swimming, for example. However, it also includes such simple possibilities as the Ping-Pong and billiard tables found in some small family resort properties.

Another type includes the nightclubs and other showplaces featuring star-quality entertainers that one finds in many mountain and shore resort properties across the country, in the major hotels and motels of Las Vegas and Atlantic City, and on such closely related facilities as cruise ships.

Still another type is gaming, a highly profitable and popular attraction in many of the hotels of Las Vegas and Atlantic City, as well as on Indian reservations, riverboats, and in some areas outside the United States. Along the same line as gaming are the bingo games, card games, and coin-operated machines of various sorts available in many properties because they appeal to guests.

The operators of lodging properties who believe the addition of one or more of these is likely to increase the appeal of the properties, their profitability, or both will probably attempt to include them.

Parking

Facilities for parking are of ever-growing importance to guests and lodging operators, as more and more travelers use automobiles—those they own and those they rent. Many properties are so far removed from public transportation that guests must have automobiles to get around the local area.

Properties surrounded by adequate land have relatively little difficulty using it for parking, whether outdoor parking near the doors to guests' accommodations or on a simple lot, or indoor parking in a purpose-built structure. By contrast, many newer properties have parking facilities within their structures, permitting guests to drive inside buildings and to park before proceeding to lobbies to check in.

A number of older hotels in the centers of cities have been forced to arrange alternative parking. Because they have no surrounding land and cannot create parking space within their structures, many make arrangements for parking with nearby garages and lots. Some provide pickup and delivery service so that guests need never go farther than the front door to leave or retrieve their vehicles. That is the case at the Kensington, where an underground parking facility is provided for guests' cars. At the Mountain Inn, a large parking lot is provided; at the Value Lodge, guests park at the entrance to their rooms.

Other Personal Services

There is any number of other possibilities for offering personal services to guests of hotels, motels, and similar lodging operations. The following sections discuss the most common.

Banking Services

For the convenience of guests, some lodging operations provide banking services at the front desk. Cashiers normally make change and, in some properties, they cash both personal checks and traveler's checks. In a growing number of establishments, they convert foreign currencies to dollars, given the increased number of international visitors entering the country. This service is provided at the Kensington.

Guest Laundry

A large number of hotels, motels, and other commercial lodging operations provide personal laundry service to guests. Guests can arrange for soiled shirts, blouses, underwear, and other clothing to be collected from their rooms, laundered, and returned. Some facilities even provide same-day service. Another approach is to provide self-service facilities for guests to attend to their own laundry—making washers, dryers, irons, and ironing boards available.

Dry Cleaning

Most properties that provide laundry service also provide dry-cleaning services. Guests can arrange to have suits, skirts, trousers, and other garments collected from their rooms, cleaned, pressed, and returned. As with laundry, some facilities provide same-day service. Dry-cleaning services in hotels are normally referred to as valet services. Because the Kensington does not have its own laundry, the hotel has an arrangement with a local service for its guests.

Hair Styling

Many lodging properties provide facilities for men's and women's hair styling. In a few properties, these are still known by the older terms *barbershop* and *beauty salon*, but these are disappearing from the lodging lexicon. Some facilities offering hair styling may also offer nail care, cosmetics treatments, and related services.

Office Services

Increasingly, hotels, motels, and other lodging properties offer an array of office services, primarily for business travelers. They provide copy machines, fax machines, computers and printers, modems, typewriters, and tape recorders for dictation. Some set up this equipment—as well as such simple items as staplers, staple removers, and paper clips—in special rooms for use by guests 24 hours a day. Many now provide Internet and E-mail services in guest rooms. A very few provide personal assistance on request.

Health Facilities

Because many guests are health conscious, and because of the increased emphasis on exercise, some lodging operations provide a variety of facilities for exercise. Some have health clubs, saunas, and steam rooms on premises. Others set up a room or an area with exercise equipment. Some maintain small swimming pools for exercise. Still others assist joggers in finding appropriate routes at various hours of the day.

Newsstands

In a lodging establishment, the term *newsstand* can refer to a small counter at which a few newspapers and magazines are sold, or to a larger enterprise selling newspapers, magazines, books, candy, cigars, cigarettes, souvenirs, and such personal articles as disposable razors, shaving cream, antiperspirants, and toothpaste.

Language Services

Hotels, motels, and similar lodging establishments that accommodate tourists and business travelers from other nations often employ individuals who are fluent in two or more languages. Such people can be helpful to visitors who are not fluent in English. The Kensington started offering language service last year in response to an increasing number of foreign visitors.

Other Shops

Hotels and other major lodging properties in large cities are likely to rent space to shopkeepers who provide various goods and services to guests as well as to residents of the surrounding area. It is not unusual to find travel agencies, jewelers, luggage shops, and clothing boutiques, among many other possible shops, in the lobby areas of these properties.

The availability of some or all of these commonly increases the appeal of a hotel, motel, or similar lodging establishment to guests. Therefore, the property offering these typically enjoys some competitive advantage over those that do not. There are several shops, including a travel agency, clothing boutique, and drugstore, at the Kensington. The Mountain Inn leases space to operators of a clothing shop, sports equipment shop, and drugstore. None of these shops are located in the Value Lodge.

THE INTERRELATEDNESS OF LODGING OPERATIONS

It should be apparent that the several operations that are the essence of a lodging facility—front office, telephone, housekeeping, and security, which comprise Group 1—as well as those that enhance the quality of the lodging operations—front service, food and beverages services, and others, which comprise Group 2—must function effectively, both individually and as a group, for the operation to achieve its goals.

Within the front-office operation, reservations must be accurately recorded if the room clerks are to know how many rooms are available to rent to persons without reservations. Room clerks must properly record information about arriving and departing guests if the housekeeping department is to have accurate data to perform its job. Housekeepers must clean and prepare vacated rooms properly and report the room numbers of made-up rooms to the front desk promptly and accurately so that newly arrived guests can be assigned to suitable accommodations.

In the front-services operation, bellpersons checking guests into rooms should note and report the numbers of rooms that are not up to standard—those with burned-out light bulbs, damaged furniture, or dripping faucets, for example. This information helps housekeeping identify problems and keep guest rooms in proper condition.

In the food and beverage operation, room service employees must accurately verify the names and room numbers of guests ordering from their rooms so the items ordered can be delivered to the correct room quickly. Similarly, employees in restaurants must verify the names and room numbers of guests who charge food and beverages so their bills can be properly charged.

Employees attending to guests' laundry and dry-cleaning requirements must be particularly careful to obtain and record room numbers correctly so garments can be returned to the right rooms and charges for the service recorded on the correct bills.

Because the operations in a lodging establishment are interrelated, all must function properly and in a coordinated way for the lodging operation to achieve its goals. When an operation is not performing as designed or intended, other operations are affected. For example, if the housekeeping operation in the Kensington fails to clean rooms quickly, the front-office operation is affected. Room clerks may be forced to tell guests that there will be a delay in assigning them to rooms, thus disappointing some guests and possibly angering others. In addition, this may affect the behavior of room clerks toward guests. If one or another of the lodging operations fails to operate properly, the overall operation will not achieve its goals.

SUMMARY

In this chapter, lodging operations are examined. Front office, telephone, housekeeping, and security are identified as the basic operations and services common to all lodging facilities. Front service, food and beverage, recreation/entertainment, parking, and personal services are identified as six additional activities not common to all lodging operations but used selectively by some to aid in achieving their goals.

Examples are drawn from three types of lodging properties—the Value Lodge, the Mountain Inn, and the Kensington Hotel. Finally, the interrelatedness of activities in a lodging enterprise is emphasized and offered as a basis for examining and understanding complex lodging operations.

KEY TERMS

Banquet	Housekeeping	Reservation
Check-in	Information activity	Room clerk
Checkout	No-show	Room service
Front office	On change	Walk
Front service	Outsourcing	Yield management
Guaranteed reservation	Overbooking	

DISCUSSION QUESTIONS

1. Name the four operations and services common to all lodging facilities.
2. List and state the goals of the four activities associated with the front office and describe the functions of each.

3. Identify five additional services offered by some, but not all, lodging operators.

4. What are the advantages of electronic locks over traditional locks and metal keys?

5. Describe three variations on checkout procedure used by hotels, motels, and similar facilities.

6. Define the terms *overbooking* and *no-show*. Describe two problems that cause some lodging operators to overbook.

7. What is the goal of housekeeping?

8. Describe ten tasks that may be assigned to housekeeping.

9. List ten tasks typically involved in making a room ready for occupancy.

10. Why would a guest room in a luxury hotel take more time to make ready for occupancy than one in an economy motel?

11. Why is it necessary to redecorate or rehabilitate guest rooms every few years? List the kinds of tasks likely to be required for the complete rehabilitation of a guest room in a luxury hotel.

12. Describe several security measures typically taken in a large center-city hotel. Contrast those with security measures typically taken in a small motel in a rural community.

13. List ten guest services normally associated with front service.

14. Identify three services provided to guests by a modern telephone system.

15. List and describe three types of facilities in which food and beverage services are available in lodging operations.

16. Of the services offered in the three types of food and beverage facilities identified in question 15, which is the most profitable? Why?

17. Is it more important for lodging properties in remote rural areas to have parking facilities for their guests than for those located in city centers? Why?

18. List eight personal services identified in the chapter that are offered by some, but not all, lodging properties.

MOMENTS OF TRUTH

1. Visit a lodging property in your community. Identify the services offered to guests. Are any services offered in the property not discussed in this chapter?

2. You are the desk clerk of a local motel. The reservation department has overbooked for the current day. Unfortunately, the anticipated number of cancellations did not materialize, and a guest with a confirmed reservation is now at your front desk. You do not have a vacant room, so it is necessary for you to walk the guest. Explain how you would do this. Describe what you would do, what you would say, how you would say it, and how you would deal with

the guest if he were angry. This guest has given the telephone number of your motel to a large number of potential buyers of his products, and many of these people will be calling to make appointments with him.

3.   You are the evening desk clerk at a motel located in a remote area in the western part of the United States. At 9:00 P.M., you have no vacant rooms left except for one you are holding for a Mr. Pool, an individual with a guaranteed reservation who has not yet arrived. Your records show that the anticipated arrival time for the guaranteed reservation was 6:00 P.M. A woman without a reservation is at your front desk asking if any rooms are available. You check with other lodging establishments in the area, but find they have no vacant rooms either. She is desperate, because the next area with lodging facilities is over 100 miles away. She is too tired to attempt that long a drive at this hour. What would you do?

INTERNET EXERCISES

1.   Go to http://www.bristolhotels.com. Find the Four Points Hotel in Leominster, Massachusetts, on that Web site. What services do they offer beyond the basic ones listed in this chapter?

2.   Go to http://www.choicehotels.com. Compare the services offered for three of their brands—Comfort, Quality, and Sleep hotels.

PART V
Hospitality
Management
Perspectives

Hospitality Operations Management

▶ Learning Objectives

After reading and studying this chapter, you should be able to:

1. Define the term *operations management*.

2. List and define the functions of management.

3. List the six steps in the organizing process.

4. Discuss the significance of an organization chart.

5. List and discuss the four steps in the control process.

6. Define *marketing*, as used in hospitality operations.

7. List and describe the four elements of marketing.

8. Define the term *human resources management* and describe the activities it includes.

9. Identify three important steps taken by management to enhance employee safety in the workplace.

10. Define the term *accounting* and identify the two major financial statements derived from accounting records.

11. Define the following terms:
    • Asset
    • Current assets
    • Fixed assets
    • Liability
    • Current liability
    • Long-term liability
    • Owner's equity
    • Income statement
    • Revenue
    • Expense
    • Profit
    • Loss

12. Identify the formula for calculating each of the following:
    • food cost-to-sales ratio
    • beverage cost-to-sales ratio
    • labor cost-to-sales ratio
    • percentage of occupancy

13. Identify each of the following:
    • Inventory turnover
    • Return on sales
    • Average sale per customer
    • Average rate per occupied room

14. Define the term *budget*.

15. Describe the importance of cost control to the management of a hospitality operation.

16. Identify benefits that computers can provide for hospitality operations.

INTRODUCTION

Previous chapters identified various types of hospitality establishments, discussed hospitality facilities, and described basic elements common to hospitality operations. This chapter introduces operations management in the hospitality enterprise.

Operations management is a term that requires some explanation. In the hospitality industry and in this text, operations management is defined as the day-to-day activities that managers engage in to achieve the goals of the operations they manage. People with experience in professional hospitality operations are likely to be familiar with some or all of the areas that these activities encompass. They are known to hospitality managers by such traditional business terms as *marketing*, *accounting*, and *human resources management*. These, and others similar to them, are areas in which managers must be able to apply certain specific skills: planning, organizing, directing, and controlling. These four are known as the functions of management.

THE FUNCTIONS OF MANAGEMENT

In formal texts devoted to the subject, management at all levels is often said to have four functions:

1. Planning

2. Organizing

3. Directing

4. Controlling

Planning

Planning is the primary task of managers at all levels. At the highest level—many refer to it as top management—planning is the process of defining goals and objectives for an organization and determining the appropriate means for achieving them. In its broadest sense, planning is an attempt to define the organization's future, to determine today what the state of organization should be in the future—one year or five years from now. In the hospitality industry, top management must make plans today for the future. These are likely to center on such considerations as the service products that will be offered, the rate of expansion for the organization, the rate of sales increases necessary to sustain that growth, and the means for financing the expansion.

To illustrate planning in one hospitality organization, we cite several examples from Marecki Foods, the business and industry hospitality organization described in Chapter 5. In the Marecki organization, top management is developing plans to enlarge the business. These plans include increasing the number of clients by 10 percent per year and expanding the company from its present regional base to one more national in scope. This is an example of the type of high-level and long-range planning that top managers do.

At the next-highest level—middle management—planning tends to be more pragmatic and more short range. In the Marecki organization, the middle managers are the district managers. Their plans are linked to the day-to-day realities of the units they oversee. In Marecki Foods, the district manager of the area that includes the Mountain Bank and six other units is one of several middle-level managers. She works with unit managers to plan annual budgets to submit to the main office once a year. She also makes plans for unit renovations as needed and for such major purchases as kitchen equipment and computer systems.

At the lowest management level—the supervisory level—planning tends to be for the very near term. Supervisory managers must make plans for today, tomorrow, and next week. Their plans deal with such problems as having adequate staff and sufficient food available in the kitchen to prepare and serve the next meal and meals for the balance of the week. They commonly make plans, for example, for having enough servers and linens on hand in the dining room to prepare for heavy demand for the next three days. In the Mountain Bank unit, the manager plans menus, as well as the food purchases to prepare those menus, and he plans staffing levels for the operation, including the daily work schedules for employees.

Organizing

Organizing follows planning as the next logical step in the management process. It is the second function of management. After a manager develops plans designed to achieve some objective, those plans must be carried out. That is the purpose of the additional steps in the management process—organizing, directing, and controlling.

Organizing means coordinating the use of resources, human and otherwise, to achieve established objectives. To organize work in a hospitality operation, a manager determines how human and other resources will be combined and activated to achieve established objectives.

Organizing is accomplished by means of the following steps:

1. Determine what work must be done to execute plans and achieve objectives.

2. Arrange that work into logical patterns or structures.

3. Assign the work to specific jobs.

4. Allocate the resources required to accomplish the work.

5. Coordinate the work activity.

6. Evaluate the results of the organizing process.

Assume that in the Steak Shack, the restaurant described in Chapter 5, the chef has completed plans to feed the expected number of customers for the following week. The first step in the organizing process is to determine what must be done to carry out the plans. Clearly, food must be ordered and a staff schedule set up. The second step is to group the work into logical patterns. To do this, the chef must decide which menu items should be prepared by each of the stations in the kitchen. The third step is to assign the preparation of the various menu items to specific cooks. Next, each cook is told the number of portions of each item to prepare and given recipes to use. Additionally, the chef makes provision for the ingredients to be on hand when needed. Next, he coordinates the work activity, synchronizing the efforts of all personnel so that the established goals are achieved—the menu items are ready on time. He specifies the times at which roasts and potatoes are placed in ovens and soup and sauces cookery begins so that all these items are properly done at the time needed. As the work proceeds, he continually evaluates the results of the organizing process to determine whether or not changes or alterations are required.

Once the organizing process is completed, each of the six steps does not necessarily have to be repeated each day. When work is satisfactorily organized, it simply becomes a daily routine. Although daily routines should be reevaluated regularly, they are unlikely to be changed unless new, more effective or efficient ways are found.

Hospitality Organization

The work in a hospitality enterprise can be organized in any of several ways. One way is to create departments in which the focus is on employees whose work is logically grouped. For example, all the employees working in the dining room of the Steak Shack can be grouped into one department known as the dining room service department. This department is headed by a dining room manager and includes all servers and bussers. Similarly, all employees working in the front-office of the Kensington Hotel can be grouped into a front-office department headed by a front-office manager.

Organization Charts

An **organization chart** is simply a diagram of the formal structure of the business organization. In a small organization like the Steak Shack, an organization chart shows the departments in the organization and the relationship of the departments to one another. In Figure 10.1, the organization chart of the Steak Shack, the lines connecting the departments show the reporting structure. The reporting structure in an organization indicates to employees which workers report to particular supervisors. From Figure 10.1, it is clear that the dining room manager and the chef both report to the general manager of the restaurant. It is also clear that cooks and dishwashers report to the chef, while servers and bussers report to the dining room manager. The owner/manager of the Steak Shack considered other possible organizational structures before settling on the one illustrated, but rejected them as unsuitable for this specific operation.

It is especially important in an organization to ensure that no employee has more than one immediate supervisor—a practice identified as unity of command.

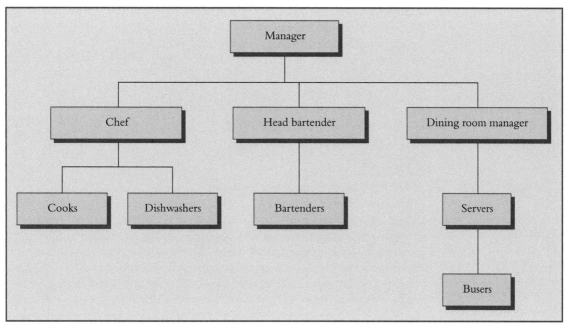

FIGURE 10.1
Organization chart for the Steak Shack

If an employee reports to more than one manager, there is a strong possibility—even a probability—that the employee will be given opposing or contradictory instructions by these managers, resulting in conflict and confusion. If, for example, the chef identified in Figure 10.1 were to begin giving instructions to servers to serve plates of food from the right, although the dining room manager had instructed them to serve from the left, the servers could become confused and frustrated. Some would be angry at being criticized by the two managers for failing to follow directions. If the chef wanted an item served in a particular way, the correct procedure would be to discuss the matter with the dining room manager, who would, in turn, instruct the servers. Similarly, if the manager wanted to change a standard recipe, she would be wrong to go directly to the cook preparing that item. Proper procedure would be for the manager to discuss the change with the chef, who would, in turn, instruct the cooks. When one employee has two or more bosses giving him contradictory orders, confusion and conflict are sure to result.

Directing

The third management function is directing. **Directing** is the process of achieving organizational goals by leading, motivating, and supervising subordinates. Directing is important at all levels of management, but it is particularly important at the supervisory level. Compared with many other businesses, hospitality operations tend to be labor intensive. This means that a large proportion of hospitality employees report to managers at the supervisory level.

In the Mountain Inn, the front-office manager is the supervisory manager with responsibility for leading, motivating, and supervising the front office staff. One of her activities aimed at fulfilling this responsibility is to hold regular meetings with staff to deal with a range of important topics, including procedures for handling credit cards, dealing with complaining guests, selecting and assigning rooms for arriving guests, and plans for room renovations over the next six months. In addition, because the front-office manager is normally at the front desk during periods of heavy arrivals, she is in an excellent position to observe employees and to make note of problems that should be addressed during the meetings. This is just a small sample of the dozens of activities required of the front-office manager in the Mountain Inn, who has an important and complex job.

The vast majority of hospitality employees report to chefs, front-office managers, dining room managers, and other supervisory managers. In hospitality operations, the employees who report to supervisory managers are those whose job titles are best known to the public, including servers, desk clerks, cooks, reservationists, dishwashers, housekeepers, and bartenders. Employees reporting to supervisory managers account for as much as 90 percent of all hospitality employees.

Controlling

The fourth function of management is **controlling**. Control is a process used by managers to regulate and, sometimes, restrain the actions of people in order to achieve desired goals. Controlling consists of decisions and actions taken by managers to assure that desired goals are achieved.

Assume that plans are made to achieve goals and objectives, the enterprise is organized, and managers direct the efforts of employees. It is unlikely that goals and objectives will be achieved unless managers exert control over those efforts. In part, they do this by preventing incidents and problems.

The Control Process

The control process consists of four steps:

1. Establish standards and standard procedures for operation.

2. Train employees to follow established standards and standard procedures.

3. Monitor employee performance and compare actual performance with established standards.

4. Take appropriate action to correct deviations in performance.

One example serves to illustrate. In the Steak Shack, one of the three soups listed on the menu is an onion soup served with a small toasted slice of rye bread covered with mozzarella cheese. The item is placed briefly in a broiler just before service to melt the cheese. In recent years, the restaurant has earned a reputation for having the best onion soup in the area, and the owner/manager wants to keep that reputation. To do so, he must be sure that all portions of onion soup are identical to one another, day after day after day. The best way to achieve this is to establish a standard procedure for preparing the item. This is done by writing a standard recipe, a recipe that kitchen personnel are required to use each time the item is prepared. The recipe is printed on a card and accompanied by a color photograph of one portion prepared as it is to appear to each customer. Staff members must be trained to follow the recipe. If they do so correctly and see that every portion looks like the example in the photograph, there is some reasonable assurance that all portions will be identical and the reputation for excellent onion soup maintained. The chef must monitor employee performance, comparing actual portions of onion soup with the standard portion defined by the standard recipe and photograph. If portions do not measure up, steps must be taken to correct performance. The nature and type of corrective actions depend on what goes wrong.

OPERATIONS MANAGEMENT

As indicated earlier in this chapter, operations management is defined as the day-to-day activities that managers engage in to achieve the goals of the operations they manage. These activities cover key areas including marketing, human resources, accounting, budgeting, cost control, and computers. In this chapter, we suggest how all these key areas are linked to an operations manager's job in the hospitality industry. Successful performance as an operations manager in hospitality requires considerable knowledge of these key areas. In the course of demonstrating this, the chapter conveys a sense of the broad range of daily activities that face the typical manager in the hospitality business.

KEY AREA 1: MARKETING

The best manager cannot make an enterprise meet its financial goals if too few customers patronize it. Restaurants must serve a given number of customers per week and hotels must ensure that a given number of rooms are occupied if these hospitality operations are to be financially healthy. Our discussion of marketing focuses on the activities associated with obtaining the number of customers or guests required for a foodservice or lodging operation to achieve the necessary degree of financial health.

Definition of Marketing

The American Marketing Association defines marketing broadly. It states that marketing is "the process of planning and executing the conception, pricing, promotion, and distribution of ideas, goods, and services to create exchanges that will satisfy individual and organizational objectives."

While this definition is entirely suitable for organizations that manufacture and sell goods that customers use in their homes and businesses, it needs to be adjusted slightly to apply to service products that customers consume in hospitality establishments. Our adjusted definition for hospitality operations is as follows: **Marketing** is the process of planning service products, finding the right place to locate, and pricing and promoting products to attract sufficient numbers of customers/guests and to create exchanges that will satisfy both their needs and the goals of the hospitality enterprise.

Elements of Marketing

The above definition has four key elements:

1. Product

2. Place

3. Price

4. Promotion

Product

One basic decision to be made in hospitality marketing is the nature of the service **product** or products to be offered. To some extent, that is defined by the characteristic type of establishment one intends to operate. Some of the many possible foodservice types were discussed in Chapter 4, including fast-food restaurants, family restaurants, specialty restaurants, fine-dining restaurants, cocktail lounges, and taverns. A number of lodging types were identified in Chapter 7.

Each characteristic type of foodservice or lodging enterprise is associated with some general type of service product line. Based on that knowledge, customers seeking a particular type of service product are likely to look for the type of establishment they expect offers it.

Among the foodservice examples cited, the Steak Shack characterizes itself as a neighborhood family restaurant and has a product line consisting of eight entrées that are among those most favored by residents of the area. By contrast, Frog's Pub, which caters to an entirely different group of people, has chosen to emphasize imported beers—36 varieties—and to treat food as secondary.

Among the lodging examples, the Kensington is a luxury hotel offering the full range of services and amenities normally associated with that type of property, while the Value Lodge is clearly a budget operation offering clean, comfortable sleeping accommodations but few additional services.

Place

The second element in hospitality marketing is **place**. In the hospitality world, place is a synonym for location. The location of a hospitality operation can be an essential element in its marketing effort. Physical location is critical to the success of many hospitality operations. A family restaurant like the Steak Shack must generally be located within a reasonable driving distance of the population it intends to serve. By contrast, fast-food restaurants must be in the immediate vicinity of their customers to attract great numbers of them. In the lodging industry, it is well known that location is probably the single most important consideration. If the Value Lodge were not situated within sight of an exit from a major interstate highway, it probably would not attract enough customers to survive.

For marketing managers, physical location is a fact of life that cannot normally be changed; hotels, motels, restaurants, and bars do not normally change locations. One of the major challenges of marketing is to develop a product line that is suitable for the existing location.

Price

The third element in hospitality marketing is **price**—the prices charged for hospitality service products, including menu prices in a restaurant and room rates in a lodging operation. In general, customers and guests are more easily attracted to operations with lower prices and rates than to similar establishments that charge more. Price is only one consideration, however, in the consumer's decision to purchase a service product from one operation rather than another. The three other elements of marketing—product, location, and promotion—may also play important roles in the decision-making process.

Establishing the price structure for hospitality operation is a difficult process. Unfortunately, no simple formula enables one to do so. Many judgments must be made, most of which are subjective. Room rates and menu pricing are among the most difficult challenges facing hospitality operators. If prices are too high, customers may go elsewhere. If they are too low, the establishment may not be profitable.

At the Mountain Bank, where operating costs are subsidized, menu prices are kept low to encourage bank employees to use the facility and to remain on premises throughout the working day. At the Steak Shack, which has earned an excellent reputation for superior food, menu prices can be somewhat higher than would be possible without that reputation.

The same basic problem faces operations managers in the lodging industry. If room rates are higher than those in similar operations nearby, customers may patronize the competing establishments. If, for example, the room rates in the Value Lodge were $10.00 per night higher than those in a comparable new motel just across the highway, the Goodsons would lose considerable business.

To establish menu prices for food and beverages or rates for hotel rooms, operations managers take the following factors into account:

- Product costs: ingredient costs in a restaurant, or such costs as bed and bath linen in a hotel or motel
- Labor costs, including benefits and payroll taxes
- Overhead costs
- Prices at competing establishments
- The effect of prices on the numbers of customers or guests likely to patronize the establishment

It should be obvious that hospitality operations cannot operate profitably if the prices or rates charged are less than product costs. Further, operating costs are not limited to product costs. Other factors include labor costs and such overhead costs as real estate taxes, telephone, insurance, heat, gas or electricity for cooking, electricity for lighting, and cleaning supplies, to name just a few. All of these costs must be taken into account before setting menu prices and room rates, because revenue from product sales must be adequate to cover all costs of operation. Labor cost reflects both the levels of skill and the amounts of employee time required to prepare service products for sale. These must be factored into the menu prices and room rates. For example, fine-dining establishments employ talented and highly paid chefs and cooks because they have the high-level skills required to prepare the menu items. In contrast, most fast-food restaurants can operate successfully with relatively unskilled employees who earn far lower wages. The menu prices at both these types of establishments reflect the levels of difficulty and amounts of employee time required to prepare menu items. These differences help to account for the higher menu prices charged in fine-dining establishments, compared with those of the fast-food restaurants.

The same considerations are important in lodging operations. In luxury hotels like the Kensington, which offer extensive personal services, labor costs are much higher than in budget motels like the Value Lodge. The higher room rates charged by luxury hotels reflect greater numbers of employees and the higher levels of skills they bring to their jobs.

For the majority of hospitality operations, neither menu prices nor room rates should be established until one has considered prices in competing operations. Those who ignore the prices of their competitors risk having potential customers and guests go elsewhere. Hospitality operators who seek to attract a large number of customers or guests usually establish low prices. For example, one of the major reasons for the success of fast-food hamburger chains is this ability to attract many customers by pricing products low. The chains are able to make a satisfactory level of profit by instituting strict controls over costs. For many food-service operations, low pricing is a key element in marketing. This is also the case in a number of the successful budget motel chains.

Promotion

The fourth element in hospitality marketing is **promotion**. For hospitality operators, promotion is the process of informing, influencing, and persuading customers to purchase their service products. The five types of promotional activities are:

1. Personal selling

2. Advertising

3. Sales promotion

4. Merchandising

5. Public relations

PICK A HOTEL PRICE, ◀
LET NET DO THE BIDDING

Two of the more popular sites on the Web are Priceline.com and Expedia.com. They allow travelers to pick an unspecified hotel by location and quality rating, then bid on the rate. If the nonrefundable, nonchangeable offer is accepted, the traveler's credit card is charged and the name of the hotel is revealed. Hotels say this allows empty rooms to be filled without lowering their published price, and travelers can sometimes get real bargains.

For example, one traveler got a room at the Hilton Crystal City in Arlington, Virginia, for only $100, where the lowest rate published is $169.95. Another traveler received an acceptance of an offer of $90 for a room at the Grand Hyatt in downtown Washington, D.C.—where the cheapest rate they found was $199.

So, if you are looking for the cheapest rate, try using one of the above Web sites. The worst thing that can happen is that the hotel will say no to your bid.

Personal Selling. **Personal selling** requires personal contact between buyer and seller. It typically takes place in a face-to-face encounter. Personal selling enables a salesperson to communicate directly with a buyer—to ask and answer questions and to use personal powers of persuasion to sell the service product. In restaurants, servers come in direct contact with customers. Each server is in an excellent position to engage in personal selling—to make suggestions and respond positively to questions with the aim of increasing sales. In addition, servers can be trained to promote the sale of items with the highest profit margin—the items that it is in the best interests of the establishment to sell in greater quantities. In lodging operations, desk clerks come in direct contact with guests. The desk clerk is also in an excellent position to engage in personal selling—to suggest accommodations that may be larger, more luxuriously appointed, or better located, and charge higher rates than for the more basic accommodations. Personal selling can be a major sales tool in hospitality operations.

Advertising. **Advertising** is paid, nonpersonal communication directed to potential buyers. A vast number of hospitality organizations promote their service products by advertising. Advertising is costly, however, and most organizations have limited amounts of money to spend on it. One of the important goals in advertising is to reach specific potential customers and to avoid reaching those who cannot or will not purchase the advertised service product. The familiar term *market* refers to a group of people who are willing and able to purchase a product. The owner/manager of the Steak Shack has identified as his market, families living within easy driving distance and having upper-middle-class incomes. The Goodsons, owners/managers of the Value Lodge, have identified transient travelers on Interstate 80 as their market.

Once a hospitality operator decides to advertise his establishment, he must then decide where to advertise. He may choose among broadcast/cable television, radio, newspapers, magazines, outdoor ads, direct mail, the Internet, and even the Yellow Pages—a directory of business telephone numbers readily available to everyone. Both advantages and disadvantages are associated with the use of each of these for hospitality advertising.

Sales Promotion. A **sales promotion** is an inducement offered by a seller to persuade a buyer to make an immediate purchase. Sales promotions are intended to persuade consumers to take action immediately rather than to wait. In hospitality operations, sales promotions are intended to attract customers to an establishment immediately, or at least to make reservations immediately for dining or lodging.

Hospitality operators frequently offer sales promotions to increase business. Some restaurants offer entrées at reduced prices on specific nights. For example, the manager of the Steak Shack developed a sales promotion for his slowest night, Monday, offering a 50 percent discount on all fried shrimp dinners. One aim is to attract business during slow periods. By contrast, Frog's Pub offers a 50 percent discount on the special imported beer of the week on Monday and Tuesday afternoons between 4:30 P.M. and 6:00 P.M. This would be illegal in some places, but not in the area where Frog's Pub is located. In the lodging industry, sales promotions are also common. In the Kensington, a center-city property where weekend business is light, a discounted weekend package for two includes a room for two nights, breakfast from room service, dinner in the dining room, and theater tickets, is offered on Friday and Saturday nights.

An important promotional tool used by hotels to attract and retain loyal guests is the **frequent-guest program**. These programs reward guests for staying at particular hotels by giving frequent-flyer miles or points for each stay. Hotel chains purchase miles from airlines at discounted rates and frequently give the guest the option of receiving air miles or hotel points for each stay. Hotel points can be exchanged for a variety of benefits—free lodging, upgrades to better rooms, car rental discounts, and so on. Frequent-guest programs build brand loyalty and are a powerful incentive for travelers to stay at the same brand hotel each time they need hotel accommodations.

Merchandising. **Merchandising** is a term used to describe actions taken to increase sales to customers already in the establishment. Merchandising differs from sales promotion, which is aimed at attracting new customers to the establishment; merchandising activities are designed to increase sales to existing customers— diners seated at tables in the dining room, or guests who are passengers in hotel elevators, for example.

Merchandising tools used by hospitality operators include posters, carefully written menus, literature placed in guest rooms, table tent cards in a dining room, and displays of breads, desserts, fruits, and wines. Some restaurants use dessert carts; others use tent cards to merchandise specific desserts. In the Steak Shack, tent cards on tables promote the sales of desserts, especially fruit pies. In the Kensington,

WHO BENEFITS FROM HOTEL PREFERRED-GUEST PROGRAMS? IT DEPENDS ON WHICH SIDE OF THE DESK YOU ARE

Hotel preferred-guest programs are emerging from the long shadow cast by the airline industry frequent-flyer programs. Sophisticated travelers realize that hotel rewards are as generous, if not more generous, than airline counterparts. However, do they pay for themselves?

Hotel loyalty programs are complicated and expensive. They require considerable training for staff and the rewards are costly. For example, one estimate of costs to franchisees is that franchise fees dedicated to frequency programs amount to an average of 9.5 percent of total fees.

Further, the strong human element required in developing loyal customers requires costly training. For example, a Marriott official states, "The program is highly automated, but we have an extensive training program because hotels do take responsibility in certain key activities, such as arranging for upgrades, preparing express check-in, enhancing customer service, and more."

Given the complexity and cost of the loyalty programs, how effective are they? Most experts agree that they are not as effective as airline counterparts because they do not have the universal appeal of airline programs. However, chains look at them as long-term investments in building brand awareness. Not only that, loyalty programs might actually drive rates up in a positive way because repeat guests tend to be at a higher tier and will pay more.

After all, these programs are primarily marketing costs, and most experts agree that hotel loyalty programs are strong marketing tools. Nevertheless, the varieties of hotel products can make it challenging for frequent travelers to figure out exactly what they are entitled to.

Source: Adapted from an article in *Lodging*, 3 December 1999.

signs in the elevator promotes reservations in the gourmet dining room, while literature in the rooms promotes the hair stylist.

Public Relations. **Public relations** is a term used to refer to activities and efforts designed to do one of the following: (1) improve or enhance the image or reputation of an organization; (2) promote the organization's name; or (3) improve its relations with employees, customers, suppliers, stockholders, or other individuals or groups thought to be important to the organization.

Public relations activities and efforts can take many forms. Supporting local charities or sponsoring worthwhile activities is one form. The owner of Frog's Pub sponsors a Little League team by purchasing uniforms, and the management of the Kensington hosts a fund-raising dinner once each year, with the proceeds going to purchase equipment for the local hospital.

All of the four elements of marketing discussed above—product, place, price, and promotion—are important components in the marketing efforts of hospitality organizations of every size and type. Decisions about marketing are major concerns in operations management, so managers of hospitality establishments must understand the components of marketing and be prepared to use them effectively.

KEY AREA 2: HUMAN RESOURCES

The hospitality industry is labor intensive, meaning that many people are needed to do the work required in the hundreds of thousands of hospitality operations in the United States. Of all the resources available to hospitality managers, none is of greater value than human resources.

This industry is known to have a high rate of employee turnover, a term that refers to the number of new employees required to replace employees who have left, expressed as a percentage of all employees. It is not unusual for a hospitality operation to have an employee turnover rate of 100 percent during the course of a year.

Because of the ongoing need to retain present employees as well as to hire and train new employees, hospitality managers commonly spend considerable amounts of time with activities commonly grouped under the heading of human resources.

Human Resources Management Defined

Dr. Mary L. Tanke, in her text *Human Resources Management*, defines **human resources management** as "the implementation of the strategies, plans, and programs required to attract, motivate, develop, reward, and retain the best people to meet the organizational goals and operational objectives of the hospitality enterprise."

From this definition, it is clear that human resources is a broad field that includes planning staff requirements, recruiting suitable applicants, selecting new employees, orienting them to the organization, providing them with the proper training, conducting performance appraisals, developing suitable compensation and benefits packages, attending to employees' health and safety considerations, and making every reasonable effort to retain the services of personnel in whom a great deal of time and effort has been invested. In organizations with employees covered by contracts negotiated by labor unions, labor relations constitutes yet another specialized challenge.

The activities cited above are the major responsibilities of a human resources manager. In one sense, all managers are human resources managers, because working with people and supervising their activities is a human resources activity and a major part of every supervisor's job. In large organizations with extensive human resources departments, such as the Kensington, supervisory managers are relieved of the need to attend to all the details of recruiting, selecting, and training employees for their departments. However, in smaller organizations, such as the Steak Shack and the Value Lodge, human resources activities are somewhat limited because managers have little time to devote to them. We discuss the human resources activities to which managers in these circumstances are most likely to devote their limited time.

Recruiting Applicants

Recruiting is a process used by managers to find suitable applicants to fill vacant jobs. It may begin when there are actual vacancies to be filled because employees have left. Alternatively, it may begin in anticipation of vacancies likely to occur in the near future. This is a wise approach in an industry with high rates of employee turnover. Hospitality managers have found that job applicants can be found by means of recommendations made by current employees, unsolicited resumes received in the mail, walk-ins, classified advertisements in newspapers, public and private employment agencies, vendors, unions, colleges and universities, trade journals, and competitors.

The decision whether or not to use any of these sources depends on the nature of the jobs to be filled. Many hospitality operations with labor contracts are required to seek new employees for jobs covered by the union contract through the union hiring hall. Applicants for jobs other than those covered by a union contract may be obtained through classified advertisements in the help-wanted sections of newspapers. In contrast, entry-level management trainees can often be recruited at colleges and universities. Candidates for supervisory positions and for such skilled positions as chef and front-office manager often come from employment agencies.

Job Descriptions

Before attempting to recruit applicants for a position, a manager must have a clear idea of the specific duties and tasks that someone in that position will be required to carry out. This is to say that a job description should be written for every job in the hospitality enterprise. As the term implies, **job descriptions** are detailed written statements that describe jobs. In many instances, job descriptions list specific duties and directions for performing jobs. The job description for any job should answer three important questions:

1. What is to be done?

2. When is it done?

3. Where is it done?

A job description typically has three parts:

1. A heading that states the job title and the department in which the job is located. In some organizations, the heading may include such information as the number of positions with that job title, the specific hours, days, or shifts worked by employees with the job title, and the supervisor to whom they report.

2. A summary of the duties of the job, typically written in paragraph form. The summary enables the reader quickly to gain a basic understanding of the nature and purpose of the job. By reading the summaries of all the jobs in a particular department, one could obtain a great deal of information about the department in a very short period. This might be of great benefit to a new manager, for example.

3. A list of the specific duties assigned to the job. These should be as detailed as possible, to the point that well-written job descriptions can be used as step-by-step instructions for doing the work.

Having job descriptions can be of great value to managers charged with appraising employee performance. A job description is particularly important for prospective employees. By having detailed descriptions of the duties required, job applicants and newly hired workers know specifically what is to be done by someone holding a particular job.

Job descriptions are also important for employers. They enable employers to hold employees accountable for doing the work assigned to a job. Employees who have read job descriptions but fail to perform the assigned work cannot successfully use the age-old excuse "Nobody ever told me I had to do this." Job descriptions offer the added benefit of forcing managers to assign specific work to each job holder. When all the normal duties of a department are identified with specific job descriptions, the department is better organized and operates more smoothly than it would otherwise.

Figure 10.2 is an example of a job description that one might find in a food-service enterprise. Note the degree of detail provided.

Selecting Applicants for Employment

One purpose of the recruiting effort is to develop a sizable pool of applicants from which the best person for a job can be selected. The value of job descriptions for this purpose should be evident. In their efforts to obtain sufficient information about applicants to ensure the selection of the best one, human resources personnel use a number of common tools. These include application forms, resumes, selection tests, interviews, and background checks. The following constitutes a standard selection process used by many organizations:

1. Preliminary interview

2. Application form

3. Selection test

4. Interview

5. Reference checks and background investigation

6. Selection

7. Physical examination

Some or all of these are normally included in the selection process followed by managers in hospitality firms. However, each hospitality firm tends to develop a preferred routine for selecting the best candidate.

Job Title: Server

Supervisor: Dining Room Manager

Working Hours: Schedule varies: Hours and days vary each week.

Job Summary: Server greets seated guests, takes orders, serves food and drinks, presents check with last service, and clears and resets table.

Duties:

1. Server reports to supervisor one hour before meal period to assist in preparing dining room for opening.
2. Server is assigned station in dining room by dining room manager. Schedule is posted each Friday for the following week, which begins Sunday.
3. Server pours water, takes food and drink orders, places orders in kitchen and at bar, picks up and serves food and drink, presents check(s) to guest(s), and clears and resets tables.
4. Service procedures: Food is served from guest's left; beverages from right. All china, glassware, and silver are removed from guests' right.
5. Fifteen minutes before the scheduled opening of the dining room, servers are briefed on daily specials, service techniques, and other matters of importance.
6. Tips are pooled. Ten percent of the tip pool goes to bartenders, and the remainder is divided equally among servers.
7. Servers provide own uniforms as follows: black pants or skirt; white dress shirt with long sleeves and buttoned cuffs; black bow tie; polished black shoes with flat heels (no high heels). Servers are given an allowance of $5 per week to care for their uniform.
8. Standards for personal appearance: shower or bathe prior to work; must use underarm deodorant; clean fingernails; hair must be clean and neat; no excessive jewelry.

Males:

1. Clean-shaven preferred. Moustache permitted if neat and trimmed.
2. No facial or ear jewelry.
3. Hair cannot extend beyond shirt collar.

Females:

1. No excessive jewelry, makeup, or perfume.
2. Long hair must be in hair net.
3. No long, false nails.

FIGURE 10.2
Steak Shack Job Description

Orienting New Employees

All new employees should be given a suitable **orientation** to the organization prior to their first day of work. New employees normally have some concern and uncertainty about beginning a job, and it is important to get them started with as little uneasiness as possible. In addition, basic information should be given to every new employee. In most well-managed hospitality organizations, basic orientation includes:

1. Organization policies, procedures, and rules. Among the concerns to be addressed are wages, work hours, overtime, sick leave, time cards, insurance, and keys. In the hospitality industry, answers must be provided for such common questions as "What meals do employees get?" "How do I get a clean uniform?" "Where do I change into my uniform?" "How does the health insurance plan work?"

2. Mission and objectives of the organization. It is important that every employee in the organization work toward the same goals—and that the goals be understood by every employee from the first day on the job.

3. A tour of the work area to point out offices and facilities with which all employees should be familiar. The tour should include opportunities for the introduction of such personnel as the chef or the front-office manager—any manager with whom workers should be acquainted.

Some organizations rely on a mentor system to provide each new employee with a more complete orientation. A new employee is paired with an experienced employee who shows him the ropes. For example, a cook who has been with the Steak Shack for ten years is made the mentor for a new cook. The experienced cook gives the new cook an orientation tour of the property and kitchen, pointing out such details as the locker room, storeroom, specific pieces of equipment, requisitions, recipes, uniforms, and refrigerators. The experienced cook also explains the chef's policies for reporting to work, cleaning equipment, laundering uniforms, and other matters. In the Kensington, a new desk clerk is paired with an experienced one who gives the new employee a tour of the property, pointing out elements with which the desk clerk should be familiar.

Training Employees

Training is generally required of all new employees—even those who come to an organization with considerable experience. Every hospitality operation has its own way of doing things, its own methods for performing tasks and accomplishing work. It is important, therefore, that people who already know how to perform a job be shown the specific methods and procedures used by the organization for which they have just started to work. For inexperienced employees, more formal training is likely to be needed.

Training can be done on an individual basis or in groups. Individual training is undoubtedly more effective, but it is very expensive. The trainer must devote time to training only one person at a time.

Training can be done on the job or off the job. On-the-job training is commonly used with experienced workers, who need only be shown the methods used by the hospitality operation. For example, a new cook in the Steak Shack is put to work immediately under the guidance of an experienced cook, who shows the new cook such details as how requisitions for supplies are filled out, how orders are placed for menu items, and how the establishment garnishes particular menu items. For inexperienced employees, on-the-job training can be used effectively when their work can be easily monitored and corrected before it has negative impact on customers, or when new employees can work side by side with experienced workers. For example, a new desk clerk in the Mountain Inn can be trained effectively if assisted by an experienced clerk. The experienced clerk can show the new employee the normal routine for checking in new guests and checking out departing guests.

Employee Safety

Another important human resources concern in hospitality operations is employee safety. Accidents are costly to both employees and employers—costly in terms of lost wages, medical bills, and higher insurance premiums, among the many possibilities. Therefore, when feasible, responsible employers prefer to develop educational campaigns and training programs aimed at improving safety in the workplace and reducing the number of accidents. Efforts to do this normally come under the heading of human resources.

One agency of the federal government, the Occupational Safety and Health Administration (OSHA), sets safety and health standards for workers in the United States. The basic standard is that an employee's workplace should be free from recognized hazards—those that are likely to cause physical harm to the employee. Most states have also adopted legislation aimed at protecting workers from physical hazards.

The potential for physical harm in the hospitality industry is at least as great as that in many other industries. Such areas as kitchens, bars, stairwells, guest rooms and baths, boiler rooms, elevator shafts, and many others present great potential for physical harm. Management must take three important steps to enhance employee safety in the workplace:

1. Know the applicable federal, state, and local safety regulations, and take all necessary and appropriate actions to comply.

2. Develop policies, procedures, methods, guidelines, and work rules aimed at maintaining a safe work environment for all employees.

3. Conduct appropriate safety training for all categories of employees, giving special emphasis to those who work with potentially dangerous materials and equipment.

Human resources issues are major concerns in operations management, so managers of hospitality establishments must have considerable knowledge and understanding of this broad subject and be prepared to make critical decisions in this all-important area.

KEY AREA 3: ACCOUNTING

Accounting is broadly defined as "the process of identifying, measuring, and communicating economic information to permit informed judgments and decisions by users of the information." In practical terms, it is the process of analyzing, recording, classifying, reporting, and interpreting financial information that reflects the financial condition of an organization. **Accounting principles** are the rules generally accepted by the accounting profession for analyzing, recording, classifying, reporting, and interpreting financial information.

A hospitality manager should have sufficient knowledge of accounting principles to be able to look at information provided by an accountant, understand it, and make judgments about the financial condition of the organization. This is one reason that educational programs in hospitality management commonly include at least one course in financial accounting.

Financial Accounting

Financial accounting is a branch of accounting concerned with analyzing, recording, classifying, and summarizing the day-to-day transactions of an organization. Analyzing means preparing data to be recorded. Recording means entering data into the formal records of the organization. Classifying is arranging the data into useful categories so that data are reported in a way that can be understood. Reporting is summarizing the information into statements for managers, owners, and others.

Some people think of financial accounting as bookkeeping and, indeed, bookkeeping is one part of financial accounting. Bookkeeping is record keeping. It is clerical in nature and a fundamental element in accounting.

The Accounting Cycle

Accounting cycle is a term that refers to a sequence of procedures used to record and summarize transactions for an accounting period; to organize the summary data into financial reports, called statements; and to prepare for the next sequential accounting period. The normal accounting period is one year. Accounting data, however, are typically summarized monthly and used to prepare monthly statements.

The two most important financial statements prepared by accountants are balance sheets and income statements.

Balance Sheet

A **balance sheet** is a financial statement that lists the assets, liabilities, and the value of ownership claims to the assets of a business on a specific date. Figure 10.3 shows a balance sheet for the Steak Shack; Figure 10.4 shows a balance sheet for the Value Lodge.

Assets

On the left-hand side of the balance sheet are the assets of an organization. An **asset** is anything of value. Any asset belonging to an organization belongs on the organization's balance sheet. Examples of assets are cash, food, beverages, furniture, and automobiles. Assets are classified as either current or fixed.

Current Assets. **Current assets** are those that are not expected to last beyond one year. They are normally used up in the course of doing business. Current assets are listed on the balance sheet in order of liquidity. The term *liquidity* refers to the capacity to be converted into cash. Obviously, cash is the most liquid of all assets, so it is listed first. In Figures 10.3 and 10.4, accounts receivable (money owed to a business) are listed second and are followed by such other current assets as food in the Steak Shack and cleaning supplies in Value Lodge.

Fixed Assets. **Fixed assets** are those that will last beyond one year. In Figure 10.3, the fixed assets of the Steak Shack are identified as furniture and equipment, and an automobile. In Figure 10.4, the fixed assets of the Value Lodge are listed as land, building, furniture and equipment, and an automobile. Note that the values of some of the fixed assets are reduced by amounts shown on the balance sheets as accumulated depreciation.

Accumulated depreciation is a bookkeeping figure that indicates a theoretical lessening in value of those assets from the time they were purchased. It should be noted that accumulated depreciation is only a bookkeeping figure and that the real value of fixed assets—their market value—may be either higher or lower than shown on the balance sheet. For example, the furniture and equipment shown on the balance sheet of the Steak Shack as having a value of $243,600 less $23,678 in accumulated depreciation may really be worth more or less than shown if it were sold. Assets are listed at cost because it is impossible to know their true market value unless and until they are actually sold.

Liabilities

Liabilities are financial obligations to others. Stated another way, liabilities indicate what the business organization owes. Liabilities are generally incurred and are a normal consequence of doing business. They are classified as either current or long term.

Current Liabilities. **Current liabilities** are financial obligations that are due to be paid within the next accounting period. The illustrated balance sheets show several current liabilities, including accounts payable, wages payable, sales tax

Assets			Liabilities and Owners' Equity		
Current Assets			**Current Liabilities**		
Cash	$9,322		Accounts payable	$4,250	
Accounts receivable	3,893		Wages payable	2,312	
Food	16,891		Sales taxes payable	1,567	
Liquor	9,633		Rent payable	2,000	
Supplies	4,540		**Total Current Liabilities**		$10,129
Office supplies	561				
Total Current Assets		$44,840	**Long-Term Liabilities**		
			Note payable		2,355
Fixed Assets			**Total Liabilities**		$12,484
Furniture and equipment	$243,600				
Less accumulated depreciation	23,678	$219,922	**Owner's Equity**		
Automobile	18,700		Capital at January 1, 19XX	$211,100	
Less accumulated depreciation	6,400	12,300	Net income for 19XX	53,478	
Total Fixed Assets		$232,222	**Total Capital**		$264,578
Total Assets		$277,062	**Total Liabilities and Capital**		$277,062

FIGURE 10.3
Steak Shack Balance Sheet, December 31, 19XX

	Assets			Liabilities and Owners' Equity		
Current Assets			**Current Liabilities**			
Cash		$3,560	Accounts payable	$2,300		
Accounts receivable		2,575	Wages payable	350		
Cleaning supplies		620	Sales tax payable	375		
Office supplies		75	**Total Current Liabilities**		$3,025	
Total Current Assets		$6,830				
			Long-Term Liabilities			
Fixed Assets			Mortgage payable		$993,000	
Land	$1,500,000	$65,000	**Total Liabilities**		996,025	
Building	$1,500,000					
Less accumulated			**Owner's Equity**			
depreciation	100,000	1,400,000	Roger and Jane Goodson			
Furniture and equipment	50,000		Capital at January 1, 19XX	$314,467		
Less accumulated			Net income for 19XX	$115,233		
depreciation	14,285	35,715	**Total Capital**		$429,700	
Automobile	12,500					
Less accumulated						
depreciation	5,000	7,500				
Total Fixed Assets		$1,508,215				
Total Assets		$1,515,045	**Total Liabilities and Capital**		$1,515,045	

FIGURE 10.4

Value Lodge Balance Sheet, December 31, 19XX

payable, and rent payable. *Accounts payable* refers to amounts owed to suppliers for goods and services. *Wages payable* refers to wages earned by employees but not yet paid to them. *Sales tax payable* refers to sales taxes collected from customers but not yet remitted to the government agency that collects the tax. *Rent payable* refers to amounts owed to a landlord for use of the premises but not yet paid to that landlord.

Long-Term Liabilities. **Long-term liabilities** are financial obligations due beyond the accounting period. The Steak Shack has a note payable, and the Value Lodge has a mortgage payable. The amounts remaining on these are shown on the illustrated balance sheets as long-term liabilities.

Owner's Equity. **Owner's equity** is the term used to describe an owner's claims to the value of assets listed on a balance sheet. The term **capital** is sometimes used as a synonym. In the Steak Shack, capital (the owner's claim to the assets) at the beginning of the year was $211,100. The restaurant made a profit of $53,478 last year, and that amount is added to the start-of-year capital to arrive at the total figure of $264,578 at the end of the year. In the Value Lodge, capital at the beginning of the year was $314,467. The motel had a net income of $115,233 for the year, making the end-of-year capital figure $429,700.

The Income Statement

The second important financial statement is the income statement. An **income statement** shows sales (or revenues) and expenses of an organization for a given time period. That period is normally one year, but income statements can be prepared for any period. The income statements of the Steak Shack and the Value Lodge are shown in Figures 10.5 and 10.6. **Sales** and **revenue** are the terms used for the income an organization receives as a result of doing business. **Expenses** are the costs of doing business. Note the differences between the income statements of the Value Lodge and the Steak Shack. The income statement of the Steak Shack uses the term *sales* rather than *revenue*. This is simply a difference in terminology and is not significant. The income statement for the Steak Shack indicates two sources of revenue: food sales and beverage sales. The income statement also has a section labeled cost of sales, in which the food and beverage costs are subtracted from total sales to determine gross operating profit. This is customary in hospitality operations whenever expenses can be attributed directly to a specific revenue source.

The Value Lodge also has two sources of revenue. The major source is identified as room sales—income received from renting accommodations to guests. The secondary source is identified as miscellaneous income—that received from selling postcards, maps, and food in the vending machines.

Expenses on income statements are commonly grouped into two categories: operating (or controllable) expenses and fixed expenses, sometimes identified as fixed charges. **Operating** or **controllable expenses** are those that managers can control or change. They are direct expenses, which tend to increase and decrease as business volume increases and decreases. These expenses include wages, laundry, cleaning supplies, and office supplies. **Fixed charges**, by contrast, are those that managers cannot change in the near term. Fixed charges include rent, mortgage payments, and property taxes—expenses that must be met even if the business has no sales revenue. In the Steak Shack, fixed charges include occupancy costs, interest, and depreciation; in the Value Lodge, they include property taxes, insurance, interest expense, and depreciation.

The income statements of the Steak Shack and the Value Lodge are comparatively simple and provide useful information about financial operations to the owners (Figures 10.5, 10.6). The total dollar amount in each category listed on an income statement can be compared with the amount anticipated or budgeted for that category. For example, if the amount shown for wages is higher than anticipated or budgeted, the owners can attempt to determine a reason and take precautions to hold wages to a lower figure in the next operating period.

If revenues exceed expenses for the period covered by an income statement, the result is termed *profit*. If expenses exceed revenues for the period, the result is termed *loss*. The value of accounting information is not limited to the specific figures listed on income statements and balance sheets. Additional useful information can be obtained by anyone willing to spend a few moments performing simple calculations, several of which are described below. There are literally dozens of ratios, averages, and other figures that managers can calculate from financial reports and use to analyze business performance. The following are just a few, selected to suggest the broad range of possibilities.

Ratios

Ratios compare one number to another for purposes of making judgments. Most students are familiar with the concept, if not the term. For example, if there are ten questions on a test, a student who answers eight correctly can be said to have performed well. Her ratio of correct answers to total questions is eight to ten, written numerically as:

$$8/10 = .8, \text{ or } 80\%$$

Thus, we determine that the student's grade—an evaluation of performance—is 80 percent. Ratios are used commonly in hospitality operations to evaluate financial performance. The following are a few of the ratios that managers calculate and use. Note that all answers are rounded.

Cost-to-Sales Ratios: Cost Percents

Food and Beverage Cost-to-Sales Ratios. The ratios of food cost to food sales and beverage cost to beverage sales are considered important by hospitality managers. The ratio of food cost to food sales is also known as the **food cost percent;** the ratio of beverage cost to beverage sales is known as the **beverage cost percent.** Managers believe these two ratios, or cost percents, indicate how well

Income Statement Year Ended December 31, 20XX	
Sales	
Food	$853,066
Beverage	223,355
Total Sales	**$1,076,421**
Cost of Sales	
Food	$349,757
Beverages	51,372
Total Cost of Sales	**401,129**
Gross Profit	$675,292
Other Income	4,356
Total Income	**$679,648**
Controllable Expenses	
Salaries and Wages	$333,548
Employee Benefits	78,692
Direct Operating Expenses	45,187
Energy and Utility Services	48,341
Administrative and General	16,528
Repairs and Maintenance	8,976
Total Controllable Expenses	**$531,272**
Income Before Occupancy Costs, Interest, Depreciation, and Income Taxes	$148,376
Occupancy Costs	80,025
Income Before Interest, Depreciation, and Income Taxes	$68,351
Interest	1,258
Depreciation	13,615
Restaurant Profit	$53,478

FIGURE 10.5
The Steak Shack

these important costs are being kept under control. Cost-to-sales ratios are calculated as follows:

$$\text{Cost/Sales} = \text{Cost-to-sales ratio, or cost percent}$$

For the Steak Shack, food and beverage cost-to-sales ratios are calculated as follows:

Income Statement Year Ended December 31, 20XX		
Revenue		
Room sales		$ 584,040
Miscellaneous		3,682
Total Revenue		**$587,722**
Operating Expenses		
Wages	$51,162	
Employee benefits	7,665	
Laundry	57,838	
Cleaning supplies	25,632	
Uniforms	1,820	
Office supplies	5,591	
Repairs and maintenance	15,267	
Energy costs	26,722	
Telephone	11,115	
Automobile expense	4,451	
Commissions	3,334	
Reservation network fees	4,245	
Franchise fees	23,368	
Credit card fees	6,379	
Total Operating Expenses		**$244,589**
Income Before Fixed Charges		$ 343,133
Fixed Charges		
Property taxes	$34,600	
Insurance	26,500	
Interest expense	99,300	
Depreciation	67,500	
Total Fixed Charges		**$227,900**
Net Income Before Income Taxes		$ 115,233

FIGURE 10.6
The Value Lodge

$$\text{Food cost/Food sales} = \text{Food cost-to-sales ratio}$$
$$\$349,757/\$853,066 = 0.4099, \text{ or } 41.0\%$$

$$\text{Beverage cost/Beverage sales} = \text{Beverage cost-to-sales ratio}$$
$$\$51,372/\$223,355 = 0.23, \text{ or } 23.0\%$$

The food cost percentage is .4099, or 41 percent. This figure can be compared with planned cost percentage and with industry averages for other restaurants of the same characteristic type.

The beverage cost percentage is .23, or 23 percent. As in the case of the food cost percent, a manager compares this figure with the planned cost percentage and, perhaps, an industry average. In this instance, both the food cost percentage and the beverage cost percentage compare favorably with industry averages.

Labor Cost-to-Sales Ratio. From Figure 10.5, the dollar figure appearing on the line marked salaries and wages is $333,548. That on the line marked employee benefits is $78,692. The sum of these, $412,240, is the cost of labor for the period. Using this figure, one can calculate a labor cost-to-sales ratio or **labor cost percentage** by dividing the cost of labor by total sales, $1,076,421:

$$\$412,240/\$1,076,421 = 0.38297, \text{ or } 38.3\%$$

This figure, 38.3 percent, is the labor cost percent. As with food cost percent, a manager would compare labor cost percent with that planned and with industry averages. In this case, the labor cost percent compares favorably with industry averages for these types of establishments.

Some additional ratios that can be calculated simply using readily available figures include the following.

Other Operating Ratios

Operating ratios measure overall performance in specific areas. Four ratios commonly used in hospitality are percentage of occupancy, seat turnover, inventory turnover, and profitability.

Percentage of Occupancy. **Percentage of occupancy** is used in lodging operations to express the ratio of occupied rooms to total rooms available for sale. It is calculated as follows:

Occupied rooms/Total rooms available for sale = Percentage of occupancy

We illustrate with the Value Lodge, which has 50 rooms. On a given night, 40 of those rooms are occupied, so the percentage of occupancy for that night is 80 percent, calculated as follows:

40 occupied rooms/50 rooms available for sale = 0.8, or 80%

Lodging operations normally determine the percentage of occupancy each night. Managers then make comparisons with their percentages of occupancy the same night the previous week and the same night the previous year. By doing so, they are able to make some general assessment about the state of business for that one night, compared with other nights. In some major cities, night managers in the major hotels normally exchange information about percentages of occupancy so that managers of the properties can compare their percentages of occupancy to those of their competitors.

Seat Turnover. **Seat turnover** relates the number of diners served in a given time period to the number of seats available in the dining room. Viewed another way, it indicates the average number of customers served per seat in the time period. Often called *turns* in the hospitality industry, it is calculated as follows:

Number of diners served/Number of seats available for diners = Seat turnover

In the Steak Shack, with 100 tables seating 250 persons, the number of customers served on a given Friday night was 575. Seat turnover for that night is calculated as follows:

575 diners served/250 seats available for diners = 2.3 turns

Foodservice managers often keep records of turns so that comparisons can be made between days and dates.

Inventory Turnover. **Inventory turnover** ratio measures the rate at which inventories are used up and replaced during an operating period. The ratio is calculated as follows:

Cost of goods sold/Average inventory = Inventory turnover rate

The Steak Shack has two inventory turnover ratios to calculate: one for food, the other for beverage. Food inventory turnover rate is calculated as follows:

Cost of food sold/Average inventory = Inventory turnover rate

The inventory figures from the balance sheet of the Steak Shack are shown as $16,891 for food and $9,633 for beverages. We assume that these represent the average inventories for the restaurant. Costs are shown on the income statement as $349,757 for food and $51,372 for beverage. Given this information, the inventory turnover rates would be calculated as follows:

$349,757/$16,891 = Food inventory turnover rate
Food inventory turnover rate = 20.71

$51,372/$9633 = Beverage inventory turnover rate
Beverage inventory turnover rate = 5.33

The food inventory rate is 20.71 times per year, or just under two times per month. This rate is considered about right for many restaurants. Because food is perishable, it should be used up and replaced about every other week.

The beverage inventory turnover rate is 5.33 per year, or about every other month. Except for beer, alcoholic beverages are not considered perishable. Therefore, it is not uncommon for foodservice establishments to have large liquor inventories. This is particularly true for those that stock fine wines.

Profitability Ratios.   Profitability ratios are said to measure the efficiency of organizations. They are important to both investors and managers because they can
indicate the quality of management. One important ratio is **return on sales**, or
net profit margin, which shows the portion of each sales dollar that an organization earns as a profit. It varies considerably from one type of business to another.
Return on sales is calculated as follows:

$$Profit/Sales = Return\ on\ sales$$

For the Steak Shack, this is calculated as follows:

$$\$53,478/\$1,076,421 = 0.04968,\ or\ 5.0\%$$

For the Value Lodge, this is calculated as follows:

$$\$115,233/\$587,722 = 0.196067,\ or\ 19.6\%$$

The ratio for the current year can be compared with those for prior years
and with industry averages. For the Steak Shack, the ratio is probably somewhat
lower than the owner would like; for the Value Lodge, many would consider it
reasonable for that type of property.

Averages

In addition to ratios, owners and managers of foodservice and lodging operations
commonly use averages to evaluate business operations. An **arithmetic average**,
the kind most commonly used, is determined by adding a series of figures to obtain a total, then dividing that total by the number of figures it includes. Suppose,
for example, one wanted to determine the average grade earned by a student
whose scores on four quizzes were 68, 82, 88, and 90. To determine the arithmetic average, one would add the scores on all quizzes and divide by the number of scores:

$$68 + 82 + 88 + 90 = 338\ total\ of\ all\ scores$$
$$328\ total\ of\ all\ scores/4\ scores = 82\ average\ score$$

Two of the most common arithmetic averages in hospitality operations are
average sale per customer in restaurants, and average rate per occupied room in
hotels.

Average Sale per Customer

Average sale per customer is calculated by dividing total dollar sales for a given
time period by the number of customers served in that period.

$$Total\ dollar\ sales/Number\ of\ customers = Average\ sale\ per\ customer$$

In the Steak Shack, for example, total sales on a given day were $3150.40. The number of customers served on the day was 220. Therefore the average sale per customer on that day was $14.32, calculated as follows:

$3150.40 total sales/220 customers = $14.32 average sale per customer

Average Rate per Occupied Room

Average rate per occupied room is calculated by dividing the room revenue for a given period by the number of rooms occupied in that period.

Total room revenue/Number of rooms occupied
= Average rate per occupied room

In the Value Lodge, total room revenue for a given night was $1640, and 40 rooms were occupied. Average rate per occupied room was $41.00, calculated as follows:

$1,640 room revenue/40 occupied rooms
= $41.00 average rate per occupied room

A variety of useful averages can easily be calculated, and many hospitality managers do so regularly. Possibilities include average sale per waiter, average rate per guest, average food sale, and average beverage sale.

Accounting is generally described as "the language of business," and hospitality managers should have more than a passing knowledge of the subject. Accounting questions are major concerns in operations management, and managers of hospitality establishments must be prepared to make full use of accounting information in making critical decisions in operations management.

KEY AREA 4: BUDGETING

Budgeting is a necessary element in business operations. A **budget** is a financial plan developed for a period in the future. Therefore, a budget can be viewed as a manager's attempt to project future financial performance. Successful businesses need to look ahead and make specific plans to reach revenue targets while keeping expenses within predetermined bounds. Without financial planning, management is leaving the future health of a business to chance.

Types of budget include operating budgets, capital budgets, sales budgets, advertising budgets, and cash flow budgets. For a hospitality manager, the most important of these is likely to be the operating budget.

Operating Budget

An **operating budget** is a financial plan for generating a given amount of revenue at a given level of expenditure in a coming period. Operating budgets are usually based on income statements from the most recent operating periods. Normally, one assumes that past performance is the best indicator of future performance and that the enterprise will continue to operate more or less as it has been operating. If one could assume no change of any kind, then a recent income statement could be adopted as a future budget. However, changes are always being planned and trends becoming evident. Changes include rewriting a menu, increasing the number of servers in a dining room, and raising menu prices or room rates to offset increasing costs. Trends include increases or decreases in sales revenue due to the opening or closing of other hotels or restaurants in the area and, in the case of restaurants, to increases or decreases in the number of people living in the surrounding area. The manager of the Steak Shack, for example, has noted that the number of customers has been increasing at approximately 5 percent per year, a figure that matches the increase in population in the neighborhood the restaurant serves.

One element in budgeting is to identify tomorrow's changes and trends today because they will obviously affect tomorrow's revenues and expenses. The more difficult task is to quantify the changes and trends—to identify the net effect in dollars that these changes and trends will have on various categories of revenue and expense. In the budgeting process, managers attempt to project the effects all changes will have on each. Figure 10.7 illustrates a budget for the Value Lodge for the coming year. Before preparing it, Roger and Janet Goodson analyzed revenues and expenses for the year just ending, then identified changes anticipated in the coming year—such items as the normal effect of inflation on expenses, planned increases in hourly wages for employees, an increase in reservation network fees, and a decrease in local real estate taxes reported in the local newspaper.

The Goodsons plan to increase wages to the staff by 10 percent, which will increase the expenses for both wages and employee benefits, which is normally a percentage of wages. They anticipated that most other operating expenses will increase by approximately 4 percent, except for reservation network fees, which are expected to rise by 10 percent. The remaining three operating expenses—commissions, fees to franchisor, and credit card fees—are expected to remain the same percentage of revenue. Fixed charges are expected to remain the same, except for property taxes, which will decrease by 3 percent, and insurance costs, which will increase by $10,000. Next, having considered the general overall increase in expenses, the Goodsons decided to increase room rates by 5 percent. Finally, they quantified these changes and have prepared the budget shown in Figure 10.7.

Once an operating budget is prepared, managers and others who need to purchase supplies and hire personnel have guidelines for doing so. The guideline is the budget. For example, once the budget is prepared for the Value Lodge, the Goodsons have a budgeted figure for employees' wages for the year—a figure to be used as the guide for spending in that category for the period. From that budgeted figure, the Goodsons can determine the number of housekeepers and other employees they can have on the payroll.

Without budgets, managers have limited means of assessing whether or not operations are progressing satisfactorily and whether or not financial objectives are likely to be reached. Budgets are important to operations managers, so people in-

Year Beginning January 1, 20XX		
Revenue		
Room sales		$613,242
Miscellaneous		3,682
Total Revenue		**$616,924**
Operating Expenses		
Wages	$56,278	
Employee benefits	8,432	
Laundry	60,151	
Cleaning supplies	26,657	
Uniforms	1,893	
Office supplies	5,815	
Repairs and maintenance	15,878	
Energy costs	27,791	
Telephone	11,560	
Automobile expense	4,629	
Reservation network fees	4,670	
Commissions	3,508	
Fees to franchisor	24,536	
Credit card fees	6,700	
Total Operating Expenses		**$258,498**
Income Before Fixed Charges		$358,426
Fixed Charges		
Property taxes	$33,562	
Insurance	36,500	
Interest expense	99,300	
Depreciation	67,500	
Total Fixed Charges		**$236,862**
Net Income Before Income Taxes		$121,564

FIGURE 10.7
Budget for the Value Lodge

tending to follow careers in hospitality management must have some reasonable level of knowledge of this important subject and be prepared to develop and work within budgets throughout their careers.

KEY AREA 5: COST CONTROL

Cost control activities are important to managers in hospitality operations. **Cost control** is the process of regulating costs and guarding against excessive costs. Managers need to know the costs of the hospitality service products they sell to customers and guests. For example, a hotel manager needs to know the total cost of preparing a vacated hotel room for the next guest. That total cost has many elements, including the wages of the housekeeper who will clean the room and the costs of the bed linen, bath linen, soap, and other supplies that go into it. Restaurant managers need to know the costs of the ingredients in the menu items they prepare so that suitable prices can be established and printed in menus. Some need to know the labor cost of preparing standard quantities of particular menu items. One example will suffice.

One of the items on the luncheon menu at the Steak Shack is a charcoal-broiled hamburger served on a sliced sesame-seed bun. The standard portion size for a hamburger is 6 ounces. Hamburgers are made from ground chuck, which is purchased at $2.40 per pound. Hamburger buns are purchased fresh daily at $1.50 per dozen. The cost of the 6-ounce hamburger is $.90, determined by dividing 16 ounces into the $2.40 cost per pound to find the $.15 cost per ounce, then multiplying by 6 ounces in each portion.

$2.40 cost per pound/16 ounces in each pound = $.15 cost per ounce

$.15 cost per ounce x 6 ounces per portion = $.90 cost per portion

The cost of the bun is $.125, determined by dividing the cost of the dozen,

$1.50, by the number of buns in the dozen, 12.

$1.50 cost per dozen/12 buns per dozen = $.125 per bun

Thus, the basic food cost per portion for the hamburger and bun is:

hamburger	$ .90
bun	.125
total	$1.025

To this, one adds the costs of other items accompanying the hamburger—ketchup, mustard, pickles, and so on—to determine the total cost of the item. If the other items are assumed to cost $.225, the total cost of the item is $1.25.

It should be obvious that foodservice operators should know the basic cost of every item on a menu before setting menu sales prices. If the hamburger above is listed on the menu at $1.50, the cost of the food alone uses up all but $.25 of the sales price. However, if the item can be priced at $2.50, the sale price is twice the food cost.

In the first case, food cost percent would be 83.3, calculated thus:

Food cost $1.25/Sales price $1.50 = 0.833, or 83.3%

In the second case, food cost percent would be 50.0, calculated thus:

Food cost $1.25/Sales price $2.50 = 0.5, or 50.0%

Once the portion cost for an item is determined, the manager has a responsibility to control the cost of all portions of that item prepared in the kitchen. In general, this means that the manager must establish procedures aimed at regulating portion costs and guarding against excessive costs. Those procedures should ensure that:

- Purchases of specified ingredients of specified quality are made in appropriate quantities and at proper prices in a timely manner.
- Foods purchased are received, stored, and issued under secure conditions and in a manner that preserves their quality until they are needed for production.
- Food production is accomplished with minimal waste and results in appropriate numbers of portions of correct quality and quantity, prepared according to specific recipes.

For example, the manager of the facility in the Mountain Bank must limit the spending for food purchases to the amount specified in the budget. This requirement has led him to take four steps aimed at controlling the cost of hamburgers. These include:

1. Specifying that the only beef to be used for hamburgers is ground chuck, U.S. Choice, with fat content not to exceed 10 percent.

2. Estimating the amount of ground chuck needed each week and ordering only enough for one week at a time.

3. Seeing that beef is moved to refrigerated storage immediately after it is received and that it is stored securely and under proper conditions until needed.

4. Installing a machine to make hamburger patties that features a dial to control the number of ounces per hamburger.

Many operations managers devote considerable time to setting up and overseeing extensive procedures for keeping costs under control. Cost control is of critical concern to operations managers in this industry, so anyone intending to pursue a career as a hospitality manager must have a firm understanding of the subject and be prepared to establish and maintain control over costs at every stage of her career.

KEY AREA 6: COMPUTERS

In the hospitality industry today, computers are of critical importance to operations managers. Operations managers rely on computer systems principally because they provide the kinds of information and control measures that owners and managers require to help ensure efficient operation. In fact, it is becoming difficult to find a hospitality operation of consequence that lacks some type of computer system.

At this point, it is useful to describe the computer system used in the Steak Shack, which is typical of many found in foodservice operations today.

Figure 10.8 illustrates the floor plan of the restaurant, showing the following system components linked together on a network:

- In the manager's office, a large-capacity microcomputer used as a file server, which is the hub of any computer network
- Terminals with keypads and printers at two servers' stations
- One microcomputer with monitor and printer at the manager's desk as well as at the bar
- Remote printers at the service station at the front bar and at the cooks' station

Operations proceed along the following lines. Servers arriving for work change into uniforms, then proceed to their side stands in the dining room. On each of the two side stands is a small terminal with keypad and printer, which dining room personnel use to log in. In other words, they record their arrival for work much as they would with a traditional time clock. Other personnel log in at the terminal in the manager's office. Guests enter by the front door and leave their coats in the coat room. They are seated by the dining room manager, who leaves menus at the table. Servers greet the guests and take their orders for drinks; the orders are written on ordinary white pads rather than on guest checks. Each server proceeds to a terminal and opens an account in computer memory. This account is equivalent to a guest check. The process requires that the server enter his personal code, the table number, the number of guests, and a special code used for creating a new account. With the account opened, the server uses a numerical code to enter the customers' orders for drinks. This information, together with the time of the order, is stored in computer memory. The computer is programmed with correct prices for each drink.

The system is programmed to send the recorded drink orders to the service station at the front bar. There, the bartender gets the drink orders on a remote printer. The hard copy provided by the remote printer is an order for the bartender to prepare the drinks. This hard copy includes the server number, table number, and order time. The bartender removes the hard copy of the order from the printer and places it on the tray with the prepared drinks, thus eliminating questions about which drinks are for which server and what time the orders were entered. At the appropriate time, the server follows similar procedures for placing food orders. With different codes used for foods and drinks, the computer is programmed to send food orders to the remote printers at the cooks' station. All menu items ordered are stored in memory, but the only items appearing on the remote printer at any specific preparation station are those appropriate to that station. Thus, food orders are not sent to the service bar, and orders for coffee, handled by the servers themselves, do not appear on any remote printers.

After a diner finishes her meal, the server obtains her guest check by going to the terminal and printer at the side stand and requesting one. With this system, the guest check is a hard copy of the data stored in the computer, accessed by table and server number. This hard copy is removed from the printer and given

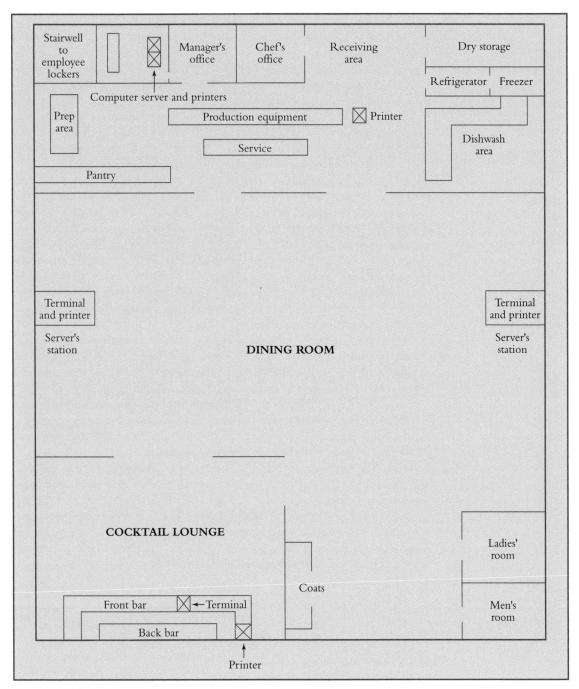

FIGURE 10.8
Layout of the Steak Shack, showing the elements of the restaurant's computer system, with terminals and workstations at several key locations: manager's office, dining room, bar, and kitchen

to the diner. In the Steak Shack, each server acts as a cashier for his own checks, and settlement for each check is recorded at the terminal as the server receives cash or a credit card.

At the end of a shift, the server reports to the manager's office to turn in the cash, checks, and credit card vouchers for his sales. The manager uses his terminal to print out summary data showing charge and cash sales for that particular server. He collects the appropriate amount of cash and all charge vouchers from the server. The totals collected from each must, obviously, equal the amounts recorded on the printout. Finally, each server logs out, using the manager's terminal, before changing out of uniform and leaving the premises.

At the end of the day, the manager obtains a detailed breakdown of the day's business on a computer printout. The system provides considerable information, including total dollar sales categorized into cash sales and charge sales, with the charge sales divided by type of credit card; total dollar sales separated into food sales and beverage sales, with the food sales broken into dollar sales by menu category and by individual menu items; average dollar sale per customer, per server, per seat, per table, and per hour; seat turnover; number of orders of each hospitality item sold; total dollar sales per hour; sales in any category for the period to date; total payroll cost for the day, for any part of the day, or for the period to date; and a vast amount of hospitality cost data.

Using this system, the manager of the Steak Shack can monitor operations as the day progresses. Such data as gross sales volume, number of customers served, number of checks outstanding, number of portions of particular items sold, and many other tallies may be of special interest at times throughout the day.

Because computer systems are of such importance in operations management, hospitality managers should have reasonable knowledge of computer operations. Hospitality managers should be prepared to take full advantage of the capacity of the systems available in today's hospitality environment.

From the foregoing, it should be apparent that marketing, human resources management, accounting, budgeting, cost control, and computers all play important roles in hospitality operations management. Students who are planning careers in hospitality management should develop their knowledge of the topics discussed in this chapter and learn as much as possible about additional subjects and complex topics that can best be covered in the more advanced courses commonly offered in hospitality management programs.

SUMMARY

In this chapter, operations management is defined as the day-to-day activities that managers engage in to achieve the goals of the operations they manage. The four functions of management—planning, organizing, directing, and controlling—are identified as primary skills required by operations managers. Marketing, human resources, accounting, budgeting, cost control, and computers are described as key areas in operations management. Examples from the Steak Shack, Mountain Bank, and Value Lodge facilities are used to illustrate these six key areas of operations management and to provide a sense of the day-to-day work that consumes much of the time of a hospitality manager.

KEY TERMS

Accounting
Accounting cycle
Accounting principles
Accumulated
  depreciation
Advertising
Arithmetic average
Asset
Average rate per
  occupied room
Average sale per customer
Balance sheet
Beverage cost percent
Budget
Capital
Controllable expenses
Controlling
Cost control
Current asset
Current liability
Directing

Expense
Financial accounting
Fixed asset
Fixed charges
Food cost percent
Frequent-guest program
Human resources
  management
Income statement
Inventory turnover
Job description
Labor cost percentage
Liabilities
Long-term liability
Marketing
Merchandising
Operating budget
Operating expenses
Operating ratios
Operations management
Organization chart

Organizing
Orientation
Owner's equity
Percentage of
  occupancy
Personal selling
Place
Planning
Price
Product
Promotion
Public relations
Ratio
Recruiting
Return on sales
Revenue
Sales
Sales promotion
Seat turnover
Training

DISCUSSION QUESTIONS

1. Define the term *operations management*.

2. Define the term *planning* as used in management.

3. What does the term *organizing* mean?

4. List the six steps in the organizing process.

5. What does the term *reporting structure* refer to?

6. What can be the negative consequences of failure to follow the practice known as unity of command?

7. What is an organization chart?

8. What does the term *directing* mean?

9. What does the term *control* mean?

10. List and discuss the four steps in the control process.

11. Define *marketing* as used in hospitality operations.

12. List and describe the four elements of marketing.

13. List five factors taken into consideration in establishing menu prices.

14. List and describe five types of promotional activities.

15. Define the term *human resources management*.

16. What does the term *recruiting* mean in hospitality?

17. What is a job description?

18. List and discuss the three parts of a job description.

19. Identify ten possible sources from which human resources personnel can recruit applicants for employment.

20. List and discuss the seven basic steps that constitute a standard procedure for selecting the best candidate for employment.

21. Identify three principal elements that should be included in a basic orientation for new employees.

22. Identify three important steps taken by management to enhance employee safety in the workplace.

23. How is *accounting* defined in the chapter?

24. Identify the two major financial statements derived from accounting records and list the principal parts of each.

25. Define the following terms:
    a. Asset
    b. Current assets
    c. Fixed assets
    d. Liability
    e. Current liability
    f. Long-term liability
    g. Owner's equity
    h. Income statement
    i. Revenue
    k. Expense
    l. Profit
    m. Loss

26. Identify the formula for calculating each of the following:
    a. food cost-to-sales ratio
    b. beverage cost-to-sales ratio
    c. labor cost-to-sales ratio
    d. percentage of occupancy

27. Given the following information, determine seat turnover for the Steak Shack for March 15:
number of diners: 900
number of seats available for diners: 250

28. Identify each of the following:
 a. Inventory turnover
 b. Return on sales
 c. Average sale per customer
 d. Average rate per occupied room

29. What is a budget?

30. Discuss the importance of cost control to the management of a hospitality operation.

31. Determine the portion cost for each of the following:
 a. 5-ounce portion of tomato juice if tomato juice is purchased in 46-ounce cans costing $1.38 each
 b. an order of toast consisting of 2 slices of bread from a loaf of 24 slices costing $1.44, plus 1 ounce of butter purchased at $1.60 per pound
 c. an order consisting of 2 eggs and 3 strips of bacon where eggs cost $0.96 per dozen, bacon costs $3.36 per pound, and each pound of bacon consists of 16 strips.

32. Identify the benefits that computers provide for hospitality operations managers.

MOMENTS OF TRUTH

1. You are the assistant manager of a fine-dining restaurant located in a midsize city. The chef has developed two new entrées that are unique and exciting. You have been asked by the manager to suggest ways of promoting these new entrées. Make a list of suggestions, explaining each in as much detail as possible.

2. You have just been hired as the front-office manager for a 200-room motel. During your first day on the job, you notice that the procedure for selling rooms is performed differently by each desk clerk. Some clerks explain which types of rooms are available and the rates for each, then ask which type the guest would prefer. Others offer only the highest rates and suggest lower-rated rooms only if the prospective guest refuses the highest-rated room. Still others offer only the lowest rates in an attempt to sell as many rooms as possible. How do you deal with this problem?

3. Write a job description for the most recent full-time or part-time job you have held.

4. Go to a nearby restaurant or hotel. Interview a supervisor to learn in detail about the work he or she does, then write a job description for the job.

INTERNET EXERCISES

1. Go to http://www.marriottrewards.com/awards/. What rewards are available to frequent guests? Compare this program to another rewards program of your choosing.

2. Go to http://florida-hotels-motels.com/hotels/tallahassee.fl. Compare the room rates and quality ratings of ten hotels at this site. Are the rates for three- and four-star properties generally higher than for one- and two-star properties? If not, what reasons can you give for this?

PART VI
Travel and Tourism Perspectives

Dimensions of Travel and Tourism

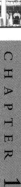

▶ Learning Objectives

After reading and studying this chapter, you should be able to:

1. Identify at least ten travel motivators.

2. List and discuss eight social and economic changes that have led to increased travel.

3. Explain the role of local, state, and federal governments in travel and tourism.

4. List the four criteria used to establish the status of an individual as a traveler or a tourist.

5. Define the terms *traveler* and *tourist*.

6. Identify the three segments of the travel industry.

7. Discuss the size and scope of international travel.

8. Identify the nations that are the world's leading travel destinations.

9. Identify the nations whose citizens spend the most on international travel.

10. Discuss the conditions and documents that make international travel possible.

11. Identify the nations that send the most visitors to the United States.

12. Describe the importance of domestic travel to the U.S. economy.

13. Define and describe the economic, cultural, social, and environmental impacts of tourism.

14. Identify several nations, states, areas, and localities that rely on tourism for jobs and income.

INTRODUCTION

Earlier chapters pointed out the close relationships that four significant areas have: economic progress, the development of roads and transportation, the scope of hospitality facilities, and the extent of travel. We indicated that those nations with the most advanced economies have the most highly developed transportation networks and the greatest numbers of travelers. We showed that hospitality enterprises develop as a direct consequence of the development of transportation and that, as transportation modes change, so, too, do the locations of hospitality operations. We discussed the foodservice and lodging industries in detail and described characteristic types of operations in each.

In Part VI, we turn our attention from the specifics of food, beverage, and lodging operations to the larger industry of which hospitality operations are a part: travel and tourism. In this chapter, we discuss the importance of travel and tourism to various nations and states, then take a close look at the economic, social, cultural and environmental impacts of travel and tourism on them.

In the second chapter, we describe travel services. In the third, we describe recreation and entertainment facilities to which people travel for a major non-business purpose: pleasure.

TRAVEL MOTIVATORS

People travel for many reasons. The list below includes just a few of the many possibilities.

Convention attendance

Visiting family or friends

Business

Health problems

Climate

Rest and relaxation

Theme parks

Exhibits

Concerts

Sports events

Sightseeing

Education

Visiting the birthplace of parents or grandparents

Weddings

Funerals

"Getting away"

Recreation

Entertainment

Some of these were unknown before the twentieth century. In the 1600s and 1700s, for example, few people had the time or the money to travel just because they wanted to go to a warmer climate. No one traveled to ski or to visit a theme park: ski slopes and theme parks were not developed until the twentieth century.

In recent years, important social and economic changes have led to increased travel. The following sections discuss these changes.

Early Retirement

The retirement age for a large part of the population is earlier than it used to be. The Social Security system in the United States grants retirement benefits as early as age 62, and many retirement programs are linked to years of service rather than age. In some retirement programs, particularly government programs, it is possible to retire at age 55 with substantial benefits after working 25 or 30 years. Early retirement leads to greater numbers of travelers as the retirees set out to see the world.

Longer Life Span

The average person in a developed nation can now expect to live well into his or her seventies, and many live considerably longer. This is in contrast to conditions a few generations ago, when the average life span was considerably less. A growing population of people over 60 provides a larger base of travelers, many of whom can afford extended periods of travel.

Shorter Workweek

In the first third of the twentieth century, the six-day week was standard for most workers. Today, the five-day week is standard, and a four-day week is not uncommon. The resulting longer weekends, combined with faster and easier transportation, enable many workers to take weekend trips. This may include driving to visit friends and relatives, attending weddings and receptions, and traveling to places and events that people did not have time for only a few years ago.

More Leisure Time

Workers have greater amounts of leisure time today than ever before. American, Canadian, and Western European workers have more vacation time than any groups of workers in history. Most receive a minimum of two to four weeks each year, and many work for organizations that offer additional vacation time for employees with greater numbers of years of service. Some of the leisure time available to Americans is in the form of holidays, many of which are now scheduled to fall on Mondays and Fridays. These create three- and four-day weekends that make it possible for people to get away. One example is the addition of Martin Luther King Day, celebrated on a Monday in mid-January. This created a long weekend that has had a major impact on travel destinations. In the northeastern United States, for example, it has turned a relatively quiet weekend into a record weekend for the ski areas.

Greater Disposable Income

Many families have more disposable income available than ever before. Higher wages and two-earner households account for much of this increase. The 1990s and the first years of the twenty-first century have been prosperous for many households. This makes it possible for consumers to spend more for goods and services, and travel appears to be one of the services that consumers want most.

Greater Mobility

Improved roads and better transportation make travel easier and more comfortable each year. The American interstate highway system is now virtually complete,

America's highways and bridges are the most modern in the world. This helps promote travel within the United States. Shown in this picture is the Golden Gate Bridge.
(Photo courtesy of San Francisco Convention and Visitors Bureau. Photo by Phil Coblentz.)

making road travel faster between points distant from one another. Most people in the United States are near a major airport or one that provides service to a major airport.

Smaller Families

The average size of American families has decreased significantly, making it easier and cheaper for the average family to travel. With fewer family members, travel costs less.

Change in Consumer Spending Patterns

The growth in public and private retirement programs has prompted a "live now" attitude and a feeling that the future will take care of itself. Many people are not as concerned as their parents were with saving for retirement; they are more willing to spend their growing incomes on travel. Significantly, travel has become a major element in the lifestyle of many people.

GOVERNMENT ROLE IN TRAVEL AND TOURISM

In many countries, the national government plays an important role in travel and tourism. Many national governments own and operate airlines as well as national rail systems. Some also own and operate hotels, motels, and other tourist facilities. In addition, most national governments establish tourism goals, gather statistical data, regulate tourist facilities, and advertise internationally to promote tourism.

In the United States, the national government takes a much more limited role. Prior to 1996, the official United States government travel office was the United States Travel and Tourism Administration (USTTA), which was responsible for marketing U.S. tourism abroad. However, Congress never provided sufficient funds for it to do its job properly. The most it received was $17 million per year to fund the entire agency. By comparison during a similar time, Canada's National Tourism Organization was funded with $104 million and 33 other countries, including some very small ones, funded their national tourism organizations in greater amounts. In April 1996, the USTTA went out of business, and Congress set up an organization called the United States National Tourism Organization. It is essentially a planning organization, as it has never received funding from Congress to support its work. Many of the functions of the old USTTA were picked up by other branches of the federal government, but the important work of promoting travel to the United States was taken over by the **Travel Industry Association** (TIA). The TIA is a nonprofit organization comprising over 1000 member organizations, including various state travel offices, lodging and restaurant organizations, airlines, and convention and visitors' bureaus. It funds programs designed to attract foreign visitors to the United States and engages in research, lobbying, and training.

The International Trade Administration, part of the U.S. Commerce Department, gathers trade data and provides assistance businesses to American firms trading overseas. Part of its work involves gathering data on international tourism to the United States, and much information for the illustrations in this chapter comes from this organization.

Statistical data concerning travel within the United States is gathered by the Bureau of the Census and by several other agencies. However, most people interested in obtaining travel-related data about the United States tend to rely on information from private agencies. The principal private organization providing data in this area is the U.S. Travel Data Center, based in Washington, D.C.

In the United States, the responsibility for promoting and regulating travel and tourism in each state falls to state governments. All state governments have offices charged with that responsibility, but their names and the departments to which they report vary from one state to another. Some states have an independent state travel department; in others, the office responsible for travel and tourism is part of a larger department—commerce or transportation, for example.

At the local level, most American cities and regional areas have chambers of commerce, which promote tourism in communities where the industry is important. City governments frequently have convention and visitors' bureaus that promote travel to the city. These bureaus receive inquiries that they refer to hotels and motels for follow-up. They provide services to meeting planners such as orientations to the city and introductions to convention hall managers, hotel convention managers, and other suppliers of hospitality services. These bureaus frequently act as housing coordinators for groups that come to the city, referring delegates to hotel properties. In some instances, convention and visitors' bureaus are funded by a tax added to hotel bills in the city. This is not the only approach to funding these bureaus, however. In other cases, their operating costs are met by some combination of funds contributed by tourism-related businesses and matching funds from state or local government.

Definition of a Traveler and a Tourist

A **traveler** is someone who goes from one place to another. Thus, a person who goes from Boston, Massachusetts, to Phoenix, Arizona, is categorized as a traveler. However, when someone drives from her home to a shopping mall 10 miles away, should she be considered a traveler? If someone goes from Hartford, Connecticut, to New York City to see the Yankees play baseball, should that person be considered a traveler? These types of questions cause considerable discussion and concern among people who count travelers for statistical purposes.

Most people also agree that a **tourist** is a person who travels for pleasure. If one accepts that opinion, it is obvious that a tourist is also a traveler. Thus, the person who travels from Boston to Phoenix is a traveler and also a tourist, providing that the person is traveling for pleasure. However, when one examines that definition critically, it becomes apparent that categorizing a specific traveler as a tourist is not as easy as it first appears. For example, suppose the person going to Phoenix is on a business trip but takes a day out of his schedule to sightsee or play golf. Is that person considered a tourist?

Government agencies, including state government tourist offices, promote tourism to their areas. The Virginia Travel Guide is one of the pieces of advertising that helps promote tourism in that state. *(Photo courtesy of Virginia Tourism Corporation)*

Four criteria are used to establish the status of an individual as a traveler or a tourist.

1. Distance
2. Residence
3. Purpose
4. Length of stay

Governments, states, and organizations concerned with travel and tourism tend to develop their own definitions of a traveler or a tourist based on these criteria. The definitions are important. They are used to count and categorize travelers. Unfortunately, governments, states, and organizations still disagree on both the definitions of *traveler* and *tourist* and on the importance of each of the four criteria in those definitions.

To be counted as a traveler by the U.S. Bureau of the Census, a person must travel to a place at least 100 miles away from home and return. The U.S. Travel Data Center uses a broader definition: A traveler is "any resident of the United States, regardless of nationality, who travels to a place 100 miles or more away from home within the United States or who stays away from home one or more nights in paid accommodations and who returns home within 12 months, except for commuting to and from work or attending school." Of the 50 state governments within the United States, a majority have now adopted this U. S. Travel Data Center definition, although some use a distance of 50 rather than 100 miles.

Because travel and tourism are important to the economic health of so many nations of the world, even the United Nations has become involved in establishing definitions. In 1993, the United Nations Statistical Commission adopted "Recommendations on Tourism Statistics," proposed by the World Tourism Organization (WTO). Included in the document were definitions aimed at establishing uniform approaches to collecting data. One definition is for tourism. It stated that tourism comprises the activities of persons traveling to and staying in places outside their usual environment for not more than one consecutive year for leisure, business, and other purposes. Some travelers who are not considered tourists are persons immigrating to another country and people who commute to another country to work, as well as others. All travelers engaged in tourism are described as visitors, and visitors are separated into two groups—domestic visitors and international visitors. Note that persons traveling for both business and pleasure are considered tourists, because it is difficult to distinguish between the two. Thus, the terms *traveler* and *tourist* are often used interchangeably. The two terms are quickly becoming synonyms. In this text, our definition of the word *traveler* is that of the U.S. Data Travel Center, explained above, and the words *traveler* and *tourist* are used interchangeably.

MAKEUP OF THE TRAVEL INDUSTRY

The **travel industry** is made up of firms and people who serve the needs of travelers. Professor Chuck Gee, a well-known authority in the field, divides the travel industry into three segments:

1. Direct providers of travel services

2. Support services

3. Tourism development

Direct Providers of Travel Services

Direct providers of travel services are firms and people who are in direct contact with travelers and who provide the services necessary for their travel. They include:

Airlines

Bus companies

Camps

Car rental companies

Credit card companies

Cruise lines

Entertainment and recreation centers

Hotels/motels

National and state parks

Railroads

Rental companies specializing in campers and recreational vehicles

Restaurants

Shops selling goods and services to travelers/tourists

Travel agents

This is not a complete list of all direct providers of travel services. However, it does offer a good cross section of firms whose primary business activity is to provide a travel service. It is important to emphasize that this category of the travel industry is not restricted to transportation, lodging, and foodservice. It includes any firm that provides a travel service directly to the traveler—travel agents who make travel arrangements; shops that sell souvenirs to travelers; tour guides; entertainers who provide music and cultural activities for tourists; businesses that supply rental bicycles, rowboats, or sailboats for tourists; and many, many others. The keys to determining if a business belongs in this segment are that the business caters directly to travelers and the bulk of its business is from travelers.

Support Services

Support services is a segment that includes the firms and individuals who provide services and supplies to the direct providers. These firms and individuals depend on the travel market for all of their business, or for a large part of it. They provide the necessary goods and services that make it possible for direct providers to perform travel services.

A list of support service firms includes purveyors of food and beverages to hotels and restaurants, laundries that supply the linen for lodging properties, firms and individuals who supply the travel mementos to gift shops, employment agencies that specialize in providing hospitality workers, management firms that run hospitality operations, foodservice firms that provide the food for airline passengers, and many, many others.

Tourism Development

Tourism development is a term used to identify the individuals and organizations that have an impact, direct or indirect, on direct providers, support services, and individual travelers. This category includes people and groups with an interest in travel and tourism who are not classified as direct providers, support services, or travelers. Examples of individuals and organizations in tourism development include:

1. Organizations associated with direct providers, such as the American Society of Travel Agents, the American Hotel and Motel Association, the National Restaurant Association, the International Air Transportation Association, and the Cruise Lines International Association. Each of these organizations represents its respective hospitality or travel industry and consists of member firms from those or allied industries. They provide a voice for their industries to the U.S. Congress and to the public, provide information about their industries to their members, and, in some cases, make policy decisions relating to sales of their services, the business or professional practices of their members, or both of these. For example, the International Air Transportation Association establishes international air fares for member airlines.

2. Government agencies, including state and local travel offices. These government organizations promote travel and tourism to their states and localities and are important components of the travel industry.

3. Private agencies that promote travel and tourism and gather statistical data. One example is the World Tourism Organization, a private organization located in Madrid, Spain. The WTO promotes international tourism, gathers statistical data on world tourism, and is an official consultant to the United Nations. Another important private organization is the World Travel and Tourism Council, located in Brussels, Belgium.

4. Schools, colleges, and universities—public, private, and proprietary—that prepare individuals for careers in hospitality and tourism. Numerous public and private institutions train cooks, chefs, desk clerks, and travel agents, among many other hospitality workers. In addition, more than 800 two- and four-year colleges offer majors in foodservice, lodging, or tourism. Among the first colleges to develop such programs were Cornell University, Michigan State University, and Pennsylvania State University. One of the first to develop a culinary program was the Culinary Institute of America in Hyde Park, New York, whose program has won national and international acclaim. The oldest of the four-year colleges offering a comprehensive program in travel industry management is the University of Hawaii.

The travel industry is made up of a broad range of private and government firms and agencies. It is a collection of organizations serving the needs of travelers. Many firms in the travel industry have little in common except their dependence on travelers for their primary business.

THE SIZE AND SCOPE OF THE TRAVEL INDUSTRY

Travel is the world's largest industry. In 1998, the WTO estimated that world spending on international tourism reached about $445 billion. The WTO predicts that receipts from international tourism will reach $1.55 trillion by the year 2010.

Worldwide, travel and tourism employs more than 200 million people. Students should note that the data in this chapter are the latest available as this revision is prepared. The presentation of data is always delayed by at least two years because of the time required to collect, tabulate, analyze, and publish it.

THE SCOPE OF INTERNATIONAL TRAVEL

International travel is travel between countries. There has been continued growth in the number of people traveling internationally, as shown in Tables 11.1 and 11.2.

The data in Tables 11.1 and 11.2 include international arrivals only. The many millions of travelers who travel within their own countries are not included.

Some readers will note that these two tables appear to offer conflicting information. Table 11.1 shows a sizable increase in the number of arrivals over the years, while Table 11.2 indicates a decline in the percentage of increase in international tourism for each of the periods shown. For example, between 1950 and 1960, the increase in international tourist arrivals was 44,038,000 (69,320,000

TABLE 11.1

Growth of World Tourism—International Tourist Arrivals

Year	Arrivals
1950	25,282,000
1960	69,320,000
1970	165,787,000
1980	285,997,000
1990	458,229,000
1999	657,000,000 (pe)
2010	1,047,000,000 (p)

(pe) = preliminary estimate

(p) = projection

Source: World Tourism Organization

TABLE 11.2

Annual Increase in World Tourism

Period	Average Annual Increase in International Arrivals
1950–1960	10.6%
1960–1970	9.1%
1970–1980	5.5%
1980–1997	4.6%

Source: World Tourism Organization

minus 25,282,000), and the percentage increase per year for that period was 10.6 percent, while between 1970 and 1980, the increase in international tourist arrivals was 118,495,000 (284,282,000 minus 165,787,000) but the annual increase for that period was only 5.5 percent. The reason is that the base numbers used to calculate the annual percentage increases were larger in the latter period, and this results in a smaller percentage increase. For example, an increase of 500 in the number of visitors to an area from 1000 to 1500 is a 50 percent increase. Yet that same increase of 500 in the number of visitors the next year, from 1500 to 2000, is only 33 percent.

For purposes of this chapter, it is important to note that the increase in international travel has been significant and steady. One of the primary reasons is the decreased cost of transportation relative to income, making transportation more affordable for great numbers of people. Others include greater periods of vacation time and greater number of holidays in many countries.

WORLD'S LEADING TOURIST DESTINATIONS

The world's leading tourist destinations are shown in Table 11.3. A destination, as used in this table, is a country that receives visitors, regardless of whether they come by plane, ship, train, or automobile.

France receives more international arrivals than any other country. One reason is its central location in western Europe. Residents of western Europe frequently travel from one country to another, and France is both an excellent destination in itself and a country through which travelers must pass when driving to other countries. France's central location means that the statistics include people passing through on their way to Germany, Italy, Spain, or other destinations.

Second on the list is Spain. Its sunny, warm climate and relatively low prices make it a popular travel destination, particularly for residents of colder climates. It is, thus, perhaps the leading vacation country for European travelers. The Spanish government has made a consistent effort to keep the monetary rate of exchange favorable for visitors in order to attract as many tourists as possible.

TABLE 11.3

World's Leading Tourist Destinations, 1999

Rank	Country	Number of Arrivals
1	France	71,400,000
2	Spain	51,958,000
3	United States	46,938,000
4	Italy	35,839,000
5	China	27,047,000
6	United Kingdom	25,740,000
7	Mexico	20,216,000
8	Canada	19,556,000
9	Poland	17,940,000
10	Austria	17,630,000

Source: World Tourism Organization

Third is the United States. Travel to the United States is discussed later in this chapter.

Italy, the fourth leading tourist destination, is important historically, particularly because the Vatican is located there, and there is much more to see in Rome as well as in the rest of the country. Many tours of Europe start or end in Rome.

Perhaps most surprising is China's position as fifth most common tourist destination. China has made great strides in attracting tourists over the past few years. However, the figure also reflects the recent inclusion of Hong Kong as part of China. Hong Kong has always been a favorite international tourist destination.

In nations high on the list of tourist destinations, many jobs are created to provide food, lodging, and other travel services for tourists. The jobs created by tourism are important to the economies of these nations, as discussed in greater detail later in this chapter.

Table 11.4 shows the amount spent on international trips by residents of countries ranked as the top ten in spending for international travel. The United States leads the list of international spenders. U.S. spending abroad is discussed later in the chapter. Germany is second on the list. The Germans have always been frequent travelers. A primary reason is the country's economic prosperity and high standard of living. In addition, German workers typically have considerable time for travel. On average, they receive ten holidays and six weeks of paid vacation annually.

Third on the list is Japan, a leading economic power that exports automobiles, televisions, cameras, computers, radios, and many other products. Japan has become a significant member of the world community, and its citizens are leading international travelers. The average Japanese worker now receives more vacation time than the average American, and the Japanese government actively encourages its citizens to travel abroad.

TABLE 11.4

World's Leading Spender Nations on International Travel, 1997

Rank	Country	Amount Spent[a]
1	United States	$51,220,000,000 ($59,800,000,000 in 1999)
2	Germany	46,200,000,000
3	Japan	33,041,000,000
4	United Kingdom	27,710,000,000
5	Italy	16,631,000,000
6	France	16,576,000,000
7	Canada	11,268,000,000
8	Netherlands	10,232,000,000
9	China	10,166,000,000
10	Austria	10,124,000,000

[a]Excludes international transportation.

Source: World Tourism Organization

It should be noted that the list of leading tourist spenders is made up of the most developed nations. None of the so-called underdeveloped nations are included. This has been the pattern historically.

Current trends suggest that travel will continue to increase. Recent political changes in Eastern European nations have allowed many people who were formerly prohibited from traveling by their governments to join the world's growing number of travelers. In addition, these former Eastern-bloc countries are becoming attractive destinations for growing numbers of international travelers. The world is fast developing a global economy. As nations become more and more dependent on one another, travel will increase.

CONDITIONS AND DOCUMENTS REQUIRED FOR INTERNATIONAL TRAVEL

Before international travel can take place, nations must recognize each other through formal diplomatic channels, certain specific agreements and arrangements must have been made, and the travelers themselves must have proper documentation.

Diplomatic Recognition

The first requirement for international tourist travel is diplomatic recognition between countries. This recognition can take two forms:

1. **De jure recognition:** The government of one country recognizes that the party in power in another country is that country's legitimate government.

2. **De facto recognition:** The government of one country does not acknowledge the legitimacy of the party governing another country but acknowledges, at least, that the party does govern.

When discussions between two nations result in diplomatic recognition, government officials from each take up residence in the other and additional negotiations begin to establish the procedures and routines for travel. Without diplomatic recognition, there is no suitable way to negotiate procedures for travel, so travel between the two countries is normally prohibited.

The procedures for travel are negotiated by diplomatic officials known as consuls or ambassadors, who serve as the official links between nations. Diplomats work out detailed procedures for travel between nations and for assistance and protection to travelers. Diplomats also negotiate agreements that facilitate travel, such as landing rights for aircraft.

International travelers must have appropriate documentation. The basic document needed for visits to most nations is the **passport**. Passports are issued by the government of a nation to its citizens. A passport provides specific data about the individual to whom it is issued, including name, date of birth, residence, occupation, and citizenship. It also has a photograph of the passport holder.

In addition to the passport, many nations require a **visa**. A visa is either an endorsement on the passport or a separate document showing that the passport holder has received permission from the government of the country he or she intends to visit to enter that country. Visas are usually obtained by applying to a consulate office of the country to be visited well in advance of the intended dates of travel, although in many countries that require visas, it is possible to obtain one on entering the country.

Passports and visas are stamped by immigration authorities as visitors enter a country. These official stamps show the date and port or border of entry, and indicate the permissible length of stay for the passport holder. Permission to stay in a country is normally granted for a limited period of time. U.S. citizens need only a passport to visit most Western European countries; a visa is not needed. Passports are not required for U.S. citizens to visit Canada, Mexico, or most Caribbean nations. Valid identification and proof of citizenship are required, however. For some countries, a driver's license is sufficient; for others, further proof is needed—a birth certificate, for example. A visa is required to visit most eastern European, Middle Eastern, Asian, and African countries. In many South American countries, visas are normally required for business travelers and for those staying three months or more.

Additional travel requirements exist for many parts of the world. Typical of these are vaccination certificates proving immunity to certain infectious diseases that travelers are likely to encounter in the country being visited. Cholera vaccinations are commonly required in many African nations, including Angola, Chad, Ghana, and Liberia. Cholera vaccinations are also required in many parts of the Middle East and the Pacific region.

Proof of financial ability—a return ticket or a stated amount of cash—and other documentation are also frequently required. For example, to enter Brazil, Bolivia,

Chile, Ecuador, and other Central and South American countries, a tourist must have sufficient funds, a ticket to leave, and necessary documents for onward travel. A passport is required, and a visa is necessary for a stay of three months or more.

Governments frequently prohibit citizens from visiting nations at war, those where the safety of visitors may be at risk, or those that have not been officially recognized. For many years, U.S. citizens were prohibited from visiting China because that nation did not have diplomatic relations with the United States. The United States does not officially recognize Cuba or Iraq, so U.S. tourists cannot normally visit these two countries.

Some countries restrict the amount of money their citizens can take from their country. Citizens of Indonesia, Israel, and Malaysia are restricted in this way, for example. Some countries, including India and Burma, prohibit tourists from taking local currency out of the country.

Governments sometimes prohibit some citizens of other nations from entering. Most do not allow criminals, suspected terrorists, and similar undesirables to enter, for example. Most nations restrict the types and quantities of goods that visitors can bring with them. For example, pork products, alcohol, and pornographic materials are prohibited by Saudi Arabia. Many nations limit the amounts of alcohol, tobacco, and perfumes that can be brought in.

Some countries require that departing travelers obtain exit permits. When travelers return home from abroad, governments commonly require that they show passports and any other travel documents to a government official at entry. Most also restrict both the type and value of goods that citizens can bring home. U.S. citizens must declare all articles purchased abroad and currently in their possession as well as the price paid for each. However, individuals are permitted orally to declare goods up to a total value of $400, the maximum that can be imported duty free (except for the U.S. Virgin Islands, American Samoa, and Guam, from which tourists can bring back $1200 worth of goods duty free, and Caribbean Basin countries, from which tourists can bring back $600 in duty goods duty free). If the value of goods exceeds the permissible limit, travelers are charged an import tax known as a duty. Travelers are not permitted to bring goods intended for resale into the United States without the proper permits.

Officials also verify that travelers entering a country are not bringing prohibited goods. In the United States, prohibited goods include illegal drugs, explosives, firearms, and certain plants, animals, and related items.

TRAVEL TO AND FROM THE UNITED STATES

United States citizens have always been leading world travelers. Americans spend more on international travel than any other country's citizens ($59.8 billion), as illustrated in Table 11.4. Perhaps the most significant reasons for this are:

- The United States has a large, prosperous group of middle-class citizens who can afford to travel internationally.

- Many Americans have roots in other countries. This leads many to visit the homeland of their ancestors.

- Travel is an integral part of the American heritage. Compared to citizens of other nations, Americans tend to move more frequently from one town or city to another. Because many Americans have relatives in other parts of the country, they often travel distances to see them.

- International travel is easier for Americans than for the citizens of many other countries. The United States government has relatively few travel restrictions, making it possible for most Americans to travel freely outside the country. The amount of money Americans can take along when traveling outside the country is not restricted. Neither is the amount of time they can spend outside the country or their frequency of travel.

- English is the most widely spoken of the international languages, making it easier for Americans to travel without having to know other languages. In many countries, English is a nearly universal second language, required in schools and used by many. Employees in hotels, restaurants, airline offices, and other travel services throughout the world speak English.

The United States is also the leading country for tourism receipts ($73.3 billion), as illustrated in Table 11.5.

The United States is a vast country with innumerable sights and attractions for foreign visitors. Its many features include such imposing cities as New York and Chicago, with their tall buildings and cultural diversity; the impressive scenery in the national parks; excellent facilities for such sports activities as golf and

TABLE 11.5

World's Top International Tourism Earners, 1997

Rank	Country	Amount Spent[a]
1	United States	$73,268,000,000
2	Italy	29,714,000,000
3	France	28,009,000,000
4	Spain	26,651,000,000
5	United Kingdom	20,039,000,000
6	Germany	16,509,000,000
7	China	12,074,000,000
8	Austria	11,073,000,000
9	Canada	8,763,000,000
10	Switzerland	7,902,000,000

[a]Excluding international transportation.

Source: World Tourism Organization

TABLE 11.6

Foreign Visitor Arrivals to the United States, 1999

Origin	Number
Canada	14,110,000
Mexico	9,915,000
Overseas	24,466,000
Western Europe	10,847,000
Eastern Europe	396,000
Asia	6,935,000
Middle East	625,000
Africa	274,000
Oceania	667,000
South America	2,733,000
Central America	731,000
Caribbean	1,258,000

Source: Tourism Industries, International Trade Administration

TABLE 11.7

Overseas Visitor Arrivals to the United States, 1999

Country	Number
Japan	4,826,000
United Kingdom	4,252,000
Germany	1,985,000
France	1,059,000
Brazil	665,000
Italy	626,000
Venezuela	552,000
Netherlands	527,000
Argentina	502,000
South Korea	499,000

Source: Tourism Industries, International Trade Administration

skiing; and places of special interest, such as Disney World, historic Williamsburg, and Sea World.

It is interesting to note which countries send the most visitors to the United States (see Tables 11.6 and 11.7).

The largest numbers of foreign visitors to the United States come from Canada and Mexico. The proximity of these two countries to the United States is the obvious reason. It is both easy and inexpensive to drive across the American border, compared with the distance and cost associated with overseas travel.

The pattern of travel to the United States from overseas has changed in recent years. Table 11.7 shows where most overseas visitors to the United States originate.

In recent years, the Japanese have traveled to the United States in large numbers and now lead the list of overseas visitors. This is indicative of both the role of Japan in the world economy and the importance of the United States as an importer of Japanese goods. Americans have strong economic ties to Japan. The Japanese have invested heavily in the United States, and Americans purchase more goods and services from Japan than from any other country. The Japanese people come to the United States for many reasons, not the least of which is to play golf, a sport they embrace with a passion. Golf is an expensive sport in Japan and is therefore available to relatively few people there. Nevertheless, most Japanese golfers join driving ranges in their own country and play on courses outside of their country.

The United Kingdom is second in the number of visitors. Britain has always accounted for many travelers to the United States. A major reason appears to be a common heritage and language. America also received large numbers of immigrants from the United Kingdom in past centuries, so many Americans can trace their family roots there.

TRAVEL WITHIN THE UNITED STATES

The scope of travel/tourism in the United States is truly impressive. According to the TIA, total spending for tourism services in the United States was estimated at $481.5 billion for 1997. However the total economic impact, as explained in the following pages, was $1.16 trillion.

Table 11.8 reveals interesting information about travel patterns in the United States. The data shown below is the most current available as of this writing.

Several observations can be drawn from these data. Nearly all travelers in the United States use family automobiles or trucks, recreational vehicles (RVs), or air-planes to reach their destinations. Seventy-seven percent of all travel over 100 miles is by automobile and almost 20 percent by airplane. About 97 percent of all trips taken use these two modes of transportation. Trains and buses are rarely used for long-distance travel. It appears that their primary use is for commuting to and from work. The major reason that people travel long distances within the United States is to visit friends and relatives (see Chapter 13).

Thus, the statistics confirm the importance of the family automobile to the traveling public. This is in contrast to many other nations, particularly the less de-

TABLE 11.8

U.S. Trip Profile

Mode of Transportation	% of Trips
Auto, truck, RV	77.0
Airplane	19.7
Bus	2.6
Train	.6
Ship	.1
Trip Duration	
No nights	25.0
1–3 nights	48.9
4–7 nights	18.5
8 nights or more	7.6
Type of Lodging	
Homes of friends or relatives	43.6
Hotel or motel	41.4
Rented cabin or condo	3.6
Owned cabin or condo	4.2
Camper, trailer, RV	2.5
Other	4.8

Source: U.S. Bureau of Transportation, Statistics

veloped nations, in which comparatively few people own automobiles, roads are poor, and trains, buses, and bicycles are still the primary means of transportation.

THE IMPACTS OF TOURISM

Tourism affects every nation and many localities. For some nations and localities, tourism has a major impact on the economy, the culture, the society, and the environment. The effects can be both positive and negative and are greater in some countries and areas than others. Let us examine these effects in more detail.

The Economic Impact of Tourism

Economic impact of tourism refers to the increased level of economic activity in an area as a result of tourism. It is generally measured in additional jobs and income to an area. Travelers and tourists purchase goods and services. They spend money for transportation, lodging, food, drink, and entertainment. They also purchase other goods and services in the areas they visit. The money they spend comes from outside the area and is brought to the area in the form of cash, traveler's checks, and credit cards. It is "new" money, not generated from internal economic activity. It is money that would not get into the local economy without travel and tourism.

The direct, or immediate, effect of this additional spending is likely to be an increase in the number of jobs in the area and an increase in the income of many local citizens. For example, in an area being developed for tourism, new hotels, motels, and other lodging establishments must be built to accommodate travelers. This creates construction jobs. Once the facilities are built, staff must be hired to operate them. Wages are paid to employees, and these wages are spent in the area to purchase housing, food, clothing, and many other goods and services. Retail establishments selling these items receive income that they would not have had if the hotels, motels, and other lodging facilities had not been built. In addition, the lodging properties must purchase supplies, including food, beverages, linens, and a host of other items. If these goods are bought locally, the food purveyors and suppliers of other goods gain income they would not have earned otherwise.

Besides these immediate effects, important ripple effects also take place. The additional income going to local businesses as a result of tourism enables their owners to hire more employees to handle the extra business. The new employees also spend their wages locally, so more jobs are created and more income is generated as a secondary effect of the original new spending. The cycle does not stop there. Third, fourth, and additional rounds of new jobs may be created as these new employees spend their money locally. Where there was only one restaurant in the area, for example, several may now cater to the tourists, and to the growing and more prosperous local population.

The total economic impact on an area is the sum of this increased economic activity. It may be greater than the original amount spent or it may be less, depending on how much of the original new money is spent locally and how much

Tourism helps preserve a culture when large numbers of people travel to observe that culture, as shown in the accompanying photograph.
(Photo courtesy of Hong Kong Tourist Association)

of it is spent outside the area. For example, suppose that a new hotel hires workers who commute from a distance away and that the hotel also purchases its goods and services from firms outside the local area. Under these circumstances, the economic impact on the immediate area is limited because little of the new money is spent there. This was the case in Atlantic City, New Jersey. The legalization of casino gaming led to the construction of many new hotels, but the economic impact on the immediate area was minimal. There were three principal reasons for this:

1. Gamblers tended not to leave the casino hotels and, consequently, spent little in other Atlantic City businesses.

2. Comparatively few casino hotel employees established residence in Atlantic City, so they tended to shop for goods and services outside the city.

3. The casino hotels purchased a major portion of their goods and services from vendors located outside the city.

The economic impact of tourism varies considerably from one part of the country to another and from one location to another. The relative economic impact of travel and tourism is high in some areas and low in others. For example, tourism is the most important industry in the state of Florida. In one recent year, $51.6 billion was spent by tourists in that state. This spending directly and indirectly created about 1.1 million jobs, which accounted for 18 percent of the state's civilian labor force. The relative economic impact of tourism is high in Florida because most of the wages paid to workers are spent in the state, and a large proportion of the goods and services purchased by the travel industry come from Florida businesses. By contrast, in Bermuda, the economic impact of tourism is relatively low when one considers that a large percentage of Bermuda's income is from tourism, which accounts for about 60 percent of the jobs. The relative impact is lower than in Florida because Bermuda grows little food and manufactures few products for the travel industry. Although employees do spend their wages in the local community, hotels, shops, and other businesses must purchase food and other goods from suppliers outside Bermuda. In both Florida and Bermuda, tourism is the most important economic activity. The economic benefits from tourism are greater in Florida because the direct and indirect economic impact is greater.

Another important economic benefit is the increased government income from taxes. Every state in the United States imposes taxes on tourists. Most have sales taxes on rooms, meals, and rental cars. These are frequently higher than the sales taxes imposed on other goods and services. For example, the state of New Hampshire has an 8 percent tax on rooms and meals, yet it has no sales tax on other goods and services sold in the state. Several states impose a sales tax as high as 23 percent on rental cars. New York City imposes special sales taxes on hotel rooms. A traveler staying in a New York hotel may be charged as much as 15 percent in state and city taxes for hotel accommodations.

Finally, the foreign exchange earned as a result of tourism is a major economic benefit to many nations. A nation needs foreign exchange to pay for goods and services imported from abroad, and tourism may be a principal means of earning it.

The Cultural Impact of Tourism

Tourism can have a significant **cultural impact** on a nation—the customary beliefs, social forms, and daily life of a racial, religious, or social group. Culture manifests itself in art, dance, religion, food, drink, and other aspects of a society. Tourism may help preserve native culture but, at the same time, it speeds the process of cultural change.

Tourism helps preserve a culture when large numbers of people travel to observe that culture. Music and dance, religious rites, and other ceremonial activities are performed for tourists and, thus, become profitable. The repetition of these performances and the income they provide offers an incentive to preserve the culture. It is said that traditional ceremonies still performed on several Caribbean and South Sea islands would have disappeared if tourists had not been drawn to the islands to see them.

One reason travelers go to other countries is to sample the local food and drink. Irish stew, German sauerbraten, Italian cannelloni, and Japanese sukiyaki and sashimi are dishes served in the traditional way for tourists. Many are convinced that these dishes somehow have different and more authentic flavors in their homelands.

Travelers also go to other countries to see the remains of past civilizations. The Roman Coliseum and the excavated ruins of Pompeii, for example, attract large numbers of visitors, and the money spent by tourists helps preserve them. Over the long term, tourism may bring about changes in the culture of a region or a country. Two important areas that may be affected are food and clothing.

Food

Tourists bring their social and cultural attitudes and values with them when they visit other countries. They may be eager to sample the food of the countries they visit, but they commonly seek food similar to foods served at home. Hotels and restaurants willingly accommodate them. The local residents discover these foreign foods and begin to try them, and some of them eventually become part of the local culture. For example, imported frozen foods and American whiskey are now popular throughout the Caribbean. This was not the case before Americans began to visit in large numbers.

Fast-food hamburger chains are now spreading throughout the world. McDonald's is all over the world, and Burger King has expanded into China. There are American-style restaurants in Japan. Eventually, the American foods served in these restaurants will be included in the diets of those countries, and their cultures will be altered. It is said that many Puerto Rican dishes have all but disappeared from the diets of people living on that island. The Puerto Rican diet now clearly resembles that of the American mainland. San Juan has many fast-food restaurants offering typical American mainland cuisine.

Clothing

Tourism also can change the manner in which local populations dress. Tourists wear clothing that is popular at home. Local shops begin to sell clothing that appeals to tourists, and it is noticed by the local residents, some of whom begin to adopt it. As it becomes more popular with local residents, traditional clothing may become less common. It may be replaced gradually by the new styles from abroad. A classic example of this has taken place in Russia, where Levis and other jeans are popular and command high prices.

The Social Impact of Tourism

Tourism can also have dramatic—and often negative—effects on the social climate in a country. It can affect the way the host society feels about citizens of other countries, and it can affect the behavior of citizens of the host country. The **social impact** manifests itself in many ways, including:

- Resentment
- Family problems
- Social problems
- Crime and violence

Resentment

Tourists going to poor, less developed countries sometimes create feelings of resentment and jealousy among the local population. They do this by being demanding—sometimes demeaning—and by seeming to spend excessive amounts of money.

Local workers see tourists check into first-class and luxury hotels. The rates paid by these tourists are usually high by local standards. The room rate charged for one night in some of these properties may be the equivalent of several weeks' wages for a local worker. Some tourists can be demanding, requiring instant service or a special service not readily available in the area. Other tourists can be demeaning, talking to the hotel staff as if they were inferior.

The considerable amount of money spent by the tourists can create jealousy. Tourists sometimes appear to spend money as if it means little. Native workers with lower standards of living become jealous of the more affluent tourists and develop a dislike for them.

If the behavior of tourists is grossly inappropriate, local workers are likely to become resentful and react by being impolite. These feelings are transferred to the local population as workers go home and discuss events with family and friends. Americans have poor reputations in some countries because some American tourists behave inappropriately and insultingly. Thus, local residents assume that all Americans are like the unpleasant ones they see at the hotels.

This problem is not restricted to other nations. It can be seen within the United States. For example, tourists from large cities, such as New York, who go to rural areas in New England may appear to local residents to throw money around. Given the high cost of living in major cities, New Yorkers, for example, are accustomed to spending more for goods and services, but they appear to spend more than the local population feels these goods and services are worth. The prices of goods and services generally rise in response to this. In reality, prices in rural areas may be considerably cheaper than in large cities such that tourists do not feel they are paying too much. Nevertheless, the native population resents them for driving up prices, crowding the highways, polluting the area, and generally acting superior, and, although local residents typically are willing to take tourists' money, they resent the presence of the outsiders.

Family Problems

Tourism can affect the family relationships of local residents when one or more members of the family work in the tourist industry. Several years ago, a study of Hawaiian families showed that the divorce rate of workers involved in tourism was rapidly rising. The study concluded that women who dressed in native Hawaiian costumes to greet and entertain tourists sometimes faced jealousy from their husbands, who accused the women of carrying on with the tourists. In addition, many of the women began to earn higher wages than their husbands, which led to further domestic conflict.

Social Problems

Tourism obviously creates the need for labor to work in hotels, restaurants, and other businesses catering to travelers. Many of these workers are drawn from the local population, but some may come from other areas and settle locally. Communities that have always been of a single culture find that people of different backgrounds, beliefs, values, and lifestyles are now living in their neighborhoods. The new residents act differently, go to different churches, may speak a different language, and even eat different foods. Past social patterns are upset and cultural collision occurs. If the new residents are accepted by the community, the dissimilar cultures can exist peaceably together. If not, there may be conflict.

Crime and Violence

When areas grow in population as a result of tourism, negative changes can take place. A once peaceful rural community may become a busy town or a small city. Tourists, who tend to carry larger amounts of money than they would when not traveling, become targets for amateur and professional thieves. Houses and stores are broken into, a larger police force is required, and local residents who had never found it necessary to lock their homes and cars find an urgent need to do so.

The Environmental Impact of Tourism

The **environmental impact** of tourism can be positive or negative, depending on the specific area and one's personal views. On the one hand, everyone agrees that some tourist areas, such as Atlantic City, Miami Beach, and Waikiki, do not now have the natural beauty that existed prior to development. On the other hand, many people argue that resort areas such as Bermuda, Nassau, and Maui are nicer, cleaner, and more charming than they were prior to their development for tourism.

Some people feel that more people in an area and such changes as new roads, hotels, and restaurants are harmful to the environment. To them, all tourism is harmful to the environment. The general arguments for both the positive and negative points of view are as follows.

The Positive Argument

Development of all kinds has a tendency to destroy natural as well as historical and cultural elements in an area. One cannot develop an area without building new roads, creating hotels and other structures, and installing power lines for electric power. In the process, some historical or cultural symbols may be destroyed. Many countries and areas lack the incentive or the economic means to undertake large-scale projects for the conservation of beautiful scenery, rare and interesting natural environments, or historically important sites. The local population may have little use for unspoiled nature and want to develop these areas in ways that will bring in the most money—whether it be for factories, mining, or some other kind of business.

Tourism changes all that. It encourages the restoration of ancient monuments and archaeological treasures. It provides a reason for the preservation of historical buildings and the creation of museums. The Roman Coliseum would not be preserved if there were no tourists to see it; the same can be said for the Acropolis in Greece—probably the best-known ruins in the world. Natural scenery and historical sites, as well as traditional towns, become economic assets. In fact, some attractions may be more beautiful than the natural land—golf courses and parks, for example.

Tourism provides not only the incentive but also the economic means to preserve the environment. It discourages the development of heavy industry and other unsound uses of the land.

The Negative Argument

The benefits of tourism are overshadowed by its side effects. The development of tourism often brings large numbers of people accustomed to relatively high standards of amenities to a previously secluded natural or cultural environment. Tourism necessitates the development of roads, airports, foodservice, lodging facilities, and shops.

In the process, many tourist sights are inevitably transformed. At best, their natural attractiveness is lost as they become regulated tourist attractions with parking lots, food outlets, and bathrooms. At worst, major and often irreversible environmental damage is caused by a rush to build tourist facilities on the most attractive sites. In many instances, the natural environment is lost forever.

Crowds of tourists litter the area and damage the fragile environment. Local water, sewage, and other facilities become overburdened, causing pollution and unclean air. In the long run, tourism, like any other industry, contributes to environmental destruction.

Most people find that both points of view are somewhat off the mark. Perhaps the most compelling argument falls somewhere between these two extremes. If development is to occur—if an area is to have economic progress—tourism is one of the best alternatives. If properly controlled and regulated, tourism can be the least damaging form of economic development and can actually improve the environment of an area. The key to preserving the environment and allowing for economic progress is in controlling the rate of growth, attending to the necessary support (water, sewage, roads), and developing a plan that preserves the best environmental assets of the area. This usually requires government involvement in tourism planning.

The Importance of Tourism to Nations, States, Areas, and Communities

Tourism is more important to some nations, states, areas, and communities than to others. In many nonindustrialized nations, for example, tourism is the single most important source of income and economic activity. This is true of Spain and most of the Caribbean islands, where tourism produces about 43 percent of the income for the region. Leading the list of income generators in the Caribbean are the Bahamas, Puerto Rico, the Dominican Republic, the U.S. Virgin Islands, and Jamaica. Taken together, these five account for over half the tourist-generated dollars in the region.

The economic importance of tourism is not limited to nonindustrialized nations. Some industrialized countries also rely heavily on tourism to provide foreign exchange. France is now the world's leading travel destination and receives about 10 percent of all international tourists. Spain is second and the United States is third on the list. Canada, Italy, and the United Kingdom also rely heavily on tourism.

Within the United States, tourism is important to some states and less so to others. Those states in which tourism is particularly important—where large numbers of tourists visit the state or where more than 20 percent of the jobs in the state can be traced directly or indirectly to tourism—are frequently labeled destination states. Heading the list of destination states is California. More tourist dollars go to California than to any other state. Other destination states include Florida, New York, Texas, New Jersey, Hawaii, New Hampshire, Vermont, Nevada, Colorado, Arizona, Maine, and South Carolina, among others. In some of the destination states, tourism is the leading industry, accounting for more jobs than any other industry in the state. This is true in Hawaii, Florida, Vermont, Maine, and Nevada.

For many states, tourism is not the leading or even the second leading industry but is still a major factor in the economy, accounting for 10 percent to 20 percent of total employment. This is true in Virginia, West Virginia, Georgia, Tennessee, Louisiana, Michigan, Missouri, Illinois, Wisconsin, Minnesota, North Dakota, Montana, Utah, Idaho, Oregon, Washington, Alaska, Massachusetts, Connecticut, and others.

In some areas and many local communities, tourism is the only significant industry. In these places, most jobs and income can be traced directly or indirectly to tourist dollars. This is true for such destinations as Cape Cod, Bar Harbor, the White Mountains, the Catskills, the Poconos, Atlantic City, Myrtle Beach, Orlando, White Sulphur Springs, Sea Island, the Great Smoky Mountains, New Orleans, Hot Springs, the Black Hills, Yellowstone, Scottsdale, Santa Fe, Las Vegas, Sun Valley, Yosemite, and Vail.

It is impossible to list all of the areas in the United States where tourism is the only significant industry. Hundreds of smaller areas, such as Boothbay Harbor, Maine, and Long Beach Island, New Jersey, are not well known outside their regions but rely heavily on tourism for employment and income.

To many, tourism is the industry of the future. As more people have greater amounts of leisure time, the number of people traveling will increase. As transportation becomes cheaper, faster, and more comfortable, travelers will venture farther and farther from home. As disposable income increases, travel will become even more a part of our lifestyle. As the population lives longer and the quality of medical care enables more people to be healthy and mobile for greater numbers of years, more older people will travel. These and other changes in society mentioned at the beginning of this chapter ensure that travel and tourism will continue to be a leading growth industry.

SUMMARY

In this chapter, the dimensions of travel and tourism are explored. The motivators for travel and changes in society that have caused people to travel more frequently are listed. The government role in travel and tourism is examined, and major government and private travel organizations are identified. The terms *traveler* and *tourist* are discussed, and definitions are provided for each. The composition of the travel industry—direct providers, support services, and tourism development—is explained. The size and scope of international and domestic travel are examined. Conditions and documents necessary for travel are described, as are the economic, cultural, social, and environmental impacts of tourism. Finally, the importance of tourism to nations, states, areas, and communities is discussed.

KEY TERMS

Cultural impact
De facto recognition
De jure recognition
Direct provider of travel services
Economic impact
Environmental impact
Passport
Social impact

Support services
Tourism development
Tourist
Travel industry
Travel Industry Association
Traveler
Visa

DISCUSSION QUESTIONS

1. List at least ten motivators for travel.
2. Describe eight social and economic changes that have led to more frequent travel.
3. How does the role of the U.S. government in travel and tourism compare to that of other nations?
4. What organization publishes most U.S. travel data?
5. List the four criteria used to determine a person's status as a traveler.
6. How does the U.S. Census Bureau define *traveler*?
7. How does the U.S. Census Bureau's definition of a *traveler* differ from that of the U.S. Travel Data Center?
8. Define tourism.
9. List ten examples of direct providers of tourist services.
10. What kinds of firms are classified as support services to the travel industry?
11. Give one example of each of the four types of organizations or agencies classified as tourism development.
12. How much money is spent on world international tourism?
13. List the countries that are the top three international tourist destinations.
14. The citizens of which five countries are classified as the top five spenders on international tourism?
15. Distinguish between de jure and de facto diplomatic recognition.
16. What basic document is required for Americans to visit most European countries? Canada? the Caribbean islands?
17. What is a visa?
18. List the five nations that earn the largest amounts from international tourist spending.
19. From which two countries do the largest number of foreign tourists come to the United States? What accounts for these large numbers?

20. From which countries do the largest number of overseas visitors to the United States come?

21. How much is spent on domestic travel in the United States?

22. Which mode of transportation accounts for the greatest share of domestic travel?

23. What is the primary reason for domestic travel?

24. What does the phrase *economic impact of tourism* mean?

25. Identify three major benefits that national governments derive from tourism.

26. In what primary way does tourism preserve the culture of a nation?

27. In what ways can tourism affect human relations in a society?

28. The chapter describes the points of view of people favoring and opposing tourism. Summarize each in one short paragraph. Do you accept either? Why?

29. List five destination states for tourists.

30. List ten areas or localities where tourism is the only significant industry.

MOMENTS OF TRUTH

1. You are discussing a possible career in the travel industry with a friend. He states that he does not believe the industry will grow significantly in the coming years and, thus, would not be a wise choice for a career. What is your response?

2. You are planning a trip to Mexico. What information do you need to obtain about entering the country?

3. Select a nearby area that caters to tourists and assess the environmental impact of tourism on the area. Is it positive, or negative, or mixed? Respond in an essay of suitable length, including as much factual information as possible to defend your position.

INTERNET EXERCISES

1. Go to http://travel.state.gov/. Are there travel warnings for the following countries? If so, what is the nature of warnings for each country?
   • Afghanistan
   • Colombia
   • Congo
   • Iran
   • Nigeria

2. Go to http://www.tinet.ita.doc.gov/free. Find the tourism statistical data for overseas travelers to the United States. Compare the number of tourists entering the United States from the top ten countries with the numbers listed in the text. What significant changes in the numbers do you see?

Travel Services

▶ Learning Objectives

After reading and studying this chapter, you should be able to:

1. Define the term *travel intermediary*.

2. Define the term *package* as used in the travel business.

3. List the advantages and disadvantages of purchasing travel packages over making travel arrangements independently.

4. Describe the contents of each of the following types of packages:
   a. All-inclusive
   b. Fly/cruise
   c. Fly/cruise/hotel
   d. Fly/drive
   e. Motor coach
   f. Accommodations
   g. Accommodations and meals
   h. Family vacation
   i. Events
   j. Special-interest
   k. Affinity group
   l. Incentive
   m. Convention and meeting

5. Explain the advantages and disadvantages of making travel arrangements directly with a supplier of travel services.

6. Describe the typical packages provided by:
   a. Airlines
   b. Bus companies
   c. Cruise lines
   d. Hotel companies
   e. Railroads

7. Identify the number of travel agencies in the United States.

8. Explain the importance of travel agents to the suppliers of travel services.

9. List the prerequisites for a travel agency to sell travel tickets.

10. Define the terms *travel wholesaler* and *tour operator*.

11. Define the term *specialty channeler*.

12. Identify and explain the role of each of the following specialty channelers in selling travel:
    a. Hotel representatives
    b. State and local tourist offices
    c. Corporate travel offices
    d. Incentive travel firms
    e. Convention and meeting planners

In the previous chapter, the dimensions of travel and tourism were explored. The travel industry was shown to consist of direct providers of travel, support services, and tourism development. Data were supplied to show that international and domestic travel has increased steadily over the years such that the travel industry is now the world's largest, accounting for more than one in every ten dollars spent at the retail level.

Mass travel—extensive long-distance travel by the middle class as well as by the wealthy—really began shortly after World War II. Prior to that time, the middle class generally had neither the time nor the money for long-distance travel, except for job-related purposes, immigration, or some urgent purpose. For many Americans, serving with the armed forces during a war provided the single opportunity for travel that they would have in their entire lives. After World War II, however, more people had greater amounts of free time to travel. They had automobiles that could be used for travel, and they were earning higher wages that gave them the disposable income for travel.

Airlines evolved into a major means of public transportation, making it possible for virtually everyone to travel long distances at relatively low prices. The age of large-scale selling of travel to the public began after World War II.

In this chapter, we provide a broad description of the travel business. We identify the two basic options for people intending to travel, then examine the roles of travel agencies, travel wholesalers, travel specialists, and other related organizations in developing travel packages and making arrangements for travelers.

Once an individual decides to travel, she has two possible options for making the necessary arrangements: seeking the help of an individual or firm in the business of making travel arrangements, or taking the do-it-yourself approach. If the traveler elects the do-it-yourself approach, she must make direct contact with the supplier or suppliers of the services required and attend to all the necessary arrangements. She must obtain detailed information about fares, schedules, and dates directly from suppliers. The difficulties associated with making these arrangements lead many travelers to take the other approach—having all arrangements made by a travel professional known as an intermediary. The term **travel intermediary** refers to a person or firm that makes travel arrangements for individuals or groups. When the arrangements are made by an intermediary, the traveler need only call or visit the intermediary, discuss the options, then leave the detailed arrangements to this professional.

One of the more familiar travel intermediaries is the travel agent. A **travel agent** is in the business of making travel arrangements for others. When travelers use the services of a travel agent, travel arrangements can be tailored to their particular needs and desires. Specialized itineraries can be prepared for them. The travel agent inquires into their needs and makes reservations for airlines, hotels, transfers, rental cars, and other requirements. If specialized travel arrangements are not required, the travel agent may recommend a common alternative: a travel package. **Travel package** is a term used to describe two or more travel services bundled together and sold at one price.

Travel packages are among the most important elements in the travel business. Travel agents typically find that sales of travel packages represent approximately 18 percent of annual bookings. Approximately 32 percent of Americans traveling to overseas destinations book travel packages. Because of the important role they play in the travel business, it is useful to examine types of packages and the firms that develop them.

TRAVEL PACKAGES

There are many kinds of travel packages. Some are group packages, arranged so that a given number of travelers are together for the duration of the trip. Others are individual packages, which enable a traveler to move about independently of others who select the same package. In some instances, the independent package requires that the individual travel at specified times; thus, the air transportation may be arranged along with others taking the tour. In other instances, the independent tour does not require a specific departure or return date. Travelers choose those dates for themselves and travel entirely independently of others taking the same package.

Packages can vary considerably. Some are vacation packages to specific locations—a hotel on a Caribbean island, for example. Others involve travel to several locations—London, Paris, Rome, and Berlin, for example. Packages may last for only a few days or for a week or longer, and they vary in price, according to the quality of the package and the length of time involved.

Some packages provide deluxe accommodations; others include accommodations in properties of lower quality. Some packages are geared to specific activities—golf, for example. Some packages include all the necessities: travel, accommodations, meals, tips, transfers, sports, and entertainment. Others include only a few—accommodations and a rental car, for example. The firm that assembles the package makes judgments about the combination of services it believes are most appealing and can best be sold to potential customers.

The following are characteristic types of packages sold to travelers.

All-Inclusive Packages

As the name implies, **all-inclusive packages** provide most or all of the necessary elements of travel. They generally include transportation, accommodations, meals, transfers (ground transportation between an airport and a hotel or similar lodging property), entertainment, sightseeing, sports, taxes, and gratuities. However, they do vary considerably. Some offer all meals; others offer a specified number of meals. Some include admission to special events; others do not. Other specifics in the travel package may also vary.

Fly/Cruise Packages

Fly/cruise packages include air transportation to and from a point of departure, transfers, and a cruise. Fly/cruise packages are almost always all-inclusive,

---

➤ BOOKING A TRAVEL PACKAGE ON LINE

One of the easiest ways to book a travel package is to go on-line. Many sites offer excellent packages of all kinds. For example, Travel Package at http://www.travelpackage.com is a World Wide Web site for Select Sport Travel, Inc., a wholesale and retail travel company specializing in vacation adventures.

One can book a cruise, a tour, a sports package, or a customized package through this Web site, which even offers packages for senior citizens and single travelers. Booking travel packages on-line is becoming a popular way to conveniently make arrangements for travel.

---

meaning that the package price includes the cost of airfare, accommodations, all meals, and entertainment. Gratuities and sightseeing are typically extra.

Fly/Cruise/Hotel Packages

Fly/cruise/hotel packages normally include air transportation, a cruise, and a specified number of nights at a hotel. These packages are typically offered by cruise line companies, such as Cunard, that own resort hotels in the vicinity of the ship's point of departure.

Fly/Drive Packages

Fly/drive packages typically include airfare and rental car only. They are intended for travelers who prefer to make their own travel plans. Fly/drive packages are usually prepared by airlines in partnership with rental car companies.

Motor Coach Packages

Motor coach packages are special-purpose bus tours for people interested in shopping, sightseeing, or attending a particular sports event, for example. They are planned by motor coach operators and other tour companies. If a tour is to take more than one day, it normally includes accommodations, meals, and entertainment.

Accommodations Packages

Accommodations packages usually include lodging only. They are really just discounts on room rates. Some are available only for particular seasons or on specified dates. Others are limited to particular numbers of nights. Many international airlines offer attractive accommodations packages for use in major cities abroad. Accommodations packages sometimes include such additional features as continental breakfasts, transit passes, and theater tickets.

This page from a Club Med brochure is one example of all-inclusive vacation packages. It includes information on accommodations, location, foodservice, activities, and other points of interest. Travel packages are often available, offering savings through volume sales and the convenience of having the most important arrangements made for the traveler.

(Photo courtesy of Club Med Sales, Inc. All rights reserved.)

Accommodations and Meals Packages

Accommodations and meals packages include hotel accommodations and meals. They vary considerably. Some include three meals per day; others include certain specified meals—full English breakfast daily, or dinner the second night, for example. Some include free access to sports facilities, such as golf courses and tennis courts. Others offer discounts on sporting activities. Some also offer sightseeing and other entertainment.

Family Vacation Packages

Family vacation packages always include accommodations at destinations and attractions that appeal particularly to families—Disney World, Sea World, and Busch Gardens, for example. They normally include other appealing features as well—some type of child care for part of the vacation, for example, so that adults can have time for themselves. These packages are typically designed to provide value to families.

Events Packages

Events packages are special packages that focus on particular events or performances: football games, festivals, theater, art exhibits, and so on. The possibilities are endless. These packages usually include transportation and admissions to the event or performance, and may include accommodations, meals, rental cars.

Special-Interest Packages

Special-interest packages are designed for groups of people who share a particular interest, such as a sport or hobby. The common interests around which these packages are developed include golf or tennis, photography, wineries, fall foliage, and many others.

Affinity Group Packages

Affinity groups are groups of people who share a common bond. They may be students in the same college, alumni of a university, members of a social club, a religious organization, or a fraternity or a sorority. They may all be in the same profession—doctors, dentists, or lawyers, for example. **Affinity group packages** enable the group to share a common experience. It can be a tour, a vacation at a resort, a cruise, or any other activity that appeals to the group.

Incentive Packages

An **incentive package** is a vacation package sponsored by a corporation and offered to employees as a reward for superior performance—high-volume sales of a product or service, or some other achievement beyond the norm. Some compa-

CHOOSING THE OPTIONS IN CARIBBEAN ACCOMMODATIONS THAT ARE RIGHT FOR YOU

When visiting the Caribbean, travelers have several options in accommodations. Choosing the right one may be the key to a successful vacation. Travel agents can best advise vacationers which accommodations are best for them.

- **All-Inclusive Resorts**—First made popular by Club Med in the 1950s, all-inclusives now offer an even wider range of activities and amenities. At the new breed of "super inclusive" resorts, the daily rate usually includes an air-conditioned room, meals, drinks, airport transfers, and activities like tennis lessons, windsurfing, and snorkeling. Base prices are higher than standard resort prices, but they are excellent values for fun-loving guests prepared to take advantage of everything these resorts have to offer. Jamaica boasts the most all-inclusive resorts. They range from those that cater to couples only to those that accept singles only to those catering to families.

- **Family-Run Inns**—These intimate resorts provide the experience of an extended family in the Caribbean. Most do not offer room service but do offer a friendly house-party atmosphere imbued with the personality of the host. Sociability is important, as regulars arrive ready to mingle.

- **Classic Resorts**—Most of these properties provide the elegant island style of the 1960s but with updated amenities, and many cater to groups. Guests are not required to participate in activities unless they want to, and, unlike at all-inclusive resorts, they pay only for food and drinks they purchase.

- **Villa Rentals**—For some, a Caribbean villa means peace, privacy, and independence—all with an ocean view. A two-bedroom house can provide ample room for two couples or a family and allow the occupants freedom to make their own schedules. Many villas come with privileges at tennis and golf facilities, and, frequently, a complex will include the amenities of a full resort.

The travel agent is best able to match the needs of travelers with the type of accommodation suited for them, and there is no cost to the traveler. Travel agents receive their commissions from direct providers of travel services.

nies offer all-inclusive vacations to Hawaii, for example. Any type of package can be used as an incentive package as long as it provides incentive for employees to improve performance.

Convention and Meeting Packages

Convention and meeting packages are typically offered by hotels and sponsoring organizations. They frequently include accommodations, meals, sightseeing, and other activities.

Packages have several advantages over individual travel arrangements. They are typically less expensive because the person or firm preparing the package purchases the travel arrangements in quantity and is able to pass on savings to the traveler. For example, an intermediary putting together a vacation package to London for 45 people might be able to obtain rooms and meals at a particular hotel for 70 percent of the normal price. The hotel manager may be glad to sell these rooms at that price because he is assured of selling a large number of rooms, and the cost of providing food for these guests might be less than for regular customers. In addition, the hotel does not have to pay a travel agency commission because the commission is paid to the travel agent by the intermediary.

It is also possible to purchase airline seats at a discount. Some of the savings that result from making these arrangements at discounts are passed on to the purchaser of the package, and sufficient profit is left for the intermediary making the arrangements. The total price of the package is considerably less than it would be for an individual to make the same arrangements on his own. Another advantage of a package is that the traveler knows precisely what the trip costs. All essentials of the trip are normally included in the price, and extra charges are stated in the promotional materials.

Finally, if the travel is complicated, the tourist traveling on a package has to make only a few decisions. Once the tour package is selected, there are normally relatively few additional choices to be made. Many people prefer to travel without having to make important decisions about where to stay and what sights to see. Good packages assure the traveler that the important events and sights will be seen.

PACKAGE DEVELOPERS

Many suppliers of travel services develop travel packages. A list of these suppliers and the packages they develop includes the following.

Airlines

Airlines create a large number of packages, the most popular of which are fly/drive packages and accommodations packages. Fly/drive packages are designed for travelers who wish to be on their own. Airlines create these packages to provide incentives for travelers to go to destinations served by the airlines. They frequently offer these packages on dates or days of the week when flights are not normally fully booked.

Accommodations packages are also popular with airlines. These are typically individual travel packages rather than group packages. Airlines work closely with hotels to provide accommodations at rates below the normal room rates offered by the hotels. Hotel companies are willing to do this because when they establish links with the airlines, they obtain bookings they might not otherwise get.

Many accommodations packages offered by airlines do not include airfare, and some do not include meals or other normal expenses. For example, American Airlines offers accommodations packages to more than 20 Caribbean islands and has established package rates with several hotels on each of these islands. The basic package rate is appealing but includes only the hotel room. Transfers to the hotel, taxes, airfare, food, drinks, entertainment, and activities are all extra. Many of the hotels participating in the American Airlines package plan, however, do allow customers to opt for an all-inclusive rate that includes drinks and some activities.

Other packages offered by airlines are more extensive and include airfare as well as other costs. For example, Northwest Airlines offers packages to Bangkok, Hong Kong, and Singapore that include airfare, hotels, land transportation, sightseeing, and entertainment. Thus, the buyer of an airline package must look closely at the contents of a package to determine if it includes the elements she is looking for.

Bus Companies

Bus packages are increasingly popular, particularly with senior citizens. These packages are offered by bus companies that own or lease buses and by many other firms that contract with bus companies for required bus service.

Bus tours vary considerably in quality, length, price, and amenities. Some are as short as a few hours, while others take days. One of the most popular tours is the gaming tour, a bus tour that takes potential gamblers to a casino and returns them to the point of departure. The casino hotels of Atlantic City, New Jersey, play host to many of these tours from the surrounding region—New York, Connecticut, Pennsylvania, Delaware, Washington, D.C., and other nearby areas. These tours frequently include bus fare, entertainment, and a number of quarters or gaming chips of sufficient value to make the cost of the tour reasonable.

Extended bus tours are, by nature, all-inclusive tours, because the people on the tour must be housed and fed. These tours, like other all-inclusive tours, vary in quality and in amenities offered. At the economy level, bus tours stay at budget lodging properties. Meals involve few, if any, menu choices, and travelers may be charged extra for admissions to events. At the luxury level, travelers on the tour are accommodated at luxury hotels, have a number of choices from the hotel menu, and do not pay for admission to events.

One of the more interesting professions is that of bus tour manager or tour guide. This person meets the travelers at the point of embarkation and stays with them throughout the tour. Duties of the tour manager include confirming that all reservations for hotels, restaurants, and events are in order, assigning seats and establishing a seat rotation plan on the bus, keeping the tourists informed of sights along the way, keeping order on the tour, making sure baggage gets to hotel rooms and back on the bus, attending to illness and other emergencies, and attending to the myriad details of a bus tour and countless needs of travelers. Tour managers typically are not paid high salaries, but they do receive tips at the end of the tour. In some cases, they also receive commissions from gift shops and other retail establishments when buses stop at these places. Thus, many tour managers are able to earn comfortable incomes and live interesting lives.

Bus Packages are increasingly popular, especially with senior citizens. Shown in the photograph is a tour bus of Tauck Tours.

(Photo courtesy of Tauck Tours)

Domestic bus tour companies generally price their package tours without airfare. International bus tour companies, however, have package prices that do include airfare. For example, Cosmos, a European-based bus tour company, offers various packages to Europe. Their 27-day escorted budget tour of Europe can include airfare and offers transfers, tourist-class hotels, private baths, 25 continental breakfasts, 12 dinners, and visits to various sights. These and other bus tours are sold directly to the public as well as through travel agents.

Cruise Lines

Major cruise lines prepare all-inclusive packages that include airfare, transfers to the ship, and the cost of the cruise. Included in the cruise are accommodations, meals, and entertainment. Passengers are required to pay only for drinks, gratuities, and excursions from the ship. Most cruise lines are noted for the quality and quantity of their food. A typical day includes breakfast, lunch, midafternoon tea or snacks, dinner, and midnight buffet.

The cruise lines use a variety of airlines to transport passengers from their homes to the ship. Interestingly, for many cruise lines, the price of the cruise, including transportation, is usually the same from any city in the United States. This means that cruise passengers coming long distances pay the same as those coming from near the port of embarkation. Usually, cruise lines deduct the airline portion of the package for passengers who choose not to take advantage of the "free" air transportation.

Some cruise lines offer packages that include one or more nights in a hotel before or after the cruise. These combinations are particularly attractive to people who wish to see the sights while they are in the vicinity of the port. Some packages include a one-week cruise and a second week at a resort hotel owned by the cruise line.

Travel agents account for 95 percent of all cruise sales, virtually all of which are packages. The packages cruise lines create are obviously the most important element in their sales effort.

Railroads

As mentioned in earlier chapters, rail travel was once the most important form of public transportation. In Europe and other parts of the world, it is still important, but in the United States, rail travel is used primarily for commuter service. Amtrak does offer rail and hotel package tours, as well as an Air-Rail program. They are subcontracted to a package tour operator. Also, Amtrak and VIA Rail Canada offer a 30-day North America Rail Pass. In Europe, a Eurailpass enables travelers to see Europe relatively inexpensively. In several South American countries, trains are a relatively popular transportation mode for excursions, although the trains are not particularly modern or comfortable. Trains may be part of packages prepared by others, but railroad companies have not been leading developers of packages.

Cruise Lines are expanding their capacity at a very rapid rate in order to meet increasing demand. Shown in the photograph is the Carnival cruise ship *Triumph*. *(Photo courtesy of Carnival Cruise Lines)*

Lodging Companies

Many of the companies operating hotels, motels, and other lodging properties create travel packages that are sold directly to customers as well as through travel agents. For example, Club Med, one of the largest chains of resort hotels, has developed all-inclusive packages for their resorts around the world. These packages include transportation, transfers, taxes, gratuities, meals, entertainment, and accommodations. Recreation is also included in the package price, although the resorts charge extra for certain sports, such as golf, horseback riding, and deep-sea fishing. In contrast to cruise packages, the price of Club Med packages is not the same from all cities. Those who travel the farthest are charged more than those who come from nearby points. Interestingly, Club Med is now also in the cruise business and offers a cruise package aboard its Club Med 1, a motor-sailing vessel, advertised as the largest and most beautiful sailing ship in the world. The vessel has 191 outside staterooms.

Other accommodations packages offered by hotels vary significantly. Many hotels offer packages that include accommodations, all meals, and recreation. Some offer only accommodations and breakfast, plus specified entertainment. Several all-inclusive resorts offer packages with accommodations, meals, recreation, sports, gratuities, taxes, and even unlimited drinks at the bar. It is almost impossible to spend money at these resorts.

Tour Wholesalers and Tour Operators

Tour wholesalers and tour operators are important developers of travel packages. As the name implies, a **tour wholesaler** prepares tours and other travel packages and distributes them through retail outlets. The wholesaler organizes the tour, prepares promotional material, and distributes it to travel agencies and other retail firms. Wholesalers may also conduct the tour. **Tour operators** traditionally have been individuals and firms that carry out ground arrangements—for bus tours or guides, for example.

One example of a tour wholesaler that prepares and operates tour packages throughout the world is Collette Travel Service, based in Pawtucket, Rhode Island. This company offers group tours and independent tours to Australia, Europe, Alaska, Africa, Asia, Hawaii, Canada, and the continental United States. The packages range from fly/drive vacations to escorted tours that include land and sea transportation, accommodations, a number of meals, and many of the tour sights. Airfare to the starting destination is additional and is arranged with TWA and other airlines. Collette relies heavily on travel agents to sell their tours.

Of course, when the wholesaler makes travel arrangements, there is a risk that not all of the available space will be sold. If tours are not sufficiently popular, the wholesaler may lose money or have to cancel the tour.

Any individual or firm can act as a wholesaler. There are virtually no government regulations or requirements for becoming a tour wholesaler. There are more than 2000 independent tour wholesalers and operators in the United States, although the largest 40 account for the lion's share of the business. One of the major problems of dealing with tour wholesalers and operators is that some of the smaller ones are not well managed. Some have gone into bankruptcy, causing serious loss to customers, travel agents, and suppliers of travel services. In recent years, several large tour wholesalers have abruptly gone out of business. The travel industry is addressing this problem. The U.S. Tour Operators Association, which represents many of the largest international tour operators, has established a bonding program that assures payment in the event of the failure of a travel wholesaler or tour operator.

In many instances, the tour wholesaler and tour operator are two separate firms. The wholesaler makes the travel arrangements for hotel accommodations, meals, and visits to sites along the way. He also prepares the promotional material and distributes it to travel agencies. The tour operator actually conducts the tour, providing the bus to meet travelers at their departing or arriving point and conducting the tour for the travel wholesaler.

There is an increasing degree of overlap in the functions of tour wholesalers and tour operators. Some tour wholesalers arrange all of the details for tours and also act as tour operators. Some tour operators act as tour wholesalers, preparing tour packages and promotional materials and distributing them to retail travel outlets. Thus, travel wholesaler and tour operator sometimes appear to be one and the same. In fact, travel wholesalers are often referred to as tour operators.

Frequently, travel agencies act as travel wholesalers. They do this by developing their own package tours and offering these both to their own customers and to those of other travel agencies. They make arrangements for airline travel, hotels, ground transportation, and all other features of the tour. One of the largest of these firms is American Express, which acts as both tour operator and travel agent.

TRAVEL AGENTS

The most important retail sellers of travel are travel agents. Interestingly, they are a relatively recent addition to the travel industry. The first travel agent was Thomas Cook, a British publisher and lecturer on the evils and sins of alcohol. In 1841, he conceived of the idea of chartering railroad trains to bring his temperance supporters to meetings; on July 5 of that year, he transported 570 passengers round trip on a train from Leicester to Loughborough, England. The distance was 12 miles each way and the reported cost to each passenger was one shilling.

The trip was successful, and others interested in group travel soon sought his services. By 1845, Cook was organizing relatively complex travel for individuals and groups over several railroad lines. In 1851, he organized tours to the Exhibition in London and, in 1855, organized similar tours to the Paris Exhibition. Shortly thereafter, he opened an office in London.

Thomas Cook was the first person to organize and conduct an around-the-world tour, a feat he accomplished in 1872. His travel agency business continued to grow, becoming one of the world's largest travel organizations. In 1994, parts of that organization were acquired by American Express, but the name Thomas Cook is still among the best known in the travel industry.

The Expertise of Travel Agents

Travel agents are professionals with expertise in arranging travel for clients. Good travel agents, like good doctors, lawyers, and accountants, are highly trained individuals. They have extensive knowledge of travel destinations, accommodations, transportation, and all other aspects of travel. They are able to find the most direct or the least expensive travel route to any destination. They can determine which hotel in a given city is most convenient to a particular site. They can advise travelers about the best time of year to travel to specific destinations. They can advise customers about the proper type of clothing to pack for a specific destination at a particular time of year. They can tell clients whether or not a visa is required to visit a particular country. They can even advise clients on the best routes from the airport to their hotel.

Like other professionals, some travel agents have specialties. Some are particularly knowledgeable about travel in specific parts of the world—Africa, China, or Russia, for example. Others have extensive knowledge of particular types of vacations—cruises or bus tours, perhaps. All travel agents have access to information about the elements of travel, and all should be able to make appropriate travel arrangements for their clients.

Good travel agents have one important trait in common—the ability to match customers with travel that is suitable. For example, assume that a customer goes

All states have tourist offices that promote hotels, motels, and other travel services. Shown in the photograph is a Virginia Travel Office.
(Photo courtesy of Virginia Tourism Corporation)

to a travel agency looking for a vacation on a cruise ship. Each cruise line and cruise ship is different. Some cruise ships are more formal than others and require formal dress at meals. Some have music and entertainment that appeals to younger people, and others are more suitable for older adults. Some cruise ships sail at night and dock during the daytime at different ports. A good travel agent can determine which cruise best suits the needs, desires, and budget of each individual. To be able to do so requires an understanding of the customer—the kinds of activities, entertainment, and food he prefers as well as the most suitable shipboard environment, type of accommodation, size of ship, and price. Only by understanding both the customer and the cruise lines can the travel agent properly match the customer and the cruise. If the travel agent does a poor job of this, the customer will not be satisfied and find the travel agent at fault.

Travel agents have immediate access to a wealth of travel information that would take customers long hours to find if they were attempting to make their own arrangements. For example, an individual intending to fly from Boston to San Francisco would have to spend considerable time on the telephone calling the airlines that fly out of Boston to determine if they fly to San Francisco, or, alternatively, search the Web to obtain that information. She would have to ask about flight schedules and fares for each airline. If she were to require a hotel room in San Francisco, she might have to obtain a guide to hotels or call someone in California who had access to the Yellow Pages for San Francisco to determine the names, addresses, and telephone numbers of local hotels. She would then have to call, fax, e-mail, or write to the hotels to inquire about reservations.

All of this information is readily available to travel agents through computers and publications on hand in their offices. Within moments, a travel agent can determine which airlines fly to San Francisco, the schedules for all flights, and the availability and cost of seats on each flight. He can also advise the customer about which hotels are located in the city, their rates, and their locations, and can easily determine the availability of rooms. All travel arrangements, including air, hotel, rental car, and travel insurance, can be made by the travel agent in a short period of time.

Frequently, travel agents can obtain travel and hotel reservations at lower prices than can a customer attempting to make individual travel arrangements. The agent's familiarity with rates and sales practices of airlines, hotels, rental cars, and other services makes it possible for him to find the lowest rates. Under most circumstances, travelers are wise to use the services of travel agents for travel that requires public transportation, accommodations, rental cars, or other travel services. Good travel agents have the expertise to advise clients on the best travel arrangements and can usually make these arrangements at equal or lower cost than arrangements made independently.

Travel agents gain their expertise in a variety of ways. Most study at postsecondary institutions—some at colleges and universities offering degree programs in travel and tourism, others at schools that offer shorter professional training programs for travel agents. They complete courses in travel agency management, geography, computer operation, ticketing, customer relations, and other professional subjects.

However, course work alone is normally not enough. Experience is a major element in the development of an expert travel agent. Travel knowledge and expertise is gained on the job and by means of **familiarization trips**, commonly known as FAM trips. These are trips to resorts, cities, sights, and the like that are sponsored by airlines and by other travel suppliers at the destination. The cost of these trips is usually absorbed by the airline and the sponsoring organization. The organizations that sponsor FAM trips do so with the obvious objective of creating referrals and bookings from the travel agencies.

Cost of Travel Agency Services to Clients

Many agents perform services at no cost to the client. This is because their primary income comes in the form of sales commissions paid by airlines, hotels, and other suppliers of travel services. These sales commissions are normally a stipulated percentage of the price of the particular travel service arranged. However, in recent years, travel agency commissions have become smaller because airlines are limiting the amount that they pay in commissions. This has caused many travel agents to charge a fee for making airline and other reservations.

The Number of Travel Agencies and Their Size

Although travel agencies have been in existence since the mid-1800s, when Thomas Cook started the first one, the number was comparatively small until after World War II, when the era of mass travel began. The increase in the number of travel agencies kept pace with the growth of travel until the latter part of the twentieth century. With more people making their own airline reservations on airline Web sites and the efforts of the airlines to reduce travel agent commissions, the number of travel agencies in the United States is beginning to decline. Table 12.1 shows the growth in the number of travel agencies in the United States.

Supplier Dependence on Travel Agents

Airlines rely heavily on travel agents for a large percentage of their business. Historically, about 80 percent of domestic business and 85 percent of international

TABLE 12.1

Number of U.S. Travel Agencies[a]

Year	Number of Travel Agencies
1985	27,193
1987	30,169
1990	37,807
1993	42,709
2000	42,593

[a]Including satellite ticket printer locations.

Source: Airlines Reporting Corporation

business has come from travel agents. However, that is changing rapidly. Major airlines now have Web sites that allow passengers to search destinations and make reservations on their office or personal computers. When passengers do this, the airline, obviously, does not pay a travel agent commission. To encourage use of office and personal computers, many airlines grant cheaper fares when reservations are made via their Web site. Further, they limit the maximum amount a travel agent can receive when reservations are made. Thus, travel agent commissions from airlines are decreasing, causing much distress for most travel agencies.

Cruise lines are almost totally dependent on travel agencies, and some international hotels are heavily agency dependent. Some domestic hotels are also heavily dependent on travel agencies for a large part of their business, but most are not.

For most suppliers of travel services—tour operators, cruise lines, hotels, car rental firms—there are several critical reasons to promote the use of travel agencies. One of the most important is that travel agents act as one's sales representatives in all parts of the country. It was shown in Table 12.1 that there are over 42,000 travel agencies in the United States. If the average travel agency has six employees, that means more than 250,000 salespeople are working to sell travel. This is a powerful incentive to promote their use, particularly when one considers that agencies are paid only when the agents are successful in selling travel.

The use of travel agents is particularly important for suppliers of travel services that cannot afford to have sales representatives in all parts of their marketing areas. For example, a 200-room resort hotel in the Caribbean obviously cannot afford to maintain offices in all the major cities in the eastern United States.

Travel agencies are equally important for the larger suppliers of travel services. Travel agencies enable them, in effect, to expand the number of offices selling their services without increasing their overhead costs. For example, cruise line operators might be forced to consider having a sales office in every city of the United States if no travel agents were available to represent them.

Prerequisites for a Travel Agency to Sell Travel Tickets

One cannot open a travel agency and sell airline, cruise line, or other travel tickets as easily as one can open other types of retail establishments. This is because the travel agency receives its income from the suppliers of transportation services, and most of these suppliers will not pay commissions to organizations that they have not approved or that have not been approved by a travel association. Approval to sell tickets for transportation services is given to a travel agency only when it receives an appointment to one or more of the conferences that represent travel services. The term *conference* does not mean a meeting, as one might think; in this context, it is a regulatory body that sets standards for travel agencies. The following are the most important conference approvals needed by travel agencies:

ARC: The Airline Reporting Corporation
CLIA: Cruise Lines International Association
IATA: The International Air Transport Association

Each conference has specific requirements that travel agencies must meet in order to gain approval and the right to sell the services offered by conference members. Conference requirements are strict because travel agents issue tickets and collect funds that must be turned over to the companies whose services they sell. Requirements for conference approval typically include the following:

- The travel agency must have a manager with at least two years' experience and at least one employee with one year's experience as a travel agent.

- The agency must have a net worth of about $100,000 or a bond—a type of insurance policy—covering the normal amount of business expected for a period of time.

- The agency must be clearly identifiable to the public and open for business a given number of hours (typically, at least 35) per week.

- The agency must pay an application fee and annual fees to the conference, plus additional charges for blank ticket forms and for computer and other costs.

Each conference has its own requirements, but those listed above are representative. After receiving conference approval, travel agents can issue tickets and are entitled to commissions on the sale of tickets.

Computer Use in Travel Agencies

Just a few years ago, travel agents used telephone, telex, and the mails to make all travel arrangements. A travel agent booking an airline seat looked up the airline schedule in a publication known as the Official Airline Guide, then called the airline to find out about seat availability. Today, virtually all full-service travel agents make these travel arrangements using one of the computer programs that airlines have developed. American Airlines, with its Sabre system, has a greater number of network users for its program than any other system. United has the Apollo system, and TWA has a system called PARS. These programs make it possible for travel agents to determine which airlines fly between any two points and to obtain the schedule of flights between those two points for any given day. They enable the travel agent to determine seat availability for each flight and the prices for various classes of tickets. If a customer wants to reserve a seat, the travel agent can make the reservation by computer. The computer prints the ticket in the travel agent's office and the agent issues it to the customer. The entire transaction may take as little as five minutes.

New computer programs now available enable travel agents to obtain information about many hotels, motels, and resort properties. Agents can even obtain layouts and floor plans of properties as well as information about special features they offer. Telephone calls and the mail still have their place, of course; but fax machines and computers have largely replaced older methods of communication at travel agencies.

The Outlook for Travel Agencies

Although there is and always will be a strong need for travel agencies, many experts are predicting that the number of travel agencies will continue to decline. The reasons for this can be found in the increasing use of the Internet by travelers and the continuing limitations on commissions that airlines and, possibly, other travel suppliers are willing to pay.

All major airlines and most other suppliers of travel have Web sites, and they are making major efforts to get their customers to book directly with them. To the extent that these efforts are successful, travel agencies will lose business. Additionally, many larger travel agencies are now creating their own Web sites. As more and more travelers make their travel arrangements on-line—directly with suppliers or through Web sites of travel agencies—and as commissions continue to be limited, smaller agencies will not be able to book sufficient business to remain profitable. Thus, experts predict that many of them will go out of business. However, many travel agencies are aggressively seeking new business to offset declining commissions. Additionally, while many customers are making airline and hotel reservations over the Internet, most travelers who go on extended vacations still use travel agents to book their arrangements. Travelers going on extended trips by and large still prefer the personal service and advice of the travel agent.

OTHER TRAVEL SPECIALISTS

In addition to the direct providers, travel wholesalers, tour operators, and travel agents discussed above, yet more specialists assist travelers by making arrangements for some or all of their needs.

Specialty Channelers

Specialty channelers are individuals or firms that represent either buyers or sellers of travel services. They make travel arrangements for the parties they represent and do so either directly with a travel supplier or through a travel agent. Because specialty channelers deal directly with travel customers, they can have great impact on where travelers go and how they get there. There are two types of specialty channelers: (1) those that represent sellers of travel services and (2) those that represent buyers of travel services.

Specialty channelers that represent sellers of travel services include hotel representatives and state and local tourism offices.

Hotel Representatives

A **hotel representative**, usually called a hotel rep, is an individual or firm that represents hotels—usually a number of them in many locations—and sells the services of those hotels directly to individuals, businesses, and groups. Hotel reps are not employees of the hotels; they usually have contractual agreements with the hotels they represent, and they develop and book both individual and group business for these hotels. Hotel representatives may be individuals, travel agencies, or other firms, and they are normally located in large metropolitan areas such as New York, Chicago, and Los Angeles.

Hotel representatives seeking group business have detailed knowledge of the businesses and groups in their area that require hotel facilities for meetings and conventions. Many maintain close contact with travel agencies and thus provide a link between the hotels they represent and local travel agencies.

Hotel reps are able to meet the needs of the businesses and groups they contact because they represent a great number of hotels in many areas. This means they can offer service products that meet the specific needs of the business and groups they contact. Some hotels have representatives in several parts of the country. Their compensation comes in the form of retainers—fees paid to professionals for services rendered—and commissions for the business they book in the hotels.

State and Local Tourism Offices

All states have tourist offices that promote hotels, motels, and other travel services in their state. They advertise travel opportunities and attempt to connect potential customers with appropriate properties and organizations. They often maintain information offices, called **visitor centers**, that direct customers to appropriate travel destinations, properties, and businesses. Visitors centers are often located on highways.

Chambers of Commerce. **Chambers of commerce** act for local areas as state tourism offices do for states. They advertise the local area and refer inquiries to appropriate properties and businesses. Most chambers of commerce have offices that provide information and assistance to travelers and refer them to local hotels, motels and other properties.

Convention and Visitors Bureaus. Most cities with populations over one million have **convention and visitors bureaus**. These bureaus typically focus their attention on attracting groups, businesses, conventions, tours, and the like to their cities. They frequently assist in convention arrangements and often act as housing coordinators for convention groups.

Specialty channelers that represent buyers of travel services include corporate travel offices, incentive travel firms, and convention and meeting planners.

Corporate Travel Offices

Corporate travel offices are an example of a specialty channeler who represents the buyer of travel services. A company employs a corporate travel officer who makes travel arrangements for corporate personnel. Corporate travel officers may make the arrangements directly with suppliers of travel services, or they may book through travel agencies. Corporate managers, sales personnel, and employees in other positions account for a considerable amount of travel, and many corporations establish travel departments to make the necessary arrangements. These travel departments are generally not official travel agencies because they are not members of the travel conferences and cannot receive commissions on their travel arrangements. Frequently, however, they make the same arrangements as travel agencies—booking transportation, accommodations, and other required travel services directly with the suppliers of those services. Some make travel arrangements through travel agencies in just the same way as other travel agency customers.

A number of reasons explain why firms establish corporate travel offices. Sometimes they are set up as a convenience for employees, providing a central office where travel arrangements can be made. Frequently they are established as a means for corporations to control travel costs. Travel departments have information indicating which personnel are permitted to travel at company expense, which may be permitted to travel first class, how much each employee is allowed for accommodations and meals, and related matters. It should be obvious that corporate travel departments have great influence over the airlines and hotels used by company employees.

Incentive Travel Firms

As part of a program aimed at encouraging personnel to work toward achieving company goals, many organizations provide rewards for employees who exceed specific targets. These are called incentive programs because employees are offered incentives to perform above and beyond some norm. Sometimes the rewards offered are in the form of company-paid travel. Firms that specialize in developing—and, sometimes, administering—such programs are called **incentive travel firms**. They specialize in assembling incentive packages—transportation, accommodations, meals, and entertainment, for example.

Incentive travel firms are of two broad types: those that charge fees for their services and those that receive their fees in the form of commissions from the travel suppliers. Those that charge fees are called full-service incentive companies. They are employed by corporations to establish incentive programs, prepare promotional material, supervise the operation of the programs, and make the travel arrangements. They make travel arrangements either directly with the suppliers of travel services or through travel agencies.

The second type of incentive travel company does not charge fees but receives commissions directly from the travel suppliers. Travel agencies sometimes have incentive travel departments that specialize in making these travel arrangements. These departments typically do not establish the incentive programs or supervise their operation as a full-service company would. Instead, they limit their activity to providing advice to interested companies on establishing incentive programs and making the travel arrangements. Incentive travel firms of both types obviously have great influence over the travel arrangements of the incentive packages they book.

Convention and Meeting Planners

Convention and meeting planners are employees of or consultants to corporations, government agencies, and other large organizations. Their profession is planning and running conventions and meetings.

Convention and meeting planners organize meetings and conventions ranging from small board meetings to conventions attended by thousands of people. They typically attend to all planning details, including budget, travel, accommodations, meeting programs, and billing. They supervise the meetings or conventions and ensure their success. Conventions and meetings account for more than $50 billion per year; thus, these individuals and firms have influence over large expenditures for travel. They make travel arrangements directly with travel suppliers, or they may work through travel agencies.

Given this broad description of the travel business, it should be apparent that the selling of travel is a major and growing industry in the world today. The roles of travel agents, travel wholesalers, tour operators, and other travel specialists are of greater importance than ever, both to the industry and to the economies of the communities and nations that are coming to rely heavily on the tourism dollar as a source of income.

SUMMARY

In this chapter, the individuals and businesses that sell travel services are examined. The term *package* is defined, and characteristic types of packages are identified and explained in detail. The advantages and disadvantages of travel packages are described. The terms *tour wholesaler, tour operator,* and *specialty channeler* are defined, and their roles in travel are described.

The role of travel agents and their importance and significance are examined. The size and scope of the travel agency industry, supplier dependence on travel agents, requirements for a travel agency to sell transportation, and the importance of computers in modern travel agency operation are discussed in detail. Finally, the role of such specialty channelers as hotel representatives, state and local tourist offices, corporate travel offices, incentive travel firms, and convention and meeting planners are described.

KEY WORDS

Accommodations and meals package	Convention and meeting planner
Accommodations package	Convention and visitors' bureau
Affinity group package	Corporate travel office
All-inclusive package	Events package
Chamber of commerce	Familiarization trip
Convention and meeting package	Family vacation package

Fly/cruise package
Fly/cruise/hotel package
Fly/drive package
Hotel representative
Incentive package
Incentive travel firm
Motor coach package
Special-interest package

Specialty channeler
Tour operator
Tour wholesaler
Travel agent
Travel intermediary
Travel package
Visitor center

DISCUSSION QUESTIONS

1. Identify five direct providers of travel services.

2. When did the era of mass travel begin?

3. What is a travel package?

4. List three advantages of purchasing a travel package over making arrangements directly with the providers of the travel services included in the package.

5. Describe each of the following characteristic types of packages, identifying the features normally included.
   a. All-inclusive
   b. Fly/cruise
   c. Fly/cruise/hotel
   d. Fly/drive
   e. Motor coach
   f. Accommodations
   g. Accommodation and meals
   h. Family vacation
   i. Event
   j. Special interest
   k. Affinity group
   l. Incentive
   m. Convention and meeting

6. What are the advantages to the traveler of making arrangements directly with the supplier of travel services rather than making arrangements indirectly through a travel agent? What are the advantages to the direct supplier?

7. List and describe the typical packages provided by:
   a. Airlines
   b. Bus companies
   c. Cruise lines
   d. Hotels and motels

8. Who is generally considered to have been the world's first travel agent? For what purpose did he organize his first group tour?

9. When was the first round-the-world tour? Who arranged and conducted it?

10. List six reasons why it is advisable to use a travel agent to make travel arrangements.

11. What is the approximate number of travel agencies in the United States?

12. What percentage of sales of airline tickets have been historically booked through travel agents? What is likely to happen to that figure in the future?

13. Why are conference appointments necessary for travel agencies? What are the typical requirements for a travel agent to obtain a conference appointment?

14. Name two computerized airline reservations systems used by travel agents.

15. Define the terms *tour wholesaler* and *tour operator* and distinguish between them.

16. Define the term *specialty channeler*.

17. Define and explain the role of each of the following in the travel industry.
    a. Hotel representatives
    b. State and local tourist offices
    c. Corporate travel offices
    d. Incentive travel firms
    e. Convention and meeting planners

MOMENTS OF TRUTH

1. You are preparing family vacation packages for Disney World. Of the travel packages described in this chapter, which would you prepare to appeal to families coming from a distance?

2. You have a friend interested in a job as a bus tour guide for a tour company in the United States. He tells you that he sees the job as relatively easy because his primary job is to entertain the customers on the bus and he will have little else to do. Is he correct? If not, what other types of duties is he likely to have if he takes the job?

3. You are interested in going to Mexico for your vacation. What advantages do you see in making your travel arrangements through a travel agent rather than directly with the airline, hotel, and car rental firms?

INTERNET EXERCISES

1. Go to http://www.taitrips.com. Find the lowest round-trip airfare offered from New York's Kennedy Airport to Los Angeles for two persons departing on a date of your choice and returning one week later. Make note of the airline for the fare quoted. Then go to the Web site of that airline and compare the airfare for the same trip. If one is lower than the other, why do you suppose there is a difference in price?

2. Go to http://www.expedia.com. Find the lowest round-trip airfare offered from Washington, D.C., to London for two persons departing on a date of your choice and returning two weeks later. Make note of the airline for the rate quoted. Then go to the Web site of that airline and compare the airfare for the same trip. If one is lower than the other, why do you suppose there is a difference in price?

Recreation, Entertainment, and Other Tourism Attractions

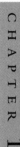

▶ Learning Objectives

After reading and studying this chapter, you should be able to:

1. Distinguish between recreation and entertainment.

2. Identify the types of national parks operated by the U.S. National Park Service.

3. Distinguish among primitive, transient, and vacation camping.

4. List five resort areas and identify the recreational activities for which they are noted.

5. Define the term *theme park* and list several well-known examples, identifying the theme commonly associated with each.

6. Define the term *entertainment area* and list several nationally known examples, citing the types of entertainment for which each is best known.

7. Distinguish among economy, standard, and luxury motor coach tours.

8. List ten kinds of performances, musical and nonmusical, that bring tourists to an area?

9. Identify several national and international fairs and festivals that take place each year.

10. List several annual parades and ceremonies that have positive economic impact on tourist businesses.

11. Discuss the importance of legal gambling to the economies of some regions of the United States.

12. List ten forms of gambling that are legal in at least one state.

13. Identify five types of special events that have positive economic impact on the areas where they are held.

14. Specify the four principal features of cruises that make them appealing to vacationers.

15. Describe how shopping serves as a tourist attraction for some areas.

INTRODUCTION

Some of the major reasons for travel were identified in earlier chapters: business; vacations; attending conventions, conferences, exhibits, concerts, or theatrical performances; sports events; sightseeing; education; visiting the birthplace of parents or grandparents; and attending weddings or funerals, among the many thousands of possibilities. This chapter focuses on some of the major attractions that draw tourists to an area—recreation, entertainment, and other significant attractions that induce travel.

In recent years, important social and economic changes have made it possible for greater numbers of people to travel. These include early retirement, longer life span, shorter workweek, more leisure time, increased disposable income, greater mobility, smaller families, and changes in spending patterns. In fact, as the figures in Table 13.1 indicate, a total of 56.8 percent of U.S. travel was for pleasure purposes. More specifically, 27 percent was for leisure purposes, including sightseeing, outdoor recreation, and entertainment. It is quite clear that recreation, entertainment, and similar activities account for an important share of travel.

Given the definition of a traveler—"any resident of the United States, regardless of nationality, who travels to a place 100 miles or more away from home within the United States or who stays away from home one or more nights in paid accommodations and who returns home within 12 months, except for com-

TABLE 13.1

Travel in the United States

Main Purpose of Trip	
Business	29.3%
Pleasure	56.8%
Personal Business	13.9%
Total	100.0%
Pleasure Travel	
Visit friends, relatives	29.8%
Leisure	27.0%
Total	56.8%
Leisure Travel	
Rest or relaxation	9.9%
Sightseeing	3.7%
Outdoor recreation	6.1%
Entertainment	5.7%
Other	1.6%
Total	27.0%

Source: U.S. Bureau of Transportation, American Travel Survey, 1999.

muting to and from work or attending school"—it is clear that many travelers contribute to the economic health of the areas to which they travel and the businesses they patronize while traveling.

A list of the activities that generate tourism—recreation, entertainment, and others—would be nearly endless. Think of the possibilities.

- Visiting theme parks
- Going to resort areas
- Gaming
- Attending performances—theater, concerts, dance
- Witnessing events—religious, parades, patriotic ceremonies
- Engaging in hobbies—photography, collecting
- Going on cruises
- Watching sporting events—football, baseball, races (horse, dog, automobile, bicycles, and so on), the Olympic Games, etc.
- Visiting national, state, and local parks
- Engaging in outdoor activities—golf, tennis, skiing, hiking, climbing, fishing, hunting, boating, swimming, surfing, snorkeling, waterskiing, beaching, sunning, bird watching, taking nature walks
- Attending festivals
- Camping, RVs
- Taking tours to see landmarks, sights, museums, fall foliage
- Shopping at major malls or discount shopping centers

While there are no universally accepted definitions for the terms *recreation* and *entertainment*, it is useful to attempt some differentiation at this point in the chapter. **Recreation** is an interesting term meaning to create anew, to restore, or to refresh. The idea of activity is commonly linked to recreation; people often refer to recreational activities. Thus, recreation has to do with activities aimed at restoring or refreshing one's mind, or body, or both, presumably after some sort of work. The annual vacations that working men and women look forward to each year are often of a recreational nature, used to restore their minds and bodies in ways they find interesting.

By contrast, **entertainment** is a term commonly used to refer to something diverting or engaging, presumably something that holds one's attention and occupy one's mind for some period. It does not normally suggest physical activity of the type that one associates with recreation. Limited physical activity may be associated with reaching the entertainment, but once at the entertainment site, the individual is commonly said to be watching, or seeing, or viewing, or hearing—all verbs that suggest something more passive than the real physical activity associated with such recreational activities as tennis and swimming.

Because of the extent to which recreation and entertainment in the United States affect the travel and tourism industry, including the hospitality industry, a

➤ EVEN TELEPHONES CAN BE ENTERTAINING

Entertainment comes in many forms. One of the most unusual is the Georgia Rural Telephone Museum, located in Leslie, Georgia. It is housed in a 1920s brick building located across the street from the Citizens Telephone Company, an independent telephone company. The museum exhibits telephones from the entire span of telephone history. Tommy C. Smith, creator of the museum, claims it is the world's largest collection of telephones and telephone memorabilia. Over 1500 phones are on display.

A guide conducts the tour through the museum, explaining every facet of telephone history. One of the more interesting telephones is the McKinley telephone (1897), the same type of phone used to make the call to report that President McKinley had been shot. Other interesting telephones include a jukebox phone, a hush-a-phone, and a graba-phone.

The Georgia Rural Telephone Museum certainly fits the definition of entertainment. It is an engaging and educational display that holds one's attention for an extended period of time.

Source: **Adapted from an article in** *USA Today,* **9 June 2000.**

number of the better-known examples are examined below. We present three lists—one for locations or activities associated with recreation, a second for those associated with entertainment, and a third for others, by which we mean some that could be described as either recreation or entertainment, or both recreation and entertainment, or neither recreation nor entertainment, but a third classification instead. An example is a family trip to one of the largest shopping centers in the world, the West Edmonton Mall in Alberta, Canada.

RECREATION

People visit many sites for the purpose of recreational activity. The most significant are discussed in the following sections.

National and State Parks

National and state parks have become popular destinations for American travelers. The national park system, operated by the National Park Service, part of the U. S. Department of the Interior, includes recreation parks, recreation areas, battlefields, historic sights, monuments, and memorials, and brings to mind such well-known parks as Yellowstone, Glacier, Sequoia, and Grand Teton. The majority of the parks are entirely traditional, but some of the newer parks might best be described as innovative. One national park is actually under water! The John Pennekamp Coral Reef Park, in Florida, offers an underwater lodge for tourists. Jules' Undersea Lodge, reached only by diving and passing through an airlock, is a bit small, with just two suites available for travelers. In 1999, the National

The National Park Service operates 379 sites. Shown in the photograph is the Grand Canyon, one of the most heavily visited of the national parks.
(Photo courtesy of Corbis Digital Stock)

Park Service reported over 250 million visits to the 379 sites in the national park system.

The U. S. Forest Service operates 155 national forests and 20 grasslands in 42 states, Puerto Rico, and the Virgin Islands, on 191 million acres of land encompassing 8.5 percent of the total area of the United States. More than 300 million recreation visitor days are recorded each year in national forests. There are over 5000 state parks in addition to national parks and national forests. State parks have well over 700 million visitors each year.

It is quite clear that people visit these parks in great numbers for various recreational and educational purposes: to experience the natural landscape; to see plants and animals in their natural environment; to view the Grand Canyon, Old Faithful, and other major sights; to learn about significant battles in the wars fought in North America and about other significant events from history. Visitors also take advantage of the recreational activities available in the parks, such as skiing, hiking, boating, fishing, swimming, skating, and so on.

Many parks have excellent facilities—hotels, motels, lodges, and campgrounds, as well as foodservice facilities of many kinds. The foodservice and lodging facilities are all licensed by the National Park Service. Some of the lodging facilities are quite modern, while others are somewhat rustic. For example, in Everglades National Park, the nation's only tropical national park, tourists can stay at the

Flamingo Lodge, a relatively modern property, privately operated, with 102 rooms and 24 bungalows. Guests can take advantage of such activities as watching flocks of waterbirds, seeing alligators and crocodiles, and taking guided tours of the park, then return to the relative comfort of a modern inn.

One hotel in Yosemite National Park offers an interesting contrast. Built in 1879, the Wawona Hotel was once a stagecoach inn. The two-story property has 105 rooms and is a national historic landmark. It is not modern; only half the rooms have private baths, and none have telephones or television.

People have found that the park systems provide excellent opportunities for recreational activities of all kinds. Many entrepreneurs have developed businesses outside the parks to meet the needs of the growing numbers of tourists. Hotels, motels, inns, lodges, and foodservice operations of all kinds abound near the parks, offering travelers sleeping accommodations and meals at a wide variety of rates and menu prices.

It is interesting that the number of visitors to some parks has grown to the extent that many people are now concerned about the potential threats to the environment they pose. In fact, in some parks, no new tourist facilities are being developed, in spite of growing demand, in order to prevent further damage to the environment. Existing tourist facilities are even being shut down to reduce the risk.

Campgrounds

The national and state park systems offer excellent opportunities for camping. Camping has become increasingly popular, particularly for families, partly because it is comparatively inexpensive. Camping is by no means restricted to national and state parks; many private campgrounds thrive from coast to coast. In general, there are three kinds of camping.

Primitive Camping

Primitive camping is normally associated with public lands—forests and large national parks. The areas set aside are normally unimproved and appeal only to dedicated backpackers who are willing to make the best of it for a few nights. Visitors choosing to hike along the Appalachian Trail, which runs from Maine to Georgia, have no camping choice other than the primitive.

Transient Camping

Transient camping is for people who intend to remain for no more than a few nights. The areas set aside for transient camping are somewhat improved, with electricity, bathing facilities, and toilets available. The campsites are more or less organized, and many are privately run. This type of camping is more likely to appeal to individuals who are put off by the rigors of primitive camping.

Vacation Camping

Vacation camping is for people who plan to spend a greater number of nights at a single site—from four nights to several weeks or more. Vacation camps are improved, with electricity and bathroom facilities. Some even provide cabins that can be rented by the day or the week. Improved camps commonly have stores that sell basic supplies and recreational facilities for such activities as baseball, volleyball, swimming, boating, and water-skiing, among others.

Camping has led to the growth of tourism-related business in some areas. Many people on camping trips patronize foodservice and lodging facilities before, during, or after the camping activity. Some stay overnight in a motel before setting out early in the morning on a trip into the wilderness; others do so on their return. Many campers are especially eager to find foodservice facilities after several days of cooking over a campfire.

One interesting element in the growing popularity of camping is the accompanying increase in the popularity of **recreation vehicles**, commonly known as RVs. These wheeled vehicles with temporary living quarters include motor homes, travel trailers, park trailers, truck campers, folding camping trailers, and van campers. They are a significant part of the American scene. About 8.5 million people in the United States own some form of RV, and about 25 million people regularly use them—on an average of about 23 days per year. About one in ten families own at least one RV.

Recreation vehicles, commonly known as RVs, are increasing in popularity. About 8.5 million people in the United States own some form of RV. *(Photo courtesy of Winnebago Industries)*

When RVs first became popular in the early and mid-1970s, many were sold. However, gasoline prices increased significantly in the late 1970s and early 1980s, when there was a recession, and interest rates on automobile loans were high. This led to a dramatic drop in the number of RVs sold. In recent years, sales have not only recovered considerably but have begun to climb to new heights. Nevertheless, because RV sales appear to be tied closely to the cost of fuel, sales and rentals will undoubtedly fluctuate with the price of fuel.

RVs range in price from just a few thousand dollars to over a hundred thousand. The many types of RV include fold-down trailers, large trailers pulled behind automobiles and trucks, campers that fit into the back of pickup trucks, and self-motorized vacation vans of many sizes that are actually homes on wheels.

Resort Areas

Resort areas are geographic areas that have become well known regionally, nationally, and, in some cases, internationally as centers for some recreational activity. Like national and state parks, resort areas offer opportunities for recreational activities of various kinds. Some resort areas are noted for specific activities. Scottsdale, Arizona; Palm Springs, California; and both Hilton Head Island and Myrtle Beach, South Carolina, all have strong reputations as golf resorts. Many communities on the Atlantic and Gulf coasts of Florida—Miami Beach, Daytona Beach, and Panama Beach, for example—are known as beach resorts. Aspen and Vail, Colorado; Taos, New Mexico; the White Mountains in New Hampshire; and Killington, Vermont, are all known as ski resorts. Parts of Maine and Minnesota are well-known fishing areas, while Newport, Rhode Island, and San Diego, California, are noted for sailing.

In some cases, the reputations these areas enjoy have been carefully developed and nurtured. In any event, their reputations have encouraged considerable tourist travel over the years, and this has generated considerable income for individuals and businesses.

ENTERTAINMENT

People enjoy entertaining experiences. Those experiences take various forms, and seeking some form of entertainment has long been a primary reason for travel. Entertainment in one form or another can be found at the following types of site.

Theme Parks

Of all the recent developments in tourism, perhaps the best known and most interesting is the creation of that modern entertainment center known as the **theme park**. One of the first of these was Hershey Park, founded in the early twentieth century by Milton S. Hershey, the founder of the Hershey Corporation, internationally known for chocolate products.

The term *theme park* refers to a tract of land on which a developer has created a series of exhibits, rides, and other elements that tend to be designed around some unifying idea. Knott's Berry Farm, in California, uses the Old West as a theme; Busch Gardens, in Florida, uses wild animals; Walt Disney World uses the cartoon characters created by Walt Disney. While theme parks have some such unifying theme, they commonly have other elements that are not related to the theme in any way. These may include exciting or entertaining rides, interesting and educational exhibits, or both of these. Knott's Berry Farm, for example, has 135 attractions, including roller coasters. In addition to over 3000 wild animals, Busch Gardens has trained animal shows, reconstructed African villages, and roller coasters, monorails, boats, miniature trains, and other rides. It also offers Broadway-style shows and a tour of an Anheuser-Busch brewery.

The term *theme park* has come to be used rather loosely to refer to operations that were once known as amusement parks. These lacked a unifying theme and were usually little more than collections of rides, with or without such accompanying elements as minor shows and exhibits. Many amusement parks provided wonderful opportunities for a day's entertainment and attracted substantial numbers of tourists to their respective areas. Some of today's theme parks are really old-style amusement parks with a new name.

Examples of the better-known theme parks are discussed in the following sections.

Sea World

In Orlando, near Walt Disney World, Sea World offers indoor and outdoor exhibits of sea life, including sharks and sea turtles, as well as shows featuring dolphins, sea lions, and whales.

Six Flags Great Adventure

Located in central New Jersey, this 1700-acre theme park offers over 100 attractions, including carousels, giant roller coasters, and other exciting rides, as well as vaudeville shows and a drive-through safari zoo. It is one of many theme parks operated by Six Flags.

Universal Studios

This popular park in Orlando, Florida, offers thrill rides based on well-known motion pictures, such as *King Kong, Jaws, E.T.,* and *Back to the Future.* Other attractions include a theater offering screen tests to audience volunteers and a walk-through back lot featuring set locations for a New England village, a San Francisco street, and New York City's Upper East Side. It is one of many parks operated by Universal Studios. Others are located in Hollywood, Japan, Spain, and China.

Tivoli Gardens

Located in the center of Copenhagen, Denmark, this special park, considered the oldest theme park in the world, features miniatures of such famous sites as the Eiffel Tower in Paris and Mount Rushmore National Monument in South Dakota.

Cinderella Castle, shown here, is the world-renowned magical icon of the Magic Kingdom theme park, as well as the inspirational symbol of the entire Walt Disney World Resort.
(Copyright 2000. THE WALT DISNEY COMPANY.)

Tivoli is also a world-class amusement park with rides, games, and theaters for shows, plays, pantomimes, and concerts.

Disney Theme Parks

Among the best-known and most popular theme parks today are four created by the Disney organization—Disneyland, in Anaheim, California; Walt Disney World, near Orlando, Florida; Disneyland Paris, in France; and Tokyo Disneyland in Japan.

Disneyland. Disneyland is the original Disney theme park, opened in 1955 by the late Walt Disney. Although smaller than the more recent Disney operation in Florida, it is considered the archetype of modern theme parks and has been visited by over 300 million people. Among the 60 attractions featured are Fantasyland, Pirates of the Caribbean, Frontierland, Adventureland, Sleeping Beauty's Castle, and Carnival of New Orleans. Several of these names were later used in Walt Disney World. One of the more recent additions is Star Tours, an outer-space Disneyland.

Walt Disney World. Walt Disney World is the largest and most famous theme park, or amusement park, in the world. It covers over 27,000 acres—an area twice the size of the island of Manhattan, the best known of New York City's five boroughs. It really is more than a theme park, for it contains four separate amusement parks—the Magic Kingdom, EPCOT Center, Disney–MGM Studios, and the Animal Kingdom—as well as water parks and resorts, all linked by road and monorail.

The Magic Kingdom is organized into six miniature villages: Adventureland, with a boat tour through the jungle; Fantasyland, which features Walt Disney characters; Frontierland, with a traditional Far West theme; Liberty Square, which features presidents of the United States; Main Street, U.S.A., a turn-of-the-century small town; and Tomorrowland, with a space adventure theme.

EPCOT, an acronym for Experimental Prototype Community of Tomorrow, is based on a twenty-first century theme. It features Window on the World—recreations of famed elements of many nations—as well as theme pavilions sponsored by world-class industrial corporations, the world's largest aquarium, and a huge 18-story sphere that is universally recognized as the symbol of EPCOT.

Disney–MGM Studios, based on motion-picture themes, offers such features as film-making, backstage studio tours, and ride-through attractions transporting visitors through such classic films as *The Wizard of Oz*, *Raiders of the Lost Ark*, *Alien*, and *Singing in the Rain*.

The Animal Kingdom is the newest of Disney's theme parks. It offers encounters with real, imaginary, and extinct animals. Its major attraction is a safari ride through a prehistoric world, but it also features a variety of stage shows, including "Festival of the Lion King," and "Pocahontas and Her Forest Friends."

In addition to these parks, Walt Disney World includes a 7500-acre forest reserve, two artificial lakes, five golf courses, camping facilities, resources for most sports—tennis, sailing, swimming, water-skiing, fishing, and horseback riding—plus a dozen hotels and innumerable foodservice operations.

Entertainment Areas

In a very real way, Orlando, Florida—with the Disney enterprises, Sea World, and other features—has become an **entertainment area**. In fact, it is clearly the entertainment capital of Florida. Keeping in mind that Orlando is within two hours' drive of such additional tourism attractions as Cape Canaveral, Daytona Beach, and Cypress Gardens, it does not require too much imagination to think of Orlando as the entertainment capital of the southeastern United States.

Another community that has achieved status as a well-known entertainment area is Branson, Missouri. A small but growing community in the Ozark Mountains in the southwestern corner of the state, Branson has become a focal point for musical entertainment. It is home to a number of nationally known entertainers, many of whom have built and operate their own musical theaters. Over 25 theaters in Branson offer over 40 live country music and variety shows daily to growing numbers of tourists. These tourists require the usual in lodging and foodservice, and Branson now boasts over 10,000 hotel rooms, along with growing numbers of the kinds of restaurants that cater to tourists. There are no signs that growth in the area is about to slow down.

In addition to Orlando and Branson, other places in America that can be regarded as entertainment areas include New York City, known for Broadway;

Nashville, Tennessee, known the world over as the center for country music; and New Orleans, which has earned a strong reputation for performing arts, jazz, and sports. The Superdome in New Orleans is the largest enclosed stadium in the world.

Another city on the list of entertainment areas is Las Vegas, Nevada. Las Vegas draws millions of tourists each year who go there to enjoy its many features. Some visitors attend performances in the great showrooms featured in the famed Las Vegas hotels. The Hilton Las Vegas features the Moulin Rouge Revue, while Bally's–Las Vegas, Caesar's Palace, and the Dunes Hotel all have huge showrooms that feature nationally known performers. Other visitors go for the golf; Las Vegas has some of America's finest golf courses. It is also well known for its foodservice facilities—over 700 of them—which offer some of the finest food imaginable. The area has over 85,000 hotel rooms, over 5000 of which are in the world's largest hotel, the MGM Grand Hotel. In addition, gambling has been legal in Las Vegas since 1931, so the city has had many years to develop its reputation in that field. While some people classify gambling as entertainment, that view is not universal. Thus, gambling is discussed later in the chapter under "Other Tourism Attractions."

Tour Destinations

Every nation of the world has its own special collection of unique sights for tourists to see. In the United States, tourists from abroad often go to Washington, D.C., to see the important government buildings that they have seen on television and in film over the years—the White House, the Capitol, and others. Travelers may go on a bus tour through Northern California that includes a national park and several other sights. In France, tourists from abroad visiting Paris are likely to see the magnificent sights for which the city is famous—the Eiffel Tower, the Louvre Museum, Notre Dame Cathedral, the Palace at Versailles, the Champs-Élysées, and many others. In England, tourists visiting London are likely to see Buckingham Palace, the Houses of Parliament and Big Ben, St. Paul's Cathedral, Westminster Abbey, the Tower of London, and the British Museum. Similarly, in the minds of tourists, Egypt is always linked to the Sphinx and the Great Pyramids, India to the Taj Mahal, China to the Great Wall, Japan to Mount Fuji, and Rio de Janeiro to Copacabana Beach. These all are characterized as **tour destinations** because they tend to be focal points for tourists and, thus, important locations for the development of businesses that cater to the tourists.

For many vacationers, tours are the preferred way to travel. To great numbers, motor coach tours—bus tours—are an entertaining and relaxing way to spend time—any period from an hour or two to ten days or more. Some tourists take short trips—an interesting, educational, or enjoyable trip from, say, city center to a site 20 or more miles outside the city. Others take an overnight excursion that includes hotel accommodations—in order to attend a sports event in a city 100 or more miles away. Still others go on longer motor coach tours—a ten-day trip with meals and lodging to see the leaves change color in the mountains of New England.

Tourists from abroad—both Americans visiting other lands and foreigners visiting America—commonly enjoy their first views of the sights from aboard buses.

Sometimes these tours are just a few hours long and introduce tourists to well-known sights in the center of a city—a tour of central London, New York City, or Chicago, for example. After this short introduction, tourists decide for themselves which sights they will visit again to spend more time. Sometimes these tours take a full day and are designed to take tourists on excursions from a city center to some important destination outside. Examples include bus tours from central London to Windsor Castle, and from San Diego, California, to Death Valley National Monument. Sometime bus tours are several days long and can best be regarded as package tours.

Because tour and vacation packages are grouped together, it is difficult to estimate the actual number of tours. The number is significant, however. More than 2000 tour operators are in business in the United States today, and the largest share of the business is handled by the top 40. Motor coach tours are popular with citizens of all nations. Many Americans take motor coach tours that last for a week or more. So do large numbers of foreign visitors, many of whom take motor coach tours conducted in languages other than English.

Essentially, there are three classes of motor coach tours: economy, standard, and luxury. The differences can be found in the level of quality evident in the various elements of the tours as well as in the amenities included in the price.

Economy bus tours include a seat on the bus and the basics required. If accommodations are included, they are likely to be in a budget motel. If there are meals, the fare is likely to be plain; extensive menu choices are unlikely, and so is gourmet cuisine. If the tour includes admissions to events, the tickets are not likely to be the best in the house.

Standard bus tours, by contrast, are a step higher in quality. If lodging is included in the price, it is likely to be provided at a property somewhat above the level of a budget motel. Meals are likely to be tastier, with more menu choices available. Tickets to events are likely to be for better seats.

Luxury bus tours are quite different. Many offer the best of everything, and the prices are set accordingly. The motor coach is the most comfortable available. Lodging is in luxury hotels and similar superior properties, and meals are excellent. If tickets are included, they are for the best available seats. On luxury tours, everything is usually included in the tour price, so those on the tour have no need to pay for extras, except for personal needs. People who go on luxury tours are commonly convinced that there is no more pleasurable way to travel.

While a great number of tours are planned or scheduled and offered on a recurring basis throughout the year, others are nonrecurring, having been arranged to meet a particular demand at a particular time—bus tours aimed at fans of a particular baseball team who want to see their team play in another city, for example. The possibilities for these are endless. More examples are motor coach tours to see Mardi Gras in New Orleans, the Rose Bowl Parade, or a college football game played away from home. All are positive generators of tourism income for the cities or areas visited.

Another interesting variation on touring that tends to generate tourism income for an area is the automobile tour. Automobile tours are often individual family tours for the purpose of seeing sights, monuments, or anything else of interest to the particular family. Similar, in many ways, are the tours that high-school groups take to Washington, D.C., and other places of historic interest or educational value. All these tend to be individually arranged by the schools or families intending to take the tours, so data on their number and duration are limited. Regardless, individualized tours also tend to be economic generators for the cities and regions visited as the tourists spend their money on accommodations, meals, admissions, and gifts for family members and friends back home.

Performances

Literally millions of people travel regularly or occasionally to the thousands of **performances** that take place in countries all over the world each week. There are performances of every conceivable type. Some are musical—concerts by groups ranging from rock groups performing in theaters, stadiums, and other large venues to symphony orchestras playing in well-known concert halls—Lincoln Center and Carnegie Hall in New York City and Albert Hall in London, for example. Others are performances by individuals ranging from rock stars, folk singers, popular singers, and opera stars to instrumentalists and classical artists.

These kinds of musical performance are not the only ones that serve as tourism attractions. People also travel to see plays, musicals, and operas in major cities and in many more rural resort areas. Other performances that bring tourists to an area include magicians, dancers of all kinds—folk, ballet, and tap, for example—acrobats, jugglers, and circuses, including the famed Ringling Brothers Barnum & Bailey Circus. Some people even travel great distances for lectures delivered by all sorts of people—retired military leaders, politicians, self-help artists, and characters who have gained some high level of notoriety—assorted felons and con artists among them.

Fairs and Festivals

Fairs and **festivals** constitute another class of entertaining activities that tend to increase tourism in all parts of the world. Literally thousands of fairs are held each year, especially in the summer months. In the United States, there are state fairs, country fairs, village fairs, Grange fairs, and church fairs. Many of these have equivalents in countries around the world. Every few years, a World's Fair is held.

Every year sees dozens of state fairs. The Alaska State Fair features activities including wood splitting, ax throwing, bow sawing, potato digging, and water hauling. The Indiana State Fair, by contrast, features farm animal competitions, including a workhorse show. The New Mexico State Fair features a rodeo, with thousands of dollars in prize money awarded to winners, while the Big E, the regional fair for the six states of New England, features important local food products, including apples, clams, maple syrup, and cranberries.

If there are thousands of fairs, there are even more festivals! Festivals are dedicated to film, dance, music, art, religious figures, ethnic pride, heritage, the Old West, days gone by, assorted flowers and fruits, crafts, balloons, beer, wine, boats, seasons, and various fish and sea creatures, among others. There are so many festivals annually in New England alone that a list of them consumes six pages, sin-

gle spaced, in a book by Kathy Kincade and Carl Landau entitled *Festivals of New England*. Festivals range from those that are truly major, internationally renowned, and respected to many that are minor and some that are a bit unusual, with every possibility in between. For example, major international film festivals are held annually in Sydney, Australia; Tokyo, Japan; Montreal, Toronto, and Vancouver, all in Canada; Venice, Italy; Edinburgh, Scotland; London, England; and San Sebastian, Spain. There are certainly less-known film festivals in smaller cities as well. Other festivals include the annual oyster festival in Milford, Connecticut, and Log Days, in Skowhegan, Maine—a weeklong salute to the logging industry and its influence on that part of the state.

Some of the more important festivals held in the United States include:

- The music festival at Tanglewood, in the Berkshire Mountains of Massachusetts, featuring the Boston Symphony Orchestra, the Boston Pops Orchestra, and guest orchestras, artists, and conductors from around the world.

- The National Cherry Festival in Traverse City, Michigan, a weeklong festival featuring cherries from the orchards of northwest Michigan served in every conceivable way, accompanied by parades, jazz and band competitions, sports events, and nonstop live musical entertainment.

- Dodge City Days, held annually in Dodge City, Kansas, the nineteenth-century shipping point for cattle on the old Santa Fe Trail, to celebrate the area's heritage from the Old West.

- The New York Film Festival, considered one of the finest, with showings in Alice Tully Hall at Lincoln Center of over 30 films selected by a prestigious jury.

- Mardi Gras, held in New Orleans, Louisiana, on Shrove Tuesday, the day before Ash Wednesday. It includes several parades—the Rex Parade, the Zulu Parade, and the Indian Parade among them—with elaborate floats, magnificent costumes, and great revelry.

Parades and Ceremonies

Major **parades** and **ceremonies** are also important factors in the tourism equation. Both can play significant roles in bringing tourism dollars to a community, supporting employment and generating income for those in tourism-related businesses.

Some of the better-known parades held in the United States are the Thanksgiving Day Parade in New York, sponsored by Macy's; several St. Patrick's Day parades held in Boston, New York, and other cities having large populations of citizens with Irish ancestry; the Columbus Day Parade in New York; the Tournament of Roses, often called the Rose Bowl Parade, held in Pasadena, California, on New Year's Day; the Mummers' Parade, held in Philadelphia, also on New Year's Day; the Inaugural Parade, held every four years in Washington, D.C. on the day the president is sworn into office; Memorial Day, Independence Day, and Veteran's Day parades held in major cities on those holidays; and the so-called Easter Parade in New York, which is not a parade at all—just a mass of people milling about on Fifth Avenue on Easter Sunday. Each of these brings tourists from varying distances to the parade area. Once there, they watch the parade and seek the goods and services that tourism-related businesses provide.

Important ceremonies are held in areas across the country that also serve to attract tourism to those areas. Sometimes ceremonies are held in conjunction with parades, especially in the case of patriotic national days such as Memorial Day and Independence Day. Sometime they have no relationship to parades. Religious ceremonies, for example, have always been positive forces for tourism. A visit by the Pope and a Billy Graham Crusade for Christ both offer excellent examples from the religious community. Commencement ceremonies offer an example from the academic world. These and many others help enhance the role of tourism in a local economy.

Sports Events

Sports events of all kinds are also great tourism builders. Such team sports as baseball and football, in particular, as well as basketball and hockey, account for considerable travel by tourists. So do many individual sports, such as tennis and golf, and individual sports events such as the New York Marathon, the Boston Marathon, and others held across the country each year. Professional, collegiate, and other amateur sports increase tourism in varying degrees. A substantial number of college and university football teams help the economies of their local communities by winning games and thus increasing the level of tourism activity in those communities.

The Olympic Games provide another example of sports events that increase tourism. Both Summer Olympics and Winter Olympics increase the level of tourism in the areas where the games are held, and competition is always keen among cities attempting to host the games. Selection as a site for upcoming Olympic Games also leads to other economic activity in a region. It normally helps the construction industry in the region because new facilities, including stadiums, must be constructed to accommodate the athletes and the games.

OTHER TOURISM ATTRACTIONS

Some tourism attractions do not lend themselves readily to classification as either recreation or entertainment. Any list of these would certainly include gambling, special events, cruising, and shopping.

Gambling

Gambling, in one form or another, is legal in 48 of the 50 states—all but Hawaii and Utah—and examples of it are found everywhere. At present, 35 states operate state lotteries and other games of chance using such names as Lotto, Pick-3, Pick-4, and Instant Winner. Taken together, these accounted for $30 billion in revenues in 1992. One can add to that such other legal gambling as pari-mutuel betting on horse races, dog races, and jai alai; betting on professional sports; card games, such as blackjack and poker; bingo, including both charity and Indian; as well as roulette, wheels of fortune, dice games, and slot machines. The total amount bet legally in the United States in one recent year was estimated at over $300 billion. This is an enormous amount of money—considerably greater than the sum of the gross domestic products of several industrialized nations.

Some states operate lotteries, while others permit racetracks—for thoroughbred racing, harness racing, or dog racing. While these legal gambling activities have given rise to limited increases in tourism in a few areas, none has had the same impact as casino gambling.

Gaming—another term for casino gambling—is probably the fastest-growing and most powerful force today in tourism within the United States. In the years since state and local governments and various Indian tribes realized the potential for easing all sorts of financial problems with income from legal gambling, casinos have begun to appear all across the country. In fact, it has been reported that more Americans visit casinos than ballparks.

Until a few years ago, casino gambling was restricted to one state—Nevada—plus one city—Atlantic City, New Jersey. Now, however, casino gambling is well established in a number of states, including Arizona, California, Colorado, Connecticut, Iowa, Louisiana, Mississippi, and South Dakota. In many instances, the casinos are on Indian lands and operated by Indian tribes.

The casino in Foxwoods, Connecticut, is an interesting example of this relatively new development: casinos run by Native American Indian tribes. Over 150 Indian tribes are either operating some form of gambling or have plans to begin doing so in the near future.

Casino gambling is found on the water as well as in land-based locations. In some instances, it is conducted on riverboats and is known, obviously, as riverboat gambling, which is nothing more than casino gambling conducted on a boat. Riverboat gambling is available in Iowa, Missouri, Louisiana, Illinois, and Indiana. In Mississippi, casino gambling is conducted on barges that are permanently moored and have no engines or other means of locomotion.

In spite of the growth in the number of sites where casino gambling is available, the best-known centers of casino gambling activity continue to be the state of Nevada—especially Las Vegas, Laughlin, and Reno—and Atlantic City.

Las Vegas and Reno have both become well known for casinos and casino hotels—mammoth hotels of 3000, 4000 and 5000 rooms. The MGM Grand Hotel, Caesar's Palace, Bally's Grand Hotel, and the Las Vegas Hilton, all with huge casinos, feature superior rooms at reasonable rates, excellent food and beverages, and lavish stage shows with nationally known entertainers.

But the newer properties in Las Vegas are much more than fine hotels with huge casinos. Increasingly, Las Vegas hotel operators are positioning their properties to appeal to the broadest possible markets, striving to attract tourists of every kind. They have long since abandoned the idea of appealing to gamblers alone, partly because it is a comparatively small segment of the tourism market and partly because of increasing competition for the gambling dollar from other jurisdictions.

Casino gambling will continue to be available in Las Vegas, but the city offers so many additional attractions for tourists that it is difficult for other areas with casino gambling alone to compete. Attractions aimed at drawing tourists to Las Vegas include a 15,200-seat arena for sporting events and concerts at the MGM Grand; an Emerald City theme park based on the fictitious city in the *Wizard of Oz*; a replica of King Tut's tomb in the Luxor, a hotel and casino; Treasure Island, a 2900-room hotel and theme park modeled on the famed novel of that name, where a British frigate does battle with a pirate ship six times a day in the hotel lagoon. These and such additional attractions as the Excalibur Hotel and Casino, with its $290 million Camelot theme park, offer formidable competition for cities, towns, and regions attempting to build tourism and attract tourist dollars.

Special Events

Hundreds of **special events** held every day of the year serve as tourism attractions to various areas. Some are nationally and internationally known, attracting great numbers of people. Others are far smaller. Each, however, plays an important role as a tourism attraction in the area where it is held.

Many of these are quite large—too large to be accommodated in the facilities available in a single hotel or other similar facility, and thus they become area-wide events. They attract large numbers of visitors to a city, and they are often planned and managed with the cooperation of a local convention and visitors bureau. Hundreds of special events take place in cities that have the basics required to support major public events: a major airport, good local transportation, a sufficient number of hotels, and a facility large enough to accommodate the event.

A number of cities in the United States and in countries around the world have built facilities to house major events. Facilities of this type are known by a variety of names, including convention center, exhibition center, expo center, and civic center. The fact that cities spend many millions of dollars to build the facilities to attract shows is testimony to the importance of such events to the local economy. Examples of facilities constructed for this purpose include McCormick Place in Chicago, the Jacob K. Javits Convention Center in New York City, the Pennsylvania Convention Center in Philadelphia, and the Astro Arena and Expo Center in Houston. There are facilities of this nature in hundreds of American cities, including Ft. Lauderdale, Florida; San Francisco, California; Las Vegas, Nevada; and Baltimore, Maryland. In addition, growing numbers of cities in other nations have also built convention centers for the same general purposes, including Adelaide, Canberra, Melbourne, and Sydney, Australia; Toronto, Calgary, Edmonton, Montreal, Ottawa, and Vancouver, Canada; London and Birmingham, England; Frankfurt, Germany; and Acapulco, Cancun, and Mexico City, Mexico.

Convention facilities are commonly used for several types of special events, including expositions, trade shows, exhibitions, conventions, and rallies and marches.

Expositions

An **exposition** is a large show that is open to the public. Expositions are often known simply as shows. Examples of expositions held in various cities include automobile shows, boat shows, garden shows, and computer shows. Producers or manufacturers of the goods or services that serve as focal points for such expositions typically rent exhibit space in the facility in order to place their wares on view for the public. An automobile show provides manufacturers of American and foreign cars with an opportunity to display current models and prototypes of future automobiles to the consuming public. Many people are ready to pay reasonable admission fees to attend such expositions, so they can be profitable ventures for their sponsors and for those operating hospitality and other businesses that serve people attending and working at the show.

Trade Shows

Trade shows restrict admission to people who are part of a particular industry or trade. They are sometimes called expositions. Trade shows are not open to the public. Producers or manufacturers of the goods or services that serve as focal points for a trade show rent exhibit space in the convention facility to advertise or demonstrate their products to people likely to be interested in buying. The exhibitors at these shows feature goods or services of interest to those in a specific field and provide opportunities for people in the field to see and compare goods and services available from competing vendors.

Two excellent examples of hospitality industry trade shows are the National Restaurant Show, held each May in Chicago's McCormick Place and sponsored by the National Restaurant Association, and the International Hotel/Motel and Restaurant Show, held each November in New York's Jacob K. Javits Convention Center and jointly sponsored by the American Hotel and Motel Association, the New York State Hospitality and Tourism Association, and the Hotel Association of New York City. These shows feature exhibits of interest to people in hospitality as well as lectures, seminars, and other educational presentations that focus on solving current industry problems.

Admission to both of these is restricted to individuals directly involved in the hospitality industry, either working in hospitality or in some directly related field.

Exhibitions

An **exhibition** is a show, but usually a smaller show than an exposition. Exhibitions can be aimed at entertaining, enlightening, or instructing the public, or at offering specific goods or services for sale, or at providing opportunities for competition and judging. These, too, are simply called shows, in many cases. Some exhibitions are held in convention centers, but many are held in other popular venues that may be known by such names as armories, museums, and halls. Some are even held outdoors.

Many kinds of exhibitions attract people to central locations—arts, crafts, antiques, and pets, to name a few. One held outdoors in New York City each year is the Washington Square Art Show, during which Washington Square Park and the surrounding streets are lined with artworks offered for sale by their creators. A very different kind of exhibition held in New York City, at Madison Square Garden, is the annual cat show, where cat fanciers are able to see various breeds of these popular pets and to learn which has been judged best in each of the classes of competition held. Cities all across America and in every industrialized nation have any number of exhibitions of varying types and sizes throughout the year. All of them attract visitors from near and far and result in positive contributions to the economic health of the host cities.

Conventions

A **convention** is an assembly of people who are members of an organization, or delegates representing members, or simply individuals with a common interest or concern. Conventions are special events, typically held annually, and are normally international, national, or regional in scope.

Each year, many conventions are held in the United States and in many other nations around the world. A great number of these are small enough to be held in a single convention or resort hotel. Others, however, attract too many people to be accommodated in one hotel, and thus they assume larger roles in the communities that play host to them. Three of the larger conventions held in the United States are those of the American Bar Association, the American Medical Association, and the Veterans of Foreign Wars. One annual convention that is much smaller but of great significance to hospitality educators is that of International CHRIE, the International Council on Hotel, Restaurant, and Institutional Education.

Conventions are held in all kinds of key locations across the United States each year. Some are held in major cities and may be large enough to require a convention center for some of the meetings. Examples of this type include the national conventions held every four years by the Republican and Democratic parties to nominate candidates for president and vice president. By contrast, one recent convention of CHRIE was held at a single Stouffer property, the Esmeralda Resort in Indian Wells, near Palm Springs, California.

Many national organizations vary the locations of their conventions each year to be sure that the site is relatively near each member's home at least once every few years. Some organizations select a West Coast site one year, a midwestern site the next, and an East Coast site the third. This approach attempts to equalize the travel costs of members and offers some tourism-related inducements to convention attendance.

Conventions can have significant impact on the economic life of the communities selected as their site, and competition is keen for convention business among major American cities. These special events can be important contributors to the economic health of the cities that serve as their hosts as well as to hospitality businesses in the area.

Rallies and Marches

Every year, there are newspaper and television news accounts of **rallies** and **marches** held in key cities across America by groups of people interested in influencing public opinion. People sharing an opinion on a public question gather to make their views known by marching, carrying signs, and listening to and applauding speakers who verbalize their stance effectively. These marches and rallies clearly have impact on public opinion and public policy, though not necessarily the impact their supporters hope to have. However, these special events in public life can have significant impact on the economic life of the communities where they take place. People attending the rallies and marches commonly seek the same goods and services as other visitors—foodservice, lodging, and so on.

Special events of all kinds are important contributors to the economic health of the hospitality industry.

Cruises

Cruising is an important attraction that can be classified as recreation, entertainment, or both. Worldwide, about $6.5 billion is spent annually on vacation cruises, with 81 percent of it spent in North America. This represents about 3.6 million passengers. The types of people who take cruise vacations are changing. Years ago, vacationing aboard cruise ships—cruising, as it is known—was selected by older, more affluent individuals who had the time and the money for it. Cruising required both. In more recent years, cruise ship passengers have tended to be younger and the cruises they select have become shorter. The average cruise ship passenger is now less than 50 years old, with an income level more likely to be middle class, and the duration of the average vacation cruise is likely to be three or four days. Interestingly, only about 5 percent of Americans have ever been on vacation cruises. Cruise ship vacations and getaways are becoming increasingly popular, however, with a growth rate of about 10 percent each year.

Cruises are often sold as packages, with airfare, transfers, and the actual cruise all included in one price. The only additional costs for passengers on cruise packages are for shore excursions and gratuities.

New cruise ships are being built to accommodate the expanding market. There are nearly 200 cruise ships worldwide, with more being added each year. Most ships carry between 1100 and 1600 passengers, but notable exceptions exist. Some of the newer ships carry more than 2000 passengers. Examples include the world's largest cruise ship, the Royal Caribbean *Voyager of the Seas*, which carries 4000 passengers; *Sovereign of the Seas*, which carries 2280 passengers; and its sister ship *Majesty of the Seas*, which carries 2354. Carnival Cruise Line's *Fantasy* carries 2025 passengers. A number of smaller ships carry very limited numbers of passengers. For example, Cunard's *Sea Goddess I* and *Sea Goddess II* each carry 58 couples. Exploration Cruise Line's *Colonial Explorer* carries only 102 passengers, and Ocean Cruise Line's *Ocean Islander* carries 250.

As stated in Chapter 3, the appealing features of cruises have not changed over the years. They continue to be:

- Food
- Activities and entertainment
- Weather
- Elegance and comfort

The largest Cruise ship in the world is Royal Caribbean's *Voyager of the Seas*, shown in this photograph. It carries 4000 passengers.
(Photo courtesy of Royal Caribbean International)

Cruise ships normally offer large quantities of excellent food. Passengers on vacation cruises are typically offered breakfast, luncheon, afternoon tea, dinner, and a midnight buffet supper. Passengers can eat as much as they like, and the high quality of the food is a major attraction.

Cruise ships have an entertainment staff that provides activities all day long. A typical day starts with exercises or swimming in one of several pools. During the day, ongoing activities include cards, bingo, dance lessons, sports, and movies. If the ship is docked or anchored, shore excursions range from shopping to visiting rum factories to snorkeling. The evening features live entertainment, dancing, gambling, as well as more movies.

One of cruising's main attractions, for many passengers, is the weather. Most voyages take place in the warm climates of the Mediterranean, the Caribbean, or along the Mexican coast. When the weather is cold in much of the United States and northern Europe, the temperatures in the Mediterranean and the Caribbean are appealing. Vacation cruises in colder climates—Alaska, for example—are restricted to the summer months. Many ships cruise the northern waters in the summer and the warmer waters nearer the equator during the winter.

Modern ships provide a level of elegance and comfort that can be found only in luxury resort hotels and private villas. Facilities on board the larger ships include theaters, nightclubs, gambling casinos, swimming pools, saunas, exercise rooms, beauty and barber shops, gift shops, and sporting activities. Public rooms are tastefully decorated, lounge and deck chairs are plentiful, and staterooms are comfortable. Stabilizers prevent most ships from rolling in high seas, even when the weather is stormy. Thus seasickness, which used to be a problem for some passengers, has been virtually eliminated.

VOYAGER OF THE SEAS TESTS WHETHER ◄ THE BIGGEST IS THE BEST

The Royal Caribbean Line's *Voyager of the Seas* is the world's largest cruise ship. It is longer than three football fields, taller than the Statue of Liberty, and carries 4000 passengers.

In addition to three pools, a health club, showrooms, and the largest casino at sea, the ship boasts such firsts as a four-story climbing wall, an ice skating rink, an in-line skating track, a full-size basketball court, and a four-story indoor shopping/entertainment boulevard.

The *Voyager of the Seas* weighs 142 tons and cost $700 million to build. Because of its size, the number of ports it can visit is limited. It is too wide to travel through the Panama Canal and too large for many ports.

Source: Adapted from an article in *USA Today*, 19 November 1999.

The level of service on many ships is as high as that in luxury hotels. Cabin stewards are available 24 hours a day and provide turn-down service in the evening. Food and beverage service is commonly available day and night, and all sorts of recreational activities are available at any time. Pursers store valuables, cash checks, and convert currencies. Because of the high level of service, a cruise on one of these luxury liners can be an elegant and refreshing experience.

Shopping Centers

Shopping has long been a favored American pastime. Years ago, shopping was an activity that one engaged in by going downtown to a major shopping street; every village had one, and cities had more than one. The street was lined with an array of stores offering shoppers the goods they needed and wanted, and people walked along looking in the shop windows at the goods on display. Now, with automobiles the preferred mode of transportation for most Americans, retailers have moved to make shopping easier than ever. New travel-related alternatives to traditional shopping have been developed. The most significant of these are malls and discount outlets.

Malls

Major shopping **malls** are enclosed structures designed to accommodate many stores and common walkways under one roof, making shopping possible in virtually any weather. Some shopping malls are large, multilevel affairs enclosing hundreds of retail shops, several department stores, and such other varied enterprises as banks, restaurants, food markets, and movie theaters. Some have facilities for child care and arcades with computer games as well as carousels and other rides for children. Malls normally have extensive parking facilities to accommodate the hundreds or thousands of automobiles and other vehicles shoppers use to reach the malls.

While malls have been developed with retail sales as the primary focus, many people are attracted to them for the entertainment value. On hot summer days, people flock to malls for the air conditioning; on any day, numbers of people are there just to watch other people—and to look at and ask questions about merchandise they may never be able to buy. Some of the largest malls—the Mall of America in Bloomington, Minnesota, and the West Edmonton Mall in Alberta, Canada, for example—are actually tourist destinations, drawing hundreds of bus tours each year, some from thousands of miles away. In a very real way, these malls are entertainment centers for a sizable segment of the population.

Discount Outlet Centers

Rather than develop malls of the type described above, some communities have taken advantage of the American penchant for shopping by permitting the development of **discount outlet centers**—collections of retail stores specializing in the sale of name-brand merchandise at discount prices. In effect, entire areas have become entertainment centers. Reading, Pennsylvania, and Secaucus, New Jersey, have well-known discount outlet centers that attract thousands of shoppers daily. Many of these are travelers who have come a considerable distance just to take advantage of the shopping. Some arrive in their own automobiles; others come in tour buses. All bring tourism dollars to the area, spending money in hotels, motels, restaurants, and other tourism-related businesses as well as in the discount shops.

SUMMARY

In this chapter, recreation, entertainment, and other features that attract tourists to an area are identified. General definitions to distinguish between the terms *recreation* and *entertainment* are provided. Sites for recreational activities, including national and state parks, campgrounds, and resort areas, are listed and discussed. Significant forms of entertainment that can be found at theme parks, entertainment areas, tour destinations of various types and lengths, performances, fairs and festivals, parades, ceremonies, and sports events are identified and discussed. Finally, other important tourism attractions that are not usually classified as either recreation or entertainment, including·gambling, special events, cruises, and shopping, are cited.

KEY TERMS

Ceremony	Economy bus tour
Convention	Entertainment
Cruising	Entertainment area
Discount outlet center	Exhibition

Exposition
Fair
Festival
Gambling
Gaming
Luxury bus tour
Mall
March
Parade
Performance
Primitive camping

Rally
Recreation
Recreation vehicle
Resort area
Special event
Standard bus tour
Theme park
Tour destination
Trade show
Transient camping
Vacation camping

DISCUSSION QUESTIONS

1. Distinguish between recreation and entertainment.

2. Identify four types of national parks operated by the U.S. National Park Service.

3. Distinguish among primitive, transient, and vacation camping.

4. What is an RV? Why do you suppose so many Americans own them?

5. List five recreational activities and identify at least one resort area that is noted for each.

6. What is a theme park? List five well-known theme parks and identify the theme commonly associated with each.

7. What is an entertainment area? List four nationally known entertainment areas and cite the types of entertainment for which each is best known.

8. Motor coach tours are great favorites with tourists. If you were asked to develop the itinerary for a half-day tour of your local area, which sites would you include?

9. Distinguish among economy, standard, and luxury motor coach tours.

10. List ten kinds of musical and nonmusical performances that bring tourists to an area.

11. Identify the five best-known fairs and festivals that take place each year in your state.

12. Are there any annual parades and ceremonies in your area that have positive economic impact on tourist businesses? Identify them, then identify several steps that could be taken by local groups to increase the economic impact.

13. In how many states of the United States is gambling legal in some form?

14. List ten forms of gambling that are legal in at least one state.

15. Identify five types of special events that have positive economic impact on the areas where they are held.

16. What are the four principal features of cruises that make them appealing to vacationers?

17. Over the last 50 years, the age and economic status of cruise passengers have changed. How?

18. In what way does shopping serve as a tourist attraction for an area? In addition to the shopping, what other features attract tourists?

MOMENTS OF TRUTH

1. You have been hired by a group of hotel and motel owners in your area to prepare a list of interesting local attractions to include in tour packages being developed to promote business for their lodging establishments. Identify at least ten you would recommend, along with your principal reasons for selecting each. What kinds of package tours could be developed that would include these attractions? What kinds of visitors do you think would be interested in these packages?

2. You have been contacted by a group of hospitality educators looking for a site for a regional convention they intend to hold in your part of the state in early August of next year. The site must have the following:
   a. Guest rooms to accommodate up to 400 people
   b. Room rates no higher than $100 double occupancy
   c. A minimum of ten meeting rooms accommodating up to 40 people, four meeting rooms accommodating up to 100, and one meeting room accommodating up to 400, all within ten minutes of one another
   d. At least four popular priced restaurants within ten minutes of the meeting rooms
   e. A catering facility offering several banquet menus under $35 per person for groups up to 400
   f. Nearby recreation and entertainment facilities for attendees and their families.

   Determine the best site in your area for this convention, then identify the foodservice, lodging, and other facilities meeting the specifications provided.

INTERNET EXERCISES

1. Find the Web site for Walt Disney World. List the water parks and write a brief description of the recreational facilities each contains. How many resort hotels are located at Walt Disney World? What is the average cost per night at the luxury resort hotels?

2. Go to http://www.sixflags.com. How many theme parks does Six Flags operate? Where are they located? What recreational facilities do they offer in addition to theme parks?

PART VII
Future Perspectives

Hospitality and Tourism Tomorrow:

An Issues Overview

CHAPTER 14

▶ Learning Objectives

After reading and studying this chapter, you should be able to:

1. Identify six social and economic changes that suggest a bright future for the hospitality and tourism industry.
2. Describe the growth in demand for the service products of the foodservice and lodging industries.

3. Identify and discuss specific issues that tomorrow's hospitality and tourism managers are likely to face in each of the following areas: (a) marketing, (b) legal climate, (c) human resources, (d) operations, (e) consumer affairs.

INTRODUCTION

In preceding chapters, a number of significant topics were introduced, including the history of hospitality and tourism and the dimensions of its principal segments. Understanding these topics gives one an excellent foundation for planning a career in the industry. These chapters also serve as background for later course work or for the experiential learning that is so critical to anyone pursuing a professional career in hospitality.

THE BRIGHT FUTURE OF HOSPITALITY AND TOURISM

In recent years, important social and economic changes have occurred that suggest a bright future for the industry. These were addressed briefly in several previous chapters, but it is useful to review them here.

Social and Economic Changes

Early Retirement

Today, many workers are retiring at earlier ages than was the case in previous generations. Two factors contribute to making this possible:

1. Social Security provides benefits to people as young as 62 years of age.

2. Many employee retirement programs are tied to years of service rather than to age. In some retirement programs, particularly government programs, workers can retire and receive full benefits after just 25 or 30 years of service, making it possible for them to retire by age 55.

With greater numbers of people retiring early, more people now have the leisure time and the income to see and experience the world, which translates into increased sales for tourist businesses in general, including hotels, motels, restaurants, and other hospitality businesses.

Longer Life Span

The average citizen of an industrialized nation can now expect to live well into his seventies, and many will live longer. This is in contrast to earlier generations, when the average life span was considerably less. The increasing population of older retired citizens provides a larger base of potential customers for the tourism industries, including hospitality operations.

Shorter Workweek

Sixty years ago, the six-day workweek was standard for most working people. Today, the five-day workweek is standard, and the four-day workweek is not uncommon—leaving several days for other activities. The resulting increase in leisure time, combined with faster, more comfortable, and more accessible transportation, makes it possible for many people to take weekend vacations, drive to visit friends and relatives, attend weddings and receptions, and generally travel to a degree they could not have attempted just a few short years ago. Hospitality and tourism benefit immeasurably from this increase in travel.

More Holidays

Americans now celebrate greater numbers of holidays than was the case in the past, and these holidays are often observed on Mondays and Fridays. This creates three- and four-day weekends that provide people with still more opportunities to patronize hotels, motels, restaurants, and other hospitality businesses. One comparatively recent addition to the list of holidays is Martin Luther King's birthday, which is celebrated on a Monday in mid-January. This has created a long weekend that has had major impact. In the Northeast, for example, it has turned a relatively quiet weekend into a record weekend for the ski areas.

Greater Disposable Income

The average family is likely to have more money to spend than ever before. Higher wages and growth in the number of two-earner households account for much of this. A large portion of the additional disposable income is being spent on consumer goods and services, and businesses that are tourism-dependent appear to be receiving an important share of it.

Greater Mobility

Better highways and improved transportation make travel easier each year. The interstate highway system has dramatically reduced the time required for automobile travel in the United States. In addition, most Americans live close enough to a major airport to select air travel more readily than would have been the case 40 years ago. These increases in the ease of travel have had a strong positive impact on hospitality and tourism sales.

Growing Demand

Today, the foodservice industry ranks as one of the largest in the nation. A recent publication of the National Restaurant Association (NRA), the industry's principal trade association, states that "eating and drinking places are first among all retailers in the number of establishments and the number of employees." Today, over 840,000 eating and drinking establishments employ over 11.3 million people. The number of managerial and administrative positions in the industry is approaching 500,000. In fact, one out of every four retail outlets in the nation is an eating or drinking establishment.

On a typical day, U.S. foodservice establishments serve almost half (46 percent) of all adults. The typical restaurant serves 11 percent of its customers with

→ A PROMISING FUTURE FOR
THE RESTAURANT INDUSTRY

It is difficult to foresee what the future will hold in the restaurant industry, but here are a few
ideas, some of which are already starting to be used. One of the important tools of the future is
the Internet. On-line ordering of meals is already being done, and the practice is expected to
grow in the future. Some restaurants already accept table reservations over the Internet.

Technology will bring great advances to food preparation and service. Already, servers in
many restaurants have handheld point-of-service (POS) terminals that allow them to input an
order that goes directly to the kitchen. In future years, it is expected that these systems will be
widely used, cutting down the time it takes to place an order and thus decreasing the time it takes
to get food to the table. Food preparation appliances will become smarter, according to Howard
Jenkins, vice president of Red Robin International. "They'll be smart enough to do their own
self-diagnosis and send a message that says, 'My compressor is going; you need a technician.'"
Some predict that they will go a step further, calling a service technician when necessary.

Americans will consume more healthy food in the future. The good news is that it will become more flavorful and taste as good as similar high-calorie foods served today.

Source: Adapted from an article in *Restaurants USA*, March 2000.

breakfast, 37 percent with lunch, and 52 percent with dinner. Well over 70 percent of the adult population of the United States eats at a restaurant once a month.
The growth of food and beverage sales has been continuous. In 1970, figures gathered by the NRA placed foodservice sales at $42.8 billion. By 1975, sales volume
had grown to $70.3 billion. By 1980, it had increased by over 150 percent to
nearly $120 billion, and the 1980 figure nearly doubled by 1990. By 1999, it was
$354 billion. If the rate of growth continues at the current rate of approximately
4 percent per year, sales will reach $414 billion by the year 2003. Although not
adjusted for inflation, these figures still point out the extraordinary growth in foodservice. Today, food and beverage sales account for 4 percent of the gross domestic product of the United States, which is generally defined as the value of all
goods and services sold. By any measure, ours is indeed a major industry.

The demand for foodservice has grown rapidly. Today, eating in a restaurant
is a frequent experience, one parents commonly share with their children. Many
have Kid's Meals at McDonalds, then continue to patronize McDonalds and restaurants in general in their adult years. Many adults eat out several times each
week—more than ever before in our history.

In addition, the frequency of eating out is increasing. Americans are consuming ever greater numbers of meals away from home each year and, nationwide, food sales continue to increase dramatically. Experts predict that Americans
will soon be eating half of all meals away from home!

The commercial lodging industry is also growing. The American Hotel and
Motel Association reports that the commercial lodging industry in the United
States now includes approximately 51,000 properties ranging in size from small

inns with fewer than 10 rooms to giant hotels with over 5000 rooms. In total, the commercial lodging industry in the United States generates about $93 billion in sales each year, representing more than 1 percent of the gross national product. The industry employs approximately 1.16 million people, full time and part time. It is a major industry and, with the increases in leisure time and disposable income, it is continuing to increase in size and economic importance.

The tourism industry is growing as well. Internationally, the World Tourism Organization reports that world spending on international tourism reached $445 billion in 1998. By the year 2010, the figure will exceed $1.55 trillion. The industry presently employs well over 200 million people, and that number will certainly grow. Within the United States, the Travel Industry Association estimated domestic and international tourism at $481.5 billion in 1997 and had an economic impact of $1.16 trillion.

The future of the hospitality and tourism industry is bright, in spite of the temporary setbacks that any industry must endure. In one region or another, changes will always occur that have negative implications for various segments of the industry. However, these are unlikely to last. Hospitality and tourism will continue to be important to the economic vitality of most regions.

ISSUES IN HOSPITALITY AND TOURISM

Although the future of these industries is bright, it is not without problems. People pursuing careers in hospitality and tourism will find it necessary to be familiar with a number of topics and issues that will have significant impact on the industry in the years ahead. Students in degree programs commonly confront many of these in their major courses. Some problems have existed for many years, but no generally accepted solutions for them have yet been found. Others are issues that the industry has been dealing with for years but that now must be addressed differently because of changing conditions. Still others are emerging issues occasioned by social, economic, or technological change. Many of these topics are addressed below—not exhaustively, but to the extent that indicates the significance of each and the areas in which the impact is likely to be felt most.

The topics addressed in this chapter are distributed under the following headings:

- Marketing
- Legal
- Human resources
- Operations
- Consumer affairs

The issues identified and discussed in this chapter are certainly not the only matters of concern to hospitality and tourism managers. They are, however, among the major topics that men and women planning managerial careers in this field should know about. Many are discussed in daily newspapers, in general periodicals, in trade publications, and at industry conferences. Sometimes they are the subjects of programs on broadcast television or on cable networks. They are often central topics for discussion at meetings of hospitality-related organizations. Numerous owners and managers are genuinely concerned about them. Many issues have to do with the social responsibility of people who own and operate foodservice, lodging, and other tourism-oriented enterprises—social responsibility toward customers, employees, the community, and the environment. People planning managerial careers are likely to discover that they, too, become increasingly aware of these and similarly important issues as their careers progress.

Those considering these topics and the categories under which they are discussed in this chapter may disagree with the inclusion of a given issue under a particular category. Some, for example, might consider it more suitable to cover questions relating to diet/nutrition/health with operations issues rather than with consumer issues. The difference would have more to do with the degree of emphasis given one or another of the topic's elements.

We certainly would not disagree with anyone seeking to categorize these issues differently. We are less concerned about classification than about the significance of the issues. We are particularly interested in promoting the idea that responsible hospitality and tourism managers should know about and be engaged in constructive consideration of the issues that face the industry. In our view, all the issues discussed here will be of considerable significance to managers in the years ahead.

Marketing

Changing Demographics

The population of America is aging. The median age is now 33 years and projected to go higher in the coming years. The so-called baby boomers, born in the years following World War II, are now 50 and older. An older population has preferences that differ significantly from those of a younger population, and hospitality providers will find it necessary to adjust their service products to the changing preferences of the market. Thus, changing demographics is an issue of dramatic importance to the industry.

Another changing demographic characteristic is the increase in the number of single-parent households. Single-parent households traditionally have lower levels of discretionary income and thus are not as able to support hospitality and tourism businesses. To reach this market, providers will have to continue developing new service products at affordable prices that appeal to this demographic segment.

A third demographic change is the continuing growth in the number of people traveling for personal rather than for business purposes. As indicated in Chapter 13, approximately 57 percent of domestic travelers travel primarily for pleasure. This group has accounted for growing percentages of the travel market in the past 45 years, and the growth is sure to continue.

The fourth demographic change is the growth in the number of international travelers in general and in the number of international travelers to the United States in particular. International travelers account for an ever-growing share of hospitality and tourism revenues in the United States. The number of international visitors to the United States is likely to reach 75 million by the year 2005.

In the coming years, hospitality and tourism marketing executives will find it important to take these demographic changes into account as they develop marketing plans for the service products the industry offers.

Changing Vacation Patterns

The length of vacations taken by Americans is changing. The traditional once-a-year vacation of two weeks or more is declining in popularity. For growing numbers of people, vacations are becoming shorter and more frequent. Today, people are more likely to plan minivacations. Some, for example, add two of their annual vacation days to a three-day holiday weekend to make a five-day minivacation. By doing so, they manage to get away for several days while using only two actual vacation days.

Vacation destinations are changing as well. The demise of the communist bloc makes it possible to plan vacations in countries that were usually considered off limits in the past. The Czech Republic, Hungary, Russia, Romania, and Bulgaria are becoming more popular sites for American and European vacationers. With industrialization and improvements in transportation, other nations are becoming more popular as well. The People's Republic of China was not a common destination just a few years ago. Today, China is just one of many nations seriously engaged in efforts at tourism development.

Market Segmentation

In the years since 1980, a key term in hospitality marketing has been **market segmentation.** Until the late 1970s, lodging establishments attempted to appeal to broad, general markets; their aim was to appeal to as broad a group of potential guests as possible. In more recent years, the success of limited-service properties has led to the development of other properties designed to appeal to carefully selected market segments of the guest spectrum. Types of lodging properties to emerge include all-suite properties, residence properties, sub-budget properties, and budget properties differentiated by their varying services and amenities.

Examples of market segmentation are also evident in foodservice, particularly in the past ten years. Restaurants that traditionally offer extensive something-for-everyone menus have begun to see reductions in business as customers choose to patronize restaurants offering specialized service products. As new market segments are identified, properties designed to appeal to those segments are likely to be developed.

Frequent-Guest Programs

With the proliferation of properties and the growing competition among them, some lodging operators have begun to develop programs to gain repeat business.

Modeled on the frequent-flyer programs used successfully by many airline companies, these plans typically give credits to regular guests. Credits can be redeemed in the form of reduced rates, upgrades, free accommodations, free meals, or any of a variety of amenities. In many cases, they can be translated into frequent-flyer miles and used for air travel. As competition becomes keener, the number of these programs is likely to grow. Many experts believe that these programs will gain in the lodging business the same degree of favor they achieved among airline customers.

Food and beverage service operators have long known that it pays to reward regular customers. Many restaurants and bar owners give their regulars complementary appetizers, desserts, glasses of wine, and other rewards for regular and continuing patronage. However, they do not follow the formalized approaches adopted by the airline and lodging companies, which require an elaborate recordkeeping. In most instances, rewards are a matter of independent restaurant and bar owners making spur-of-the-moment decisions when seeing frequent customers in their establishments. In some cases, departing customers are given discount coupons that can be redeemed on their next visit. This approach is more common with chain operations, some of which have taken an additional step, setting up promotions to offer discounts to all customers purchasing specific menu items during a limited period—several days in midweek, or the third week of a given month, for example. One aim of food and beverage operators adopting these approaches is to build repeat business. This aim is identical to that of the lodging operator with a frequent-guest program or the airline company with a frequent-flyer program.

Maturation of Segments of the Fast-Food Industry

Segments of the fast-food market are no longer expanding as quickly as was possible in the past. The demand for hamburgers is not growing as fast as it once did, and operators are finding it necessary to develop new products to maintain desired sales levels. Today, for example, establishments that once offered few products other than hamburgers are now test marketing or offering such products as pizza, salads, and poultry or other meat products. As public tastes continue to change, foodservice operators will need to keep pace—to develop new specialty products to retain an adequate share of the market.

Consolidation in the Commercial Lodging Industry

Some experts now suggest that the number of large international and nationwide lodging companies will decrease in the years to come. They predict that a relatively small number of firms will dominate the lodging industry by acquiring smaller chains of regional or national properties. This will enable successful firms to obtain the funds required to expand their operations internationally. It appears that this trend has already started. Examples include the following: Rock Resorts has been purchased by Olympus Real Estate Corporation and Park Plaza International; Accor, a French hotel company that acquired Motel 6 in 1990, has purchased Red Roof Inns; MGM Grand, Inc., has purchased Mirage Resorts; Starwood Hotels has purchased Vistana, Inc., a time-share company; Bass Hotels and Resorts, a London company, already includes Holiday Inn, Inter-Continental, and Crown Plaza in its portfolio and plans to double its size by 2004 through other hotel chain purchases. Other international chains are already quite large. For example, Choice Hotels, Inc., has over 4100 franchised properties in 37 countries. Its brands include Comfort, Clarion, Quality, Rodeway, MainStay Suites, and Econo Lodge.

This trend toward consolidation will have significant impact on all commercial lodging operations. Both independent operations and smaller chains will have increasing difficulty competing with heavily advertised national and international brands.

Legal

Liquor Liability

In recent years, public concern has been growing over the alarming number of alcohol-related automobile accidents. Today, substance abuse is a factor in over half of all automobile accidents, and a vast number of these have been attributed to alcohol abuse. This has led to increasing public pressure on state legislatures to act. Although the specifics vary from one state to another, it is generally true that legislators have responded by lowering the levels of blood alcohol at which an individual is considered intoxicated and by increasing penalties on offenders. In addition, many states have imposed new regulations on the serving of alcoholic beverages. In at least one state, new regulations have made the discounting of drink prices illegal, thus bringing an end to the so-called happy hour. In many states, establishments and their owners can be held financially accountable if they serve alcoholic beverages to an intoxicated individual who causes damage or injury after leaving the establishment. In some places, this has caused such huge increases in

Because of the increasing popularity of nonalcoholic drinks, some restaurant and bar owners are now featuring them on their menus, as shown in this photograph.
(Photo courtesy of Ocean Spray Cranberries, Inc.)

the cost of liability insurance that some bar and tavern owners have chosen to go out of business. It has caused some restaurant owners to stop serving alcoholic beverages.

Some restaurant and bar owners have changed market strategy; they now feature and promote nonalcoholic drinks. Others encourage groups of their patrons to select a designated driver and provide incentives for them to do so.

As societal attitudes toward alcoholic beverages continue to change, it will be necessary for foodservice and lodging operators to adjust.

Receiving and Evicting Guests

Under common law, an innkeeper who operates a transient establishment must receive all who apply for a room providing that (1) there is a vacancy, (2) the persons come in a condition to be received (not drunk or disorderly), and (3) they are willing to pay the established rate. Also, the innkeeper does not have to accept anyone with property that might harm other guests, such as snakes and firearms, or those of whom there is reason to believe might harm the property of the inn. Innkeepers do have the right to refuse pets and to refuse accommodations to persons with bad reputations, such as prostitutes and thieves.

They do not, though, have the right to refuse accommodations because of a person's race, religion, sex, or age. Fortunately, since the passage of the 1967 Civil Rights Act, innkeepers with more than five rooms have not generally discriminated on the basis of race or religion. However, many innkeepers still refuse accommodations to people under the age of 21. Historically, these innkeepers have justified their positions by stating that minor children are not responsible for contracts and may do damage to the property. Under common law, minor persons have the same rights to food, clothing, and housing as adults. As long as a minor person is, indeed, a transient traveler and can comply with the above-stated qualifications, he must be treated in the same way as adults.

Guests can be evicted for the same reasons they may be refused accommodations. Someone who is loud or disorderly and disturbs other guests can be evicted. If guests are taking part in illegal or immoral activities, they can be evicted. When a guest's contract is up and the innkeeper needs the room because the inn is full, the guest can be asked to leave.

Some hospitality managers are unaware of their full rights and obligations as innkeepers. Those who do not fully understand them or who purposely establish policies violating the law find that the ensuing lawsuits can cost the establishment dearly.

Impact of the Americans with Disabilities Act of 1990

The Americans with Disabilities Act (ADA) prohibits discrimination against anyone with a disability, defined as a physical or mental impairment that substantially limits one or more major life activities. While this landmark legislation has had significant impact in many facets of American life, the effect has been especially powerful in hospitality and tourism. In this industry, the ADA applies to both employees and guests. In lodging, it applies to establishments of more than five rooms; in foodservice, to all restaurants, bars, and similar establishments serving food or drink. In tourism generally, the ADA has had significant impact on every type of business.

The ADA prohibits discrimination in hiring on the basis of disability. It requires that builders of new facilities design and construct them to accommodate people who are disabled; by contrast, owners of existing facilities must make reasonable accommodation efforts. In general, it holds that people who are disabled are entitled to full and equal enjoyment of goods, services, facilities, privileges, advantages, and accommodations.

Although the language of the ADA is subject to varying interpretations, these will, no doubt, eventually be resolved in the courts. In the meantime, both the National Restaurant Association and the American Hotel and Motel Association have developed publications to guide their members in their effort to comply with the law. Hospitality and tourism managers are likely to be addressing questions arising from this act for many years to come.

Ethics in Hospitality

Ethics is an academic discipline that addresses codes of moral conduct. *Business ethics* refers to the application of a particular moral code to relationships, activities, and decision making in business and industry. It is the code that enables an individual in business to distinguish right from wrong—to distinguish between ethical and unethical behavior.

Ethics has been an issue in hospitality and tourism for thousands of years—since the tavernkeepers of earliest recorded history first diluted the drinks of unsuspecting customers. Although this and similar practices are illegal today, it is possible to question the business ethics of some hospitality operators. The following are a few examples: a manager of a new restaurant hires 20 servers, intending to keep only the 12 most able after the second week of operation; a room clerk accepts bribes to register guests without reservations, even when the property is overbooked; an owner fails to report all sales on her income tax returns; a server attempts to cheat on his income taxes by failing to report all tips; an owner misrepresents his hotel, using idealized artists' renderings rather than photographs in his advertising; an employee in a purchasing department accepts gifts from vendors in return for purchasing inferior products; an owner cheats on his taxes by charging personal expenses to the business. The examples go on and on. Business ethics will forever be high on everyone's list of important hospitality issues.

Human Resources

Diversity

More than most other industries, the hospitality and tourism industry has long been known for its diverse workforce. **Diversity** is a hallmark of our industry, which includes men and women of every age, race, ethnic, and religious group. In fact, throughout our history, immigrants to the United States have always been able to find employment in foodservice, lodging, and other tourism-related fields. But while the workforce was diverse, management was inclined to treat all members of all groups identically, without taking into account the characteristic cultural differences of the many groups represented. Unfortunately, this tended to create a workforce that consisted of individuals from all sorts of groups that did not get on well together and thus did not work particularly well together. In general, there was little team spirit among the employees of hotels and restaurants.

An example helps explain. Suppose that people growing up in one culture are taught to be quiet and reserved, not to speak unless someone else speaks first, never to differ with anyone in authority. When an individual with that cultural background is hired to work in a restaurant, some on the staff are likely to assume, on the basis of his behavior, that their new coworker is unfriendly and unwilling to fit into the group. The new employee, by contrast, may decide that many on the staff are rude and offensive. The truth is that the new employee and the others on the staff simply do not understand one another. Neither has experience dealing with people from cultural backgrounds other than their own, so neither can accept the other as coworkers.

One of the great challenges to managers today is finding ways to manage diversity in the workforce. This requires education. Ideally, everyone in the workforce learns to respect, understand, appreciate, and value the array of differences among their coworkers. To that end, there is a growing trend toward diversity training for hospitality and tourism employees. Many managers find that this training brings immediate and tangible benefits to the workplace, including competitive advantages in the changing economic environment.

Sexual Harassment

The federal Equal Employment Opportunity Commission defines **sexual harassment** as "unwelcomed sexual advances, requests for sexual favors, and other verbal or physical conduct of a sexual nature that takes place under any of the following conditions:

1. Submission is made a condition of the person's employment;
2. Submission to or rejection of such conduct is used as a basis for employment decisions affecting the person; or
3. It unreasonably interferes with the person's work performance or creates an intimidating, hostile, or offensive work environment."

Most cases of sexual harassment involve complaints by females about male coworkers or superiors, although the number of complaints by males is growing. In the last ten years, as greater numbers of employees have become willing to speak out, the number of these cases has grown.

Because employers are liable for the actions of their employees at work, it is particularly important for employers to take several important steps:

1. Institute a strict policy banning all forms of sexual harassment in the workplace.

2. Develop appropriate training programs for managers and employees so that all understand and are sensitive to the nature of sexual harassment.

3. Establish procedures for handling all complaints promptly, fairly, and sensitively.

ADDING DIMENSION TO DIVERSITY ◄━━━

Best Western, the world's largest hotel consortium, encompasses more than 3800 independent hotels and more than 300,000 guest rooms in 79 countries. It is making a concerted effort to address diversity issues. Proof of its cultural shift is director of human resources Vicki A. Winston, Best Western's first African American executive. She is increasing the number of Best Western minority vendors, increasing the African American owner population among Best Western members, forging an advertising and marketing plan geared toward minority groups, and increasing minority worker population at corporate headquarters.

Since Winston came on board, the National Association for the Advancement of Colored People (NAACP) has upped its Best Western diversity grade from F to B−. The company is typical of many hospitality enterprises putting new emphasis on diversity.

Source: Adapted from an article in *Lodging Hospitality*, October 1999.

Employers who take these steps find that the number of sexual harassment complaints decreases substantially and that the training has significant and positive impact on the behavior of employees at work.

Employee Turnover

As was pointed out in Chapter 10, **employee turnover** continues to be one of the major issues facing hospitality managers. With turnover rates averaging approximately 100 percent per year across the industry, managers are continually faced with the problem of losing experienced employees and hiring less experienced replacements. Faced with inexperienced replacements, many managers believe they have only two choices: to incur the high training costs associated with transforming new employees into valuable workers, or to suffer the equally high costs associated with operating with untrained workers. Too few are willing to acknowledge that they have a third option: to take steps directed toward retaining employees and reducing turnover.

Many hospitality managers understand the prerequisites to reduced turnover. These include adequate wages and benefits, reasonable working conditions, reasonable work schedules, and reasonable treatment of employees by enlightened managers. Comparatively few are willing to put these into practice.

Many employers and managers still attempt to treat workers as if they were cogs in some gigantic wheel—metal parts rather than people. They hire at the lowest possible wages, provide no training, then belittle and berate workers for failing to do work correctly. They assign workers to schedules without regard to personal preferences, change schedules without notice, and demand, at the last minute, that employees report for work on their days off if the need arises. Then they complain about the ungrateful workers who quit their jobs at the first opportunity to accept seemingly equal jobs with other employers.

Employers willing to change this pattern find that improving their treatment of employees and giving them a sense of importance to the organization results in significant positive impact on employee turnover.

Employee Assistance Plans

Employee assistance plans (EAPs) are included in this discussion of hospitality and tourism issues because they illustrate one of the attempts made by enlightened owners and managers to pay responsible attention to the real, human problems faced by their employees. The problems of people employed in hospitality are essentially the same as the problems of those in the general population. They include substance abuse, psychological problems, family issues, financial issues, legal problems, health issues, and educational issues.

The hospitality and tourism industry traditionally has been among the larger employers of men and women with limited education, including immigrants with limited knowledge of English. Because of this, managers in the industry have an opportunity—some would say an obligation—to be of unique assistance to workers who might otherwise not have access to help with their problems.

Managers who establish EAPs are likely to develop a more loyal workforce—one more willing to strive toward the operational goals of the enterprise. At the same time, managers with the foresight to help employees are likely to see reductions in employee turnover.

Operations

Total Quality Management

Total quality management (TQM)—tailoring service to the needs of guests and customers—has become an important topic in management circles today. One point made several times in earlier chapters is that service products cannot be mass-produced in advance; they are produced only when ordered by a customer. To an important extent, each service product is tailored to suit the guest or customer who orders it.

In many operations, managers develop extensive rules and procedures that all employees are directed to follow when dealing with customers. These can extend to the most minute details—rules forbidding free refills on coffee, strict limits on the number of hand towels per guest, directives prohibiting substitutions on special dinner menus, inflexible rules about checkout time. These, and the many others seen daily in hospitality and tourism—lead to critical moments of truth that may affect a customer's overall impression of a particular foodservice, lodging, or other tourism enterprise. The negative moment of truth resulting from a refusal to give a customer an extra half cup of coffee may be enough to offset all the positive moments of truth that precede and follow it. For some customers, it may be enough to make them decide never to return.

Many owners and managers have come to realize the futility of attempting to set strict rules to govern every detail of customer-employee service encounter. They are now revising their approach, developing policies that are service oriented and training their employees to provide as many positive moments of truth as possible. They are giving their employees some reasonable degree of latitude to tailor service products to the specific needs and preferences of guests. In effect, they are empowering their employees to make enlightened, educated decisions that improve service quality for guests without having a negative impact on operations.

Internationalization

Internationalization is a term that can be thought of in at least two hospitality contexts. One is the tendency of national hospitality firms to expand operations beyond national borders—to go global. Another is the special effort that hospitality firms are making to cater to the needs of international visitors. The former has been going on for decades. It is in the latter context that internationalization has become an important issue in hospitality operations today.

The United States has always been a favorite destination of international travelers who could afford the trip. While hotel operators were always glad to book international business, comparatively few went out of their way to provide for the special needs of foreign visitors: currency exchange; staff members fluent in languages other than English; special menus; brochures, maps, and similar materials in other languages; climate controls in individual guest rooms; and many others.

Today, the growth in international travel is bringing growing numbers of foreign visitors to the United States. Foreign visitors account for growing percentages of room revenue in many hotels—particularly in major cities on the east and west coasts—and growing numbers of hotel operators are taking steps to provide the kinds of services that make foreigners feel welcome. Some managers require that new guest service employees be fluent in at least one language other than English. Many offer international menus in restaurants, signs with international symbols, foreign newspapers in lobbies, currency exchange at the front desk, and any number of other thoughtful services.

Automation

Automation means using electronic and mechanical equipment and machinery to complete some or all of the tasks associated with a given enterprise. Three principal reasons are commonly cited for automating an enterprise:

1. To increase the speed of work

2. To reduce the cost of work

3. To standardize results

Historically, hospitality and tourism managers have always been ready to automate. A few examples of automation in the industry include peeling potatoes, washing dishes, washing tablecloths and napkins, preserving frozen foods, vacuuming carpets, recording reservations, and maintaining guest accounts.

Today, we are at the point where some foodservice and lodging establishments have automated to the extent that guests and customers no longer have direct contact with any human staff. Food and beverages are obtained from vending machines. Guests swipe a credit card through an electronic device, enabling them to check into a lodging operation without speaking to a room clerk at the desk. Using touch-sensitive screens on the television sets in their rooms, guests will soon be able to place orders for food and beverages from room service; obtain information about stores, restaurants, theaters, and other entertainment facilities in the area; make reservations for dinner at nearby restaurants; and even purchase clothing and other goods from stores, requesting immediate delivery. Guests can already use these touch-sensitive screens for reviewing their hotel bills and checking out.

It is interesting that foodservice and lodging operations at the high end of the price spectrum tend to maintain the appearance of service, even when automated devices have been installed. For example, some hotels with automatic elevators continue to employ personnel to run the elevators. Guests are still treated to a high level of service, but with more modern and efficient equipment than the older manual elevators.

Some people are beginning to question whether the industry is pushing automation too far—whether establishments that automate too extensively are offering any degree of hospitality. Have they automated themselves out of the hospitality industry, so to speak? This is a question that owners and managers of hospitality enterprises, as well as their guests and customers, will continue to ask in the years ahead. It is sure to be of growing importance as well. The technological capacity to automate grows daily, and the industry will have to determine the extent to which it should embrace the technology.

Consumer Affairs

Smoking/No-Smoking Areas

As more and more customers and guests of foodservice and lodging enterprises demand smoke-free areas for dining and smoke-free sleeping accommodations, the industry continues to make all reasonable efforts to meet these demands. This is particularly true in states and localities where legislation mandates that appropriate facilities be made available.

This trend has had great impact on both the food and beverage and lodging sectors of the industry. Most restaurants and related enterprises find it desirable, even if not required by law, to apportion sections of their dining facilities to accommodate the wishes of nonsmokers. Some also find it necessary to install or improve ventilation equipment. Virtually all mainstream lodging operations have set aside accommodations for nonsmokers—rooms that are free of the lingering effects of tobacco smoke. In some properties, smoking is prohibited in public areas—lobbies, corridors, elevators, and other areas—often as a matter of law. The prohibition of smoking in hospitality operations is an issue that will be of growing significance to owners and managers in the years ahead.

Sanitation and Public Health

No subject is of greater importance in foodservice than sanitation. Everyone agrees that all responsible steps must be taken to prevent illnesses that can be traced to the manner in which food is handled, or to the food itself.

Ensuring proper food handling has always been a vital issue in the industry. Managers must constantly check that food is purchased from responsible vendors. Food also must be kept at suitable temperatures to prevent bacterial growth or under proper conditions to prevent infestation by insects and rodents. Equipment surfaces must be cleaned effectively to ensure that food is not contaminated during preparation. Washing is an ongoing necessity in foodservice—the washing of employees' hands, the washing of some fresh foods to remove chemical residues, and the thorough washing of all china, glassware, flatware, pots, and pans used in the preparation and service of foods and beverages.

State and local governments apply strict sanitary standards to food and beverage operations. Some conduct regular inspections and impose sanctions on facilities found violating the applicable code. The sanctions range from imposing fines to publishing lists of violators in newspapers and web sites to closing flagrant violators. In an effort to ensure their compliance with local sanitary codes, many food and beverage operators hire consultants to conduct regular inspections and to assist in the immediate correction of violations. As consumers become increasingly aware of the potential for harm from improperly handled food, preventing violations of local codes will be an issue of growing importance to food and beverage operators.

The Environment

In recent years, society at large has become concerned with the natural environment. The public and the business community have become much more aware of key environmental issues, and the hospitality and tourism industry has taken a leadership role in efforts to protect the natural environment. For this industry, the key environmental concerns are recycling, energy conservation, and water conservation.

Recycling.   In recent years, there has been a gradual closing of the landfills traditionally used for disposing of solid wastes and growing awareness of the harmful effects of either burning solid waste or dumping it in the sea. This has led to major waste-disposal problems in some areas.

In some major metropolitan areas, the cost of removing solid wastes is becoming higher than government and citizens are willing and able to pay. In many of these areas, law now requires separating recyclable plastic, glass, metal, and certain paper items from other solid waste. Separating recyclables from other solid wastes greatly reduces the quantities requiring disposal.

The trend toward recycling is likely to grow. Many in the hospitality industry who have not been previously affected by this issue will soon see some change. They, too, will find the adoption of a recycling program both necessary and desirable.

Energy Conservation.   Energy in the form of electricity, gas, and oil is a major element in hospitality. Hospitality operations depend directly or indirectly on energy sources for heating, cooling, lighting, cooking, and operating all kinds of equipment, including elevators. Conservation of energy has become an important national goal and is now an important goal of many hospitality operations. Owners and managers have instituted many measures to conserve energy.

Monitoring temperature controls: Managers know that temperature controls for heating and cooling need to be monitored so that energy is not wasted. Some establishments have computer systems that automatically monitor and set temperatures to desired levels. Others set thermostats at the desired level, then lock the controls and provide keys to specific individuals. A major concern in the lodging segment of the hospitality industry is climate control in guest rooms. Policies must be established to prevent unneeded heating and cooling of guest rooms when guests are out or when the rooms are vacant. Members of the housekeeping staff are frequently trained to turn thermostats to desired temperatures after they finish their work in the rooms. Guests are asked to adjust thermostats in their rooms in order to avoid overheating in cold weather and overcooling in hot weather, particularly when they are away from their rooms. Many hotels offer extra blankets to guests in an effort to encourage them to keep room temperatures lower during nighttime hours.

Switching off unnecessary lights: Keeping lights on when not necessary is a waste of energy. Guests are reminded to turn off lights when not in their rooms, and staff are trained to turn off unnecessary lights, particularly in ballrooms and other public space when unoccupied. Some properties have installed sensing devices that automatically turn off lights when there is no motion in a room.

Preventative maintenance to increase equipment efficiency: Equipment that is properly maintained typically uses less energy. Additionally, equipment that is properly maintained lasts longer and has fewer repair problems.

Sequential start-up of HVAC equipment: Electric companies must be able to produce or purchase sufficient electrical power to service peak demand. Because of this, billing for electricity is typically based on peak usage during a given 24-hour period. Properties that start HVAC equipment in a staggered fashion do not generate as much usage at one time as they would by starting the equipment all at once. This approach leads to lower electric bills than would otherwise be the case.

Operating washing machines only when filled: Hospitality operations can reduce costs considerably by running washing machines in dish rooms and laundries only when loads are full. This can produce significant energy savings when followed consistently.

Replacing old equipment with new energy-efficient equipment: Equipment purchased many years ago was not commonly energy efficient. No one expected it to be. With today's soaring energy costs, replacing old equipment may actually save money. Replacing old equipment with new may be a large capital investment, but it frequently pays for itself in energy conservation. For example, old kitchen ovens usually have poor insulation and require excessive amounts of energy to maintain desired temperatures. New ovens typically use much less energy and can yield considerable dollar savings in energy costs.

In the hospitality industry, energy costs are an important component of total operating costs. Many owners and managers find that reducing these costs can contribute substantially to profit.

Water Conservation. Like energy conservation, water conservation has become an important element in hospitality. As much as any other industry, hospitality operations require dependable sources of clean water for many obvious purposes— cooking, drinking, cleaning, washing, and so on. Having a continuing source of water is an urgent necessity in hospitality, and owners and managers have come to understand the importance of conserving water. Conservation of water is now an important goal of many hospitality operations.

The following are typical of the measures taken in hospitality operations to conserve water:

- Reducing water consumption in bathrooms with devices that restrict the amount of water used in showers and toilets
- Serving no water to guests in restaurants unless they request it, and serving the water in smaller glasses
- Sweeping outdoor areas—primarily sidewalks and other walkways— with brooms rather than flushing them clean with running water
- Purchasing water-efficient equipment—dishwashers and laundry washers designed to consume less water
- Reusing treated wastewater for irrigation, public toilets, and cooling towers
- Offering conservation-minded guests the option of having their towels and bed linen changed every second day instead of daily

Truth in Menu

For most foodservice operators, preparing truthful and accurate menus is a normal practice that is never violated. A small minority, however, produce menus that are not entirely accurate indicators of the foods served in their establishments. Some merely abuse such terms as *fresh* and *cooked to order.* Others are more flagrant, serving U.S. Choice beef when their menus state U.S. Prime. Still others serve portions with fewer ounces than the number listed in the menu. Some do not use the actual ingredients suggested by their menus and substitute one product for another: turkey for chicken, margarine for butter, generic products for name brands, and domestic products for imported.

In some areas, enough abuses have occurred to produce a groundswell of public opinion in favor of requiring foodservice operators to be entirely truthful. Where such consumer protection legislation exists, operators who violate the regulations risk fines and loss of their licenses.

It is important that those in the industry conduct their operations ethically— in such a manner that consumers can have complete faith in the truth of their menus, the wholesomeness of their foods, and, generally, the honesty of their business practices.

Diet/Nutrition/Health

With the public becoming increasingly concerned about healthy diets that contain less fat and fewer calories, many foodservice operators are adjusting or amending their menus to accommodate these changing public tastes. Some devote sections of their menu to foods for the diet conscious; others designate certain of their menu items as appropriate for people interested in foods low in sodium and cholesterol.

Growing numbers of restaurants seek to attract health-conscious diners. Some eliminate "unhealthy" foods from their menu. The trend to healthier dining is certain to continue, and successful foodservice operators will want to give greater attention to the nutritional content of foods in the years ahead.

Fire and Safety

Fire and safety have always been issues of concern in hospitality. In earlier centuries, taverns, inns, and hotels, usually constructed of wood, were regularly demolished by fire. Many burned to the ground, and large numbers of people were killed or maimed.

During the twentieth century, various changes made hotels, motels, and other hospitality operations much safer. Improvements in design and construction made a great difference, as did improvements in the fire control systems installed in buildings—electronic smoke detectors, automatic systems to summon fire departments, better sprinkler systems, and so on. Because of these changes, hotels, motels, and other lodging operations have never been safer.

A number of dangers associated with fire remain to be addressed, however. In the event of fire, the guests in some properties today may face danger from the toxic smoke resulting from the burning of furniture, fixtures, and fibers produced from man-made materials. In a fire, many of the artificial fibers used in wall coverings, carpets, draperies, and upholstery produce toxic fumes that can be more dangerous than the flames and smoke.

Another problem relates to construction. In recent years, to reduce heating and cooling costs, new buildings were particularly well insulated. In some, the windows were not designed to be opened. Temperature and air were controlled by complex central systems. In the event of fire in such buildings, the danger exists that smoke may be quickly dispersed throughout the building. As a consequence, a shift to individual room ventilation can be seen in properties being built today.

Managers of hospitality and tourism operations universally agree that there is no consideration more important than the protection of their guests and customers from the threat of fire.

SUMMARY

In this chapter, social and economic changes likely to affect the future of the hospitality industry are described, including earlier retirement, longer life span, shorter workweek, more vacation time, greater disposable income, and increased mobility. Growing demand for the hospitality service products of both the foodservice and lodging industries is discussed. Many of the key topics and issues that will have significant impact on the industry in the years ahead are identified and categorized in five areas: marketing, legal, human resources, operations, and consumer affairs. Topics and issues in marketing include changing demographics, changing vacation patterns, market segmentation, frequent-guest programs, maturation of segments of the fast-food industry, and consolidation in the commercial lodging industry. Legal topics and issues include liquor liability, impact of the Americans with Disabilities Act of 1990, and ethics in hospitality. Those in human resources include diversity, sexual harassment, employee turnover, and employee assistance programs. In operations, total quality management, internationalization, and automation are discussed. Finally, topics and issues in consumer affairs include smoking/no-smoking areas, sanitation and public health, environmental issues, truth in menu, diet/nutrition/ health, and fire and safety.

KEY TERMS

Americans with Disability Act
Automation
Diversity
Employee assistance plan
Employee turnover

Internationalization
Market segmentation
Sexual harassment
Total quality management

DISCUSSION QUESTIONS

1. List and discuss six social and economic changes that suggest a bright future for the hospitality and tourism industry.

2. Identify the demographic changes that hospitality and tourism marketing executives will find it important to take into account as they develop marketing plans for the industry.

3. Why do hospitality businesses develop frequent-guest or frequent-customer programs? How do frequent-guest programs for lodging operations differ from frequent-customer programs for foodservice operations?

4. What is the major cause of the large increases in the cost of liability insurance to bar and tavern owners in recent years?

5. What was the primary purpose underlying passage by Congress of Americans with Disabilities Act of 1990?

6. Identify one positive outcome that diversity training should produce for a foodservice or lodging establishment.

7. How does the federal Equal Employment Opportunity Commission define the term *sexual harassment*?

8. What steps can hospitality and tourism managers take to reduce employee turnover?

9. Identify the three principal purposes of automation. Discuss the impact of automation on service.

10.   List seven key activities that foodservice employees engage in to ensure safe and sanitary conditions for food handling.

11.   List and discuss four environmental issues that have had significant impact on the foodservice and lodging segments of the hospitality industry.

MOMENTS OF TRUTH

1.   You are front-office manager in an airport motel of 150 rooms. The company you work for has just given you a promotion; you have been named front office manager of a 300-room luxury hotel located in center city. During your first week at the new job, you quietly evaluate members of staff and notice that one desk clerk is far more able than the others. He appears to be a member of a religious minority; he always wears a small neat cap to keep his head covered. It is also clear that others on the staff try to exclude him from their conversations and activities whenever possible, and this seems to be having a negative effect on communications and on team cooperation. You overhear one staff member telling another that this desk clerk is weird because he always wears a hat. What should you do?

2.   You have just taken a job as manager of a tablecloth restaurant. One of the featured items is chicken Tetrazzini, which is made with fresh chicken breast, cream, and butter. The ingredients are identified on the menu. Early in the dinner hour on Friday night, the chef informs you that he is running out of chicken tetrazzini and no more fresh chicken breasts are available. He can make more chicken tetrazzini only if he uses frozen chicken roll from the freezer. What would you direct the chef to do? What would you direct servers to tell customers in the dining room?

3.   You are in charge of the marketing department of a large hotel located in a small midwestern city that is home to two large universities, one public and one private. A large percentage of your rooms business comes from the universities. The private university has booked 50 single rooms for a group coming from Saudi Arabia for a conference. You are advised that most of these guests speak no English and have never been outside their native country. The university's conference coordinator informs you that this is a VIP group and she will gladly pay for special services to make its members comfortable. What special services would you suggest?

4.   You are food and beverage manager in a hotel with a restaurant and bar that stays open until 1:00 A.M. It is now 11:00 P.M., the dinner service is over, and you are in the foodservice area supervising the nightly cleanup. You are called to the bar, where you learn that a regular customer, a man who lives over 20 miles away, appears to have had too much to drink. The bar is crowded, and this customer is demanding another drink. The bartender does not want to serve him, and the customer is becoming loud and disruptive. What should you do?

GLOSSARY

The following terms and definitions are from material in this text. It should be noted that many of the terms have different definitions when used in other contexts. For example, the term *reservation* can have several meanings, only one of which is specific to the travel and tourism industry. Thus, many of the definitions in this glossary apply only to their use in the hospitality and travel industries.

A

Accommodations
The most basic element in the lodging service product line. Accommodations are the specific rooms, suites, or other sleeping facilities that will be offered to the public.

Accommodations and Meals Package
A travel package that includes hotel accommodations and meals. Such packages vary considerably. Some include three meals per day; others include specified meals: full English breakfast daily, or dinner the second night, for example. Some include free access to sports facilities, such as golf courses and tennis courts. Others offer discounts on sporting activities. Some also offer sightseeing and other entertainment.

Accommodations Package
A travel package that normally includes lodging alone. Such packages are really just discounts on room rates. Some are available for particular seasons only or on specified dates. Others are limited to particular numbers of nights.

Accounting
Broadly defined, "the process of identifying, measuring, and communicating economic information to permit informed judgments and decisions by users of the information." In practical terms, the process of analyzing, recording, classifying, reporting, and interpreting financial information that reflects the financial condition of an organization.

Accounting Cycle
A sequence of procedures used to record and summarize transactions for an accounting period; to organize the summary data into financial reports, called statements; and to prepare for the next sequential accounting period.

Accounting Principles
The rules generally accepted by the accounting profession for analyzing, recording, classifying, reporting, and interpreting financial information.

Accumulated Depreciation
A bookkeeping figure that indicates a theoretical lessening in the value of an asset from the time it was purchased.

Advertising
Paid, nonpersonal communication directed to potential buyers.

Affinity Group Package
A travel package designed for groups of people who share some common bond. Examples of affinity groups include students in the same college, alumni of a university, members of a social club, a religious organization, or a fraternity or a sorority, or members of a given profession: doctors, dentists, or lawyers.

Air Conditioning
Treatment of the air in a building that changes that air in any way. Heating, cooling, humidifying, de-

humidifying, and filtering are all air-conditioning processes.

Airline Catering
The business of providing food for service to passengers and crew during a flight.

Airline Deregulation Act of 1978
An act passed by Congress to increase competition and provide airlines with more freedom to choose routes and set rates. It has had a significant impact on the airline industry.

All-Inclusive Package
A travel package that provides most or all of the necessary elements of travel, including transportation, accommodations, meals, transfers (ground transportation between an airport and a hotel or similar lodging property), entertainment, sightseeing, sports, taxes, and gratuities.

All-Inclusive Resort
A resort that commonly includes sleeping accommodations, all meals, entertainment, and activities in the quoted rate, which may also include round-trip airfare, liquor, and gratuities. The best-known all-inclusive resort is Club Med.

All-Suite Hotel
A hotel that does not offer the traditional bedroom and bath accommodations provided by most hotels, only suites, which include facilities for limited cooking. Most all-suite hotels do not have traditional restaurants or bars, and most have no public meeting rooms. Many, however, provide some form of limited foodservice or beverage service, or both. Free breakfast buffets in the lobby, food vending machines in designated areas, and in-room bars are some of the possibilities.

Ambience
The aesthetic impact of an establishment on its customers. Ambience has any number of elements—furnishings, lighting, sound, decoration, theme, table setting, employees' appearances and attitudes, and so on—all aspects of the establishment's environment.

American Plan (A.P.)
A rate plan that includes three meals daily—breakfast, luncheon, and dinner—with the room rate.

American Service
Service characterized by food portioned and plated in the kitchen, then carried to diners by servers.

Americans with Disabilities Act
A key act of Congress that prohibits discrimination against people with any physical or mental impairment that substantially limits one or more major life activities. Passed in 1990.

Amtrak
The U.S. national passenger railway system established by Congress in 1971.

Arithmetic Average
Determined by adding a series of figures, then dividing the total by the number of figures it contains.

Asset
Anything of value. The term is used to identify those items listed on a balance sheet as having value to an organization. Stated another way, assets are what a business organization owns.

Automation
The use of electronic and mechanical equipment and machinery to take the place of humans in doing physical or mental work.

Average Rate per Occupied Room
Calculated by dividing the room revenue for a given period by the number of rooms occupied in that period.

Average Sale per Customer
Calculated by dividing total dollar sales for a given period by the number of customers served in that period.

B

Back Bar
A storage and display facility located behind a bartender. It is commonly used to display some or all of the wines and liquors available at the bar, and may also be used as a storage area for clean glassware. The compartments underneath are used for storage of bar supplies, which may include beers, wines, liquors, mixers, paper supplies, and any other item used at the bar. If these compartments are re-

frigerated, they may be used to store bottled beers and such food supplies used in beverage production as milk, cream, lemons, limes, and fruit juices.

Balance Sheet

A financial statement listing the assets, liabilities, and value of ownership claims to the assets of a business entity as of a specific date.

Banquet

The prearranged service of food and beverages to a group of people. Banquets are normally held in private rooms but are sometimes held in reserved areas of larger public dining rooms.

Banquet Department

The catering operation of a hotel. This department prepares and serves food to groups, usually in separate dining facilities. Most large hotels have a separate kitchen for preparing food served to groups.

Bar

That part of the front bar where customers sit or stand and consume their beverages. Bars also serve as a serving station for drinks and, frequently, as a platform for mixing drinks.

Bed-and-Breakfast Establishment

A small owner-operated lodging business that includes sleeping accommodations and breakfast in the quoted rate. Bed-and-breakfasts normally occupy the owner's home. While they vary in quality, a growing number are operated at high standards rivaling that of fine hotels.

Bermuda Plan

See Breakfast Plan.

Beverage

See Beverage Service.

Beverage Cost Percent

The ratio of beverage cost to beverage sales, expressed as a percentage. Beverages are those alcoholic and nonalcoholic drinks typically prepared by bartenders.

Beverage Service

Providing alcoholic and other beverages for consumption on premises. The term *beverage* includes all alcoholic and nonalcoholic drinks typically prepared by bartenders.

Beverage Service Establishment

An establishment that provides beverage service for its customers. In many cases, it provides food as well. Food sales may even constitute the major source of sales revenue.

Boardinghouse

A residential facility that provides lodging and meals for guests who normally consider the facility their home, whether temporarily or permanently. The services provided are typically restricted to limited housekeeping and meals, which tends to distinguish the boardinghouse from the residential hotel. Boardinghouses are inexpensive, compared with residential and other hotels.

Breakfast Plan (B.P.)

A rate plan that includes a full breakfast with the room rate. Sometimes called the Bermuda Plan.

Buffet Service

A self-service arrangement characterized by diners serving themselves from a selection of foods attractively displayed on a long table or counter. Typically, each diner carries a plate, determines selections, places desired quantities of selected foods on the plate, then takes the plate to a table to consume the food. A set price is usually charged for each person, regardless of particular foods or quantities selected.

Budget

A financial plan developed for a period in the future. Therefore, a budget can be viewed as a manager's attempt to project future financial performance.

Business and Industry Foodservice

A term used to identify organizations that provide food for employees of particular firms in their offices or factories during business hours.

C

Café

A type of foodservice establishment with roots in eighteenth-century France. Café is the French word for coffee, and it is probable that cafés were the French equivalents of the English coffeehouses.

Cafeteria Service

A self-service arrangement characterized by diners selecting foods from a complete array of all foods available. Diners typically have trays and proceed to the area where the kinds of foods they want are displayed. Items are priced separately. After the customer finishes making selections, the prices of his selections are totaled by a cashier. The customer pays the cashier and takes the tray to a table.

Capital

See Owner's Equity.

Caravanserai

Early inns established along trade routes in the Middle East. They tended to be dirty, bug-infested establishments.

Casino Hotel

A transient hotel that features gaming casinos. Major amounts of space are allocated to casino gaming, which includes games of chance using cards or dice—blackjack, roulette, and poker, for example—and slot machines.

Catering

Preparing and serving food to groups of people gathered for a specific purpose, such as attending a meeting or celebrating a wedding. Some caterers prepare and serve food only in their own halls; others prepare food in their own kitchens but serve only in premises provided by their clients. Some both prepare and serve in premises provided by the client.

Ceremony

A gathering of people for the purpose of honoring, remembering, or celebrating an event or individual(s).

Chain Restaurant

A restaurant linked to others by some common identifiable characteristic, such as their products, or their ownership, or their physical appearance. Wendy's, Pizza Hut, and Kentucky Fried Chicken are all examples of chain restaurants.

Chamber of Commerce

Organization of businesses in a specific geographical area, established to promote the area and to foster business development and growth in the area. In areas that are economically dependent on travel and tourism, chambers of commerce have offices that provide information and assistance to travelers and refer them to local hotels, motels, and other properties.

Check-in

The process by which people become guests in a lodging establishment. Check-in takes place in a reception area, another name for that part of a front office known as the front desk. Here, guests register, are assigned accommodations, and pick up keys for accommodations.

Checkout

The process by which guests terminate their status as guests of a lodging establishment. During checkout, guests surrender keys, verify the accuracy of their bills, and settle their accounts.

Club Foodservice

A term used to identify operations that provide foodservice in clubs and similar membership establishments.

Coaching Inn

Lodging establishment located along a stagecoach route. At the coaching inns, tired horses were exchanged for fresh horses, and stagecoach passengers were fed and given opportunities to rest, frequently overnight.

Coffeehouse

Foodservice establishments found in England beginning in the sixteenth century. They provided fresh-brewed coffee and light snacks.

Coffee Shop

Traditionally, an American foodservice establishment with a limited menu designed to attract customers seeking coffee and some light accompaniment—a doughnut, a sandwich, or a slice of pie. Today, most coffee shops have extensive menus more nearly resembling those of diners.

Commercial Foodservice Operation

One operated for profit.

Commercial Hotel

A specialized property that caters to business travelers, such as executives and sales personnel, in need of transient lodgings. The term dates from the early twentieth century, when a number of newly constructed hotels—Statler's Buffalo property among them—were designed to accommodate single business travelers, providing the types of rooms and services that would appeal to these anticipated guests.

Commercial Lodging Industry

That business-oriented segment of the lodging industry that provides transient accommodations to travelers. It consists of such profit-oriented lodging properties as hotels, motels, and inns.

Commissary

A central facility where food is prepared for service elsewhere. The term is used for facilities preparing airline food served to passengers on board planes as well as facilities preparing food for such establishments as schools and chain restaurants.

Communications System

System designed to enable guests, managers, staff members, and others outside the property to communicate with each other.

Concept

An imaginative and unifying idea of the food and beverage or lodging operation that serves to focus on the type of operation, its potential customers, and its location.

Condominium

A furnished housing unit that contains a kitchen, living room, sleeping area, and bath. Condominiums are distinguished from other types of lodging establishments by their ownership characteristics. Each condominium unit in a complex is independently owned, but the management of the complex provides maintenance for the outside and the common inside areas of the facility for a monthly fee. In addition, the grounds and other facilities are usually owned jointly by all of the condominium owners.

Conference Center

A facility designed to accommodate meetings and conference business. Conference centers are typically located in suburban and rural areas and are designed to provide a setting comparatively free of distractions. Thus, conference centers tend to be conducive to concentration and learning and are selected by groups that require such settings for productive work.

Contintental Breakfast Plan

A rate plan that includes a light breakfast with the room rate. The composition of the light breakfast varies from one establishment to another. In some, it is limited to juice, Danish pastry—also known as sweet rolls in some parts of the country—and a choice of coffee or tea. In others, it includes an array of juices, fruits, pastries, croissants, rolls, bagels, and doughnuts, and a choice of regular and decaffeinated coffee and tea.

Controllable Expenses

Expenses that managers can control or change in the near term.

Controlling

One of the functions of management; a process used by managers to regulate and, sometimes, restrain the actions of people in order to achieve desired goals. The process consists of managerial decisions and actions aimed at achieving desired goals.

Control Process

A process consisting of four steps:
1. Establish standards and standard procedures for operation.
2. Train employees to follow established standards and standard procedures.
3. Monitor employee performance and compare actual performance with established standards.
4. Take appropriate action to correct deviations in performance.

Convenience Food

Foods purchased in other than its original state, such as canned goods, breads, baked goods, and so on.

Convention

An assembly of members of an organization, delegates representing members, or simply individuals with a common interest or concern. Conventions are special events, typically held annually, and are normally international, national, or regional in scope.

Convention Hotel

A hotel that focuses on conventions as the primary source of business.

Convention and Meeting Package

A package, typically offered by hotels and sponsoring organizations, that commonly includes accommodations, meals, sightseeing, and other activities.

Convention and Meeting Planner

An employee of or consultant to corporations, government agencies, and other large organizations whose profession is planning and running conventions and meetings.

Convention and Visitors' Bureau

A government-sponsored agency established to attract groups, business meetings, conventions, tours, and other forms of tourism to the city or region they represent. They frequently assist in convention arrangements and often act as housing coordinators for convention groups.

Corporate Travel Office

An office that makes travel arrangements for corporate personnel traveling on business.

Cost Control

The process of regulating costs and guarding against excessive costs.

Counter Service

A type of service characterized by the service of food on a level surface known as a counter, on which servers place customers' selections. The customers may be either seated at the counter or standing, and they may consume the food at the counter or at some other location within the establishment.

Cruising

See Vacation Cruising.

Cultural Impact

The impact of tourism on the culture of an area—the customary beliefs, social forms, and daily life of a racial, religious, or social group. Tourism can help preserve the established culture, or it can aid in changing it.

Current Asset

Assets not expected to last beyond one year. For hospitality operations, they include cash, inventories, accounts receivable, food, liquor, and supplies.

Current Liability

Financial obligation due to be paid within the next accounting period.

Cycle of Service

The complete chain of events experienced by a customer, from his first contact with an organization to the point when he considers the service complete. It is the sum total of the customer's moments of truth.

D

De Facto Recognition

A form of recognition acknowledging the existence of a government without supporting the means by which it came to power.

De Jure Recognition

A form of recognition acknowledging both the existence of a government and the means by which it came to power.

Diner

A foodservice establishment that normally is moderately priced, offers full service, and is typically open long hours—sometimes 24 hours a day—serving breakfast, lunch, and dinner from a single multipage menu. In most diners, the customer can order any meal at any hour—breakfast at 11 P.M., for example.

Direct Provider of Travel Services

A business in direct contact with travelers that provides the services necessary for their travel. Examples include hotels, restaurants, airlines, travel agents, and rental car companies.

Directing

One of the functions of management; the process of achieving organizational goals by leading, motivating, and supervising subordinates.

Discount Outlet Center

A collection of retail stores specializing in the sale of name-brand merchandise at discount prices.

Diversity

The inclusion of people with differences in ethnicity, gender, religion, sexual orientation, national origin, and cultural background. Both the hospitality workforce and its customer base are diverse in this respect.

Dormitory

A lodging facility, affiliated with some educational or other institution, that provides sleeping accommodations for those in residence at the institution. This institutional affiliation differentiates a dormitory from a lodging house.

Drive-in

A restaurant with a large parking lot that features food served to customers seated in their parked automobiles. Orders are taken from customer, conveyed to the kitchen, and served when ready. The food is served on special trays that hook onto the frame of the open automobile window, and customers can eat without leaving their cars. In some drive-ins, servers are equipped with roller skates to speed service.

Drive-through

An operation at which a customer can drive a vehicle to a window to obtain and pay for food without ever leaving the vehicle. Having received the food, the customer drives away to consume the food elsewhere.

Dumbwaiter

A small, specialized elevator that carries food (no passengers) between floors of a hotel.

E

Economic Impact

The increased level of economic activity in an area as a result of tourism. It is generally measured in additional jobs and income to an area.

Economy Bus Tour

An inexpensive tour. Accommodations are likely to be in a budget motel. Meals are likely to be simple: extensive menu choices and gourmet cuisine are unlikely. If the tour includes admissions to events, the seats are not likely to be the best.

Electrical System

A system consisting of wires of various sizes, circuit breakers or fuses, switches, and outlets that facilitate the safe use of electrical power.

Elevator

A vertical transportation system designed to move people and supplies. Hotels typically have guest elevators and service elevators.

Empire Era

The period from 3200 B.C. to A.D. 476, when several empires existed around the Mediterranean Sea. The most important of these were the Egyptian, Greek, and Roman empires.

Employee Assistance Plan

The collective activities undertaken by an employer to assist employees in dealing with such problems as substance abuse and a range of issues relating to physical health, mental health, personal and family finance, the law, and education, among many possibilities.

Employee Empowerment

A service industry condition wherein employees have the power to make decisions about how best to meet the needs of a guest or customer.

Employee Turnover

The ratio of new employees to departed employees.

Energy Control System

A system designed to manage the use of energy. The four most common energy control systems are time clocks, automatic sensors, electric demand meters, and computerized systems.

English Service

Service is characterized by a main entrée—a roast of beef or lamb, or a turkey, for example—placed in front of the host at the head of the table, who then carves and plates it. A server places the plates in front of diners. Accompanying items may be put on plates by servers at a side stand, served Russian style, or passed family style.

Entertainment

Diverting or engaging sights and sounds that presumably hold one's attention and occupy one's mind for some period. Entertainment does not normally suggest physical activity of the type associated with recreation.

Entertainment Area

A geographical area that has become well known as a center or focal point for some type of entertainment.

Environmental Impact

The effect tourism has on the local environment—positive or negative, depending on one's point of view.

Escalators

Moving stairs designed to transport large numbers of people over short distances—usually one or two floors.

Ethnic Restaurant

A restaurant that specializes in foods associated with a particular culture. Among the most common of these are Chinese, Mexican, Greek, Japanese, German, Italian, Spanish, and Indian.

European Plan (E.P.)

A rate plan that includes no meals with the room rate. The European Plan is the standard in most American transient hotels.

Events Package

A travel package focused on a particular event or performance—a football game, festival, theater production, or art exhibit, among other possibilities. Events packages usually include transportation and admissions to the event or performance and may include such other features as accommodations, meals, and rental cars.

Exhibition

A show that is usually smaller than an exposition. It can be aimed at entertaining, enlightening, or instructing the public, offering specific goods or services for sale, or providing opportunities for competition and judging. It may or may not be open to the public.

Expense

A cost associated with doing business.

Exposition

A show similar to an exhibition, but larger and open to the public.

Extended-Stay Hotel

A property that caters to those who intend to stay longer than typical transient guests and who seek accommodations other than the traditional hotel accommodations of bedroom and bath. The typical extended-stay hotel provides a homelike environment and attempts to minimize its resemblance to other commercial lodging facilities. Accommodations in extended-stay hotels resemble those in a fine garden apartment complex—a suite consisting of kitchen, living room, bedroom, and bath and recreational facilities for swimming and other forms of exercise. Suites in extended-stay hotels commonly feature exterior entrances and parking by the door.

F

Fair

An assembly of amusement or carnival rides, exhibitions of educational, farm and household products, contests, activities and games of every sort, and food concessions.

Familiarization Trip

Travel to resorts, cities, sights, and the like for travel agents. The trips are sponsored by airlines and other travel suppliers; the cost is normally absorbed by the sponsoring organization. They are referred to as FAM trips.

Family Restaurant

A restaurant that caters to family groups—parents with children and other contemporary family groupings. In order to appeal to families, operators must make important decisions with respect to menu, food quality, menu prices, service, and ambience.

Family Vacation Package

A travel package that includes accommodations at specific destinations and attractions that appeal particularly to families: Disney World, Sea World, or Busch Gardens, for example. It normally includes other appealing features as well—some type of child care for part of the vacation, for example, so that adults can have time for themselves.

Fast-Food Establishment

A restaurant at which there is little or no waiting for the food. Many such establishments are beginning to identify themselves as fast-service or quick-service restaurants to emphasize that the service is fast, not the food.

Feasibility Study

An investigation of a given project's likelihood for success. It normally includes, as a minimum, an analysis of the intended location, competition, finances, local building requirements, and market.

Fee Ownership Time-Share

A form of time-share whereby purchasers own a period of time in a specific time-share facility. The time-share can be sold or willed to others.

Festival

A celebration dedicated to film, dance, music art, religion, or other purpose.

Feudalism

A system whereby land was given by a ruler in return for loyalty and service. It existed primarily during the Decline and Revival Period in Europe.

Financial Accounting

A branch of accounting concerned with analyzing, recording, classifying, and summarizing the day-to-day transactions of an organization.

Fine-Dining Establishment

A restaurant where the emphasis is on high-quality foods that are expertly prepared and professionally served. Fine-dining establishments tend to use few convenience foods, and most foods are prepared from fresh ingredients. Such restaurants are typically formal and often expensive.

Fire Safety System

A system designed to detect, contain, or extinguish fires and to alert both guests and employees to danger. Some also summon fire and police personnel to the danger.

Fixed Asset

An asset that will last beyond one year.

Fixed Charges

Expenses that management cannot change in the short run, such as rent, insurance expenses, and property taxes.

Fly/Cruise Package

A travel package that includes air transportation to and from a point of departure, transfers, and a cruise. Fly/cruise packages are almost always all-inclusive, meaning that the package price includes the cost of airfare, accommodations, all meals, and entertainment. Gratuities and sightseeing are typically extra.

Fly/Cruise/Hotel Package

A travel package that includes air transportation, a cruise, and a specified number of nights at a hotel. These packages are typically offered by cruise line companies, such as Cunard, that own resort hotels in the vicinity of the ship's point of departure.

Fly/Drive Package

A travel package that includes airfare and rental car only. These packages are intended for travelers who prefer to make their own travel plans. They are usually prepared by airlines in partnership with rental car companies.

Food Cost Percent

The ratio of food cost to food sales.

Food Quality

The degree of excellence in food products.

Foodservice

The act of providing foods fully prepared for immediate consumption on or off premises.

Foot-Candle

The amount of light that can be measured at a distance of one foot from an ordinary candle.

Fortified Wine

A still wine to which brandy has been added to enhance the flavor and to increase the alcoholic content. Sherry is among the best-known fortified wines.

Franchise

A contract between two parties—a franchisor and a franchisee—that grants the franchisee the right to use the franchisor's name, sell its products, and participate in its programs and services under set, specific conditions.

Frequent-Guest Program

A program established by a hospitality operation to reward guests for frequent stays. The rewards include free accommodations, airline miles, upgraded accommodations, and the like.

French Service

Service characterized by the use of a gueridon, a specially equipped cart or trolley on which food is transported from kitchen to dining room. The food is carved or otherwise finished in preparation, plated, then served to customers.

Frequent-Flyer Program

An incentive program that awards mileage for travel on a given airline and provides rewards for accumulated mileage. The awards may include upgrades to first-class seats, free flights, free car rentals, and free hotel rooms.

Front Bar

A fixed counter for beverage service, directly accessible to customers and open for business on a regularly scheduled basis. Front bars are permanently fixed in locations within establishments.

Front Office

The location where the front desk is situated within a lodging property. To guests, the front office represents the lodging property; it is their first point of contact on arrival and last point of contact at departure.

Front Service

A term comprising a variety of useful and desirable personal services for guests. These include attended service at the front door for handling luggage, obtaining taxicabs, and opening doors; escorting guests from the front desk to the assigned accommodations; carrying luggage for guests; opening guest room doors for those having difficulty with their keys; delivering newspapers, mail, packages, or telephone messages to guests' rooms; providing information about restaurants, theaters, shopping, and sightseeing (if this is not done at the front desk); and making reservations or providing tickets for shows, tours, sporting events, and transportation.

G

Gambling

Any form of wagering on the outcome of an event, including lotteries, racing, and casino gambling.

Gaming

Another term for casino gambling.

Golden Age of Hotels

The decade of the 1920s—popularly known as the Roaring Twenties—was an important period of hotel development. It is called the golden age of hotels because of the large number of hotels constructed, their size, and the high occupancy rates they were able to maintain.

Grand Tour

A tourist activity that began in the sixteenth century. Wealthy English parents would send their sons on a tour of Europe to finish their education. The tour lasted as long as three years.

Great Depression

The period in U.S. history from the collapse of the stock market in 1929 to the beginning of World War II, when the country was in an economic collapse.

Guaranteed Reservation

A room reservation that a lodging establishment guarantees to hold provided the guest guarantees payment for one night.

Gueridon

A specially equipped cart or trolley on which food is transported from the kitchen to dining room. It is equipped with a gas burner for tableside cooking and is used in French service.

Guest Check

The guest bill, presented to a customer for payment, on which is written items purchased by the customer and their prices.

Guest House

See Tourist Home.

Guest Ranch

A resort property that emphasizes horseback riding and related activities. Guest ranches are typically properties containing fewer than 100 rooms; they provide housekeeping services, food, and other seasonal recreational facilities—swimming, tennis, and hunting, for example.

H

Health Spa

A lodging establishment that focuses on providing beneficial health-related services. Many spas specialize—some in weight reduction, others in cosmetic therapy or drug or alcohol rehabilitation, among many others. The newest form of health spa uses a holistic approach, emphasizing relaxation, exercise, and healthy foods.

Heating System

A system designed to raise the temperature of air and water in a building. Common resources include oil, gas, electricity, steam, coal, and solar energy.

Hospital

A specialized lodging facility established to provide medical care for the sick. It offers sleeping accommodations and many of the same services provided by hotels, including housekeeping, room service, telephone, television, and a pharmacy—and, often, such additional services as hair stylists, gift shops, and lending libraries.

Hospitality

A term derived from the Latin word *hospitare*, meaning to receive as a guest—a phrase that implies a host prepared to meet a guest's basic requirements while that guest is away from home—food, beverages, or lodging.

Hospitality Industry

The industry comprising businesses that provide food, beverages, or lodging to travelers.

Hostel

An inexpensive lodging establishment that typically caters to young, transient customers. It provides little or no service and very little privacy. The typical hostel provides a bed for the night and offers no frills. Some hostels provide a community kitchen in which guests may prepare their own meals. Everyone staying in a hostel is expected to participate in keeping it clean. There is usually a limit to the number of nights an individual is allowed to stay.

Hotel

Traditionally, a lodging facility of two stories or more that provides sleeping accommodations and other services for its guests. Hotels commonly offer housekeeping services and luggage-carrying assistance as well as food, beverages, telephone, and other services. The extent of these services varies from property to property. Some hotels provide the full range: restaurants; bars; cocktail lounges; room service; hair stylists; exercise salons; computer, photocopy, and fax facilities; laundry; dry cleaners; gift shops; check cashing and other financial services; newsstands; travel agencies; drugstores; and others. Other hotels provide nothing beyond the basics: sleeping accommodations and housekeeping services.

Hotel Representative

An individual or firm that represents hotels—usually a number of them in many locations—and sells the services of those hotels directly to individuals, businesses, and groups. Usually called a hotel rep.

Housekeeping

A basic component of the lodging service product line. The principal goal of housekeeping is to serve the needs of guests by providing appropriate care for their accommodations and for other areas in a lodging property. However, many lodging operations assign additional goals to housekeeping, including uniform maintenance and care of offices.

Housekeeping Area

That part of the lodging facility occupied by housekeeping personnel. In large hotels, the housekeeping area can occupy several rooms and include storage for linen, uniforms, and housekeeping equipment, plus offices for housekeeping management.

Hub-and-Spoke Routing

A system of routing aircraft meant to fill the maximum number of seats on each flight and to simplify scheduling. Each airline has several major airports that serve as hubs and provide meeting points for planes coming from outlying cities (spokes). Flight schedules are established so that many planes arrive at the hub at about the same time. Passengers then change planes and proceed to their destinations.

Human Resources Management

The branch of managerial activity aimed at implementing the strategies, plans, and programs required to attract, motivate, develop, reward, and retain the best people to meet the organizational goals and operational objectives of the hospitality enterprise.

HVAC

An acronym formed from the first letters of the terms *heating*, *ventilation*, and *air conditioning*.

I

Incentive Package

A vacation package sponsored by a corporation and offered to employees as a reward for superior performance—high-volume sales of a product or service, or some other achievement beyond the norm.

Incentive Travel Firm

A firm that develops and/or sells incentive packages to corporations.

Income Statement
A financial statement that summarizes sales (or revenues) and expenses of an organization for a given period—normally one year, but income statements can be prepared for any period of time.

Information Activity
That part of guest service that provides information to guests about a wide range of subjects including hotel activities, services, and facilities as well as information about goods and services located outside the lodging establishment. Information about guests is also provided to designated individuals and departments of the hotel. Information activity is normally provided to guests at the front desk or through front service.

Inn
A term, brought to the United States from England in the early seventeenth century, that originally meant an establishment providing rooms, food, and entertainment to both travelers and residents of the local community. Over the years, the term came to be used for three types of hospitality enterprises.
1. A small, typically rural lodging establishment that may or may not serve food
2. A larger property—one that normally might be known as a hotel or motel—that wishes to convey an image of smallness and caring for their customers
3. A restaurant or bar that has no sleeping accommodations

Institutional Foodservice
A foodservice operation whose principal purpose is the preparation of food for those associated with a particular institution. The institution may be any of a wide range of service organizations, public and private, that attend to one of many possible public needs. Schools, colleges, hospitals, nursing homes, and prisons are common examples of institutions.

Internationalization
(1) The tendency of national hospitality firms to expand operations beyond national borders—to go global. (2) The special effort that hospitality firms are making to cater to the needs of international visitors.

Inventory Turnover
A ratio identifying the rate at which inventory is consumed and replaced during an operating period.

Issuing
The process of removing items from a storeroom and taking them to the person who requisitioned them.

J

Job Description
A detailed written statement that describes a job. The job description for any specific job should answer three important questions:
1. What is to be done?
2. When is it done?
3. Where is it done?

K

Kelly Act
Passed by the U.S. Congress in 1926, it authorized long-term mail contracts for airlines. The passage of the Kelly Act led to the founding of many airline companies.

L

Labor Cost Percentage
The cost of labor (including employee benefits) divided by total sales.

Liabilities
Items on a balance sheet identifying financial obligations to others. Stated another way, liabilities indicate what a business organization owes.

Limited-Menu
An establishment in which management has made a conscious decision to restrict the number of items on the menu.

Liquidity
The ability of an asset to be converted into cash.

Lodge
Traditionally, a lodging establishment associated with an outdoor activity, such as ski lodge or hunting lodge. This type of lodge was a small establishment, typically in a rural setting, that provided food

and housekeeping services to guests who came to be with others engaging in the same activity. A substantial number of properties are known as motor lodges. For all practical purposes, *motor lodge* is merely another name for a motel.

Lodging House

A boardinghouse that does not provide meals. See Boardinghouse.

Lodging Property

An establishment that charges a fee for providing furnished sleeping accommodations to persons who are temporarily away from home or who consider these accommodations their temporary or permanent homes. Many of these establishments also provide food, beverages, cleaning services, and a range of other services normally associated with travel and commonly sought by travelers.

Long-Term Liability

A financial obligation due beyond the current accounting period.

Lumen

A measure of light. One lumen per square foot equals one foot-candle.

Luxury Bus Tour

A tour that offers the best of everything. The motor coach is as comfortable as any available anywhere. Lodging is in luxury hotels and similar superior properties, and meals are excellent. If tickets are included, they are for the best available seats. On luxury tours, everything is usually included in the tour price, so those on the tour have no need to pay for extras, except for personal needs.

M

Mall

An enclosed structure designed to accommodate stores and common walkways under one roof, making shopping possible in virtually any weather.

March

A gathering of people who try to focus public attention on an issue by marching and carrying signs.

Marketing

The process of planning service products, finding the right place to locate, and pricing and promoting products to attract sufficient numbers of customers/guests and to create exchanges that satisfy both their needs and the goals of the hospitality enterprise.

Market Segment

A portion of a total market that a business wishes to attract and for which it designs a product or service.

Menu

A list of the items offered for sale in a food or beverage enterprise. A menu is also a sales tool that influences customers' orders and the dollar amounts they spend.

Merchandising

Actions taken to increase sales to customers already present in an establishment.

Mise en Place

A French culinary term meaning having everything in place. In other words, all advance preparation is completed.

Modified American Plan (M.A.P.)

A rate plan that includes breakfast and dinner with the room rate. Luncheon is often available for an extra charge.

Moment of Truth

Any encounter between a customer and a business, whether or not an employee of the business is present.

Motel

Traditionally, a type of lodging establishment that catered to travelers with automobiles and provided self-service parking on premises. The original motels were single-story properties providing basic sleeping accommodations to overnight travelers. They were inexpensive and offered free parking and housekeeping service, but little else. Staff was kept to a minimum to keep costs down. None of the services normally associated with hotels—room service, bellmen, restaurants, and the like—were offered. Motels were located on the outskirts of cities and towns and catered to those who did not want the expense and formality of a hotel. Later, many had adequate land to expand and to add swimming pools, which helped differentiate motels from hotels and attracted new customers. Over the years, many motels evolved into properties that so resemble hotels that it is impossible to identify differences. Many are multistoried, provide full services, and are located in the centers of cities.

Motor Coach Package
A special-purpose bus tour for people interested in shopping, sightseeing, or attending a particular sports event, for example. It is planned by motor coach operators and other tour companies. If a tour is to take more than one day, the price normally includes accommodations, meals, and entertainment.

Motor Inn
Originally, a motel property whose proprietors wished to convey both the concept of free parking and the traditions of an inn—a kind of modern inn. During the 1950s and 1960s, when older hotels were no longer in favor because of competition from motels, many hotel properties that had parking facilities on premises or nearby changed their names from hotel to motor inn in order to compete with motels.

Motor Lodge
Another name for motel.

N

National Restaurant Association
The national organization that represents all restaurants in the United States. It researches and publishes data on the restaurant industry, performs educational seminars and conducts educational programs, and acts as the lobbying arm of the restaurant industry.

Neighborhood Restaurant
A restaurant that caters to the needs, tastes, and preferences of people living or working nearby. In general, neighborhood restaurants reflect the character of the neighborhoods in which they are found.

Noncommercial Foodservice Operation
A foodservice operation established for the convenience of its clientele and not for profit.

Nonperishable
Food that keeps for extended periods before spoiling. It is typically packaged in cans, jars, bags, bottles, and boxes; it may be dried or frozen. Sometimes referred to simply as nonperishables, these foods are ordered infrequently and can be ordered in large quantities because of their long shelf life.

No-Show
A guest with a reservation who fails to check in.

Nursing Home
A residential facility that provides lodging and foodservice for people requiring nursing or related care. People residing in nursing homes tend to be temporarily or permanently infirm, physically or mentally.

O

On Change
A term describing a guest room that is vacant but not yet ready for occupancy by guests.

Operating Budget
A financial plan for generating a given amount of revenue at a given level of expenditure in a coming period. Operating budgets are usually based on income statements from the most recent operating periods.

Operating Expenses
Controllable expenses, including wages, laundry, cleaning supplies, uniforms, office supplies, repairs, energy costs, telephone expense, and various fees.

Operating Ratio
A ratio that measures overall performance in some specific area. Four operating ratios commonly used in hospitality are percentage of occupancy, seat turnover, inventory turnover, and profitability.

Operations Management
The collection of day-to-day activities that managers engage in to achieve the goals of the operations they manage.

Ordinary
An old term used originally in Great Britain to describe a midday meal served at a fixed price in a tavern to the local inhabitants. The term also came to mean the tavern itself. Throughout the colonial American period, the terms *ordinary*, *tavern*, and *inn* were all used to refer to the same basic institution—an enterprise providing food, drink, overnight accommodations, or some combination of these to travelers, local residents, or both. Over time, *tavern*

became the more common term from New England to New York; *inn* became favored in the Pennsylvania region; and *ordinary* was more common in the South.

Organization Chart

A diagram of the formal structure of the business organization, identifying positions and reporting relationships within it.

Organizing

A function of management; the process of coordinating the use of resources, human and otherwise, to achieve established objectives. To organize work in a hospitality operation, a manager determines how human and other resources will be combined and activated to achieve established objectives.

Orientation

The process of introducing new employees to an organization. Orientation typically addresses organization policies and rules and the mission and objectives of the organization, and includes a tour of the establishment.

Outsourcing

The practice of assigning work to persons or firms that are not employees of the facility. Work commonly outsourced includes security, accounting, laundry and dry cleaning, yard maintenance, and painting.

Overbooking

Taking more reservations than can be accommodated in the number of rooms currently available.

Owner's Equity

The owner's share of the value of assets listed on a balance sheet. The term *capital* is often used as a synonym.

Oyster House

A popular and inexpensive type of restaurant found in American cities in the nineteenth century. Oysters were a popular food in the period, and they were served in establishments also known as oyster cellars, oyster saloons, and oyster wagons.

P

Package

See Travel Package.

Palaces of the Public

A term used to refer to American hotels that suggests not only their public character but also their elegance.

Parade

An organized march. Most parades, such as the Rose Bowl Parade and the Thanksgiving Day Parade, feature bands, various marching personnel, and displays of every sort, and are organized to celebrate a significant event.

Passport

A document, issued by the government of a nation to a citizen of that nation, that officially identifies the individual to whom it is issued. It provides such specifics as the passport holder's name, address, date of birth, occupation, and citizenship status. It includes a photograph of the passport holder.

Percentage of Occupancy

A ratio relating the number of occupied rooms to the total number of rooms available for occupancy.

Performance

A presentation of music, play, act, lecture, or other form of entertainment to a group of people.

Perishable

Food that can be kept for just a short period before it begins to lose its quality—to spoil and become unusable. Perishable foods are typically fresh foods, such as meat, fish, fruit, and vegetables.

Personal Selling

An approach to sales that requires personal contact between buyer and seller. It enables a salesperson to communicate directly with a buyer—to ask and answer questions and to use personal powers of persuasion to sell the service product.

Pilferage

Theft.

Place

A synonym for location when used in hospitality marketing.

Planning

A function of management, perhaps the primary function of managers at all levels; the process of defining goals and objectives, then determining the appropriate means for achieving them.

Posthouse

One of the inns located at regular intervals along established mail routes during the period when the mails were transported by stagecoach. Posthouses were much like coaching inns. They were equipped to provide replacement teams of fresh horses for stagecoaches carrying mail, to feed stagecoach drivers and passengers, and, if necessary, to accommodate them overnight.

Potluck

Early rural innkeepers would go into the nearby woods, kill game, and put it into a pot to cook. This was served to guests, who called it potluck, as it could be game of almost any type.

Pourer

Measuring device that delivers a precise amount of liquor.

Price

An element of marketing; the amount charged for hospitality services.

Primitive Camping

Camping on unimproved sites without the benefit of hot and cold running water, bathrooms, electricity, cooking facilities, and similar comforts.

Producing

The process of preparing foods for consumption in the dining room.

Product

An element of marketing; a service product offered by a hospitality operation. See Product Line.

Product Line

A group of products having similar characteristics. Common examples are shoes, luggage, and jewelry. Foodservice and lodging use the term to mean a group of service products offered by a hospitality enterprise and based on the concept developed for that enterprise.

Production Sheet

A list of menu items to be prepared by a foodservice operation for a specific day or meal period, along with the quantity of each item for production personnel to prepare. Some production sheets also indicate particular recipes to be used in preparation.

Promotion

A marketing process aimed at informing, influencing, and persuading customers to purchase their service products. Five types of promotional activities are commonly used in hospitality operations: personal selling, advertising, sales promotion, merchandising, and public relations.

Public Relations

Activities and efforts designed to improve or enhance the image or reputation of an organization, promote the organization's name, or improve its relations with employees, customers, suppliers, stockholders, and other individuals or groups thought important to the organization.

Purchasing

The process of ordering goods for use in a hospitality facility.

R

Rally

A gathering of people who wish to voice their opinion about an issue and who frequently march with signs to gain the attention of the public.

Rate

The fee charged for sleeping accommodations in a lodging facility; also called room rate.

Ratio

An expression of a relationship between two numbers. In hospitality, ratios are calculated for purposes of making comparisons and judgments.

Receiving

The process of verifying that goods delivered conform in quantity, quality, and price with orders placed.

Recreation

The process or act of creating anew, restoring, or refreshing. The idea of activity is commonly linked to recreation; people often refer to recreational activities. Thus, recreation has to do with activities aimed at restoring or refreshing one's mind, or body, or both of these, presumably after some sort of work.

Recreation Vehicle

A wheeled vehicle with temporary living quarters. Examples of recreation vehicles include motor homes, travel trailers, park trailers, truck campers, folding camping trailers, and van campers.

Recruiting

A process used by managers to find suitable applicants for jobs.

Renaissance

The period in European history from the early fourteenth century to the late sixteenth century. The term is derived from the French word for rebirth.

Reservation

An arrangement by which lodging operators hold accommodations for guests who will arrive at some later time or foodservice operators hold tables for customers who will come later to dine. The guests or customers may make their reservations for the same day or for some date in the future.

Residential Hotel

A hotel offering traditional hotel services—food and beverages, laundry and dry cleaning, telephone, and the like—to people who choose to live permanently in hotels. In contrast to transient hotels, residential hotels provide accommodations for long-term guests—individuals who consider the hotel their temporary or permanent home.

Resort Area

A geographic area that is well known regionally, nationally, or, in some cases, internationally as a center for some recreational activity.

Resort Condominium

A condominium located in a resort area or on a resort property. Condominium units differ from traditional guest rooms; they have kitchen and living room facilities in addition to sleeping accommodations. Guests also have access to the recreational facilities of the resort.

Resort Hotel

A lodging establishment that features recreational activities for guests. These activities may be enjoyable, beneficial, or both. Swimming, tennis, and golf are among the most common, although many others are possible. Some resorts have all the necessary facilities for these activities on premises. Others have only limited recreational facilities on premises and provide their guests with access to other facilities nearby.

Resort Motel

A motel located in a resort area. Many resort motels offer traditional hotel services and most have recreation facilities, although these are likely to be limited compared to those offered in resort hotels.

Restaurant

A foodservice establishment with a dining room open to the public where foods can be purchased and consumed. Dozens of variations exist.

Return on Sales

The ratio of net income to net sales, expressed as a percent. It indicates the portion of each net sales dollar the enterprise earns as profit.

Revenue

A synonym for sales.

Right-to-Use Time-Share

A type of time-share that allows the purchaser to occupy a time-share unit for a certain period—one week for 15, 20, or 25 years, for example. The unit may be a specific room or facility, or, more commonly, a different unit each time the person comes to the facility.

Roadhouse

A roadside restaurant that, during Prohibition, illegally sold alcoholic beverages, alone or as accompaniments to meals, and that provided live or recorded music for dancing.

Room Clerk

A front-office staff members whose duties include checking in guests. Synonyms include desk attendant and guest service representative.

Room Service

A form of dining service, unique to lodging establishments, in which customers have their food and beverage orders delivered to and served in their rooms.

Russian Service

Service characterized by food arranged on a serving platter in the kitchen for maximum eye appeal, then transferred from the serving platter to plates previously placed before each diner.

S

Sales

The income an organization receives as a result of doing business; a synonym of revenue.

Sales History

A record of the number of customers served during past periods as well as the number of portions of each menu item sold in each past period.

Sales Promotion

An inducement offered by a seller to persuade a buyer to make an immediate purchase rather than to wait.

Seat Turnover

The ratio of the number of diners served in a given period to the number of seats available in the dining room; often called turns.

Self-Service

A service arrangement that allows customers to select foods from an array of displayed items, then carry the items, with or without a tray, to some location in the establishment to consume them. Cafeterias, buffets, and salad bars are three common examples of self-service arrangements.

Service

A basic element in the hospitality service product line. Typical examples of services include housekeeping, valet and lodging, security, parking, and front service.

Service Bar

A bar to which customers have no access. Drink orders taken by servers are given to the bartender at the service bar. The bartender prepares the drinks, which are then delivered to customers by the servers who took their orders.

Service Quality Management

See Total Quality Management.

Serving

The process of delivering portions of food or drink to customers in a manner consistent with the objectives of the establishment. Several types of service are commonly used in restaurants: American service, Russian service, French service, and several types of self-service.

Sexual Harassment

As defined by the federal Equal Employment Opportunity Commission, unwelcomed sexual advances, requests for sexual favors, and other verbal or physical conduct of a sexual nature that takes place under any of the following conditions:

1. Submission is made a condition of the person's employment;
2. Submission to or rejection of such conduct is used as a basis for employment decisions affecting the person; or
3. It unreasonably interferes with the person's work performance or creates an intimidating, hostile, or offensive work environment."

Social Impact

The effect of tourism on the social climate of an area. Negative social effects can include resentment of tourists, additional crime and violence, and changes in the social patterns of the local population.

Sparkling Wine

A wine in which the fermentation process is allowed to continue after bottling. This produces carbon dioxide, which gives sparkling wines their characteristic fizziness. Champagne is the best known of the sparkling wines.

Speakeasy

An establishment that sold alcoholic beverages illegally during Prohibition.

Special Event

An event that occurs infrequently and is sufficiently important to attract a large number of people. Some special events, such as the World's Fair, require considerable planning and money.

Special-Interest Package

A travel package designed for a group of people who share a particular interest, perhaps a sport or a hobby. The common interests around which these packages are developed include golf or tennis, photography, wineries, fall foliage, and many others.

Special-Purpose Bar

A bar that, although directly accessible to customers, is open only for a defined period to accommodate a special need. Special-purpose bars are most commonly used in banquet or catering businesses to accommodate guests at special functions—parties, dances, or the receptions preceding special events.

Specialty Channeler

An individual or firm that represents either buyers or sellers of travel services. Specialty channelers make travel arrangements for the parties they represent and do so either directly with the travel supplier or through a travel agent.

Specialty Restaurant

A restaurant that features foods of a particular type, such as seafood, pancakes, chicken, vegetables, steaks, doughnuts, omelettes, or sandwiches. The possibilities for specialties are many and varied, as are the establishments that feature them. Some limit their menus almost exclusively to the specialty, while others use the specialty item as the focal point of the menu but add other items to broaden the restaurant's appeal and attract additional customers.

Stand

A stationary, open-air foodservice establishment with no dining room facility. Customers walk to a counter to order and obtain foods, then consume the foods at the counter or elsewhere, as they prefer.

Standard Purchase Specification

A carefully considered written description of a food item to be purchased. It may include such information as grade, size, count, color, type and size of container, degree of freshness, and other characteristics that vary with the product.

Standard Recipe

A recipe established as the correct one to use each time a given item is prepared.

Standard Bus Tour

A motor coach tour that, in terms of comfort and quality, is rated above a budget tour but below a luxury tour.

Still Wine

A wine in which the fermentation process is stopped before the wine is bottled, as contrasted with sparkling wines, where the fermentation process continues after the wine is bottled.

Storing

The process of placing goods received in a dry storeroom, refrigerated storeroom, or freezer.

Suite

An accommodation consisting of two or more rooms, one of which is a living room—sometimes called a parlor—plus one or more than one bedroom and bathroom. Many have some type of kitchen facility. Some properties offer suites with several bedrooms and baths. Sometimes the term is used to describe a large one-room accommodation with a living room area and a bedroom area rather than separate rooms.

Support Services

The segment of the travel industry that includes the firms and individuals who provide services and supplies to direct providers. These firms and individuals depend on the travel market for all of their business, or for a large part of it. They provide the necessary goods and services that make it possible for direct providers to perform travel services.

Table d'Hôte

A complete meal for one price.

Table Service

A type of service characterized by orders for food and beverages taken from customers seated at tables. The server who takes the orders normally delivers the food and beverages to the customers at their table.

Table Service Restaurant

A restaurant in which customers are seated and served at tables.

Take-out/Delivery Service

Two types of service characterized by the consumption of food off premises. Take-out service means that food is taken from the premises by the customer who ordered it. Delivery service means that an employee of the establishment takes the food from the premises to an address specified by the customer.

Theme Park

A tract of land on which a developer has created a series of exhibits, rides, and other elements, usually designed around some unifying idea. Some elements may not be related to the theme in any way. These may include exciting or entertaining rides, interesting and educational exhibits, or both.

Theme Restaurant

A restaurant designed around a particular theme that is used or reflected in every element of the establishment's ambience. Possibilities for themes include railroad cars or stations, antique automobiles, colonial America, the Old West, medieval dining, World War II, kitchenware—the number is endless, limited only by human imagination.

Time-Share

Sharing the cost and use of a property with others. Time-share takes three forms: fee ownership, right-to-use, and vacation club time-shares.

Tops Restaurant

A food and beverage operation located on the top floor of a hotel or other tall building, usually situated in some part of a major city where the view is interesting or spectacular.

Total Quality Management

A management technique that gives some authority for making decisions about service to the members of staff directly responsible for providing the service. A desired outcome is the tailoring of service to the individualized needs of guests and customers. Some firms use the term *service quality management* to describe the same management technique.

Tour Destination

Any geographic location—country, state, region, area, city, town, or other—that receives appreciable numbers of visitors, regardless of the means of transportation they use to get there.

Tour Operator

A wholesaler that devises and conducts tour packages.

Tour Wholesaler

An individual or firm that devises tours and sells them through travel agents. See Tour Operator.

Tourism

As recommended by the World Tourism Organization and adopted by the United Nations, the term *tourism* comprises the activities of persons traveling to and staying in places outside their usual environment for not more than one consecutive year for leisure, business, and other purposes.

Tourism Development

One of three segments of the travel industry in the classification system proposed by Prof. Chuck Gee. The term identifies the individuals and organizations that have an effect, direct or indirect, on direct providers, support services, and individual travelers. This category includes those with an interest in travel and tourism who are not classified as direct providers, support services, or travelers. Examples of tourism development organizations include the American Hotel and Motel Association, the World Tourism Organization, and schools and colleges that train cooks, hotel workers, and so on.

Tourist

A synonym for traveler. See Traveler.

Tourist Court

A type of motel that existed during the early days of the motel industry. This type was typically a single unit, unconnected to other units.

Tourist Home

Private home in which the owner rents spare bedrooms to transient guests. Few remain in operation today. In these establishments, no meals were served to guests. They were not normally run as business ventures in the usual sense; they were more often sources of extra income for those whose primary income was derived from some other source. Tourist homes and guest houses have largely been replaced by bed-and-breakfast establishments.

Trade Show

An exposition directed toward a particular industry or trade. Trade shows are not open to the public. Admission is restricted to people who are part of the targeted industry or trade.

Traditional Resort

A resort hotel with recreational facilities on the premises. Traditional resorts may include most or all meals and activities in their rates. Most also offer entertainment as a part of their program.

Training

The process of teaching employees how to perform their jobs. Training can be accomplished in several ways—on an individual basis or in groups, on the job or off the job. Training mechanisms include classroom lectures, on-the-job training, computer programs, reading assignments, seminars, and simulation.

Traiteur
Member of a caterers guild who prepared roasts and meats for consumption in private homes during early French history.

Transient Camping
Camping for one or several nights on an improved site, with electricity, bathing facilities and toilets available.

Transient Hotel
A hotel designed to accommodate temporary guests—people who have need of temporary sleeping accommodations for one or more nights. The guests may be businesspeople, groups of sightseers, government employees, members of the armed forces, students, or other individuals or groups seeking temporary lodging.

Transportation System
Facilities used to move guests, employees, equipment, and supplies from one level of the building to another. The primary components of a transportation system are elevators and escalators.

Travel
See Tourism.

Travel Agent
A professional in the business of selling travel services in a travel agency. Travel agents have expertise in advising clients about travel and in making the necessary arrangements to meet their travel needs.

Travel and Tourism
The terms *travel* and *tourism* are commonly linked to create this special term, used to refer to businesses providing primary services to travelers, including the traditional hospitality businesses and others closely linked to them in such fields as entertainment, recreation, and transportation, plus travel agencies and tour operators.

Traveler
As defined by the U.S. Data Travel Center, any resident of the United States, regardless of nationality, who travels within the United States to a place 100 miles or more away from home or who stays away from home one or more nights in paid accommodations and who returns home within 12 months, except for those commuting to and from work or attending school. The terms *traveler* and *tourist* are commonly used interchangeably.

Travel Industry
The industry comprising firms and people who serve the needs of travelers. According to Prof. Chuck Gee, the travel industry has three segments:
1. Direct providers of travel services
2. Support services
3. Tourism development

Travel Industry Association
A nonprofit organization comprising over 1000 members of the travel and hospitality industry. It funds programs designed to attract foreign visitors to the United States and engages in research, lobbying, and training.

Travel Intermediary
A person or firm that makes travel arrangements for others.

Travel Package
Two or more travel services bundled together and sold at one price.

U

Under Bar
A work area under the bar surface containing equipment and supplies used by bartenders.

V

Vacation Camping
Camping for a substantial number of nights—from four nights to several weeks or more—on an improved site with electricity and bathroom facilities. Most vacation camps have stores that sell basic supplies and recreational facilities for such activities as baseball, volleyball, swimming, boating, and waterskiing.

Vacation Club Time-Share

The newest form of time-share. Purchasers buy points that are exchanged for stays at lodging facilities.

Vacation Cruising

Cruising designed for passengers on vacation. The cruise typically departs from and returns to the same port. Vacation cruising constitutes the primary use of most passenger ships today.

Ventilation System

System that provides fresh or recirculated air and that controls the volume of air in a building. Ventilation systems are designed to replace all of the air in a space a certain number of times each hour.

Visa

An endorsement on a passport or a separate document showing that a passport holder has received permission from a government to enter that country. Visas are usually obtained by applying to a consulate office of the country to be visited well in advance of intended dates of travel.

Visitor Center

A building established by a state or local travel department in which tourist information is provided.

W

Walk

The practice of sending guests with confirmed reservations to other lodging properties because their reservations cannot be honored.

Waste System

A system designed to facilitate the removal of solid and liquid waste from a facility. Solid waste is normally collected by employees and transported to waste containers. Liquid waste is typically transported through pipes to a sewer system.

Water System

A system consisting of those parts of the plumbing system that provide fresh water to an establishment. The water may be treated prior to distribution to users.

Wine Cellar

That part of a beverage facility where wine is stored.

Y

Yield Management

An approach to room reservations aimed at yielding maximum occupancy at maximum rates. The general approach is as follows. Future demand for accommodations is assessed based on past occupancy and current conditions. For periods of low demand, all rates are available to potential guests. For periods of high demand, only the highest rates are quoted. Presumably, only people willing to pay the higher rates are accepted during periods of high demand, and people unwilling to accept the high rates are accommodated only during slack periods.

The process is similar in the airline industry. Airlines attempt to fill seats by quoting lower rates to people who can make reservations far in advance and who are willing to meet other criteria, such as staying over a Saturday.

Z

Zeppelin

A lighter-than-air craft also known as a dirigible or blimp. Zeppelins carried passengers domestically and internationally from 1909 to 1940.

A&W, 82
Accidents, workplace, 309
Accommodations:
  defined, 234
  packages, 368, 370
  refusal of, 428
  types, 206–207
Accor, 426
Accounting:
  averages, 320–321
  balance sheet, 311–314
  financial, 310
  income statement, 314–315, 316–317
  ratios, 315–320
Accounting cycle, 310
Accounting principles, 310
Accounts payable, 314
Accumulated depreciation, 311
Adams House, Boston, 49
Advertising, 301–302
Affinity group packages, 370
Air-conditioning systems, 250
Airline Deregulation Act of 1978, 77
Airline Reporting Corporation, 381
Airline travel, 204–205, 421
  catering, 128
  Concorde, 76–77
  history of, 73–76
  hub-and-spoke routing, 78–79
  incentive programs of, 77–78
  international operations and, 94
  regulation of, 77
  resort development and, 100–101
  travel agents and, 380–381, 383
  travel packages of, 367–368, 372–373
  yield management and, 78
Airport clubs, 77–78
Albemarle Hotel, London, 41
Albrecht, Karl, 14–15
Alcoholic beverages. *See* Beverage service

Allen, Roy, 82
All-inclusive packages, 367, 369
All-inclusive resorts, 214, 371
All-suite hotels, 216, 217
Alternating watches, system of, 21
Ambience, 118, 119, 120, 149, 234–235
American Automobile Association (AAA),
  rating scale of, 225–226
American Express, 377
American Hotel, Buffalo, 49
American Hotel and Motel Association
  (AH&MA), 205, 344, 422, 429
American House, Philadelphia, 49
American Plan (AP), 223
  Modified, 223
American service, 123, 162, 189–190
American Society of Travel Agents, 344
Americans with Disabilities Act (ADA) of
  1990, 428–429
Amtrak, 72–73, 375
Amusement parks. *See* Theme parks
Animal Kingdom, 401
Antoine's, New Orleans, 59
Arithmetic average, 320
Arizona Biltmore, Phoenix, 98–99
Assets, on balance sheet, 311, 312, 313
Astor, John Jacob, 48, 52
Astor House, New York, 48
At America's Service (Albrecht), 14–15
Atlantic City (New Jersey), 355, 407
Automation, 433–434
Automobile travel, 43
  fly/drive packages, 368
  highway system and, 68, 204, 338–339, 421
  motel development and, 91
  in RVs (recreation vehicles), 397
  tours, 403–404
Average rate per occupied room, 321
Averages, 320–321
Average sale per customer, 320–321

Back bar, 166–167
Balance sheet, 311–314
Balsams, The, New Hampshire, 54–55
Banking services, 283
Banquets, 127, 190–191, 282
Bars. *See* Beverage service; Beverage
    service establishments
Bass Hotels, 426–427
Bathrooms, 246
Bed-and-breakfast establishments, 211
Beds, dimensions of, 242–243
Bellboys, 49
Bermuda Plan, 224
Best Western, 431
Beverage cost percent, 315, 318
Beverage service:
    back bar, 166–167
    defined, 132, 195
    front bar, 166, 167, 195
    layout and design for, 165–169
    legal requirements for, 131–132,
        145–146, 195, 427–428
    during Prohibition, 80–81, 131
    product line of, 146–149
    service bar, 167, 195
    special-purpose bar, 167–168, 195
    under bar, 167
    wine, 195–196
    See also Food and beverage operations
Beverage service establishments:
    concept and, 144–145
    focus of, 133–134
    location of, 145
    NRA classification of, 136
    reasons for patronizing, 132
    sales growth for, 136
Biltmore Hotel, New York, 41, 88
Bistros, 148
Boardinghouses, 47, 56–57, 96, 219–220
Boca Raton Hotel and Club, Florida,
    99–100
Boeing 314 (Yankee Clipper), 75
Boeing 747, 76
Branson (Missouri), 401
Brasseries, 148
Breakfast Plan (BP), 224
Brew Moon, 149
Broadmoor Hotel, Colorado, 97–98
Broadway Limited, The, 72
Brown Palace Hotel, Denver, 51–52

Budgeting, 321–323
Buffalo Statler, 86–87
Buffets, 127, 193–194
Building codes, 233, 245
Bureau of the Census, 222, 340, 342
Burger King, 124
Busch Gardens, 399
Business and industry foodservice, 128,
    152–153
Bus tours, 368, 373–374, 402–403

Cafés, 40
Cafeterias, 60, 126–127, 192–193
Campgrounds, 396–397
Caravansarai, 32
Career opportunities, 17–20
Caribbean resorts, 371
Carlson, Jan, 14
Carnival Cruise Line, 411
Casino gambling, 12, 96, 355, 402,
    406–408
Casino hotels, 218, 219, 355
Catering:
    airline, 128
    restaurant/hotel, 127
Catskill Mountain House, 54
Chain restaurants, 60, 81, 82–83, 84–85,
    124, 125, 357
Chambers of Commerce, 12, 384
Charing Cross Hotel, London, 41
Check-in process, 239, 261–264, 265
Check-out process, 239, 265–266
Chicago (Illinois), hotels in, 50
Childs' Restaurant, New York, 60
China, as tourist destination, 347
China Clipper, 75
Choice Hotels, Inc., 427
City Hotel, New York, 46
City hotels, 47, 86–90, 93, 238
Civil Aeronautics Board (CAB), 77
Civil Rights Act of 1967, 428
Club Med, 369, 371
Clubs, foodservice in, 129
Coaching inns, 38
Coffeehouses, 39
Coffee shops, 129
Coles, Robert, 44
Coles, Samuel, 44
Coles Ordinary, 44
Colonial Air Transport, 74

Colonial Explorer, 411
Colton, Hugh, 82
Commercial foodservice, 135, 136
Commercial hotels, 215–216
Commercial lodging industry, 205–206
Commissary, 128
Commodore Hotel, New York, 41
Communications systems, 254–255
Computer use:
    for airline reservations, 381, 383
    in food and beverage operations,
        325–328
    in lodging operations, 94–95, 254, 263,
        267
    in travel agencies, 382, 383
    for travel packages, 368
Concept, 144–145, 233
Concorde, supersonic, 76–77
Condominiums:
    rental of, 212
    resort, 214
Conference centers, 218
Congress Hotel, Cape May, New Jersey, 54
Conrad Hilton Hotel, Chicago, 88–89
Continental Breakfast Plan, 224
Controllable expenses, 314–315, 316
Controlling, in management process,
    296–297
Convenience food, 117
Conventions and meetings:
    centers for, 408
    hotels for, 216
    planners of, 386
    as tourist attraction, 410
    travel packages for, 371
Convention and Visitors Bureaus, 12, 384
Cook, Thomas, 377
Corporate travel offices, 384–385
Cosmopolitan Hotel, San Francisco, 51
Cost control:
    defined, 323–324
    food, 324–325
Cost-to-sales ratios, 315, 318
Counter service, 117, 119
Crime, 276, 359
Cruise Lines International Association, 381
Cruises, 70–71, 381, 411–413
    travel packages and, 367–368, 374–375,
        411
Culinary Institute of America, 344

Cultural impact of tourism, 356–357
Cunard, 411
Current assets, 311, 312–313
Current liabilities, 311–314
Cycle of service, 14–16

Davis, Arthur Vining, 99–100
Dawes, Charles, 99
Days Inn, 10
DC-3 aircraft, 76
Deagle's Hotel, New York, 53
Decor, lodging, 207
De facto recognition, 349
De jure recognition, 348
Delivery. *See* Take-out/delivery service
Delmonico's, New York, 59
Demographic change, marketing and,
    424–425
Depreciation, accumulated, 311
Deutsche Luftschiffahrts AG, 73–74
Diners, 80, 129
Dining area, layout and design of, 161–165
Diplomatic recognition, international travel
    and, 348–349
Directing, in management process,
    295–296
Direct providers of travel services, 343
Disabled, legal requirements and, 428–429
Discount outlet centers, 414
Discrimination, 428–429
Dishwashing area, 161
Disneyland, 400
Disney-MGM Studios, 401
Disney World, 11, 399, 400–401
Diversity, employee, 429–430, 431
Dodge City Days, 405
Dormitories, 220–221
D'Oyly Carte, Richard, 41
Drive-ins, 80
Drive-throughs, 130
Dry cleaning services, 283–284
Dumbwaiters, 252

Economy:
    impacts of tourism on, 354–356,
        360–361
    sectors of, 4
    as travel motivator, 338
Economy bus tours, 403
Educational requirements, job, 17–18

Egypt, ancient, 33
Electrical systems, 251
Electric demand systems, 254
Elevators, 252
Empire era, hospitality services in, 32–35
Employee assistance plans (EAPs), 432
Employees:
    benefits, 318
    career opportunities for, 17–20
    empowerment of, 16
    French service and, 191
    job descriptions for, 305–306, 307
    mobility of, 23
    on organization chart, 294–295
    orientation of new, 308
    people skills of, 23–24
    personal selling by, 188, 301
    qualifications and experience of, 17–18,
        19
    racial/ethnic diversity among, 112,
        429–430, 431
    recruitment of, 304–305
    safety in workplace, 309
    sanitary practices of, 434–435
    selection process for, 306
    service quality and, 12–17
    sexual harassment of, 430–431
    training of, 308–309
    travel opportunities for, 22–23
    turnover of, 431
    wages and salaries of, 20–21
    work environment of, 21
    work hours/days of, 21–22
    and workplace safety, 309
Energy control and conservation, 253–254,
    435–436
Engineering systems, 160, 163–164,
    249–255
English service, 192
Entertainment:
    areas, 401–402
    in beverage service establishments, 134
    cruises, 70–71, 411–413
    defined, 393
    fairs and festivals, 404–405
    history of, 10
    in lodging operations, 234, 282
    parades and ceremonies, 405–406
    performances, 404
    as reason for travel, 393

    sightseeing tours, 402–404
    sports events, 406
    theme parks, 11, 398–401
Environment:
    energy conservation and, 435–436
    recycling and, 435
    tourism's impact on, 359
    water conservation and, 437
EPCOT Center, 401
Equal Employment Opportunity
        Commission, 430
Equipment:
    food and beverage, 159, 163, 168–169
    lodging, 242, 249
Escalators, 252
Escoffier, Auguste, 41, 43
Ethics, business, 429
Ethnic restaurants, 122
Eurailpass, 175
European Plan, 58, 224
Events packages, 370
Everglades National Park, 395–396
Eviction, legal requirements for, 428
Exhibitions, 409–410
Exit permits, 350
Expenses, on income statement, 314–315,
        316, 317
Exploration Cruise Line, 411
Expositions, 408–409
Extended-stay hotels, 216, 218

Fairmont Hotel, San Francisco, 210, 211
Fairs and festivals, 404–405
Familiarization (FAM) trips, 380
Family restaurants, 126
Family size:
    foodservice demand and, 114
    as travel motivator, 339
Family vacation packages, 370
Fantasy, 411
Fast-food restaurants, 6–7, 121, 426
Federal Aviation Administration (FAA), 77
Fee ownership time-share, 102–103
Feiner, Elliot J., 149
Festivals and fairs, 404–405
Feudalism, 35–36
Film festivals, 405
Financial accounting, 310
Fine-dining restaurants, 123–124
Fire safety, 49, 253, 276, 438

Fixed assets, 311
Fixed charges, 315
Flagler, Henry, 55
Florida, tourist industry in, 355–356
Fly/cruise/hotel packages, 368
Fly/cruise packages, 367–368, 374–375
Fly/drive packages, 368, 372
Food:
    area, 156–161
    cost control, 324–325
    cost percent, 315–317
    quality, 116–117, 176, 179–180
    quantity, 182
    travel's impact on, 356–357
Food and beverage operations:
    basic steps in, 174–175
    computer system, 325–327
    interdependence of, 197–198
    issuing, 157, 160, 166, 180–181
    in lodging establishments, 235, 279–280
        banquet rooms, 127, 282
        history of, 41–42, 43, 60–61
        meal plans, 223–224
        packages, 370
        restaurants and bars, 280
        room service, 119, 194–195, 281
        sales of, 136
        vending areas, 280–281
    marketing and sales in, 184–188, 426
    organizing process in, 293–294
    production, 157–158, 160–161,
        166–167, 181–184
    purchasing, 156, 165, 175–177
    receiving, 157, 160, 165, 177–178
    service styles, 189–197
    storage, 157, 160, 166, 177, 179–180
Foodservice:
    and accommodation packages, 370
    airline catering, 128
    ambience and, 118, 119, 120, 149
    automation in, 433–434
    in beverage service establishments,
        133–134
    buffets, 127, 193–194
    business and industry, 128
    cafeterias, 60, 126–127, 192–193
    catering, 127
    chain restaurants, 60, 81, 82–83, 84–85,
        124, 125, 357
    characteristics of operation, 115–119

coffee shops, 129
college programs in, 344
concept of, 144
counter service, 117, 119
on cruises, 412
defined, 114–115
diners, 80, 129
drive-ins, 80
drive-throughs, 130
employment in. *See* Employees
ethnic restaurants, 122
European plan and, 58
family restaurants, 126
fast-food restaurants, 6–7, 121, 426
fine-dining, 123–124
food quality and, 116–117
history of:
    ancient empires, 34, 35
    coffeehouses, 39
    hotel dining, 41–42, 43, 60–61
    origins of restaurant, 39–40
    taverns, 39, 112
    in United States, 56–61
institutional, 127–128, 137, 138,
    152–153
layout and design, 156–165
legal requirements for, 145–146,
    428–429, 435
location of, 145, 298–299
market segmentation in, 425
menu:
    health conscious, 437–438
    items on, 115–116, 123, 146
    limited, 124
    prices, 117, 299–300
    sales-oriented, 184–188
    truthful, 437
neighborhood restaurants, 129–130
NRA classification for, 135, 138
operations procedures. *See* Food and
    beverage operations
postwar development of, 83–86
in private clubs, 129
product line of, 146–149
in Prohibition era, 80–81
reasons for demand in, 113–114
sales growth in, 113, 136–137, 421–422
sanitary standards in, 434–435
seat turnover in, 319
self-service, 119

Foodservice (*continued*):
  smoke-free areas and, 434
  specialty restaurants, 122–123
  stands, 129
  table d'hôte meals, 57–58
  table-service restaurants, 117, 121–122
  takout/delivery, 119, 130, 194
  theme restaurants, 125
  tops restaurants, 125–126
  types of establishments, 6–8, 120–128
  See also Beverage service; Operations
    management; Service
Foot-candle of light, 160
Forest Service, U.S., 395
Fortified wines, 196
Foxwoods (Connecticut), gambling casino
  in, 407
France, as tourist destination, 346
Franchises:
  hotel, 92–93
  restaurant, 82–83, 85
Fraunces, Samuel, 46
Fraunces Tavern, New York, 45–46
French restaurants, 148
French service, 123, 191–192
Frequent-flyer programs, 77
Frequent-guest programs, 302, 303,
  425–426
Front bar, 166, 167, 195
Front office:
  layout and design of, 239–242
  procedures in, 241, 261–269, 285
Front service, 279

Gambling casinos, 12, 96, 355, 402,
  406–408
Gee, Chuck, 342
Geist, Clarence H., 99
Georgia Rural Telephone Museum, 394
Goode, Thomas, 54
Government role in travel and tourism,
  12, 339–340, 341, 344, 384
Government sector of economy, 4
Grand Hotel, Mackinac Island, Michigan,
  55
Grand hotels, 47–52
Grand National Hotel, Lucerne, 42
Grand tour, 37–38
Great Depression, lodging industry during,
  89–90

Greece, ancient, 34
Greenbrier, The, West Virginia, 54
Guaranteed reservations, 269
Gueridon, 191, 192
Guest check, 121–122, 167, 326–327
Guest houses, 91, 211
Guest ranches, 215

Hair styling facilities, 284
Hancock's Tavern, Boston, 44
Happy hour, 427
Hapuna Beach Prince Hotel, Hawaii, 102
Harvey, Fred, 60
Health codes, 145
Health spas, 219, 220
Heating systems, 249–250
Hershey Park, 398
Highways and roads, 68, 204, 338–339,
  421
Hilton, Conrad, 89
Hilton Hotels, 10, 88–89, 94, 95
Holiday Inn, 10, 92, 204
Homestead, The, Virginia, 53, 54
Hospitality, defined, 5
Hospitality industry:
  career opportunities in, 17–20
  comparison to other service enterprises,
    5–6
  environmental issues and. *See*
    Environment
  ethics in, 429
  growth of, 4–5
  scope of, 6–10
  in service sector of economy, 4
  See also Food and beverage operations;
    Foodservice; Lodging industry;
    Lodging operations; Operations
    management
Hospitals, 212
Hostels, 211–212
Hotel representatives, 383–384
Hotels:
  all-suite, 216, 217
  casino, 218, 219, 355, 407
  chain, 92–93, 101
  characteristics of, 209
  city, 47, 86–90, 93–94, 238
  commercial, 215–216
  convention, 216
  dining in, 41–42, 43, 60–61, 136

extended-stay, 216, 218
residential, 213
transient, 212–213
See also Lodging industry; Lodging
    operations; Resort hotels
Housekeeping:
    layout and design, 246–248
    procedures, 270–275
Howard Hotel, New York, 49
Howard Johnson's restaurants, 82–83
Hub-and-spoke routing, 78–79
Human resources management:
    defined, 304
    and disabled, 429
    of diverse workforce, 429–430
    and hiring process, 304–307
    orientation of new employees, 308
    sexual harassment and, 430–431
    training programs of, 308–309
    turnover and, 431
    workplace safety and, 309–310
HVAC system, 250, 436
Hyatt, 10
Hyatt Regency, Chicago, 96

Incentive packages, 370–371
Incentive travel firms, 385
Income levels:
    foodservice demand and, 113–114
    as travel motivator, 338, 421
Income statement, 314–315, 316–317
Industrial Revolution, 40–41, 204
Information sources:
    front-office, 234, 239, 264–265
    travel agents, 379
    visitor centers, 384
Inns, 8, 34, 35, 205
    coaching inn, 38
    in colonial America, 44, 45
    family-run, 371
    motor inn, 10, 212
    types of, 209
Institutional foodservice, 127–128, 137,
    138, 152–153
Interior Department, 394
International Air Transport Association,
    344, 381
International Council on Hotel,
    Restaurant, and Institutional
    Education, 410

International Trade Administration, 340
International travel:
    destinations of, 346–348
    documents and conditions for, 348–350
    scope of, 345–346
    to U.S., 351–353, 433
    from U.S., 350–351
Inventory turnover rate, 319
Issuing procedures, food and beverage,
    157, 160, 166, 180–181
Italy, as tourist destination, 347

Jackson, Nelson, 68
Japan, as tourist destination, 347
Jenkins, Howard, 422
Jet aircraft, 76
Job descriptions, 305–306, 307
Job opportunities, 17–20
Johnson, Howard, 82

Kelly Act, 74
Keys, room, 263–264
Kincade, Kathy, 405
Kirby, J. G., 80
Kitchen:
    equipment, 159
    layout and design of, 156–161
    production procedures in, 181–184
Knott's Berry Farm, 399
Kroc, Ray, 84, 85

Labor cost percentage, 318
Landau, Carl, 405
Language services, 284
Las Vegas (Nevada), 12, 13, 96, 402,
    407–408
Laundry service, 274, 283
Layout and design:
    beverage facility, 165–169
    foodservice facility, 150–165
    lodging facility, 239–249
Legal requirements:
    alcoholic beverages and, 131–132, 195,
        427–428
    building and zoning codes, 233, 245
    disabled and, 428–429
    discrimination and, 438
    for eviction, 428
    health codes, 145
    sanitary standards, 435

Leisure travel, 337–338, 392, 421, 424
Liabilities, on balance sheet, 311–314
Life span, longer, impact on travel and
    tourism, 337, 420
Lighting, restaurant, 160, 163, 169
Limited-menu restaurants, 124
Linen, caring for, 247–248, 273–275
Local tourism offices, 384
Location, 145, 298–299
Lodges, 210
Lodging houses, 220
Lodging industry:
  accommodation refusal, 428
  accommodation types, 206–207
  automation in, 433–434
  bed-and-breakfast establishments, 211
  boardinghouses, 219–220
  classification of establishments, 221–223
  commercial segment of, 205–206
  computerized operations of, 94–95
  concept in, 233
  condominiums, 212
  conference centers, 218
  consolidation in, 426–427
  decor of, 207
  dormitories, 220–221
  employees in. See Employees
  engineering systems in, 249–255, 436
  in entertainment areas, 96, 402
  evictions and, 428
  fire safety in, 49, 253, 276, 438
  frequent-guest programs of, 302, 303,
    425–426
  health spas, 219, 220
  hospitals, 212
  hostels, 211–212
  international operations of, 94, 433
  job opportunities in, 18, 19
  layout and design in, 239–249
  legal requirements for, 233, 428–429
  lodges, 210
  lodging houses, 220
  major companies, 10
  market segmentation in, 95–96, 425
  motels, 90–92, 209–210, 236–237
  motor inns, 212
  in national parks, 395–396
  new construction, 94, 96
  nursing homes, 221
  occupancy rate in, 318

product line of, 233–236
ratings of establishments, 225–226
room rates in, 207, 223, 268, 299, 300,
    301
sales growth of, 206, 422–423
smoke-free areas and, 434
target clientele of, 208
tourist homes/guest houses, 211
travel packages of, 368, 370, 376
types of establishments, 8–10, 208–221
See also Hotels; Lodging operations;
    Operations management; Resort
    hotels
Lodging industry, history of, 30–31,
    204–205
  Egyptian empire and, 33
  in feudal age, 35–36
  Greek empire and, 34
  hotel dining and, 41–42, 43, 60–61
  railroad travel and, 40–41, 55–56
  in Renaissance, 36–38
  Roman Empire and, 34–35
  in seventeenth and eighteenth centuries,
    38–40
  Sumerians and, 31–32
  in United States, 42–55, 204–205
    city hotels, 47, 86–88
    colonial period, 44–46
    fire danger in, 49
    first hotel, 46
    grand hotels, 47–52
    Great Depression and, 89–90
    resort hotels, 52–55
    in Roaring Twenties, 88–89
Lodging operations:
  basic, 260–261
  foodservice in. See Food and beverage
    operations, in lodging
    establishments
  front office, 239–242, 261–269
  housekeeping, 246–248, 270–275
  interrelatedness of, 285–286
  parking, 283
  personal services, 206, 232, 234, 279,
    283–285
  recreation and entertainment, 282
  security, 275–278
  telephone service, 269–270
  See also Reservations
Lodging properties, defined, 205

Long-term liabilities, 314
Luchow's, New York, 59
Lumens, 160
Luxury bus tours, 403

McArthur, Albert Chase, 98
McDonald, Richard and Maurice, 84–85
McDonald's, 84–85, 113, 422
Majesty of the Seas, 411
Management. *See* Operations management
Marches and rallies, 410–411
Mardi Gras, New Orleans, 405
Marketing:
    advertising, 301–302
    defined, 297–298
    demographic change and, 424–425
    menu and, 184–188
    merchandising tools, 188, 302–303
    personal selling in, 188, 301
    place and, 298–299
    price and, 299–300
    product and, 298
    public relations, 303
    sales promotion, 302, 425–426
Market segments, 95–96, 425
Marriott, J. Willard, 82
Marriott Corporation, 10, 82, 95–96, 101, 303
Marriott's Desert Springs, California, 101–102
Marriott's Ihilani Resort, Hawaii, 214, 215
Meal plans, 223–224
Menu:
    health conscious, 437–438
    items on, 115–116, 123
    limited, 124
    prices, 117, 299–300
    sales-oriented, 184–188
    truthful and accurate, 437
Merchandising tools, 188, 302–303
Metropolitan Hotel, New York, 49
MGM Grand, Inc., 426
MGM Grand Hotel, Las Vegas, 96, 402
Military foodservice, 138
Mise en place, 181–182
Mizener, Addison, 99
Mobil Travel Guide, rating scale of, 225, 226
Moments of truth concept, 14
Monasteries, lodging in, 37

Motels, 8, 10
    budget, 236–237
    defined, 209–210
    history and development of, 90–92
    resort, 215
Motor coach tours, 368, 373–374, 402–403
Motor Inns, 8, 10, 212
Motor lodges, 210
Mount Washington Hotel, New Hampshire, 56
Musical performances, 401, 404
Music festivals, 405

National Cherry Festival, Michigan, 405
National Park Service, 12, 394–395
National Restaurant Association (NRA), 112, 113, 135, 138, 344, 421, 422, 429
National and state parks, 12, 394–396
Navigator, 71
Neighborhood restaurants, 129–130
New Orleans, restaurants in, 59
Newsstands, 284
New York:
    hotels in, 46, 47, 48, 49, 52, 87
    restaurants in, 59
    tourist attractions in, 404, 405–406, 409–410
New York Film Festival, 405
New York Hotel, 49
Noncommerical foodservice, 137
Nonperishables, 176
North America Rail Pass, 375
No-shows, 268
No-smoking areas, 434
Nursing homes, 221

Occidental Hotel, San Francisco, 51
Occupancy:
    average rate per room, 321
    percentage of, 318
Occupational Safety and Health Administration (OSHA), 309
Ocean Cruise Line, 411
Ocean Islander, 411
Office services, 284
Olympic games, 406
On change, 271
Operating budget, 321–323

Operating expenses, 314–315, 317
Operating ratios, 318
Operations management:
  accounting, 310–321
  budgeting, 321–323
  computer systems, 325–328
  controlling function of, 296–297
  cost control, 323–325
  defined, 292
  directing function of, 295–296
  human resources, 304–310, 429–431
  marketing, 184–188, 297–303, 425–426
  organizing function of, 293–295
  planning function of, 292–293
  service quality management, 12–16
  total quality management (TQM),
    16–17, 432
Ordinaries, 39, 44, 112
Organization chart, 294–295
Organizing, in management process,
  293–295
Orientation, employee, 308
Orlando (Florida):
  Disney World in, 11, 399, 400–401
  as entertainment area, 401
Outsourcing, 261
Overbooking, 268–269
Owner's equity, 314
Oyster houses, 57

Packages. See Travel packages
Packaging, fast-food, 121
Palace Hotel, San Francisco, 51, 61
"Palaces of the public," 47
Palmer House, Chicago, 50, 88
Panama Limited, The, 72
Pan American Airlines, 74–75, 76, 94
Parades and ceremonies, 405–406
Parker, Robert, 50
Parker House, Boston, 49, 60
Parker House, San Francisco, 50–51
Parking facilities, 283
Passenger ships, 69–70
Passports, 349
Pennekamp (John) Coral Reef Park,
  394–395
Pennsylvania Hotel, New York, 88
Penrose, Spencer, 97, 98
Percentage of occupancy, 318
Performances, 401, 404

Perishables, 176
Personal selling, 188, 301
Pilferage, 179
Planning, in management process, 292–293
Planters' Hotel, St. Louis, 49
Plaza Hotel, New York, 87–88, 205
Point-of-service (POS) terminals, 422
Portion size, 121
Posthouses, 39
Pourers, 169
Prices:
  European plan, 58
  marketing and, 299–300
  menu, 117, 299–300
  purchasing, 177
  room rate, 207, 268, 299–300, 301
  table d'hôte, 57–58
Primitive camping, 396
Prince Resorts, 102
Private clubs, foodservice in, 129
Production:
  goals, 181
  layout and design, 157–158, 160–161,
    166–167
  procedures, 181–184
Production sheets, 182–184
Product line:
  defined, 146, 233
  foodservice, 146–149, 159, 169
  lodging, 233–236
Products sector of economy, 4
Profitability:
  item gross profit, 187–188
  ratios, 320
Prohibition era, 80–81, 131
Promotion, marketing and, 300–303
Prostitution, 276
Public relations, 303
Purchasing procedures, 156, 165, 175–177

Qualifications, job, 17–18, 19
Quality Inn, 10
Queens Hotel, Birmingham, 41

Railroad travel, 40–41, 51
  Amtrak, 72–73, 375
  decrease in passenger traffic, 71–72
  railroad networks and, 55–56
  resort hotels and, 52
  station hotels and, 41, 88

station restaurants and, 60
travel packages for, 375
Rallies and marches, 410–411
Ramada, 10
Ratios, 315, 318–320
Receiving procedures, food and beverage,
157, 160, 165, 177–178
Recipes, standard, 183–184
Recreation, 10–11
camping, 396–398
cruises, 70–71, 411–413
defined, 393
in lodging operations, 234, 282, 284
in national/state parks, 394–396
as reason for travel, 393
in resort areas, 11, 398
Recreation vehicles, 397
Recruitment, employee, 304–305
Recycling, 435
Refrigeration, 157, 166, 179–180
Registration card, 262
Renaissance, hospitality services in, 36–38
Rent payable, 314
Reservations:
airline, 381, 383
defined, 239, 266
guaranteed, 269
overbooking and, 268–269
procedures, 266–267
through travel agents, 379, 380
yield management and, 267–268
Residential hotels, 213
Resort areas:
entertainment and recreation in, 11, 398
travel agents and, 12, 371, 381
Resort condominiums, 214–215
Resort hotels:
all-inclusive, 214, 371
characteristics of, 213
development of, 100–102
fly/cruise packages, 368
grand resorts, 97–100
meal service in, 224
nineteenth century, 52–55
ski resort, 237
time-shares, 102–103
transportation modes and, 100–101
types of, 214–215
vacation time and, 97
Resort motel, 215

Restaurants. *See* Foodservice
Retirement, early, impact on travel and
tourism, 337, 420
Return on sales, 320
Revenue, on income statement, 314, 317
Revere House, Boston, 49
Right-to-use time-share, 103
RIHGA Royal Hotel, New York, 246
Ritz, César, 41, 42
Ritz-Carlton, 17, 42, 88
Roadhouses, 81
Rock Resorts, 426
Rogers, Isaiah, 47, 48
Roman Catholic Church, 36
Roman Empire, 34–35
Room clerk, 262
Rooming houses, 47, 57, 96, 220
Room keys, 263–264
Room rates, 207, 268, 299, 300, 301
Rooms:
housekeeping operations and, 271–272
layout and design of, 242–244
refurbishment of, 275
size of, 207, 244, 245
Room service, 119, 194–195
Russian service, 123, 190–191
RVs (recreation vehicles), 397
Ryan Airlines, 74

Safe deposit boxes, 276, 277
Safety, workplace, 309
St. Charles Hotel, New Orleans, 49
St. Enoch's Hotel, Glasgow, 41
St. Louis Hotel, New Orleans, 49
St. Nicholas Hotel, New York, 49
St. Pancras Hotel, London, 41
St. Petersburg-Tampa Airboat Line, 74
Salaries, 20–21
Sales:
average sale per customer, 320–321
cost-to-sales ratios, 315–317
on income statement, 314, 316
return on, 320
Sales growth:
food and beverage, 113, 136–137,
421–422
lodging, 206, 422–423
Sales histories, 182
Sales operation. *See* Marketing
Sales promotion, 302, 303, 425–426

Sales tax payable, 314
San Francisco:
    hotels in, 50–51
    restaurants in, 59
Savoy Hotel, London, 41, 43
Sea Goddess I/II, 411
Seat turnover, 319
Sea World, 399
Security systems, 275–278
Self-service, 119
Sensors, automatic, 254
Service:
    cycles of, 14–16
    European plan and, 58
    goal of, 188–189
    layout and design and, 162
    moments of truth concept of, 14
    personal selling and, 188
    in product line, 148–149
    quality management and, 12–17
    styles of:
        American, 123, 162, 189–190
        buffet, 127, 193–194
        cafeteria, 126–127, 192–193
        English, 192
        French, 123, 191–192
        room service, 119, 194–195
        Russian, 123, 190–191
        take-out/delivery, 119, 130, 194
    table d'hôte meals and, 57–58
    types of establishment and, 120–131, 197
Service bar, 167, 195
Service sector of economy, 4
Serving, defined, 158
Sexual harassment, 430–431
Sheraton, 10
Ships:
    fly/cruise packages, 367–368
    transatlantic passenger, 69–70
    vacation cruising, 70–71
Shopping centers, 413
Shopping malls, 413–414
Signs, tavern, 37
Six Flags Great Adventure, 399
Ski resort, 237
Smith Travel Research, 222–223
Smoking/no-smoking areas, 434
Social impact of tourism, 357–359
Sovereign of the Seas, 411
Spain, as tourist destination, 346

Sparkling wines, 196
Spas, health, 219, 220
Speakeasies, 80–81
Special events, 408
Special-interest packages, 370
Special-purpose bar, 167–168, 195
Specialty channelers, 383
Specialty menu items, 115–116
Specialty restaurants, 122–123
Sports events, 406
Sprague, Reginald, 83
Staff. *See* Employees
Stagecoach travel, 38, 41
Standard bus tours, 403
Stands, open-air foodservice, 129
State fairs, 404
State and national parks, 12, 394–396
State tourism offices, 384
Station Hotel, Perth, 41
Statler, E. M., 86, 88
Statler Hotels, 86–87, 88
Still wines, 196
Storage, food and beverage, 157, 160, 166, 177, 179–180
Storeroom, 157
Suite, 216
Sumerians, 31–32
Super Chief, The, 72
Support services, travel industry, 343–344

Table d'hôte meals, 57–58
Tables:
    size, 162–163
    space between, 163
Table service, 117, 121–122
Take-out/delivery service, 119, 130, 194
Tanglewood music festival, 405
Tanke, Mary L., 304
Taverns, 8, 10
    in ancient empires, 32, 34, 35
    in colonial America, 44–46
    ordinary (meal) in, 39, 112
    signs, 37
    See also Beverage service establishments
Telephone service, 269–270
Television, closed-circuit, 278
Theme parks, 8, 11, 398–401
Theme restaurants, 125
Time clocks, 253
Time-shares, 102–103

Tivoli Gardens, 399–400

Tops restaurants, 125–126

Total quality management (TQM), 16–17, 432

Tourism. *See* Travel and tourism; Travel services; Travel packages

Tourism development, 344–345

Tourism offices, 384

Tourist, defined, 340–342

Tourist attractions. *See* Entertainment; Recreation; Travel and tourist attractions

Tourist courts, 91

Tourist homes, 211

Tour operators, 12, 376, 377, 403

Tour wholesalers, 376–377

Trade shows, 409

Traffic flow:
   in dining area, 164–165
   in food area, 161

Training, employee, 308–309

Traiteurs, 39

Transient camping, 396

Transient hotels, 212–213

Transportation. *See* Airline travel; Automobile travel; Railroad travel; Travel and tourism

Transportation systems, in lodging establishments, 252

Travel agents, 11–12, 366, 377–383

Traveler, defined, 340, 392–393

Travel Industry Association (TIA), 339

Travel intermediary, 366

Travel opportunities, employee, 22–23

Travel packages, 11–12
   airline, 367–368, 372–373
   bus tours, 368, 373–374, 402–403
   in Caribbean resorts, 171
   cruise lines, 367–368, 374–375
   lodging company, 376
   railroad, 375
   of tour operators/wholesalers, 376–377
   types of, 366–372

Travel services:
   convention and meeting planners, 386
   corporate travel offices, 384–385
   direct providers of, 343
   hotel representatives, 383–384
   incentive travel firms, 385
   specialty channelers, 383

state/local tourism offices, 12, 384
   support services, 343–344
   tourism development and, 344–345
   tour operators, 12, 376–377, 403
   travel agents, 11–12, 366, 377–383
   See also Travel packages; Travel and tourism

Travel and tourism, 10–12
   airline. *See* Airline travel
   automobile. *See* Automobile travel
   cruises, 70–71, 367–368, 374–375, 381, 411–413
   cultural impact of, 356–357
   definition of traveler and tourist, 340–342, 392–393
   destinations, 346–348, 360–361, 425
   early history of, 34, 35, 36–38, 41
   economic impact of, 354–356, 360–361
   environmental impact of, 359
   government role in, 12, 339–340, 341, 344, 384
   international:
      destinations of, 346–348, 425
      documents and conditions for, 348–350
      scope of, 345–346
      from U.S., 350–351
      to U.S., 351–353, 433
   mass travel and, 68–69, 366
   motivators for, 336–339, 392, 420–421
   paid vacation and, 97
   passenger ships, 69–70
   pros and cons of, 359–361
   railroad. *See* Railroad travel
   size and scope of, 345–346, 423
   social impact of, 357–359
   stagecoach, 38, 41
   within U.S., 353–354, 360–361
   See also Travel packages; Travel services

Travel and tourism attractions:
   conventions, 410
   discount outlet centers, 414
   exhibitions, 409–410
   expositions, 408–409
   gambling, 12, 96, 355, 402, 406–408
   rallies and marches, 410–411
   shopping centers, 413
   shopping malls, 413–414
   special events, 408
   trade shows, 409
   See also Entertainment; Recreation

Tremont Hotel, Boston, 47–48, 49
Twentieth Century Limited, The, 72

Under bar, 167
United Nations Statistical Commission, 342
United States National Tourism Organization, 339
United States Travel Data Center, 340, 342
United States Travel and Tourism Administration (USTTA), 339
Universal Studios, 399

Vacation camping, 396–397
Vacation club time-shares, 103
Vacation cruising, 70–71
Vacations:
    change in patterns of, 425
    paid, 97
Vending machines, 280–281
Ventilation systems, 160, 163–164, 250
Video systems, 183
Villa rentals, 371
Visas, 349
Visitor centers, 384
Volstead Act, 131
Voyager of the Seas, 411, 413

Wages, 20–21
    payable, 314
Waldorf-Astoria Hotel, New York, 52, 60–61, 90
Walked guests, 268

Walt Disney World, 11, 399, 400–401
Warren and Wetmore, 97
Washington House, Philadelphia, 49
Waste systems, 252–253
Water conservation, 437
Water systems, 251–252, 437
Web sites:
    airline reservations and, 381, 383
    travel packages and, 368
Weston Hotels, 17
White Castle, 81, 82
Wilson, Kemmons, 91–92, 204
Windows on the World, New York, 126
Wine cellars, 166
Wine service, 195–196
Winston, Vicki A., 431
Work environment, 21
Work hours/days, 21–22
Workweek, shorter, impact on travel and tourism, 337, 420–421
World Tourism Organization (WTO), 342, 344, 345, 423
Wright, Frank, 82
Wright, Frank Lloyd, 98
Wrigley, William, Jr., 99

Yankee Clipper, 75
Ye Olde Union Oyster House, 57, 58
Yield management, 78, 267–269
Yosemite National Park, 396

Zeppelin airships, 73–74
Zoning regulations, 233, 245